Faulkner's Families
FAULKNER AND YOKNAPATAWPHA
2019

Faulkner's Families

Edited by
Jay Watson
and
James G. Thomas, Jr.

University Press of Mississippi
Jackson

The University Press of Mississippi is the scholarly publishing agency of
the Mississippi Institutions of Higher Learning: Alcorn State University,
Delta State University, Jackson State University, Mississippi State University,
Mississippi University for Women, Mississippi Valley State University,
University of Mississippi, and University of Southern Mississippi.

www.upress.state.ms.us

The University Press of Mississippi is a member
of the Association of University Presses.

Any discriminatory or derogatory language or hate speech regarding race,
ethnicity, religion, sex, gender, class, national origin, age, or disability
that has been retained or appears in elided form is in no way an
endorsement of the use of such language outside a scholarly context.

Copyright © 2023 by University Press of Mississippi
All rights reserved
Manufactured in the United States of America

First printing 2023
∞

Library of Congress Cataloging-in-Publication Data

Names: Faulkner and Yoknapatawpha Conference (46th: 2019: University of
Mississippi) | Watson, Jay, editor. | Thomas, James G., Jr., editor.
Title: Faulkner's families / edited by Jay Watson and James G. Thomas.
Description: Jackson : University Press of Mississippi, 2023. | Includes
bibliographical references and index.
Identifiers: LCCN 2023007511 (print) | LCCN 2023007512 (ebook) | ISBN
9781496845030 (hardback) | ISBN 9781496845863 (trade paperback) | ISBN
9781496845047 (epub) | ISBN 9781496845054 (epub) | ISBN 9781496845061
(pdf) | ISBN 9781496845078 (pdf)
Subjects: LCSH: Faulkner, William, 1897-1962—Criticism and
interpretation—Congresses. | Faulkner, William,
1897-1962—History—Congresses. | Families in literature. | LCGFT:
Essays. | Literary criticism.
Classification: LCC PS3511.A86 Z7832255 2023 (print) | LCC PS3511.A86
(ebook) | DDC 813/.52—dc23/eng/20230405
LC record available at https://lccn.loc.gov/2023007511
LC ebook record available at https://lccn.loc.gov/2023007512

British Library Cataloging-in-Publication Data available

Contents

Note on the Conference   vii

Introduction   3
   JAY WATSON

Whiteness, Childhood, and Faulknerian Gothics
in "That Evening Sun" and Sally Mann   25
   KATHERINE HENNINGER

Across the Ditch: Race, Childhood, and the
Machinery of Fate in Faulkner   47
   MAUDE HINES

Faulkner's Future Americans   58
   REBECCA NISETICH

"It Takes Two People to Make You": Brotherhood
and Loss in *As I Lay Dying*   73
   JOSEPHINE ADAMS

Undutiful Daughters: Women, Kinship, and Monument
beyond Family in *Absalom, Absalom!*   86
   JULIE BETH NAPOLIN

White Noise/Black Codes: Inscription and
Representation in *The Unvanquished*   107
   JEFF ALLRED

When Will We Be Extinct? Faulknerian Cosmopolitanism
and the Family Network   122
   ROBERT JACKSON

Faulkner's Subversive Genealogies   136
   GEORGE PORTER THOMAS

Beasts in the Mississippi Jungle: Ike McCaslin's
Queer Animal Kinship 147
   JOHN N. DUVALL

The Jefferson Outbreak: An Epidemiological
Reading of the Snopes Family 168
   MAXWELL CASSITY

"Faulkner Wasn't 'Our People'": Faulkner's "Negroes,"
the McJunkinses' Faulkner, and Our Search for Greenfield Farm 194
   GARRY BERTHOLF

"The Family of Man": William Faulkner, Atomic Diplomacy,
and US Visual Education in Post-Occupation Japan 215
   YUKO YAMAMOTO

About the Contributors 235

Index 239

Note on the Conference

The Faulkner and Yoknapatawpha Conference, sponsored by the University of Mississippi in Oxford, took place Sunday, July 21, through Thursday, July 25, 2019. Twelve presentations on the theme "Faulkner's Families" are collected as essays in this volume. Brief mention is made here of other conference activities.

The program began on Sunday afternoon with a reception at the University Museum. Following the reception, Hortense J. Spillers delivered a keynote lecture in Nutt Auditorium on the subject of "The Family, Our Beloved Crisis: Faulkner's Version." Following Spillers's lecture, John N. Duvall presented a lecture on "Beasts in the Mississippi Jungle: Ike McCaslin's Queer Animal Kinship."

Following a buffet supper at Rowan Oak that evening, Ivo Kamps, the chair of the University of Mississippi English Department, and Jason Bailey, Oxford's mayor pro tem, welcomed participants, and Jenna Grace Sciuto, secretary-treasurer of the William Faulkner Society, introduced winners of the 2019 John W. Hunt Scholarships. These fellowships, awarded to graduate students pursuing research on William Faulkner, are funded by the Faulkner Society and the *Faulkner Journal* in memory of John W. Hunt, Faulkner scholar and emeritus professor of literature at Lehigh University. Rebecca Lauck Cleary from the Center for the Study of Southern Culture presented the 2019 Eudora Welty Awards in Creative Writing. A conversation between professional genealogist Kenyatta D. Berry and Jodi Skipper concluded the evening.

Monday's program began with James Carothers, Terrell L. Tebbetts, and Theresa Towner leading the first "Teaching Faulkner" session, "Faulkner's Genealogies," followed by a panel on the theme of "Affinities and Affiliations, Familial and Otherwise," with Sage Gerson, Aili Pettersson Peeker, Maite Urcaregui, and Madeleine Roepe presenting. A panel on "Daughters and Siblings" followed and included papers by Julie Beth Napolin, Josephine Adams, and Thomas L. McLaughlin Jr. The day's program also included a Brown Bag Lunch update on the Digital Yoknapatawpha project; a keynote lecture, "Faulkner's Age: Age in Faulkner's Work," by Caroline Levander; and presentations on the topic of "Faulkner's Black Families in Oxford and Lafayette County," presented by Kenyatta D. Berry and Jeffrey Jackson, Garry Bertholf, and Rhondalyn

Peairs. The evening concluded with a screening and discussion of *The Sound and the Fury (April Seventh, 1928)* by members of the New York-based Elevator Repair Service theater company.

Tuesday's program included the second "Teaching Faulkner" session, led by Brian McDonald, followed by a panel on "Breeding, Feuding, and Forging Families" that included papers by Isadora J. Wagner, Wallis H. Tinnie, and Jeff Allred. The panel "Toxic, Contagious, and Stressed: Family Pressures in Faulkner," which included Geri Harmon, Margaret Mauk, Michael Wainwright, and Maxwell Cassity, closed the morning sessions. That afternoon, John Howard delivered the keynote lecture "Feeling and Pining: Mortality, Inequality, and Impiety in Deep South Woodlands," followed by a panel on "Space, Place, and Race: Geography and Genealogy in Faulkner's Yoknapatawpha" with Taylor Hagood, Jennie J. Joiner, and Rebecca S. Nisetich. A cocktail party at the Oxford Depot completed the day.

Wednesday's program began with Kristi Rowan Humphreys, Maude Hines, and Anne MacMaster delivering papers on the theme of "Family as Fate and Fantasm." A panel on the theme of "Family beyond Fiction" included presentations by Tyler Mercer, Chris Dieman, and Elizabeth Cornell; Yuko Yamamoto; and Marianna Sonntag Whitmer. A panel on "Subversive, Transnational, and Functional Genealogies" followed with presentations by George Porter Thomas, Hyoseol Ha, and Terrell Tebbetts. Thomas L. McHaney then delivered the 2019 Library Lecture on "Faulkner Family Reading and the Compsons" in the J. D. Williams Library. Katherine Henninger's lecture, "Whiteness, Childhood, and the Faulknerian Gothic," and a panel on "The Region, the Globe, the Cosmopolitan," including presentations by Pardis Dabashi, Robert Jackson, and Michael Zeitlin, with Sarah Gleeson-White moderating, followed in Nutt Auditorium. A late-afternoon walk through Bailey Woods ended at Rowan Oak, where the annual picnic on the grounds concluded the day's events.

Guided tours of north Mississippi, including Oxford, the Mississippi Delta, New Albany and Ripley, and African American heritage sites in Lafayette County, took place on Thursday. The conference ended with a closing party and book signing at Off Square Books.

The Faulkner and Yoknapatawpha Conference at the University of Mississippi is sponsored by the Department of English and the Center for the Study of Southern Culture and coordinated by the Division of Outreach and Continuing Studies. The conference planners are grateful to all the individuals and organizations that support the Faulkner and Yoknapatawpha Conference annually. In addition to those mentioned above, we wish to thank the University of Mississippi Slavery Research Group, the College of Liberal Arts, the Office of the Provost, Square Books, the City of Oxford, and the Oxford Convention and Visitors Bureau.

Faulkner's Families
FAULKNER AND YOKNAPATAWPHA
2019

Introduction

JAY WATSON

In one of his typically evasive moves with journalists, Faulkner told interviewer Marshall J. Smith in 1931, "I was born in 1826 of a negro slave and an alligator—both named Gladys Rock. I have two brothers. One is Dr. Walter E. Traprock and the other is Eaglerock, an airplane."[1] Beyond its dubious taste, Faulkner's jesting reveals as much as it conceals. There is, of course, that fierce desire for privacy for which the writer was noted over and over in his career, which led him to withhold access to his personal history and offer up fictional biographies in its place. Moreover, beneath the absurd hyperbole of this particular bit of leg-pulling, there's a lingering echo of the comic Al Jackson material that the author had developed with Sherwood Anderson in the 1920s, bits of which trickled into Faulkner's second novel, *Mosquitoes*. But beyond all that, the quote attests, all frivolity aside, to the relentless hold of family relations on Faulkner's imagination and sensibility. Even in jest, who he is—who a man is—is a matter of *who*, as much as *where*, he comes from—be that north Mississippi slaveholders like the author's great-grandfather or "a negro slave."

Nor is even this ridiculous lineage itself entirely a flight of fancy. To be brother to an airplane, as it were, is arguably a fate shared by numerous Faulkner characters and more than a few Fa(u)lkner men, including the author, all three of his brothers, his stepson, and his nephew Jimmy. And the immediate forebears—an alligator and negro slave—anticipate the lineage of a character like Ike McCaslin, at once the interspecies child of a mystic buck and a three-toed bear from the swampy river bottoms of north Mississippi (as John N. Duvall notes in these pages) and, by virtue of his repudiated McCaslin heritage, a thoroughly slave-made man as well, literally engendered out of the wealth and power that Mississippi slavery created. Even the writerly kiss-off, then, inadvertently lets us in, witnessing to the power of family ties in the crucible of Faulknerian identity.

Now let's turn for a moment to the cover photo for this volume. It's one of my favorite Faulkner images: four Falkner children, circa 1905, posed in front of the Trigg-Doyle-Falkner house at the corner of

Buchanan Street and South 11th Street in Oxford, Mississippi, the house where first Billy Falkner's grandparents and then his parents lived during his childhood. But wait—the fourth Falkner brother, Dean, is missing from this grouping, since he won't be born until 1907. Here the place that Dean will come to occupy in the family assemblage has fallen to cousin Sally Murry Wilkins, who tomboyed it around the neighborhood with the Falkner boys in the years before Dean arrived on the scene. No doubt the foursome wandered by the Thompson-Chandler house, only three blocks away on South 13th Street, on their local rambles, and perhaps caught a glimpse of intellectually disabled adolescent Edwin Chandler behind the iron fence that surrounded the property.

And here, of course, I'm giving the game away. For in this photo we are seeing the constellation that will become the Compson children in Faulkner's first modernist masterpiece. Sally and her cousins will become Caddy Compson and her brothers in *The Sound and the Fury*. I like to think, or at least wish, that one of the ponies in the photo was named Fancy and went on to find a namesake in the Compson stable of Faulkner's novel. If photography is a technology not only of looking and seeing but of memory, as so many students of the medium have claimed, we are looking in this photo at something like what Faulkner must have been remembering as, from his second-story turret room in the old Delta Psi house on the University of Mississippi campus, where he still lived with his parents in 1928, he imagined his way into section one of *The Sound and the Fury*. And what he was remembering, above all else, was *family*.

• • •

In June of 1928, a University of Maryland professor named A. E. Zucker published an essay in *PMLA*, the journal of the Modern Language Association, identifying "a new genre of the novel" that had arisen in response to developments in Darwinian biology and, as the genre matured, to the early twentieth-century rediscovery of Mendelian genetics.[2] The new genre, which Zucker traced to Zola's *Les Rougon-Macquart* cycle (1871-1893) and Samuel Butler's *Way of All Flesh* (published posthumously in 1903), was defined by a "panoram[ic]" account "of several generations, which link together the leading figures in the story," and often by an additional interest in the workings of heredity across those generations, in a version of "biological determinism" (553) that updated the ancient Greek conception of Fate for a modern era "ruled by science" (551). Zucker christened this new form—whose own lineage stretched across several literary generations, from Zola to contemporary writers such as Rose Macauley, John Galsworthy, Edgar Lee Masters, Joseph Hergesheimer,

Kathleen Norris, G. B. Stern, Maxim Gorky, and Thomas Mann (whose *Buddenbrooks* Zucker declared "the finest example so far produced in the genre" [556])—the *genealogical novel*.

Little did Zucker know that at the very moment his essay was finding its way into print, another contemporary novelist (and youthful reviewer of Hergesheimer), writing in and about a small Mississippi town several hundred miles southwest of College Park, was working furiously on what would become one of the century's signature exercises in Zucker's new genre, one of the most influential modern novels of multigenerational family. Launched by the death of a grandmother and more or less brought to completion by the elopement of her seventeen-year-old great-granddaughter three decades later, *The Sound and the Fury*, comprising the interior monologues of a trio of brothers and an externally narrated chronicle of Easter Sunday 1928, spans thirty years, four generations, and half a continent, providing the panoramic sweep Zucker attributes to his genre. The novel's running flirtation with contemporary eugenics theories and themes, which I have documented elsewhere, evinces its interest in heredity as a principal biological determinant of character and action.[3] Characters like Quentin and Jason Compson voice anxiety about, and their disabled brother Benjy appears to embody, a family lineage in decline—in both social status and biological vigor—over successive generations, raising the issue of "decadence" that for Zucker (556) preoccupies twentieth-century genealogical novelists like Mann (whose work Faulkner admired) and Gorky, and that of course also preoccupied the eugenics movement throughout this period. Had Zucker waited another year or so to publish his essay, then, he might have been forced to reconsider his verdict that *Buddenbrooks* represented the culmination of the modern genealogical novel. If *The Sound and the Fury* was, as Philip M. Weinstein argues, the breakthrough novel in which Faulkner discovered the implications of childhood as a literary resource, it was also, and in part for this very reason, the novel in which he first delivered on the full literary potential of family.[4]

It was in fact his *second* foray in Zucker's just-christened genre. First had been *Flags in the Dust*, the novel in which Faulkner introduced the fictional county of Yoknapatawpha in his oeuvre, and his first novel to sprawl beyond filial and sibling dynamics to encompass a century's worth of Mississippi kinsmen and kinswomen, five generations in all, giving family the full weight of regional and national history in his fiction. The discovery/invention of Yoknapatawpha and that of genealogy, then, were coeval phenomena in Faulkner's mature understanding of novelistic form and theme. He would go on, like some of Zucker's exemplars, to append a genealogical table—if not quite an actual tree diagram—for the Sutpen family, again five generations strong, to *Absalom, Absalom!*, a table that would suggestively include Quentin Compson and Shreve McCannon, those intrepid historians of the Sutpen saga, alongside (or, more suggestively, *among*?) Sutpen's own kin. Six years later the novelist would outdo himself with the seven-generation McCaslin lineage in *Go Down, Moses*, though this time he would leave the heavy lifting of genealogy construction to his critics.[5]

Family in Faulkner, however, can't be reduced to the vertical, intergenerational phenomenon of genealogy alone. In leading Yoknapatawpha clans like the Sutpens, McCaslins, and Snopeses, it also achieves a formidable horizontal sweep, enfolding, exacerbating, or ever so occasionally annealing differences of race, class, religion, sexuality, language, region, nation, and, in some of the Civil War fictions, political allegiance. With two wives and two additional consorts, the wealthy planter Thomas Sutpen, for example, fathers five siblings and half-siblings, marrying transnationally, crossing the color line sexually at least twice, and, in his last-ditch liaison with Milly Jones, descending the class ladder into the same poor-white stock from which he had struggled to lift himself back in antebellum Tidewater, Virginia. The Snopeses elevate male cousinhood to an art form, though without creating much in the way of family loyalty along the way. Such bonds loom larger in the ethos of McCaslin cousins like Lucas Beauchamp, Ike McCaslin, and Cass Edmonds, as their various relationships and mutual responsibilities bear out. Occupying a kind of limbo between matrilineal and patrilineal form, as Patricia Galloway has shown, the lineage of Chickasaw patriarchs Issetibbeha and Ikkemotubbe rests uneasily, and sometimes fractures, along fault lines of sibling- and cousinhood; indeed, in some accounts Ikkemotubbe must murder one of his cousins to assume the mantle of The Man in the tribal community.[6] Other horizontal networks reach beyond blood ties to assemble familylike structures held together by affiliation rather than strictly by filiation: the yachtful of bohemian brethren and sistren in *Mosquitoes*; the barnstorming troupe of *Pylon*, where a mechanic and a newspaper reporter supplement the sexual *ménage* of Roger, Laverne, and Jack; the Mahon household of *Soldiers' Pay*, where Great War veterans Joe Gilligan and Margaret Powers do their best to stand in for missing mothers, siblings, and lovers; or the peculiar Civil War sisterhood, half desperate, half utopian, among Judith, Clytie, and Rosa in chapter five of *Absalom*. A place of honor might additionally be reserved for the interracial, intergenerational troika of grave-emptying sleuths in *Intruder in the Dust* among what Duvall might have called the invisible, outlaw, and unspeakable *families* of Faulkner's fiction.[7]

For all modernism's vaunted obsession with the deracinated, fragmented individual subject, set adrift amidst the maelstrom of global capitalism in the absence of the master narratives that once supplied ontological coherence and purpose, the family also figures prominently in the modernist literary imagination, for a number of overlapping reasons.[8] Certainly, as Zucker hints, Darwinian biology and genetics called attention to the family as the crucible of human evolution, where the reproduction of the species took place and moreover where the young were nurtured until they reached biological maturity and produced offspring of their own. For better or worse, the modern interest in heredity went hand in hand with concerns about the status of the modern family.[9] Even before Darwin, though, the rise of nationalist ideology enshrined family as the crucible of the modern nation, the sacred fount of the nativity that gave nation its etymological and demographic underpinnings.[10] As such, the welfare of the nation rested on the state's biopolitical management of the national population, and as Michel Foucault and others have detailed, the family provided the state with one of its crucial access points to, and purchase points over, the larger population under its care and jurisdiction, a key site for the governance of sexuality, fertility, nutrition, hygiene, and labor discipline, the proverbial "habits of industry" that ensured productive contributions to the capitalist economy—and that often began at home.[11]

For the modern discipline of psychoanalysis, on the other hand, the family proved the birthplace of psychopathologies engendered in early childhood. The Freudian family, for instance—whether essentialized as perennial and universal or historicized as modern, European, and bourgeois—was a hotbed of sexuality, violence, and rivalry from which few children emerged unscathed. As it made inroads into the intellectual and popular cultures of modernity, Freudian thought helped position the family as *bête noire* for modernism's antinomian streak, a nexus of stultifying energies, outworn values, and soul-sapping heteronormative conventions against which the rebellious modernist spirit both directed and defined its rebellion: another of the insidious "nets," along with language, nation, and religion, above which the Stephen Dedaluses of modern literature—among them not a few Faulkner characters—sought to soar.[12] In a diverse array of ways, then, family is vectored through modernity, and modernity through it, in Yoknapatawpha County and its various elsewheres in Faulkner country.

Family is also in key respects vectored through region, due in part to the legacy of paternalism, an ideology, forged in the smithy of plantation slavery, that represented the southern class and racial order as an extended patriarchal family: headed by elite white men and women, with African

Americans, working-class whites, and the poor of all stripes cast, alongside actual juveniles, in the role of dependent children, subject to the authority and oversight, and reliant on the largesse, of their social superiors, who bemoaned the burden of responsibility for their ostensible dependents even as they congratulated themselves for assuming it.[13] Whether as received social wisdom or as a crippling impediment to racial equality and social progress—staging interracial kinship as regional allegory, for example, instead of the biological actuality it so often was in the plantation's shadow, and in Falkner family history—paternalism worked itself deeply into the imagination and worldview of nineteenth- and twentieth-century southerners, and into the warp and weft of the region's literature as well, including a great deal of Faulkner fiction.[14] Jason Compson *frère*, for instance, repeatedly invokes the discourse of paternalism in bolstering his self-image as the patriarch and breadwinner who "keep[s] the flour barrel full" for his Compson *and* Gibson charges in *The Sound and the Fury*, even as events unfold to reveal the extent of his actual dependence—financial, emotional, practical, biological—on the women and African Americans (and, in Dilsey's case, both) in his life.[15] Paternalism similarly informs the ease with which white planter Roth Edmonds inserts himself into the economic, domestic, and conjugal affairs of his Black elders (and tenants, and kinsmen), Lucas and Mollie Beauchamp, in *Go Down, Moses*, as well as the breezily superior attitude that Gavin Stevens adopts toward *his* elder Lucas throughout *Intruder in the Dust*.[16] And as other scholars have noted, paternalist ideology is a guiding principle behind the education, or *bildung*, of young Lucius Priest, the narrator-protagonist of Faulkner's final novel, *The Reivers*: an elite white boy whose adolescent exploits in the company of African American Ned McCaslin, working-class white (and part-Chickasaw) Boon Hogganbeck, and salt-of-the-earth white sex worker Everbe Corinthia lay the groundwork for his assumption of the privileged role to which his status as gentleman-in-the-making entitles him in the novel's turn-of-the-century social, racial, and political milieu.[17]

Southern paternalism shaped William Faulkner's own self-fashioning and self-understanding as well as his writings. Especially after the death of his father in 1932, he was acutely aware, as eldest son, that the mantle of paterfamilias, responsible for a trigenerational clan encompassing multiple households in Oxford, had passed to him. Later that year, he wrote his friend and agent Ben Wasson, "Dad left mother solvent for only about 1 year. Then it is me."[18] To editors, he liked to lament the toll that such obligations, financial and otherwise, took on his imagination and art. By 1940, for instance, the stoic tone he had struck with Wasson eight years before had yielded to a more self-pitying, and self-dramatizing, one in a letter to Robert K. Haas at Random House, wherein the novelist complained:

> Beginning at thirty I, an artist, a sincere one and of the first class, who should be free even of his own economic responsibilities and with no moral conscience at all, began to become the sole, principal and partial support—food, shelter, heat, clothes, medicine, kotex, school fees, toilet paper and picture shows—of my mother ... [a] brother's widow and child, a wife of my own and two step children, my own child; I inherited my father's debts and dependents, white and black without inheriting yet from anyone one inch of land or one stick of furniture or one cent of money...[19]

The references to "kotex," his dead father's "black" dependents, and "school fees" none too subtly feminize and racialize the author's paternal charges as well as infantilize them. Yet two years earlier, on optioning the film rights to *The Unvanquished* to MGM in 1938—a novel that conducts its own ambivalent interrogation of plantation paternalism in the Civil War and postbellum South—Faulkner had applied a substantial amount of the unprecedented windfall to acquiring a 320-acre property in eastern Lafayette County that he christened Greenfield Farm, which immediately plunged him into a new and extensive network of paternalistic relations involving not only his brother John, whom he installed as overseer, but several African American tenant families who raised crops on the land and contributed to the mule-breeding operations there. And while Faulkner sometimes griped about the everyday challenges of managing Black dependents on the farm—not to mention a fraternal factotum with ideas of his own about farming and farmhands—he just as clearly drew to fruitful effect on his personal experiences with the vagaries of southern paternalism in crafting and choreographing the Roth Edmonds–Lucas Beauchamp relationship in *Go Down, Moses* and the Gavin Stevens–Lucas relationship in *Intruder*.[20]

During this period, the novelist's lifelong bond with Caroline Barr, profoundly shaped and misshaped by a paternalistic ethos that he imposed on their relationship and she by turns accommodated and resisted there, left its indelible mark on the *Go Down, Moses* material in at least two important respects: in the character of Mollie Beauchamp, including her own efforts to achieve agency and preserve dignity in her dealings with two generations of paternalistic Edmonds landlords, one of whom she nursed in infancy, and with an equally condescending if well-meaning Jefferson attorney; and in his dedication of the novel, his deepest and most unsparing dive into southern race relations, to Barr's memory. From the extensive childhood time he and his brothers spent with Barr, including forays into her local Black world and among her Black kin, young Faulkner might well have come to an appreciation that, far from the "tangle of pathology" implicated in American academic sociology and in policy documents like the infamous Moynihan Report of 1965, the Black family was actually, in Hortense J. Spillers's words, "one of the supreme social *achievements* of African Americans under conditions of enslavement" and in the long afterlives of American slavery.[21] For the enslaved and their descendants, family was never a given but had to be painstakingly and continually *made*. In Faulkner's work, families like the Gibsons of *The Sound and the Fury* and the Black Beauchamps of *Go Down, Moses* attest to the difficult, ongoing, and ultimately successful work of that making.

At the same time, the adult Faulkner's sense of his rights and responsibilities toward the woman he called "Mammy Callie," and of her place in the Faulkner family and in his household, entitled him, in his own eyes and no doubt in the white community's eyes as well, to make the arrangements for her funeral, hold the service in his parlor at Rowan Oak, release his eulogy for her to the national wire services ("it turned out to be pretty good prose," he later observed), and place a marker on her grave in St. Peter's cemetery memorializing her as "Mammy" and declaring further that "her white children bless her."[22] In this way the dictates of white paternalism ensured that what her loss meant to the Faulkner family would be allowed to take precedence, in the private space of a white home and the public space of a Jim Crowed graveyard, over what it meant to the Barrs themselves.[23] Any attempt, then, to reckon with the legacy and significance of what we could loosely call William Faulkner's "Black families"—the domestic workers and families who labored for him and his kin, the farm families who lived and worked at Greenfield, and others, like the African American Falkners of Tippah County, who remained outside the Faulkner fold, unacknowledged by the white descendants of the novelist's slaveholding great-grandfather William Clark Falkner—must proceed, carefully, amidst such ironies, ambivalences, and disavowals.

For all these reasons and many more, family is a topic that has long preoccupied Faulkner scholarship. Cleanth Brooks, for example, played amateur genealogist in the appendices to *William Faulkner: The Yoknapatawpha Country*, trying his hand at family trees for the county's leading dynasts.[24] Arthur F. Kinney edited a series of essay collections in the 1980s and 1990s that came at the author's work by way of the great (white) families of Yoknapatawpha County: Compson, Sartoris, McCaslin, Sutpen.[25] French scholar Gwendolyn Charbrier dedicated an entire monograph to the subject, *Faulkner's Families: A Southern Saga* (1993), which employed biographical and textual criticism to trace a changing vision of family relations across Faulkner's career.[26] For Édouard Glissant, it is above all in family and lineage that the great dialectical drama in Faulkner plays out between the "atavistic" yearning for stable roots, legitimate origins, and pure bloodlines and the "composite" realities of New World societies founded in trauma, dispersal, and "digenesis."[27] Glissant's fellow Caribbeanists George B. Handley and Valerie Loichot have addressed the respective roles of genealogy and orphanhood in major Faulkner novels like *Absalom, Absalom!* and *Light in August*.[28] Thadious M. Davis recentered *Go Down, Moses* around L. Q. C. McCaslin's shadow family, and above all around McCaslin's African American son, Terrel ("Turl") Beauchamp, in one of the boldest revisionary readings of a Faulkner text to date.[29] John T. Irwin, Andre Bleikasten, and Carolyn Porter have singled out Faulknerian fatherhood for special scrutiny as a keystone in his artistic vision, while Noel Polk and Deborah Clarke have taken motherhood as their special optic on the work of gender in Faulkner's writings.[30] The list could—and will—go on. Starting in these very pages.

The dozen essays collected here extend the longstanding and always generative focus on family in Faulkner into new and surprising territory. We begin with a trio of essays that address the role of the child in Faulkner's vision of family and regional society. Katherine Henninger takes up the convergence of the Gothic genre and the figure of the child as technologies of racial disavowal that, in the hands of William Faulkner and his fellow southern artist Sally Mann, can be wielded against themselves to expose the workings of a white supremacy they elsewhere collude to sublimate. "Whiteness, Childhood, and the Faulknerian Gothic in 'That Evening Sun' and Sally Mann" faults Southern Gothic in its more spectacular manifestations (including *Absalom, Absalom!*) for overrepresenting the nation's constitutive racial traumas to the point of rendering them utterly alien or, worse, enjoyable in their monstrosity. At the same time, the genre displaces national legacies of racial violence and haunting onto regional ground, acknowledging the work of American racism in the South while disclaiming it elsewhere. Within the familial dramas on which so many Southern Gothic texts hinge, childhood becomes a vehicle alternately for the ascription of racial innocence and for the exploration of fault lines in the massive labor of unknowing on which such ascriptions rest. Faulkner's story "That Evening Sun" is a key text for Henninger in laying out dual paths in its author's "engagement of the Gothic": a "canonical" version, with its problematic "figurations and displacement," and a counterhegemonic version "deploy[ed] in service of unmasking and registering the very work" that the canonical version performs. In this alternative Gothic, the dozens and dozens of unanswered questions that the Compson children put to the adults of their world in the face of sexual mystery and racial terror bring into clearer view the processes by which "whiteness and its history becom[e] un-thought" within the white family and white Jefferson more generally. Mann, long known for photographing her own children in situations and environments evocative of Southern Gothic, achieves a similar stereoscopic effect with the genre in bringing together her daughter Virginia and her family's African American caregiver, Virginia Carter, in a series of photos, "The Two Virginias," that "do a double duty, representing both the assertion of racial innocence" in the vulnerable white child "and the fraught landscape" of racialized southern work arrangements "that leads to the desperate need to assert innocence in the first place." That landscape includes a third Virginia, that of Mann's native state, itself no stranger to gothicization in both regional and national histories of representation. These artists take both childhood and the Gothic South to new places, reclaiming them as resources "for exposing and analyzing *the ways* that whiteness becomes unthought" rather than resources "for making it so."

Like Henninger, Maude Hines focuses on the Southern Gothic child, whom she finds to be "a palimpsestic figure haunted by the past and focused on futurity," at once "a repository of inherited pain and guilt" and "a haunting evocation of the continuation of those injuries." "Across the Ditch: Race, Childhood, and the Machinery of Fate in Faulkner" follows figures like Jason Compson of "That Evening Sun," Joe Christmas of *Light in August*, and Sarty Snopes of "Barn Burning" as they "undergo an iterative assimilation of white supremacy's violence" and the "complex and oppressive social machinery" through which it imposes itself on their lives. Staged in the form of intense racialized encounters that seem to bear the overwhelming force of fate yet challenge immediate comprehension, the process of racial initiation, everywhere mediated by the nation's most explosive racial epithet, gives Faulkner's fiction "a Gothic and stultifying atmosphere in which the past haunts the present and circumscribes the future." As Hines demonstrates, Faulkner carefully orchestrates time to create "layers of temporal distance" through which readers, if not always the children themselves, can catch "glimpses of the social machinery" that both "produce[s] and frustrate[s] them." The oft-quoted phrase with which *Light in August* introduces us to the childhood world of Joe Christmas—"Memory believes before knowing remembers"—models this complex temporal work, which allows the narrative quite literally to "[pull] the curtain aside" and reveal the roots of Joe's tortured existence in the early encounters with the work, at once brutal and banal, of white supremacy and Black denigration at the orphanage. Touched by racism in very personal ways, Faulkner's white children quickly, and tragically, learn to deflect its threat by projecting it onto others: young Joe practices this strategy on the orphanage groundskeeper, while young Jason Compson employs it against Dilsey and Nancy in "That Evening Sun," a story where, as Hines puts it, "whether or not one is a 'n[-----]'" becomes "a matter of life or death," a fact apparent even, or perhaps especially, to the Compson children. "Faulkner's use of the juvenile gaze" across a wide body of writings invites readers "to remember the encounter[s] with ideology" that formed them socially, psychologically, and racially—lest the past, object of long, hard unthinking and unseeing, "come uncannily forward, distorting our perceptions of the present."

"At the center" of Faulkner's greatest novels of race, writes Rebecca Nisetich, "miscegenation seems inextricably linked to death and destruction." Yet at their margins, we find a younger generation of "racially liminal figures" who bring a "tentative optimism" to their texts, an optimism, however, that flirts problematically with untenable forms of what we now call postracialism. "Faulkner's Future Americans" focuses on three of these marginal figures—Lena Grove's baby in *Light in August*, Jim Bond in *Absalom, Absalom!*, and Roth Edmonds's child with his mixed-race Beauchamp cousin in *Go Down, Moses*—to argue that Faulkner, like his precursor Charles W. Chesnutt, experiments with the idea of racial mixture as a path beyond the nation's one-drop racial politics toward a raceless future. These characters, writes Nisetich, share two important qualities. "First, they do not know their racial ancestry," which relieves them from the burden of racial guilt and anxiety and thus helps ensure their survival. Second, "they *escape* the physical space of Yoknapatawpha," which for Faulkner remains "unchanging" and racially retrograde compared to the "new geographies" that might offer hope that "racial identities might be granted a greater degree of fluidity." Significantly, these factors also work to loosen the grip of family and ancestry on racial destiny. They thus point toward "a future where a more broadly defined conception of the family" might open up beyond the domain of "blood," so readily racialized across the social landscapes of Faulkner's South. Around Lena's newborn, for instance, family exceeds blood kinship to become surprisingly "expansive and inclusive," while around the child of "Delta Autumn" it becomes "hybrid and communal." Yet Nisetich concludes with a caution: both Faulkner's and Chesnutt's scenarios present as postracial futures what are in fact simply post-Black ones. As such, they leave the structural dominance of whiteness—the farthest thing from an unraced or raceless position—untroubled "as the norm against which all other differences," including the supposedly disappearing racial ones, "are defined." There's wisdom here, and a warning, for our own Obama-era national fantasies of postracialism as a substitute for the harder work of reconciliation and repair.

From Faulknerian children we move on to the subject of sibling relations in one of Faulkner's best-known novels of family. Tracking the competing forms of desire that circulate within the Bundren family to propel the clan toward Jefferson and the reader toward narrative resolution, Josephine Adams argues that Addie Bundren "in all her forms—alive, dead, somewhere in between"—should not be considered "the narrative's determining force" in Faulkner's fifth novel. In "'It Takes Two People to Make You': Brotherhood and Loss in *As I Lay Dying*," Adams contends that young Vardaman Bundren's interior monologues in particular are "haunted" by the absence of his brother Darl, institutionalized in Jackson as the novel comes to a close. Adams traces across these monologues "a subconscious series of attempts to name and to fill the void" created by Darl's loss. Reminding us of the retrospective dimension of the character monologues, narrating events completed months earlier but still bearing the evocative force of the now, Adams suggests that Vardaman spends the entire narrative mourning Darl. He is the one Bundren, she claims, to experience Darl's loss "*as* a loss" (emphasis added), "an absence that produces grief and longing." And this is in part because Darl is the one Bundren who responds with love and understanding to Vardaman's traumatic efforts to process his mother's death. In the boy's "unwitting ode to his brother's care" in a time of crisis, we can see Vardaman *and Faulkner* working toward a new model of brotherhood, formed in language and metaphor, in which the siblings "become so woven together that they slip into each other's monologues." Throughout the novel, Vardaman's voice dips at times into a poetic, ontological register suggesting no other speaker more than Darl. So much does Darl become "a part of Vardaman's after-Addie identity" (emphasis omitted) that when the older brother is sent away to Jackson, the younger feels not only the loss of a sibling but "the loss of a piece of himself." The brothers' final monologues powerfully underscore this discursive reinflection of kinship: Vardaman is repeatedly interrupted by italicized fragments that recall the banished Darl to consciousness and the page; and Darl is peppered with insistent Vardaman-like questions as he refers to himself in the third person, as if seeing his catastrophe through his brother's eyes. Modern literature holds few scenes wherein family bonds are more estranging yet achingly intimate than this.

"The paradoxical power of monumentality," writes Julie Beth Napolin, is that "it coerces not memory, but forgetting." As it offers up historical screen memories and official histories for public contemplation and valorization, it places deeper historical wounds and defeats off limits, preventing citizens from "recognizing loss as loss such that it may be named, laid to rest, and futurity opened." Faulkner recorded the efforts of the southern civic order to direct "memory and mourning" toward its own Lost Causes, but the author was equally sensitive to "defiant acts," emerging from the civic margins of family and homeplace, "that might embody an alternative or counter-monumentality" oriented toward forms of kinship, grief, duty, and care unacknowledged, if not proscribed, by the state. "Undutiful Daughters: Women, Kinship, and Monument beyond Family in *Absalom, Absalom!*" finds in Sophocles's Antigone the paradigmatic example of Napolin's titular figure, the undutiful daughter and sister who defies both patriarchal power and the edicts of the state by burying and publicly mourning her exiled brother Polynices. In refusing to place civic affiliation ahead of kinship, *polis* above *oikos*, she not only memorializes forms of injury that the state would prefer to forget (the nightmare of civil war) but forges new ties between the living and the dead, in a public theater that invites the reopening of foreclosed pasts. In *Absalom, Absalom!*, Rosa Coldfied, Judith Sutpen, and especially Clytie Sutpen all perform versions of the Antigone role. If Sutpen arrives in Yoknapatawpha County as "someone who has sworn to forget" the histories of trauma both undergone in Virginia and inflicted in Haiti, the novel's undutiful daughters introduce a rival "narrative economy" and temporality, a feminine one "defined by the insistence upon remembering," and indeed upon grieving and monumentalizing, those victimized as collateral damage in the Sutpen Design. Though for Napolin, Rosa ultimately falls short of a counter-monumentalizing mode of *action*, "new arrangements of kinship" nonetheless "blossom" in and through her narration, especially in chapter 5: between Clytie and Judith, Clytie and Henry, Bon and Rosa herself, Rosa and Clytie, Clytie and Bon—what Napolin calls "family by other means." Judith and Clytie go even farther, first raising Valery Bon and then monumentalizing his memory within the genealogy and built environment of the dynastic plantation. And Clytie's climactic act of burning down the Sutpen mansion performs an ambiguous "mourning" of *both* of the brothers to whom slavery's obliteration of kinship ties denies her the title of sister: "in burying Henry Sutpen" in the holocaust, "she names him as kin; in destroying Sutpen's Hundred, she names Charles Bon as kin." In all of three of these rebellious "not-sisters" and "not-daughters," then, Napolin finds "emblem[s] of a politically transformative kinship."

Drawing on paradigms from media studies, two essays approach Faulknerian family relations via a network model. For Jeff Allred, modern discursive technologies reconfigure one of Faulkner's Civil War–era families in ways that ultimately exceed blood ties. "White Noise/Black Codes: Inscription and Representation in *The Unvanquished*" utilizes the theoretical model of the discourse network, brainchild of German media theorist Friedrich Kittler, and the historical paradigm of systematic management, a modern inscription system with roots in Civil War–era military communications and corporate railroad operations, to unpack the surprising complexity of the media landscape of *The Unvanquished* and its equally surprising implications for the Sartoris family network. When Granny Millard and Ringo "hack" the Union Army's communications system to appropriate mules and money for redistribution among their war-ravaged neighbors in Yoknapatawpha County, we see how the military's written chain of command becomes vulnerable to "occupation" not only by southern sympathizers but by members of marginalized social groups—women, children, African Americans, the elderly—headquartered in a plantation slave cabin rather than a formal command center. Here Faulkner demonstrates "the activity and agency available to users of modern media," working to empower "uncredentialed subjects" in an "unlikely space"—but also to turn a slaveholding family into "a little corporation" with its own sophisticated inscription practices. The ironies continue in a pair of framing narratives, "Ambuscade" and "Skirmish at Sartoris," in which white masculine power reasserts itself, in wartime and postbellum scenes, by forcibly recapturing the technologies of inscription from rogue elements threatening the plantocratic status quo, and moreover through the "weaponization" of white noise—the Rebel yell—to drown out forms of Black knowledge and political agency that surface within unstable wartime and Reconstruction-era regimes. In Allred's revisionist reading, *The Unvanquished* is less a nostalgic venture in "reuniting the national 'family' by revising white supremacy and patriarchy . . . in an ostensibly kinder, gentler form" than "a forward-looking exercise in thinking about creative occupation of media infrastructure," and about the "postpatriarchal and/or transracial" affiliations that might result from such efforts.

Robert Jackson finds in "family estrangement," a problem ubiquitous in Faulkner but nowhere more so than in *Go Down, Moses*, a conceptual tool that allows the author to interrogate "the model of the heteronormative, genealogically blood-obsessed family" that served as "the dominant template" of his regional society. "When Will We Be Extinct? Faulknerian Cosmopolitanism and the Family Network" proposes a new concept, the family network, to get at the media properties of genealogy itself, the way that, for the blood-haunted families and communities of Faulkner's South, genealogy serves as a system for the transmission and storage of crucial information across not only space but time. At the same time, Faulkner's deeply dysfunctional, unconventional families—mixed, queered, splintered, involuted—disrupt this transmission process, pointing at once to "deeply problematic origins" and to "the prospect of their own extinction." Blood connects and perpetuates, yet blood dooms. For Jackson, the site where "the mobile, irrepressible blood of the genealogy and the biological prospect of extinction" collide is the Faulknerian family, "transforming the genealogy into a medium that foretells its own demise." Yet Jackson doesn't see these family fables as ultimately defeatist. He calls attention to the way they point beyond themselves toward alternative forms of affiliation and "sustainable models of human community" unavailable to so many of the novelist's inward-looking protagonists, who often glimpse these new forms of kinship or attachment but are unable to affirm or attain them. According to Jackson, it's ultimately to more cosmopolitan models, emerging out of widely shared global conditions of mortality and vulnerability, that we must turn to arrive at "alternative futures" and a "genealogical awareness that both grounds and liberates." Jackson locates that cosmopolitan ethic in the work of philosopher Kwame Anthony Appiah—and within the tangled circuitry of some of Faulkner's most fraught family networks.

George Porter Thomas is also preoccupied with the work of what he calls "Faulkner's Subversive Genealogies." Thomas takes the concept of "subversive genealogy" from Judith Shklar, by way of historian Michael Rogin, to remind us that "all genealogies begin with a crime," an exercise of power that the bloodline is invoked, indeed constructed, to legitimate and explain. Yet the "backwards tracings" of descent lines inevitably lead us back to the crime, the "brutal origins" of the ruling class. Faulkner's genealogies prove no exception. As a case study in genealogical *form* removed "from the more familiar *content* of the 'white' houses of Yoknapatawpha," Thomas turns to the cycle of narratives surrounding the Chickasaw chief Ikkemotubbe: *Go Down, Moses*, certainly, but also "Red Leaves," "A Justice," "A Courtship," and the Compson Appendix from Malcolm Cowley's *Portable Faulkner* volume of 1946. Ikkemotubbe's genealogy proves one of the most self-subverting in all of Faulkner. It points to brutal origins, what Thomas calls the coup d'état that Ikkemotubbe orchestrates against his uncle and nephew: an unsettling reminder that "Yoknapatawpha begins with murder." It is also epistemologically self-subverting, varying across the tales with what Thomas argues is "a purposeful sketchiness" meant to lend both "opacity" and "contingency" to the past, and to enlist the reader in the enterprise of disambiguation and interpretation. When we take up that errand, though, we arrive at further ambiguity—did Ikkemotubbe sire Sam Fathers with an enslaved woman or didn't he? But we also implicate ourselves in the same genealogical labors whose pernicious ideological work the texts expose. Framing the past in familial terms proves a hard habit to break, and Faulkner's fiction forces an awareness of "how invested we remain in bloodlines," and above all in their premise "that what matters most about the past are the ways it led to us." A healthier skepticism toward genealogy might enable us to "imagine a past not shaped by descent and inheritance," one whose "radical alterity" includes "not only our lost ancestors but those hazy generations who did not lead to us at all."

The next two essays turn to a pair of unlikely tropes to defamiliarize the function and impact of kinship in Faulkner: animality and contagion. Why, asks John N. Duvall, is Ike McCaslin, "having . . . recognized his kinship with African Americans and chosen a former McCaslin slave," Sam Fathers, "as his spiritual father," nonetheless unable "to defy a southern racial prohibition by proudly claiming and openly socializing with his Black relatives" in *Go Down, Moses*? Surprisingly, the answer lies in part in the young man's seemingly radical turn to the interspecies affiliations of the Big Woods to break the cycle of the plantation's racial injustices and create an alternative genealogy and future for himself. Duvall's "Beasts in the Mississippi Jungle: Ike McCaslin's Queer Animal Kinship" argues that the blandishments of a fetishized whiteness ultimately override the painful racial knowledge Ike gleans from the family plantation ledgers and lead him to fashion a lineage founded in Indigenous and animal kinship and in the "nonbiological homosocial" bonds of the hunting camp—in effect closing rather than balancing the books on the Black McCaslins and ethnically cleansing his own ancestry. As Duvall goes on to show, however, the nominally all-male, non-Black world that Ike seeks in the Big Woods proves far too unstable to prop up his project. Instead, it teems with unpredictable, uncontrollable energies, particularly in the intimacy between Boon Hogganbeck and the great hunting dog Lion, which singlehandedly introduces interracial, intersex, and homoerotic overtones into the "mutual, interspecies pleasure" on display in their relationship. Duvall meticulously demonstrates that such racially fluid, gender-bending, multiply queered, and anatomically shape-shifting intensities surface repeatedly across the hunting stories of *Go Down, Moses*, giving the lie to any stand Ike might hope to take in the Big Woods against the "incestuous miscegenation" that morally and racially tainted his heritage by creating his Black kin back on the plantation—kin who, over and over, refuse to stay in their assigned social or genealogical places. For Duvall, the "fantasy of Indianness" that Ike indulges in the Mississippi wilderness, along with his efforts "to privilege an animal kinship over any possible relation to African Americans," constitutes the real tragedy of *Go Down, Moses*: "the failure of whites to acknowledge the open secret of their Black kin."

Maxwell Cassity's thought experiment is to take seriously the textual and critical troping of the Snopes family's incursions into the economy and society of Yoknapatawpha County as a plague or scourge, "a contagious pattern of infection, assimilation, and corruption." "The Jefferson Outbreak: An Epidemiological Reading of the Snopes Family" pulls together data visualization tools from the Digital Yoknapatawpha project, close reading techniques, and contextual analysis into "a metaphorical and methodological framework" for following the Snopeses separately and together "across and between texts," from cameo appearances in *As I Lay Dying* and *Sanctuary* to central roles in *The Hamlet*, *The Town*, and *The Mansion*. What this methodology reveals is "an epidemiological epistemology" at work throughout the Yoknapatawpha writings—from "civilian epidemiologists" like V. K. Ratliff and Gavin Stevens, to the larger contingent of Snopes-watchers that monitors the movements and machinations of Flem and his kinsmen against the overall health of the community, and outward to interpellate the Faulkner reader as well—framing the Snopeses "as contagious 'others,' outsiders who, in their invasion of structures and hierarchies of upwardly mobile whiteness, defy and disrupt social norms." As an epidemic event, the Snopes "outbreak" moreover points to "endemic social conditions" (emphasis omitted) underway in the turn-of-the-century South, first and foremost "the fragmentation of whiteness as a racial construct" as the rural white poor migrated to the region's villages, towns, and cities and made inroads "into the economic and genetic pool of middle-class and elite whiteness." As mastermind behind and chief figurehead for the Jefferson outbreak, Flem plays a variety of epidemiologically inflected roles: as a "contagious vector" in unleashing a plague of spotted horses on an unsuspecting Frenchman's Bend; as the contagion itself on his initial arrival in Jefferson; and finally, in *The Mansion*, as an epidemiologist and immunologist in his own right, helping the community detect and expunge "his more virulent family members" who have come to threaten his respectability there, before daughter Linda turns the tables on him, mobilizing the most virulent Snopes of all, Mink, "to destroy the most entrenched." Against the background of the COVID-19 pandemic, Cassity's epidemiological approach proves as timely as it is lively, and it suggests that the "emergent truths" of literature "lie not in single characters . . . but in contagiously intersecting networks and the necessary susceptibility of self and other that accompanies healthy sociality."

A final pair of essays ranges beyond Faulkner's fiction to widen the purview of family in the author's life and career. Taking a page from James Baldwin, Garry Bertholf asks how "Faulkner's Negroes"—"the real-life domestic servants and farmhands who toiled" for Faulkner at his home and farm—might have described the author, so famous and infamous for his fictional portraits of African Americans. In "Faulkner Wasn't 'Our People'": Faulkner's 'Negroes,' the McJunkinses' Faulkner, and Our Search for Greenfield Farm," Bertholf recounts his efforts to learn more about a man whose name he encountered in Faulkner's 1951 and 1954 wills. Lawrence Arenza McJunkins, known to Faulkner as Renzi, lived and worked on Greenfield Farm, the author's 320-acre property in northeast Lafayette County, in the 1940s and 1950s and was the subject of specific provisions in both wills concerning his living and farming arrangements there. Renzi's brother Charles McJunkins and nephew Alvis McJunkins are also named in the 1954 will. Bertholf's research with US Census records led him to Alvis's daughter Trudy McJunkins Young, his son Charles McJunkins, and their cousin Theron McJunkins, with whom Bertholf visited the Greenfield property, much of it now reverting to forest and its buildings dilapidated and collapsing, in 2018 and 2019. At the "Faulkner's Families" conference, Bertholf interviewed Trudy and Charles, who shared family photographs and memories. Pointing out the family's history of independent landownership in the area, the McJunkinses also discussed the "administrative work" that their father performed for Faulkner when the author was away from the farm and the "serenity" and companionship that Faulkner found at Greenfield, especially with Renzi McJunkins. Asked if the family knew about Faulkner's wills, Charles remarked that the McJunkinses "couldn't necessarily pin our lives on" the provisions there, one reason Alvis moved on to a full-time job in Oxford after Faulkner's death and set up with his family on property of their own. These Greenfield memories, along with the archival materials Bertholf consulted in his research, suggest the need for "some shifting of sights in the study of William Faulkner," toward "a more capacious history" of "the material foundations" of aesthetic production, one that stresses "collective labor" over authorial genius in the creation of canonical literary texts—the sort of labor, for example, provided by the Black minders who attended to Faulkner and cared for him while he relaxed *and wrote* on the farm. The political economy of Greenfield and the political economy of the Faulkner oeuvre thus meet in the lives and histories of the McJunkinses, putting necessary pressure on the purview, and indeed on the very notion, of Faulkner's families.

For Yoko Yamamoto, by contrast, family is a movable ideological piece in the cultural Cold War. "'The Family of Man': William Faulkner, Atomic Diplomacy, and US Visual Education in Post-Occupation Japan" examines Faulkner's 1955 appearances as a US cultural ambassador in Nagano, Japan, in conjunction with the 1956 exhibition of *The Family of Man*, a collection of images curated by photographer Edward Steichen, as twin elements of US cultural diplomacy in support of the Eisenhower Administration's Atoms for Peace initiative. Like *The Family of Man*, the short film *Impressions of Japan*, which stars William Faulkner, was sponsored by the Japanese office of the US Information Service, as what Yamamoto calls "'visual aids' in the context of atomic diplomacy." Atoms for

Peace, which proposed the donation of fissionable materials by the US and USSR for humanitarian purposes like energy production and medicine, was aimed at countering Soviet propaganda that alleged the US was interested only in the destructive power of the atom. Winning the hearts and minds of the nation where nuclear weapons were first used against a military adversary was a key objective of the campaign, crucial to "establishing and expanding the nuclear world family in which the US would reign as the rightful patriarch." The campaign had its own traveling exhibit, which came to Tokyo in 1955, the tenth anniversary of the Hiroshima and Nagasaki bombings. Into this breach stepped Faulkner, in August 1955, and Steichen's exhibit, which toured extensively between March 1956 and summer 1957. Carefully edited for its images and verbal content, *Impressions of Japan* places scenes from Faulkner's Nagano sessions—with high school students, with academics—beneath voiceover narration that steer their significance away from immediate geopolitical realities and nuclear fears toward humanistic evocations of a "multicultural world family." To similar ends, the organizing committee for the *Family of Man* exhibit removed a photo of a hydrogen bomb test ("the only color photograph in the whole exhibit") and covered up other photos of atomic disaster when the emperor visited the exhibit. These concerted efforts to "obliterate ... traumatic memories of the past" in Japan "and replace them with a therapeutic picture of a bright new future" were, as exercises in soft power, smashing successes: by 1956, Japan had formed a national Atomic Energy Commission, created a Science and Technology agency to promote "advanced science," and, perhaps most tellingly, installed the Atoms for Peace exhibit in the Hiroshima Peace Memorial Museum. In this way, Yamamoto concludes, Faulkner served his government not only as spokesperson but as "icon" of "the Cold War nuclear family of the Western Free World."

• • •

Faulkner's final novel was a long, loving reminiscence told by a grandfather to his grandchildren—one that, moreover, ends with the entrance of one of Yoknapatawpha's seemingly most inveterate bachelors, Boon Hogganbeck, into marriage, family, and futurity in his own right. All along the way to *The Reivers*, family serves again and again as a window onto the workings of history, the complexities of psychology, the exigencies of economics and class, the ordeal of race, the afterlives of slavery, the impact of modernity, and even the principles of ecology in the Faulkner cosmos. The real-life families, Black and white, of and around the author—Falkners, Butlers, Swifts, Oldhams, Barrs, Prices,

McJunkinses—played their own roles as sources of insight into the man, his work, and his world. For all these reasons, the question of family remains an inescapably generative one in Faulkner studies, destined to preoccupy current and future generations of readers and critics.

NOTES

1. William Faulkner quoted in Joseph Blotner, *Faulkner: A Biography*, vol. 1 (New York: Random House, 1974), 694. The interview originally appeared in the New York literary journal *The Bookman*.

2. A. E. Zucker, "The Genealogical Novel, A New Genre," *PMLA* 43, no. 2 (June 1928): 551. Hereafter cited parenthetically.

3. See Jay Watson, "Genealogies of White Deviance: *Mongrel Virginians*, *Buck v. Bell*, and William Faulkner, 1926-1931," in *Faulkner and Whiteness*, ed. Watson (Jackson: University of Mississippi Press, 2011), 34-42, 53-55.

4. Philip M. Weinstein, *Becoming Faulkner: The Art and Life of William Faulkner* (New York: Oxford University Press, 2010), 36-61.

5. See, for instance, the series of McCaslin genealogies developed for the Digital Yoknapatawpha project at the University of Virginia: http://www.people.virginia.edu/~sfr/FAULKNER/09gdmgen.html. Accessed March 5, 2021.

6. Patricia Galloway, "The Construction of Faulkner's Indians," *Faulkner Journal* no. 18, 1-2 (Fall 2002-Spring 2003): 9-31.

7. John N. Duvall, *Faulkner's Marginal Couple: Invisible, Outlaw, and Unspeakable Communities* (Austin: University of Texas Press, 1990).

8. See, for example, Bradley Gerhardt, "Genealogical Modernism: Family Structures, Identity, History, and Narrative in the Twentieth-Century 'Long' Novel" (PhD diss., University of Washington, 2018).

9. On Darwinian evolution as a shaping intellectual force for modernism, see William Montgomery, "Charles Darwin and the Problem of Modernism," *The Mind's Eye: A Liberal Arts Journal* (Fall 2009): 16-31; Robert Faggen, *Robert Frost and the Challenge of Darwin* (Ann Arbor: University of Michigan Press, 1997); Carrie Rohman, *Stalking the Subject: Modernism and the Animal* (New York: Columbia University Press, 2009), 1-28; and, closer to home, Michael Wainwright, *Darwin and Faulkner's Novels: Evolution and Southern Fiction* (New York: Palgrave Macmillan, 2008).

10. See, for example, Anthony D. Smith, *Nationalism and Modernism* (New York: Routledge, 1998); Pericles Lewis, *Modernism, Nationalism, and the Novel* (New York: Cambridge University Press, 2000), 1-95; Carolyn Levander, *Cradle of Liberty: Race, the Child, and National Belonging from Thomas Jefferson to W. E. B. Du Bois* (Durham, NC: Duke University Press, 2006); Leigh Anne Duck, *The Nation's Region: Southern Modernism, Segregation, and US Nationalism* (Athens: University of Georgia Press, 2006), 17-81; and Patricia Chu, *Race, Nationalism, and the State in British and American Modernism* (New York: Cambridge University Press, 2007).

11. See Michel Foucault, *"Society Must Be Defended": Lectures at the Collège de France 1975-1976* (1997), ed. Mauro Bertani and Alessandro Fontana, trans. David Macey (New York: Picador, 2003), 239-64; Foucault, *The History of Sexuality*, vol. 1, *An Introduction* (1976), trans. Robert Hurley (1978; repr., New York: Vintage, 1990), 136-45; and Foucault, *Security, Territory, Population: Lectures at the Collège de France, 1977-1978* (2004), ed. Michel Sennelart, trans. Graham Burchell (2007; repr., New York: Picador, 2007), 55-114; Chu, *Race, Nationalism, and the State*, 1-54; and Jay Watson, *William Faulkner and the Faces of Modernity* (New York: Oxford

University Press, 2019), 289-310. On late-nineteenth-century southern labor discipline, see Allen Tullos, *Habits of Industry: White Culture and the Transformation of the Carolina Piedmont* (Chapel Hill: University of North Carolina Press, 1989).

12. On psychoanalysis as a shaping influence on literary modernism, see, for example, Erich Heller, "Observations on Psychoanalysis and Modern Literature," *Salmagundi* 31-32 (Fall 1975-Winter 1976): 17-28; Peter Collier and Judith Davies, eds., *Modernism and the European Unconscious* (London: St. Martin's Press, 1990); Albert E. Stone, "Psychoanalysis and American Culture," *American Quarterly* 28, no. 3 (1976): 309-23; David Trotter, *Paranoid Modernism: Literary Experiment, Psychosis, and the Professionalization of English Society* (New York: Oxford University Press, 2001); Kylie Valentine, *Psychoanalysis, Psychiatry, and Modernist Literature* (New York: Palgrave Macmillan, 2003); Matt Ffytche, "The Modernist Road to the Unconscious," in *The Oxford Handbook of Modernisms*, ed., Peter Brooker et al. (New York: Oxford University Press, 2010); and John Farrell, "Psychoanalysis and Modernism," in *British Literature in Transition, 1920-1940: Futility and Anarchy*, ed. Charles Ferrall and Dougal McNeill (New York: Cambridge University Press, 2018), 125-42.

13. On southern paternalism, see Eugene D. Genovese, *The World the Slaveholders Made: Two Essays in Interpretation* (1969; repr., New York: Vintage, 1971), 100-101; Melton Alonzo McLaurin, *Paternalism and Protest: Southern Cotton Mill Workers and Organized Labor, 1875-1905* (Westport, CT: Greenwood, 1971); Genovese, *Roll, Jordan, Roll: The World the Slaves Made* (1974; repr., New York: Vintage, 1976), 3-7; Genovese, *From Rebellion to Revolution: Afro-American Slave Revolts in the Making of the Modern World* (Baton Rouge: Louisiana State University Press, 1979), 5-6; Jacquelyn Dowd Hall et al., *Like a Family: The Making of a Southern Cotton Mill World*, rev. ed. (1987; repr., Chapel Hill: University of North Carolina Press, 2000), 131-40, 366-75; Lee J. Alston and Joseph P. Ferrie, *Southern Paternalism and the American Welfare State: Economics, Politics, and Institutions in the South, 1865-1965* (New York: Cambridge University Press, 1999), 1-48, 119-42; Lacy K. Ford, *Deliver Us from Evil: The Slavery Question in the Old South* (New York: Oxford University Press, 2009), 7-10, 143-295, 462-69, 514-33, 535-36; Eugene D. Genovese and Elizabeth Fox-Genovese, *Fatal Self-Deception: Slaveholding Paternalism in the Old South* (New York: Oxford University Press, 2011); and Brannan Costello, *Plantation Airs: Racial Paternalism and the Transformations of Class in Southern Fiction, 1945-1971* (Baton Rouge: Louisiana State University Press, 2007), 1-15.

14. On the interracial lineage of William Clark Falkner, the novelist's great-grandfather, see Joel Williamson, *William Faulkner and Southern History* (New York: Oxford University Press, 1993), 23-29, 64-72. On representations of racial and social paternalism in Faulkner's fiction, see Kevin Railey, "The Social Psychology of Paternalism: *Sanctuary*'s Cultural Context," in *Faulkner in Cultural Context: Faulkner and Yoknapatawpha, 1995*, ed. Donald M. Kartiganer and Ann J. Abadie (Jackson: University Press of Mississippi, 1997), 75-98; Kevin Railey, *Natural Aristocracy: History, Ideology, and the Production of William Faulkner* (Tuscaloosa: University of Alabama Press, 1999), 6-17, 37-42; and Costello, *Plantation Airs*, 71-99.

15. William Faulkner, *The Sound and the Fury*, rev. ed. (1929; repr., New York: Vintage International, 1990), 196. See also 208.

16. See Pete Kuryla, "Racial Paternalism, Rawls, and the Rule of Law: *Intruder in the Dust* Part II," *US Intellectual History Blog*, May 2, 2018, Society for US Intellectual History, https://s-usih.org/2018/05/racial-paternalism-rawls-and-the-rule-of-law-intruder-in-the-dust-part-ii/, accessed November 28, 2020.

17. See Railey, *Natural Aristocracy* 168-75; Costello, *Plantation Airs* 91-99; and Richard Gray, *The Life of William Faulkner: A Critical Biography* (Malden, MA: Blackwell, 1994), 358-71.

18. Faulkner to Ben Wasson, likely September 25, 1932, in Joseph Blotner, ed., *Selected Letters of William Faulkner* (New York: Random House, 1977), 65.

19. Faulkner to Robert K. Haas, likely May 3, 1940, in Blotner, *Selected Letters*, 122.

20. On Greenfield Farm as a geographical and interracial template for the McCaslin plantation of *Go Down, Moses*, see Joseph Blotner, *Faulkner: A Biography*, vol. 2 (New York: Random House, 1974), 1036-37. On Roth Edmonds as an autobiographical figure through whom Faulkner channels, and explores, his interracial encounters at Greenfield, see Michael Grimwood, *Heart in Conflict: Faulkner's Struggles with Vocation* (Athens: University of Georgia Press, 1987), 232, 234, 297; and Judith L. Sensibar, *Faulkner in Love: The Women Who Shaped His Art* (New Haven, CT: Yale University Press, 2009), 98-99, 108, 110.

21. Hortense J. Spillers, "Mama's Baby, Papa's Maybe: An American Grammar Book," *Diacritics* 17, no. 2 (Summer 1987): 74 (emphasis added).

22. For Faulkner's appreciative review of his eulogy remarks, see his letter to Robert K. Haas, likely February 7, 1940, in Blotner, *Selected Letters*, 118.

23. See Teresa N. Washington, "Caroline Barr: Laughing behind the Myth of Mammy," *Southern Exposure* no. 25, 1-2 (Spring-Summer 1997): 51-54; and Sensibar, *Faulkner and Love*, 101, 105-9.

24. Cleanth Brooks, *William Faulkner: The Yoknapatawpha Country* (1963; repr., New Haven: Yale University Press, 1966), 447-52.

25. Arthur F. Kinney, ed., *Critical Essays on William Faulkner: The Compson Family* (Boston: G. K. Hall, 1982); Kinney, ed., *Critical Essays on William Faulkner: The Sartoris Family* (Boston: G. K. Hall, 1985); Kinney, ed., *Critical Essays on William Faulkner: The McCaslin Family* (Boston: G. K. Hall, 1990); Kinney, ed., *Critical Essays on William Faulkner: The Sutpen Family* (New York: G. K. Hall, 1996).

26. Gwendolyn Charbrier, *Faulkner's Families: A Southern Saga* (New York: Gordian Press, 1993).

27. Édouard Glissant, *Faulkner, Mississippi* (1996), trans. Barbara Lewis and Thomas C. Spear (New York: Farrar, Straus and Giroux, 1999), 114-15, 195.

28. George B. Handley, *Postslavery Literatures of the Americas: Family Portraits in Black and White* (Charlottesville: University of Virginia Press, 2000), 112-43; Valerie Loichot, *Orphan Narratives: The Postplantation Literature of Faulkner, Glissant, Morrison, and Saint-John Perse* (Charlottesville: University Press of Virginia, 2007), 117-56.

29. Thadious M. Davis, *Games of Property: Law, Race, Gender, and Faulkner's "Go Down, Moses"* (Durham, NC: Duke University Press, 2003).

30. John T. Irwin, *Doubling and Incest / Repetition and Revenge: A Speculative Reading of Faulkner* (Baltimore: Johns Hopkins University Press, 1975); Andre Bleikasten, "Fathers in Faulkner," in *The Fictional Father: Lacanian Readings of the Text*, ed. Robert Con Davis (Amherst: University of Massachusetts Press, 1981), 115-46; Carolyn Porter, "Symbolic Fathers and Dead Mothers: A Feminist Approach to Faulkner," in *Faulkner and Psychology: Faulkner and Yoknapatawpha, 1991*, ed. Donald M. Kartiganer and Ann J. Abadie (Jackson: University Press of Mississippi, 1994), 78-122; Carolyn Porter, "*Absalom, Absalom!*: (Un)Making the Father," in *The Cambridge Companion to William Faulkner*, ed. Philip M. Weinstein (New York: Cambridge University Press, 1996), 168-96; Noel Polk, "'The Dungeon Was Mother Herself': William Faulkner, 1927-1931," in *New Directions in Faulkner Studies: Faulkner and Yoknapatawpha, 1983*, ed. Doreen Fowler and Ann J. Abadie (Jackson: University Press of Mississippi, 1984), 61-93; Deborah Clarke, *Robbing the Mother: Women in Faulkner* (Jackson: University Press of Mississippi, 1994).

Whiteness, Childhood, and Faulknerian Gothics in "That Evening Sun" and Sally Mann

KATHERINE HENNINGER

The branches of Faulkner's Gothics are of a family tree—that literal tree under which Quentin Compson stands staring up at the muddy underpants of his sister as she spies on her grandmother's dead body; the generational chart of interrelation, usurpation, and repudiation that traces from Ikkemotubbe to Lucas Beauchamp to Temple Drake's smothered infant in *Requiem for a Nun*; and the broader genealogy of Southern Gothic.[1] My goal in this chapter is to explore the roots of this tree, grounded in what Leslie Fiedler called the "special guilts" of Native American genocide and African American slavery, to be sure, but even deeper, in the source of those tragedies: the historical development of *whiteness* as a concept, and the erasure of that history as personal and national history.[2] In the process, I hope to tease out some of the critical race ramifications and potentials of literary Southern Gothic, particularly as it grows into and through Faulkner's work, and as it intertwines with photography, especially as it grows into and through the work of the Virginia photographer Sally Mann. My focalizing lens for this endeavor, as it is so often in Faulkner's and Mann's work, is the figure of the child.

I came to this topic in part through a striking confluence in the near simultaneous 2015 publication of Harper Lee's controversial "second" novel, *Go Set a Watchman*, and Mann's critically acclaimed memoir, *Hold Still*. In their differing deployments of the Southern Gothic, Lee and Mann engage a familiar familial story of southern childhood that I hope to make strange enough to see differently, so that we can see through it to different effect. Near the end of *Go Set a Watchman*, twenty-six-year-old Jean Louise "Scout" Finch—a.k.a. the world's most famous southern child—has an epiphany of personal responsibility. Having discovered that her lawyer father, Atticus Finch—the paragon of truth, justice, and the American Way—is also a full-fledged, Citizens' Council-leading racist, Scout is self-righteously furious. She rages at her father's "betrayal" of the

American ideals that he himself has instilled in her, she vomits, and vows to flee Maycomb, Alabama, scrubbing Atticus and his false liberalism from her memory forever. But a strained visit to her beloved, now-retired caregiver, Calpurnia, forces what is really the most dramatic awakening in the book: Scout suddenly sees not only her father's but *her own* culpability in perpetuating the racist systems that have oppressed Calpurnia and her fellow African American southerners through the generations. This culpability, Scout begins to realize, springs from a blindness—an unthinking but nonetheless cultivated blindness—to the ways in which her own comfort, confidence, and independence spring from a whiteness that *depends* on the subjugation of Black lives. Jean Louise's anguished, mature revelation is that her relation to Calpurnia has been structured around an unthought but deeply known racism as entrenched in Atticus's American liberal rhetoric as it is in the childhood rhyme that percolates from her unconscious as the chapter ends. "*Eeny, meeny, miny, moe,*" begins the racist chant, and Jean Louise, in despair, reflects, "God help me."[3]

There is a similar moment of anguish in Sally Munger Mann's memoir, *Hold Still*. In chapters chronicling her childhood in 1950s and '60s Lexington, Virginia, Mann's tone is proud as she recounts her mother's political activism against racist voting laws and her doctor father's "color-blind" ministrations to both white and Black patients. Yet Mann realizes in late adulthood, that they—and she—never questioned the deeper culture of racism that structured their economic and personal relationships with their African American neighbors, including their beloved caregiver of fifty years, Virginia Carter. Dubbed "Gee-Gee" by one of Mann's brothers, Carter worked twelve hours a day, six days a week, attending to the physical and emotional needs of the Munger family. Carter's love, Mann insists, "was the real stuff that held our family together," and she was loved deeply in return.[4] When they travelled together, however, "Gee-Gee" never joined the Mungers for restaurant meals, never even left the car to use the bathroom. Mann, in retrospect, marvels that this seemed so natural as to be completely unquestioned: "It's that obliviousness, the unexamined assumption, that so pains me now: nothing about it seemed strange, nothing seemed wrong.... How could I not have wondered, not have asked?" (263).

Both Lee and Mann portray in these passages a moment of coming to white consciousness, or better, of "whites" recognizing that there's something to be conscious *of* in whiteness and its workings, in a direct, personal frame. Lee through her character and Mann in her memoir reflect back on childhoods that *feel* like a time of innocence but are revealed to be a space of learned obliviousness, a race-structured world so thoroughly "the way things are" as almost to defy examination. This, as Patricia

Yaeger so compellingly described it, is the world of the unseen everyday, the nonepic, humdrum world of things and children and common interactions, manifesting the "'obscene' species of racial blindness" that Yaeger calls "the unthought known." In her revolutionary 2000 treatise on southern women's writing, *Dirt and Desire*, Yaeger explodes the southern frames that have been used both to reveal and to repress American racial histories—the myriad "ways the South has helped encode *American* ways of racial knowing," by "both overconceptualizing and refusing to conceptualize" the white blindness that so shocks Mann and Lee.[5]

How can a world so deeply known escape thought, ask Yaeger, and Mann, and Lee? Toni Morrison asks this question of American literary studies from a different angle: "'What intellectual feats had to be performed by the author or his critic to erase me from a society seething with my presence, and what effect has that performance had on the work?' What are the strategies of escape from knowledge? Of willful oblivion?"[6] In this essay I focus on two such strategies that have been particularly important in the history of American literature and photography. Both have strong associations with the US South—particularly with the work of William Faulkner—and both have long traditions of simultaneously revealing and concealing the workings of whiteness in American literature: the Gothic and childhood. And while Yaeger in particular took some pains to steer her analysis away from what she felt was the overbearing influence of Faulkner (a.k.a. "The Dixie Limited") in southern literary criticism, I will argue that Faulkner's fiction is a crucial point of departure for both Lee's and Mann's engagement with childhood, to the extent that whiteness in their works is best understood in relation to a particular vision of Faulknerian familial Gothic. As I'll briefly explore here, the "southern" Gothic has powerfully registered American racial anxiety and violence, while figures of childhood register anxiety about regional and national innocence or guilt in relation to such violence. My guiding question is whether the ways that childhood has been positioned within a Southern Gothic frame, in Faulkner's and Mann's work for example, have served to illuminate, or further to sublimate, the "unthought known" of whiteness in a regional and national context.

Critics as diverse as Fiedler and Morrison agree that the Gothic genre evolved to give shape to American anxieties around racial instability and other taboo border-crossings. In her landmark study *Gothic America*, Teresa Goddu suggests thinking about the American Gothic less as a set of specific conventions than as a set of strategies for revealing "what haunts the nation's narratives": i.e., race.[7] "Obsessed with transgressing boundaries" (5), she writes, "American gothic literature criticizes America's national myth of new-world innocence by voicing the cultural contradictions that undermine the nation's claim to purity and equality" (10). Fiedler identifies the appeal of the Gothic for Americans along two main lines: its ability to project a frontier-inflected desire to avoid "civilization" (by which Fiedler means heterosexual marriage and childbearing), and the "special guilts" of racial exploitation of Native and African Americans. Reflecting this fear and guilt, Fiedler argues, "images of alienation, flight, and abysmal fear possess our fiction," such that, "until the gothic had been discovered, the serious American novel could not begin" (143).

It may therefore not be surprising that discussions of the Gothic mode in America so often center on the South. Building on American national literary traditions of southern Otherness that were firmly established by the mid-nineteenth century, the frightening (at least to whites) ideological instability of race and its threat to the nation was pictured in a southern, increasingly Gothic frame. Imagery of the literary South and the photographic South worked in tandem through a concerted visualization of the region using a Gothic iconography. Abolitionist images of slave beatings and flayed backs invoke tortured Black bodies *in extremis*, as well as white southern madness. The Civil War, or more accurately, the famous photographs of the Civil War popularized by Alexander Gardner and others, transformed the southern landscape into fields of dead bodies and collapsing ruins. These battlefield photographs have been called the beginning of American photo-documentary tradition, but what it was that they were understood to document changed alongside the needs of white national discourse. Over the post-Reconstruction period, the horror of the southern landscape they pictured transformed, largely via Lost Cause literature, from a land soaked in the sin of slavery and rebellion, to a land soaked in the blood of white brothers whose deaths could only be redeemed by a successful white national reunion. Saturated with so much death, the (pictured) land itself is surfeited, shattered, unruly. The Gothic rhetoric of hauntedness seems not only appropriate but perhaps understated.

Such photographs constitute a visual legacy that the literature most associated with the Southern Gothic draws upon, and in turn reshapes. Mark Twain, Erskine Caldwell, Charles Chesnutt, Richard Wright, Flannery O'Connor, Truman Capote, Katherine Anne Porter, Ralph Ellison, Tennessee Williams, and of course, William Faulkner: the shorter version of this list would be to substitute "Gothic" within Flannery O'Connor's famous quip on the grotesque: "anything that comes out of the South is going to be called [Gothic] by the Northern reader, unless it is [Gothic], in which case it is going to be called realistic."[8] O'Connor's point on regional perspective is a crucial one that I'll come back to, but it remains true that it is harder to make a list of southern authors *not* identified with the

Southern Gothic than of those who are. Certainly, many southern writers have pursued Gothic strategies toward various ends. Here, I want to distinguish, to the extent possible, between these literary deployments of Gothic tropes and imagery, and the expectations and ideological hopes raised by the literary-historical category Southern Gothic.[9] Further, while both white and Black southern artists use Gothic iconography in their work, I am focusing on white productions for the ways they both express and repress self-awareness of the workings of whiteness—a dance, or better, a service, that the Southern Gothic in turn has often performed for readers.[10] It is white writers, particularly Faulkner, whom Yaeger critiques for tapping into "the thrill of Gothic spectatorship" in ways that can overshadow the unthought but deeply known workings of whiteness in American culture—the everyday hauntings of racial oppression and trauma in the "humdrum," "taken for granted" world ("Ghosts," 99–100). I suspect she had in mind imagery such as the final moments of Sutpen's Hundred in *Absalom, Absalom!*, a novel often cited as an epitome of the Southern Gothic: a decaying Mississippi plantation house built by a "demon," set on fire by the emaciated, half-Black half sister of a withered ancient Confederate soldier whom she has been hiding for four years to protect him from prosecution for the murder of their (possibly) half-Black half brother who has attempted to marry his white half sister, though he is (possibly) already in a plaçage marriage in New Orleans with an "octoroon" woman, with whom he has sired a tragic mulatto child who in turn has sired a "hulking" "idiot" child, who howls somewhere in the distance as the house burns. (Breathe.)

Here we have what, fairly or not, has come to be known as the classic (again the uppercase) Faulknerian Gothic Southscape, at its center a haunted plantation in the final process of ruin, completing physically what it has already done morally: becoming its own Lost Cause, its doomed fratricidal family burying itself alive and leaving only fields of death, wild-eyed madness, and howling to those in its wake. In this Gothic, racial trauma is figured as family trauma in the most spectacular terms, firmly grounded below "the scary Mason-Dixon line," as Trudier Harris would have it, with "the child" as a pivotal figure for diverse anxieties around settler colonialism, dynastic imperialism, national legitimacy, gender and class and sexual oppression, and the deployment of race in all these, as Hortense Spillers and Caroline Levander have explored so productively from different angles.[11] The problem with this sort of "monstrous hauntology," Yaeger argues, is that "the blunt facts of racial trauma can be over-exposed, made facile," in what she memorably calls "the glam tropology of the Gothic." The answer to the questions of "what happened" in a national legacy of racial horror is constrained to regional and the extra-ordinary, resulting in a world that "becomes too scary-sexy, sensational-alienated to be reclaimed" ("Ghosts," 99–100).

It's this last word, "reclaimed," that I want to focus on for a moment here. To reclaim is to retrieve or recover, to redeem or reuse, but in a sense closer to its root word "claim," it can mean to take back possession, to acknowledge ownership or responsibility. In its sensationalism, Yaeger argues, the classic Southern—in this case synonymous with Faulknerian—Gothic enables and even encourages an alienation, a disclaiming, of the nearby, everyday mechanisms of racial domination and trauma. This is one of the chief literary strategies, as Morrison might say, for erasing or at least containing the Africanist presence at the core of American culture, and also for rendering the ways that whiteness is *dependent* on that presence unthought, unmarked, and unremark-able. Further, the spectacular visibility of the *Southern* Gothic—both in the pyrotechnic thrills of its imagery and in its spectacular prominence in American literary history—works hand in hand with regionalization to do some important ideological work for the nation as a whole.

That work is by definition intertextual, intermedial, and interregional, that is, nationalizing. Gothic icons of the literary South inform the way that the photographic South is made, and understood, from documentary images by Walker Evans and Bill Hudson, to art photography by Clarence John Laughlin, Ralph Eugene Meatyard, and Sally Mann. Together, these literary and photographic Gothic motifs create, and mutually reinforce, a set of expectations about the region; a way of seeing and thus knowing about the South, about race, about race *as* southern. And at the same time, the Southern Gothic provides a way of not-seeing and not-knowing about racial oppression in the rest of the nation. The visual dynamics of the Gothic and the ideological dynamics of southern exceptionalism ensure that the "special guilt" of American racial injustice and the systemic subjugation of Black bodies remains most sharply visible on a southern stage. Teresa Goddu's remarks on the national stakes of a Southern Gothic are worth quoting at length:

> The South's "peculiar" identity has not only been defined by its particular racial history, but has also often been depicted in gothic terms: the South is a benighted landscape, heavy with history and haunted by the ghosts of slavery. The South's oppositional image—its gothic excesses and social transgressions—has served as the nation's safety valve.... By so closely associating the gothic with the South, the American literary tradition neutralizes the gothic's threat to national identity. As merely a regional strategy, the gothic's horrifying hauntings, especially those dealing with race, can be contained. (*Gothic America*, 76)

To be absolutely clear, this is not to say that the racial violence reflected in the Southern Gothic is fake news, or overstated; if anything, it is understated, and the Gothic, southern or not, struggles to figure white racial anxiety and violence that are unspeakable. It *is* to say that being directed to see gothically in one direction—South—creates a blind spot to the ways in which whiteness constitutes the nation. A regionalized and canonized Southern Gothic structures the lens through which we are encouraged to understand, or to forget, the United States' racial past and present. In its view, the "what happened" of racial horror manifests within a range of regionalized characteristics, with certain shapes (white trash, mutilated Black bodies), at certain times (long ago, or in a "backward" present), and in a safely distinct place (below the scary Mason-Dixon line). In implicit (and sometimes explicit) contrast, the progressive nation is free, unscarred, innocent, alive.[12] Given these racist stakes and masking superpowers of the Southern Gothic, perhaps we are better off abandoning the Gothic altogether.

In a sense, this is the strategy that Harper Lee pursued in her first novel, *Go Set a Watchman*, apparently written in 1957 but published as her second novel in 2015. Lee's novel, with its insistently direct treatment of whiteness—not just a few "bad apple" whites, but *whiteness* itself—as the structural center of ongoing racial oppression in the mid-twentieth century, deliberately evokes and refuses the spectacular thrill of Faulknerian Gothic discourse. For example, a late-night visit by Jean Louise and her boyfriend Henry to the Finch's ancestral plantation is described in Gothic terms: on a high bluff, a two-rut road vanishes among dark trees, leading to an antebellum two-story white house surrounded by galleries. Nodding to the clichés of southern literature that would have this house "in an advanced state of decay" (71), Lee's narrator posits as twin surprises that the Finch house is in excellent condition (it has been purchased by a hunting club) and that Jean Louise does not mourn its loss. Jean Louise's feelings are in fact conflicted and, as I've argued elsewhere, intimately enmeshed in childhood nostalgia.[13] But in her first novelistic attempt to grapple with the ongoing legacy of southern racial oppression, before she deployed Gothic tropes to spectacular success three years later in *To Kill a Mockingbird*, Lee's literary engagement with the classic Faulknerian Gothic was largely to defuse it.

Other white writers have employed similar or related strategies. Yaeger's *Dirt and Desire* focuses on writers who in her view refuse the "monstrous hauntology" of the Gothic to focus on material residues and remnants, such as cotton detritus or dirt, to symbolize racial trauma and its repressed histories. And again, African American literature has a long history of deploying the Southern Gothic, sometimes directly against

Figure 1.1. Sally Mann, *The Ditch*, 1987, silver gelatin print, 8 x 10 inches, 20.3 x 25.4 cm © Sally Mann. Courtesy Gagosian

itself through parody, sometimes by "haunting back" or otherwise reclaiming its powers, as Goddu and many others have argued.[14] But, stipulating that it is an ambivalent tool, I would like to explore means by which we might reclaim Faulknerian Gothic as a technology for exposing and analyzing *the ways* that whiteness becomes unthought, not just as a technology for making it so. And I will make the case that it is another classic tool for revealing and disguising the workings of whiteness—"the child"—that may give us entrée to this new way of reading the Gothic.

To do this, I want briefly to return to the moments of awakening in Lee's *Go Set a Watchman* and Mann's memoir with which I opened this essay, before reading the Faulkner story that I think helps us understand them more fully. The southern child roams the Gothic literary and photographic landscape of the South, sometimes, as in Mann's 1987 photo, "The Ditch," or the "throwaway bodies" of children that Yaeger finds ubiquitous in southern women's fiction, becoming part of it.[15] (See fig. 1.1.) The Romantic era that gave rise to the European Gothic also birthed modern notions of childhood as a fleeting state of innocence, as yet uncorrupted by the demands of "civilization." In photography such as Mann's or writing like the novel Harper Lee is most famous for, *To Kill A Mockingbird*, the pastoral, the traditional free range of childhood innocence, slides seamlessly into Gothic vis-à-vis tropes of "southernness": the Gothic and childhood are sutured by or within a southern landscape always already haunted by violence, especially around race, sex, class and religion.[16] Within this landscape, which is in the deepest sense intertextual, the white southern child's innocence hovers on just "this side," or "that side" of corruption—think of Harriett Beecher Stowe's Little Eva, whose purity in the face of overexposure to the specters of slavery, one could argue, necessitates her death; or of Huck Finn's struggles to think past the graphic violence of his father's and slavery's prerogatives in order to recognize his protector Jim's humanity. Quentin Compson's view of Caddy's "muddy drawers" above him in the pear tree (the famed originating scene for *The Sound and the Fury*) might also come to mind. In Mann's photographs of her own children, published into the maelstrom of 1990s "culture wars" in her book, *Immediate Family* (1992), her daughters and son in their rural Virginia camp often appear poised before or just over the edge of some abyss—of sexual exploitation or physical violence, symbolized in the southern landscape of dark waters, plant overgrowth, and decaying architecture.[17]

While the violence in these photographs can be, and often is, explained away by everyday childhood phenomena such as a child's anger, nosebleeds, bee stings, or melted popsicles, it is deliberately allusive, referencing both photographic history and literary history—epic, mythological and regional. In this regard, Mann's oft-stated, deep rootedness in her Lexington, Virginia, homeplace plays a prominent, allusive role. The Virginia landscape as it appears in Mann's lens and memoir is a literary one, saturated with Faulknerian Gothic legacies of southern history and literature, the very air thick and dark with the ghosts of racial violence, civil war, and illicit sexuality. In *Hold Still*, based on the Massey Lectures Mann delivered at Harvard in 2011, the first reference to William Faulkner appears on page three. Mann begins her memoir with imagery of opening twine-bound boxes of family papers in the attic, wondering about ghosts of long-dead family and secretly hoping that she will find

> a payload of southern gothic: deceit and scandal, alcoholism, domestic abuse, car crashes, bogeymen, clandestine affairs, dearly loved and disputed family land, abandonments, blow jobs, suicides, hidden addictions, the tragically early death of a beautiful bride, racial complications, vast sums of money made and lost, the return of a prodigal son, and maybe even bloody murder. (*Hold Still*, xiv)

She finds, Mann proclaims, all of this and more, and it is her reading of Faulkner's familial Gothics that comes to frame her experience, both in adolescence and in the long look back that Mann makes as she writes the memoir at around age sixty. First introduced to *The Sound and the Fury*, *Light in August* and *Absalom, Absalom!* by an African American English teacher at her Vermont boarding school, Mann recalls that her "homesick romanticism thrummed to the melodrama: the violence, the undertones of sexual threat, the sense of moldering decadence, the cursed inheritance, and, of course, the inevitable haunted home place. That haunted home place, a metaphor for the South itself, was a house divided by the institution of slavery" (263). *Absalom, Absalom!*, Mann concludes, was her "awakening": "Faulkner threw wide the door of my ignorant childhood, and the future, the heartbroken future filled with the hitherto unasked questions, strolled easefully in. It wounded me, then and there, with the great sadness and tragedy of our American life, with the truth of all that I had not seen, had not known, and had not asked."

Mann is an accomplished writer herself, and indeed earned an MA in creative writing at Hollins College in Virginia before beginning her photographic career. The "inherent" (206) relation that she claims between her own place-infused writing, her photography, and Faulkner's fiction is evident throughout Mann's work, which is very much ongoing, and Mann in her memoir encourages readers to see it. To this end, she especially calls attention to work she began after the *Immediate Family* photographs, when as her children aged out of being photographed as such, Mann moved on to create haunted and haunting photographs of her farm and then of death-infused southern landscapes such as the Tallahatchie River site where Emmett Till's body was retrieved and, especially, Civil War battlefields and a so-called Body Farm, where scientists study the effects of nature on decaying corpses strewn across a Tennessee field. Of her turn to landscape photography, Mann writes in terms of aesthetic revelation of the past, that she "came to wonder if the artist who commands the landscape might in fact hold the key to the secrets of the human heart: place, personal history, and metaphor. Since my place and its story were givens, it remained for me to find those metaphors; encoded, half-forgotten clues within the southern landscape" (210).

Clearly Mann counts herself in the company of southern artists, particularly writers, who, she rightly claims, "have long been known for their susceptibility to myth and their obsession with place, family, death, and the past" (240). She aims in her photographs to find the visual metaphors that register the region's "given" haunted twinned histories of race and death in the landscape and its bodies. As Christopher Lloyd has demonstrated, Mann's formal techniques, particularly her use of large format and, later, the nineteenth-century wet-plate collodion process, reinforce and sometimes effect the Gothic content of her work; he astutely notes (though with a striking lack of irony) that, "while at first glance, the Southern landscapes may seem empty and nonsignifying, Mann's images help the sites along, revealing to us their gothic traces of a past that lingers in place."[18] However, a Gothic sensibility infuses Mann's photographs not only in their subject matter and tone—the undercurrent of sensuality, the threat of possible danger, abuse, or death, the lush darkness and otherworldly glow—but also in the questions they encourage or discourage, the associations they draw upon, and those that they bury. In this, I would argue, they reveal a rootedness less in physical place than in the canonical Faulknerian Gothic. Interestingly, Mann's most extensive ruminations on Faulkner—the ones I have cited here—occur in the chapter in which she analyzes her family's relationship with their caregiver, Virginia "Gee Gee" Carter. The moment in *Hold Still* that I have described as Mann's awakening into whiteness, where she asks the question of *how* in the world she and her family could have not questioned the everyday mechanisms of racial oppression in their own behavior, is immediately followed by a turn to familial Faulknerian Gothic, *Absalom*-style. This, I submit, is the right move, but the wrong Faulkner text. As revelatory as Faulkner's Gothic strategies in *Absalom, Absalom!* may be,[19] Mann's reading through Faulkner of her own "ignorant childhood" and "the truth of all that [she] had not seen, had not known, and had not asked" evidently channels the *type* of questions she is thus enabled to ask into a particular Faulknerian Gothic mode. Firmly ensconced in *this* Southern Gothic, questions of *how* "ignorance" (which is precisely not ignorance, but an achieved un-thinking) of whiteness takes hold in childhood through later life, or of the role of the Gothic in this un-thinking, are not only elusive but buried alive.

As many critics have so capably demonstrated, much of Faulkner's work is devoted to exposing mechanisms and effects of racism, whether they be economic, religious, political, or familial. Doubtless many readers—many of *us*—experienced Mann's same sense of awakening to and through Faulkner, a sense of revelation that I suspect is part wonderment at Faulkner's language, part wound of recognition of the "great sadness and tragedy of our American life," and part enthrallment in the spectacular thrills of the Gothic. As our teen proxies Quentin and Shreve work (or as Shreve says, "play") to piece together the murders and conflagrations of "what happened" with the Sutpen family, or as Chick Mallison and Aleck Sander and Miss Eunice dig up graves to the same end in *Intruder in the Dust*, they bring a fuller history of "what happened" in racism into visibility, into conscious thought (and of course here I mean into white conscious thought). Alongside Quentin, or young Ike McCaslin, or Scout and Jem in *To Kill a Mockingbird,* readers may experience a certain "loss of innocence," which is our somewhat melancholy way of saying that we gain a deeper understanding of the world in which they and we are obliged to live. As Yaeger and Goddu argue, however, the *Southern* Gothic's revelatory strategies come with built-in safety goggles: By locating racism as a tragic remainder of a specifically *southern* history of slavery, interracial sexual assault, Jim Crow legal and extralegal violence, and other forms of racial terror, that very *American* history can be simultaneously acknowledged and disclaimed, contained in the borders of region and time. National innocence can be preserved. The Southern Gothic's "glam tropology" allows for readerly distancing and disavowal based on the "scary-sexy" strangeness of southernness, even, and perhaps especially, for southerners like Mann. Its pleasures, perhaps, lie precisely in the loss of an innocence that can be recuperated thereby.

This is not to denigrate the revelatory powers of the Southern Gothic entirely. The truths that Mann comes to know through Faulkner are, after all, true, or as Faulkner writes, "probably true enough."[20] There is a power—and an urgent need served—in bringing the truths of racism and its histories into white conscious thought, again and again. Witness the number of civil rights lawyers inspired to their careers by *To Kill a Mockingbird*'s Scout and Atticus Finch. What I think the classic Faulknerian Gothic is perhaps less useful for understanding is *how* whiteness becomes unthought in the first place. How is it that "whites" come to know whiteness so deeply that it becomes unthought, even unthinkable?

To my mind Faulkner's text that most directly addresses the *how* of unthinking whiteness, and that provides structures for thinking through that unthought, is his short story "That Evening Sun." As critics have amply documented, this story went through several iterations and was published in its final form in 1931 in the collection *These Thirteen.*[21] In each successive revision Faulkner further highlights the retrospective point of view of the narrator, and, ironically, given this hindsight, develops the ambiguity of the ending. "That Evening Sun" features the Compson family, particularly Quentin, Caddy, Jason, and their parents, and its original version was likely written concurrently with *The Sound and the Fury.*[22] The story is centered around the children's interactions with the Compsons' regular Black washerwoman, Nancy, who is called to substitute as cook and house servant when Dilsey falls ill, but who is too recalcitrant and later too distracted by terror to do the job as they expect. Nancy is pregnant, evidently by a white man she has serviced as a prostitute, and her husband, Jesus, has left town in a rage. Now, she believes, he has returned to kill her. Nancy appeals to the Compson adults for help, and that refused, she attempts to use the Compson children as human shields in her cabin to keep Jesus at bay. This desperate plan is finally brought to an end by Mr. Compson. As he takes the children home, Nancy refuses even to close her door, apparently in existential submission to what she believes is her fate as "just a n[-----]."[23] The children can see her framed through the door in lamplight, until they cross the ditch and head up toward their own house. Readers never find out what happened to Nancy.

"That Evening Sun" uses a lens of childhood intertwined with the Gothic in ways that are both deeply familiar and decidedly strange. Instantly recognizable now and beloved by readers, including Sally Mann, is the familial Faulknerian Gothic I have outlined above, which Faulkner was in the process of developing in this story and in the novels he published during the multi-staged period of its composition, especially *Flags in the Dust*, *Sanctuary*, *As I Lay Dying*, and *The Sound and the Fury*. The story is narrated by an adult Quentin about these events that occurred fifteen years ago, when he was nine years old. That of course, makes him a twenty-four-year-old narrator, which sometimes leads readers who know him to have committed suicide at age nineteen in *The Sound and the Fury* to feel that he is narrating from the grave. The story begins with the adult Quentin's lament about the current modernized Jefferson, with paved streets and shade trees cut "to make room for iron poles bearing clusters of bloated and ghostly and bloodless grapes" (289), which we may presume are streetlights and/or transformers. Cars, rather than walking African American women or their husbands, come to pick up laundry from white folks' homes now, "the soiled wearing of a whole week now flee[ing] apparitionlike behind alert and irritable electric horns, with a long diminishing noise of rubber and asphalt like tearing silk" (289). As the story abruptly shifts into the past of Quentin's memory, it is Quentin himself who fades apparitionlike, his voice narrating almost in the third person, giving his nine-year-old child-self progressively fewer lines of dialogue until he seems almost entirely to have disappeared. Rather, it is his seven-year-old sister, Caddy, and five-year-old brother, Jason, who do most of the children's talking, and that most significantly in the form of questions, until young Quentin pipes up again at the end with a zinger of his own.

As Laurence Perrine and others have noted, questioning and uncertainty are at the core of "That Evening Sun" for its readers, and for the child characters who stand in for readerly ignorance and, perhaps, desire.[24] Of the nearly one hundred questions asked in the story, fewer than twenty-five receive anything resembling a direct answer. In her essay for this volume, Maude Hines aptly describes the Compson children's iterative "degrees of not-knowing" in "That Evening Sun Go

Down" as tied to the complex temporality of the Gothic. Faulkner only enhances these dynamics and the not-knowing *for readers* in "That Evening Sun," with its more ambiguous ending: Faulkner removes any hint of what ultimately happened, in the sense of Jesus's threat of physical violence to Nancy's Black body, although the Quentin narrating the story nine years past surely "knows." But in a larger sense, "what happened" is made crystal clear, largely through the questions that the children ask in relation to their Black caregivers, one of whom *is* and one pointedly is *not*, as the infamous phrase goes, "like one of the family." Critics of "That Evening Sun" might be divided into two main camps: those who feel it is primarily Nancy's story—a story of Blackness—and those who feel it is Quentin's, or the Compsons' more generally as representatives of a class or order: implicitly or not, a story of whiteness.[25] What unites these opposing stories is the larger story of how whiteness works, and that it must *work*. It works to render Nancy voiceless, by reducing her, in her own words, to "nothing but a n[-----]" (293). It works to solidify the children's race, and thus power, as *not* "a n[-----]." Most importantly, Faulkner reframes the familial Southern Gothic he himself is developing in this and other fictions to reveal *how* whiteness works, through a process of becoming unspoken, and eventually, unthought.

As opposed to Dilsey's initial silence and absence—she is out sick—Nancy is all presence and voice in "That Evening Sun." The Compson children encounter her as both a regular and an exotic feature of the landscape: they like to watch as she balances their laundry on her head taking it home for washing each Monday. We might consider Nancy in this story as an anti-Mammy: she is far from the glue that holds the Compson family together, and is indeed the repeated occasion for splitting them apart.[26] Nancy *voices* her unrest, either to the children when they are sent to summon her to make breakfast (for which refusal she is accused of being drunk)—or on the street when she confronts the Baptist deacon, Mr. Stovall, about not paying her the last three times he has hired her for sex (for which she is counseled by Mr. Compson to "just let white men alone" [295]). For this impertinence, Stovall knocks out her teeth but cannot stop her laugh, even as she lies bleeding in the road.[27] In jail, Nancy still refuses silence well into the night, before attempting suicide, after which she is revived and beaten again. For this, she is surmised to be on cocaine, "because no n[-----] would try to commit suicide unless he was full of cocaine, because a n[-----] full of cocaine wasn't a n[-----] any longer" (291). It is *after* all this that Nancy is called to sub for Dilsey and her terror begins.

As Hines surmises, the tension in the story lies between the children's noncomprehension (the "particular brand of innocence" that Hines identifies as "layered degrees of *not-knowing*") and the reality—and I would add, the *discourse*—of the adult situation around them. This discourse comes from two directions, both gothically inflected: from Nancy's declarations about Jesus, her maniacal laughter, moaning, bleeding hogbone signs, and emptied eyes, and from the tortured *work* that white characters such as the Compson parents, Mr. Stovall, and the jailor must do to try and re-moor the always unsteady category of "n[-----]"—to keep it attached to Blackness. Little Jason's repeated questions and declarations about "n[-----]"-hood (others' and his own increasingly confident negative self-assessment), alongside Caddy's questions ("Let what white men alone? . . . How let them alone?" [295]; "Are you afraid of father, mother?" [299]), serve as a classic child refraction, their "naiveté" revealing the absurdities and instabilities of Blackness as it is created to shore up whiteness. As Laurel Bollinger has argued, confoundingly loud and independent Nancy is gradually stripped of power in direct proportion to the children's increasing mastery of racial discourse over the course of the story's six sections. Quentin's final question, one of the most brutal lines in American literature—"Who will do our washing now, Father?" (309)—is perhaps the apotheosis of racial un-thinking: Nancy disappears, not by physically dying (she is still "not singing and not unsinging"), but by being rendered a disappeared *thing*.

And yet the adult Quentin's own disappearance, and his and Faulkner's refusal to say what happened to Nancy, reframes the Gothic of the story. In a way that the nine-year-old Quentin comes to *know* but not to think, and that the twenty-four-year-old Quentin's narration invites readers to think but cannot and does not say, Nancy's abandoned, haunted eyes are an ideological boon, distracting from the radically unstable and contingent state of his "whiteness." It is only in the long look back—the attempted "footlog" to childhood that Hines describes elsewhere in this volume—that Quentin *may* perceive this.[28] Readers are perhaps more enabled. Yoshio Hasegawa suggests that the function of the story's first paragraph is to force readers "to be conscious of the older Quentin's point of view hidden behind the story proper": "our very consciousness of this Quentin induces . . . readers, taking the role of the older Quentin, rather than the older Quentin himself, [to] 'modify' the child's memories" (45-46). The older Quentin sets the Gothic terms of modernity in the first paragraph, and then sublimates all further commentary on their roots in the past within an ironizing "younger" narrative voice that is nearly third person: a sort of free indirect discourse in reverse that invites readers (since Quentin himself cannot or will not say) to think through the young Compsons' learned unthinking. Thus presented, the "what happened" enacted in "That Evening Sun" is not a Southern Gothic history, epitomized in Jesus's possible murder of Nancy, or even in the Compsons' refusal to protect her, but the *process* of whiteness and its history becoming unthought, a process that is accomplished, in part, by directing our vision to the Gothic. The ethical gesture of the story is for readers to make. Do we follow along unthinking, or do we recognize this gothicizing strategy for what it is, and use it to *think through* and beyond the process of whiteness formation?

"That Evening Sun" charts two paths of Faulkner's engagement of the Gothic: that which would become the canonical Faulknerian Gothic, with its tropic figurations and displacements, and a Gothic that Faulkner deploys in service of unmasking and registering the very work that this Gothic performs. Both are designed to raise questions, and to direct the ways those questions can and should be asked. The unasked questions that Mann is inspired to ask after reading *her* Faulknerian Gothic are necessary ones. It is the structures that that Gothic provides for answering those questions that are potentially limiting. So "scary-sexy," so able to set the romantic heart thrumming, to enable *certain* questions to be asked, that it can bury the very ones that need asking. Like Jean Louise Finch, Mann comes to this epiphany only in deep retrospect, while reflecting on a childhood nourished by the near-constant physical and emotional support of an African American female caregiver. Not *after* her reading of Faulkner, but perhaps in spite of it. Can this recognition—for Mann, but more importantly for us—reframe the way we can read Mann's family photographs?

As I've said, the southern family landscape as it appears in Mann's lens and memoir is a literary one, saturated with the Gothic legacies of southern history and literature, the very air thick and dark with the ghosts of racial violence, civil war, and illicit sexuality. In a photograph like Mann's *The Terrible Picture*, the white child's body may displace yet evoke regional, visual legacies of lynching, as Lloyd has argued, with "the specter of lynching" standing in for wider southern legacies of racial trauma (87).[29] But I suggest that, in a more powerful way, the function of Mann's photos of white southern childhood in a Gothic frame is to perform (or to enable a performance of a version of) what Robin Bernstein calls "racial innocence."[30] For Bernstein, figures of innocent childhood in the US—often girls and always raced white—are addressed to white hegemonic anxieties to preserve all-too-porous racial borderlines. As natural, or naturalizing, innocents, children are uniquely able to perform a tricky dance of "holy ignorance": an innocent ability to call attention to but "not-notice" racial difference. In theories of national formation like Bernstein's, the "persistent longing" for childhood innocence represents the mechanisms of a national racial innocence that inscribes racial boundaries even as it appears to transcend them, enabling whiteness and its power never to have to speak its own name (*Racial Innocence* 6–8). In Mann's photographs of her children, the "innocence" of the child hovers as a provocation and a dare to what can be thought and pictured: Sexual innocence here is explicitly fraught, but racial innocence left in place, such that Lloyd, for example, can argue that it "scarcely matters" whether the bodies Mann pictures in her regional Gothics are Black or white (109).

The workings of racial innocence are perhaps clearest in the series of photographs Mann made of her childhood caregiver, Virginia Carter, with her young daughter, Virginia Mann. In The Two Virginias, Mann's overdetermined title for this series, Mann juxtaposes extreme youth and old age, rounded and craggy bodies, Black and white, all within an almost mythological frame of bodily intimacy and of Virginia, the state, itself. (See figure 1.2.) Here Virginia Carter's body, face obscured, functions as the Gothic, always racialized Virginia landscape against which little Virginia's body, grubby or unconscious as it may be, can be read in intimate connection. Drawing upon the literary and photographic legacy of Southern Gothic, Mann's figures of southern childhood do a double duty, representing both the assertion of racial innocence and the fraught landscape that always already threatens its corruption, that leads to the desperate need to assert innocence in the first place. The Virginia-ness of the two (really three) Virginias evokes a racial history that, little Virginia's body says, doesn't matter.

But of course, as I think "That Evening Sun" invites us to recognize, it very much matters. Some implications can be seen in the learned obliviousness exposed by "That Evening Sun," and in the moments of revelation depicted by Lee and Mann with which I opened this essay. In her memoir, Mann, like Jean Louise Finch, comes to recognize the moral stakes of retaining a childlike racial innocence focused on the feelings of intimacy and fundamental innocence surrounding her relationship with her Black caregiver, all the while actively not-seeing and not-thinking, and thus enabling and perpetuating, the exploitative economic and personal racial hierarchies that are the fundamental structure not only of southern culture but national culture as a whole. The dawning consciousness of Quentin's readers, and both Jean Louise and Mann, transforms *their* Faulknerian Gothics—the underlying mode of Lee's writing and Mann's photography—into a newly haunted frame. In my most optimistic reading, what this new frame makes visible is the *function* of Southern Gothic and childhood as filters: filters that sharpen some racial dynamics—what I'll call southern "epic" Faulknerian racial dynamics—and screen out others, the humdrum, unthought everyday of American racism. Alongside Yaeger, I want to assert that the haunted everyday of racism becomes obscured,

Figure 1.2. Sally Mann, *The Two Virginias #4*, 1991, gelatin silver print, 8 x 10 inches, 20.3 x 25.4 cm © Sally Mann. Courtesy Gagosian

becomes actively unthought, through the scary-sexy thrills of the Southern Gothic.[31] And further, that there's an analogous relationship between the ways that childhood racial innocence within the Gothic creates the unseen everyday, and the way the Southern Gothic filters out dynamics of racial complicity in and for the nation.

Yaeger directs our attention to writers who refuse the "monstrous hauntology" of the Southern Gothic, who instead use figures of detritus or remnant to evoke the everyday, everywhere haunting of racism. I find her argument utterly compelling, but I don't think it's necessary to jettison the "glam tropology" of the Gothic entirely. Rather, I suggest that recognizing the Southern Gothic and childhood *as* filters offers an opportunity for re-vision. For asking further questions about what it is that we—authors, photographers, readers, and audiences—*want* from the Gothic "southernness" of photographs and literature. And possibly, in the process of getting answers, for figuring out ways to read differently a series of photographs like The Two Virginias. Instead of filtering over multiple layers of the unthought known, Southern Gothic childhood can make the meant-to-be-unseen visible.

NOTES

This essay is dedicated to the late Patricia Yaeger and Toni Morrison, whose work so informs it. Previous versions of this research were presented at the Faulkner and Yoknapatawpha Conference in July 2019, the American Comparative Literature Association conference in March 2019 and at the National Gallery of Art in April 2018. I am grateful for audiences in these venues for their enlightening and sharpening comments, and especially to Jay Watson for his insightful editorial suggestions. Research for this work was funded in part by a fellowship from the National Endowment for the Humanities.

1. In this broader genealogy I mean to include the long history and varied ways that southern writers, including Faulkner, have deployed Gothic tropes and imagery in their work, as well as the generic profile of the Southern Gothic as a literary historical category, however broadly defined: the former is a technique of production, and the latter an orientation for reception. Jay Watson has most recently traced the beginnings of Southern Gothic as a named "school" to a speech given by Ellen Glasgow in 1935, published later that year in the influential *Saturday Review of Literature.* See Watson, "So Easy Even a Child Can Do It: William Faulkner's Southern Gothicizers," *Mississippi Quarterly 72, no. 1* (2019): 1-23. Glasgow named Faulkner as an inheritor and propagator of a fatal southern romanticism that she saw as distracting from the necessary dose of "blood and irony" her own work offered southern literature. For more on Glasgow's complicated relationship with the Gothic, see Mark A. Graves, "Ellen Glasgow's Gothic Heroes and Monsters," in Susan Castillo Street and Charles L. Crow, eds., *The Palgrave Handbook of the Southern Gothic* (London: Palgrave Macmillan, 2016), 351-63. For a recent overview of the history and characteristics of the canonical Southern Gothic, see Christopher Lloyd, "Southern Gothic," in Joel Faflak and Jason Haslam, eds., *American Gothic Culture: An Edinburgh Companion* (Edinburgh: Edinburgh University Press, 2016), 79-91. The introduction and essays in Street and Crow exemplify more recent theorizations.

2. Leslie Fiedler, *Love and Death in the American Novel* (McLean, IL: Dalkey Archive Press, 1997 [1966]), 143. Hereafter cited parenthetically.

3. Harper Lee, *Go Set a Watchman* (New York: HarperCollins, 2015), 162. Hereafter cited parenthetically.

4. Sally Mann, *Hold Still* (New York: Little, Brown and Company, 2015), 250. Hereafter cited parenthetically.

5. Patricia Yaeger, *Dirt and Desire* (Chicago: University of Chicago Press, 2000), xii, emphasis added. Hereafter cited parenthetically.

6. Toni Morrison, "Unspeakable Things Unspoken: The Afro-American Presence in American Literature," *Michigan Quarterly Review* 28, no. 1 (1994): 12.

7. Teresa Goddu, *Gothic America: Narrative, History, and Nation* (New York: Columbia University Press, 1997), 10. Hereafter cited parenthetically.

8. Flannery O'Connor, "Some Aspects of the Grotesque in Southern Fiction," *Mystery and Manners*, eds. Sally and Robert Fitzgerald (New York: Farrar, Straus and Giroux, 1969), 40.

9. Often, as several critics have argued, authors engage Gothic tropology precisely in order to critique these generic expectations. Watson makes such an argument for Faulkner's Gothics in *Sanctuary*, *Absalom, Absalom!*, and "That Evening Sun." For other examples, see the introduction and essays in Eric Gary Anderson, Taylor Hagood and Daniel Cross Turner, eds., *Undead Souths: The Gothic and Beyond in Southern Literature and Culture* (Baton Rouge: Louisiana State University Press, 2015).

10. Patricia Yaeger offers one delineation of white and Black southern women's deployment of the Gothic, with white writers figuring a return of the oppressed and Black writers figuring the return of the dispossessed. See Yaeger, "Ghosts and Shattered Bodies, or What Does It Mean to Still Be Haunted by Southern Literature?" *South Central Review* 22, no. 1 (Spring 2005): 101–2. Hereafter cited parenthetically. Project MUSE. doi:10.1353/scr.2005.0026. For more expansive treatments of African American Gothic strategies, see Maisha Wester, *African American Gothic: Screams from Shadowed Places* (New York: Palgrave Macmillan, 2012); Goddu's chapter, "Haunting Back: Harriett Jacobs, African-American Narrative, and the Gothic," *Gothic America*, 131–52; and most recently, Sheri-Marie Harrison, "New Black Gothic," *Los Angeles Review of Books* (June 23, 2018), https://lareviewofbooks.org/article/new-black-gothic/, accessed July 12, 2020.

11. Trudier Harris, *The Scary Mason-Dixon Line* (Baton Rouge: Louisiana State University Press, 2009). See also Hortense Spillers, "Mama's Baby, Papa's Maybe: An American Grammar Book," in *Black, White, and in Color: Essays on American Literature and Culture* (Chicago: University of Chicago Press, 2003), 203–29, and Carolyn Levander, *Cradle of Liberty: Race, the Child, and National Belonging from Thomas Jefferson to W. E. B. Du Bois* (Durham, NC: Duke University Press, 2006).

12. Extended evidence for these dynamics from the literary origins of the US through the modernist period are offered in Jennifer Rae Greeson, *Our South: Geographic Fantasy and the Rise of National Literature* (Cambridge, MA: Harvard University Press, 2010), and Leigh Anne Duck, *The Nation's Region: Southern Modernism, Segregation, and US Nationalism* (Athens: University of Georgia Press, 2006).

13. See Katherine Henninger, "My Childhood Is Ruined! Harper Lee and Racial Innocence," *American Literature* 88, no. 3 (September 2016): 597–626.

14. See note 11.

15. See Yaeger, *Dirt and Desire*, especially 61–87.

16. This dynamic has held true in cinema as well, as the film version of *To Kill a Mockingbird* (dir. Robert Mulligan, 1962), Charles Laughton's *Night of the Hunter* (1955), David Gordon Green's first feature, *George Washington* (2001), and the recent Sundance phenomenon, Phillip Youmans's *Burning Cane* (2019) exemplify.

17. The 1990s popular critical reception of *Immediate Family* has been amply documented, and at times reembodied, in scholarly criticism regarding Mann in the years since. Sociologist James Davison Hunter's 1991 *Culture Wars: The Struggle to Define America* identified a growing political polarization around "hot-button" issues such as abortion, homosexuality, gun rights, and separation of church and state, issues loosely grouped under the rubric of "family values" by the Republican Party. Pat Buchanan's nomination challenging speech to George H. W. Bush at the 1992 Republican National Convention, alongside North Carolina Senator Jesse Helms's sustained attacks on the National Endowment for the Arts and the

long decade of public anxiety around child sexual molestation analyzed by James Kincaid in *Erotic Innocence: The Culture of Child Molesting* (Durham, NC: Duke University Press, 1998), epitomize the 1990s cultural context in which Mann's work was published and received as controversial. For a discussion of Mann's photographs and their reception in a larger context of contemporary visual representations of childhood, see Anne Higonnet, *Pictures of Innocence: The History and Crisis of Ideal Childhood* (London: Thames & Hudson, 1998). Mann's fullest account of the creation and publication of photographs of her children appears in *Hold Still*, 105-65.

18. Christopher Lloyd, *Rooting Memory, Rooting Place: Regionalism in the Twenty-First-Century American South* (New York: Palgrave Macmillan, 2015), 100. Hereafter cited parenthetically.

19. Watson compellingly shows how Faulkner depicts storytelling characters who themselves deploy Gothic strategies for "their particular ends" in *Absalom, Absalom!*, *Sanctuary*, and "That Evening Sun," to conclude that the adept "gothicizers of Yoknapatawpha allow Faulkner not only to exploit the work of southern terror but to historicize and critique that work as well" "So Easy Even a Child Can Do It," (20). My argument, focused on the role of the Gothic as a technology of unthinking whiteness, complements his: by revealing the two-way filtering function of the Gothic for and through the child characters of "That Evening Sun," Faulkner encourages readers to see and to see through Gothic filtrations how whiteness becomes known and then unthought, and thus to engage with its affects critically.

20. William Faulkner, *Absalom, Absalom!* rev. ed. (1936; repr., New York: Vintage International, 1990), 268.

21. Norman Holland Pearson was one of the earliest critics to engage the composition and publishing history of "That Evening Sun," in "Faulkner's Three 'Evening Suns,'" *Yale University Library Gazette* 29 (1954): 61-70; and critics routinely note differences in the four extant versions in the years since. "That Evening Sun Go Down," discussed by Maude Hines in this volume, was published in the *American Mercury* in 1931, after Faulkner made several changes requested by the editor, H. L. Mencken: Jesus's name was altered to Jubah and the suggestive allusion to a watermelon vine was removed. See William Faulkner, "That Evening Sun Go Down," *American Mercury* 22, no. 87 (March 1931): 257-67. Faulkner restored these elements in the version published in *These Thirteen*, but made other changes including, most significantly for my argument, a conclusion that eliminates a more adult Quentin voice describing the family's passing through the ditch as "walking out of Nancy's life ... dividing the impinged lives of us and Nancy" (267).

22. Critics supporting this necessarily speculative composition timeline include Joseph Blotner, *Faulkner: A Biography*, vol. 1 (New York: Random House, 1974), 565-66; David Minter, *William Faulkner: His Life and His Work* (Baltimore: Johns Hopkins University Press, 1997), 283n6; James Ferguson, *Faulkner's Short Fiction* (Knoxville: University of Tennessee Press, 1991), 33; and Yoshio Hasegawa, "Two Quentins in 'That Evening Sun': Faulkner's Revision toward *The Sound and the Fury*," *Faulkner Studies* 2, no.1 (1994): 43, 48n3. Hereafter cited parenthetically.

23. William Faulkner, "That Evening Sun," in *Collected Stories of William Faulkner* (New York: Vintage International, 1995 [1950]), 309. Hereafter cited parenthetically.

24. Laurence Perrine, "'That Evening Sun': A Skein of Uncertainties," *Studies in Short Fiction* 22, no. 3 (1985): 295-307.

25. Perrine provides a summary of such criticism pre-1985, which Laurel Bollinger updates in 2012 in establishing a history of "readerly discomfort" with the story. See Bollinger, "Narrating Racial Identity and Transgression in Faulkner's 'That Evening Sun,'" *College Literature* 39, no. 2 (Spring 2012): 53-72. Hereafter cited parenthetically.

26. Deborah Barker describes the character of Nancy Mannigoe in *Requiem for a Nun* (a 1951 incarnation of "That Evening Sun"'s Nancy) in similar terms, arguing that Mannigoe functions as a "modern mammy" in that novel but that Nancy's murder of Temple Drake's child may "signal the ultimate symbolic rejection" of that role. See Barker, "Demystifying the Modern Mammy in *Requiem for a Nun*," in *Faulkner and Film: Faulkner and Yoknapatawpha, 2010*, ed. Peter Lurie and Ann J. Abadie (Jackson: University Press of Mississippi, 2014), 94.

27. As Bollinger argues ("Narrating" 59), Faulkner added "laughing" to the original manuscript to emphasize that Nancy's beating does not mean her defeat.

28. See Maude Hines, "Across the Ditch: Race, Childhood, and the Machinery of Fate in Faulkner," in this volume. The question of how much Quentin, younger or older, understands has divided critics. Watson's characterization of Quentin's storytelling, for instance, as "a record, perhaps inadvertent, perhaps all too aware," epitomizes the ambiguity created by Faulkner's narrative structure ("So Easy Even a Child Could Do It," 17).

29. *The Terrible Picture* (1989) is a black-and-white medium shot of Mann's four-year-old daughter, Virginia, standing grubby, closed-eyed, and unclothed with a narrow vertical object in the background behind her back that has variously evoked a lynching rope or meat hook for some viewers. Although Mann granted publication permission, the University Press of Mississippi declined to include this image in the present essay.

30. Robin Bernstein, *Racial Innocence: Performing American Childhood from Slavery to Civil Rights* (New York: New York University Press, 2011), 4. Hereafter cited parenthetically.

31. My thanks to Jay Watson for the suggestion that "That Evening Sun" dramatizes even this occlusion, in the way that Dilsey (the nonepic everyday of Compson racism) is withdrawn from the foreground she would normally occupy "due to illness," as it were. On these terms, "making" Dilsey sick amounts to a narrative disavowal, by Quentin, who has chosen to tell *this* story, and, perhaps, by Faulkner. One might also argue that Faulkner's choice is strategic: Faulkner deploys the filter of Nancy's gothicness (and gothicizing) to reveal the degree of horror the quotidian *should* inspire, but that whiteness renders unthought. Regardless, only Dilsey's out-sick-ness makes this story possible. It is the children's formational encounter with the everyday presumption that one "negress" can/will substitute for another, and their increasingly competent resistance to Nancy's attempts to disrupt that presumption, that make the process of unthinking—and the Gothic filter—visible.

Across the Ditch

Race, Childhood, and the Machinery of Fate in Faulkner

MAUDE HINES

When Jason Compson announces, "I'm not a n[-----]," he is told, "You're worse.... [Y]ou are a tattle-tale."[1] He is five years old. When Joe Christmas announces, "I aint a n[-----]," he is told, "You are worse than that. You dont know what you are."[2] He too is five years old. I'll revisit these strikingly similar scenes in William Faulkner's 1931 short story "That Evening Sun Go Down" and his 1932 novel *Light in August* later, but first I'd like to stop and acknowledge the violence of the word "n[-----]," to sit with it for a moment.

As Koritha Mitchell powerfully demonstrates, the word confronts listeners differentially, demanding extra labor from those of us in whom it produces a "mountain of feeling."[3] Recognizing its correlate potential effects for readers, the editors of *Faulkner's Families* have elected to represent the word as "n[-----]" in this and future books in the *Faulkner and Yoknapatawpha* series, and it will appear that way in this essay. This delineation is especially appropriate here, as the dashes and brackets suggest the word's spectral attributes, following the first letter like protean baggage.

"N-----" haunts the present through its invocation of the past, reflecting the system of white supremacy necessary to commit the crime of American chattel slavery, the projection of responsibility onto its victims, and an insistence on perpetuating both the crime and its perverse justification in the present in which it is uttered. The word likewise haunts Faulkner's fiction, appearing again and again, wielding its performative power. Faulkner's particular use of it deserves its own treatment, read through and beyond Quentin Compson's famous ruminations on its significance (both as a child in "A Justice" and as an adult in *The Sound and the Fury*) to include competing functions in works like "Ambuscade" (in

The Unvanquished) and "That Evening Sun" (in the distorted perspective of Nancy's jailer). As Wallis Tinnie put it in her July 23 presentation, "Jefferson was built on a collective racial brutality encoded in the systems, laws, customs, and language that sustained it."[4] Filtered through the mouths of children, those codes threaten to infect the future. Positioning themselves against "the n[-----]," young Joe Christmas and Jason Compson attempt to negotiate complex and oppressive social machinery that has the force of fate. In these texts and others, Faulkner uses childhood to explore the transmission and propagation of the machinery's effects. Today I will argue that three elements—childhood, encounter, and fate—consolidate in Faulkner's writing to create a gothic and stultifying atmosphere in which the past haunts the present and circumscribes the future.

Some of the child figure's effects are deployed in the Southern Gothic generally: the child functions both as a repository of inherited pain and guilt and as a haunting evocation of the continuation of those injuries. If, as several critics have argued, the history of racial subjugation and slavery that relies on an uncanny confusion of person and thing haunts American literature and history,[5] and if, as still others have demonstrated, the figure of the child engages an uncanny temporality through "unrealized time,"[6] then the two types of uncanniness coalesce in the Southern Gothic child, a palimpsestic figure haunted by the past and focused on futurity.

For Faulkner in particular, child characters are carriers of the social order, their meaning a product of adult readers' projection, associations between children and didacticism, and Faulkner's particular brand of "innocence." This innocence resists the projection of "racial innocence" that Katherine Henninger has identified in readers' fondness for the young Scout Finch in Harper Lee's *To Kill a Mockingbird*.[7] Nor is it the blameless innocence our culture maps onto childhood. Rather, Faulkner's specific type of "innocence" leverages the temporal uncertainty of Southern Gothic childhood to produce layered degrees of *not-knowing*. His child characters undergo an iterative assimilation of white supremacy's violence. A collage of temporal markers from Faulkner's 1939 short story "Barn Burning" illustrates the intimate link between time and knowledge in conveying the assimilation of culture:

> Older, the boy might have remarked this. . . . And older still, he might have divined the true reason. . . . But he did not think this now. . . . Later, twenty years later, he was to tell himself. . . . A week ago—or before last night, that is—he would have asked where they were going, but not now.[8]

The accumulating temporal shifts define Sarty Snopes's non-knowing against his own future knowledge, while presenting readers with multiple degrees of innocence across a simultaneity of past and future moments. These moments imply a learning process that accesses associations between childhood and didacticism, encouraging readers to perceive what is being learned as "lessons."

In "Barn Burning," those lessons cover Sarty's dawning realization of the workings of the world outside his family, together with his place in the world by virtue of that lineage. The machinery of fate works through his father's machinelike qualities, as well as through Sarty's helplessness against the "the old habit, the old blood" (21).[9] While his choice to defy his father can be (and often is) read as an act of free will, it also demonstrates an understanding of the confines of his social position, of the ineluctability of his inheritance, and the assimilation of the values that restrict him.[10]

The layered temporality of "Barn Burning" relies on a distance between Sarty and the adult narrator, who knows more than he does. This distance is echoed in the distance between the text and its worldly reader. The connection between unknowing innocence and temporal shifts is a repeated formula with diverse manifestations. *As I Lay Dying*'s Vardaman Bundren narrates his own story of encounter with his social position while still a child, yet that very childishness is signaled by seamless temporal shifts that move from present to past with no signal to the reader (a technique Faulkner had already used for that other innocent, Benjy Compson):

> Pa said flour and sugar and coffee costs so much. Because I am a country boy because boys in town. Bicycles. Why do flour and sugar and coffee cost so much when he is a country boy. "Wouldn't you ruther have some bananas instead?" Bananas are gone, eaten. Gone. When it runs on the track shines again. "Why aint I a town boy, pa?" I said. God made me. I did not said to God to made me in the country. If He can make the train, why cant He make them all in the town because flour and sugar and coffee.[11]

In "A Justice," an adult Quentin narrates his own childhood memory: "That was it. I was just twelve then, and I would have to wait until I had passed on and through and beyond the suspension of twilight. Then I knew that I would know."[12]

To trace the layers of temporal distance that enable glimpses of the social machinery, I borrow the metaphor of the ditch from Faulkner's last novel, *The Reivers*. Lucius Priest, narrating as a grandfather the adventures he had when he was eleven, puts it this way:

> there are some things, some of the hard facts of life, that you dont forget, no matter how old you are. There is a ditch, a chasm; as a boy you crossed it on a footlog. You come creeping and doddering back at thirty-five or forty and the

footlog is gone; you may not even remember the footlog but at least you dont step out onto that empty gravity that footlog once spanned.[13]

In other words, we remember life's hard facts but can no longer see how we arrived at them. Growing up comes with its own type of innocence, as it becomes harder to see the structures of social systems that adults take for granted, systems to which Patricia Yaeger has famously referred as the "unthought known."[14] I propose that in presenting us with "innocent" characters confronting ideology, Faulkner provides a "footlog." Through the eyes of young characters not yet accustomed to the machinery of social systems that determine the limits of their futures, Faulkner can illustrate the machinery for readers who have already assimilated it. This is not a *protected* innocence, either: inevitably, child characters will be caught up in the machinery—indeed, in the layered present of the narratives, with their own futures bearing down on them, they already are.

In using the term "encounter" to describe Faulkner's child characters violently engaged by complex social systems that produce and frustrate them, I build on the work of Beverly Tatum, who herself builds on the "encounter" stage in William Cross's model of "Nigrescence"—or becoming Black. For Tatum and Cross, "pre-encounter" is characterized by children's unquestioning acceptance of the pervasive rules of white supremacy, while "the encounter stage is typically precipitated by an event or series of events that force the young person to acknowledge the personal impact of racism."[15] Read through the frame of "encounter," we can understand Joe and Jason as "force[d] . . . to acknowledge [racism's] personal impact," both of them terrified of falling victim to the machinery whose outlines they are only beginning to discern. Yet unlike Tatum's description of white identity development, in which assimilated white identity works to combat racism, these texts present a perverse reversal of such an assimilation: by positioning themselves *against* the word "n[-----]," Joe and Jason try to understand their place within their society by engaging its violent signifying instrument.

The boys' identical denials—"I'm not a n[-----]"—recall James Baldwin's later pronouncement on that construct's function within white supremacy:

> I'm not a n[-----], I'm a man, but if you think I'm a n[-----], it means you need it. . . . If I'm not a n[-----] here and you invented him, you, the white people, invented him, then you've got to find out why. And the future of the country depends on that. Whether or not it's able to ask that question.[16]

In other words, the *future* depends on understanding the constructions of the *past* and what motivates their continuation in the *present*. Baldwin's own layered temporalities constitute a fatal warning: uninterrupted, the cycle will continue. Both young Joe and young Jason are initially curious about the invention, "n[-----]." As I will discuss presently, Jason practices applying it to various others before distancing himself from it, while Joe asks the groundskeeper, "How come you are a n[-----]?" before doing the same (Faulkner, *Light in August* 383). Their childish curiosity has nothing in common with the persistent scrutiny Baldwin prescribes for adults, and it quickly fades as they accept the construct and work to orient themselves within it. Our definition of encounter must encompass this problem, as encounter is often followed, in Faulkner's texts, by a need to reinforce white supremacy—not by assimilated identity, but by monstrous projection onto a constituting other.[17]

The quintessential scene of Faulknerian encounter might be young Thomas Sutpen being turned away from the plantation house door in *Absalom, Absalom!* As Hortense Spillers reminded us in her keynote lecture, this is Sutpen's "supreme instance of self-difference," in which the child Sutpen enters a new symbolic order, his age is unstable (is he twelve? thirteen? fourteen?), and his "deep unknowing inscribes a deficit he is always racing to replace."[18] This characteristic scene bears all of the signatures of Faulkner's deployment of the child figure. Sutpen's "innocence" brings into brief focus the social systems that will subsume it, his ordained position reinforced by the gothic machinery of fate. More than twenty references to young Thomas Sutpen's "innocence" and to what he "didn't know" or "had not known" accumulate in the dizzying temporal shifts of the scene's narration and renarration.[19] Sutpen's encounter with the construct "n[-----]" builds on a nearly indistinguishable layering of the offending butler, the victim of mob violence, and the "balloon face" (187) that Sutpen imagines himself looking out of in a bizarrely Du Boisian double consciousness. The feeling of inevitable fate in Sutpen's design—"not what he wanted to do but what he just had to do" (178)—obligated by the overwhelming weight of his lineage "in the face [of] not only the old dead ones but all the living ones that would come after him when he would be one of the dead" reinforces the machinelike programming of his origin in factorylike "log cabins boiling with children" (179). And finally, all of this is pieced together by Quentin from his grandfather's old stories—the "ditch, the chasm" between the text and the reader amplified and echoed by Quentin's adulthood, the distance of time, and the guesswork inherent in a story twice removed.

Keeping Sutpen's particularly condensed example in mind, we return to our two five-year-olds. In *Light in August*, Joe Christmas makes his pronouncement, "I aint a n[-----]," as he tries to orient himself in the wake of a concatenation of bizarre childhood experiences. Other children in the orphanage have been using the epithet against him, his undercover grandfather stares at him accusingly from his position as orphanage janitor, and the orphanage dietitian calls him a "little n[-----] bastard" (122) out of misdirected sexual guilt (the event Aili Pettersson Peeker called "foundational" in her July 22, 2019, presentation). These are the type of "operatic" Southern Gothic rhetorical structures Yaeger compares with "less operatic forms in which fragments, residues, or traces of trauma fashion a regime of haunting" in southern women's writing.[20] But alongside these, through the child's unknowing innocence, Faulkner pulls the curtain aside, giving us the dim outlines of "traces of trauma" Yaeger considers "most frightening." Indeed, we can read the dietitian's attempt to remove the witness to her guilt (her claim that "children have a way of knowing things that grown people ... dont see" [133]) as a description of what young Joe actually witnesses: the "everyday haunting" of the structures of white supremacy.[21]

Little Joe follows the Black groundskeeper around until the groundskeeper asks, "'What you watching me for, boy?' and he said 'How come you are a n[-----]?'" (383). When the groundskeeper asks, "Who told you I am a n[-----], you little white trash bastard?" (384), Joe responds, "I aint a n[-----]," receiving the reply, "You are worse than that. You dont know what you are. And more than that, you wont never know."[22] This Socratic conversation recalls a lesson. The reader won't ever know either, an ambiguity that highlights the performative work of the racist epithet. As Richard Godden puts it, the novel "can be read as a thriller whose villain is the word 'n[-----].'"[23] This lesson happens in a place where temporal confusion and the ditch between ages—of readers, of the narrator, of Joe's adult and child selves—are writ large, as in the famous lines, "Memory believes before knowing remembers. Believes longer than recollects, longer than knowing even wonders" (119).

The oppressive feeling of inevitability in *Light in August* is impressive even for Faulkner. Joe Christmas's narrative arc is Sophoclean in its tragic irony (placed in a white orphanage to hide his suspected blackness, Joe lives the rest of his life in confusion over his ancestry, which prompts a series of events that leads to his figurative lynching). The institutional orphanage resembles a machine producing children, like the "log cabins boiling with children" that produce Thomas Sutpen: "a grassless cinderstrewnpacked compound surrounded by smoking factory purlieus and enclosed by a ten foot steel-and-wire fence like a penitentiary or a zoo," from which "orphans in identical and uniform blue denim" emerge in "random erratic surges" (119). Faulkner's description of the machinery of the orphanage is echoed in descriptions of Joe as an automaton ("two severed wireends of volition and sentience ... waiting to touch, to knit anew so that he could move" [220]). Added to all this is Gavin Stevens's narration of Joe's white and black blood vying for control of his actions, and dozens of metaphorical depictions of characters as actors in a play, or as chess pieces manipulated by a player or opponent. In this context, the epithet "n[-----]" is a sentence without parole. The performative, crippling violence of the novel's Jim Crow backdrop makes his place in the social order a life-or-death question for this child, one whose uncertain answer propels the novel.

In adulthood, Joe Christmas oscillates between what Tatum calls "oppositional identity" and internalized oppression, inflicting white supremacy's violence on himself and others.[24] Among so many metaphors for fate and inevitability, Joe's moment of childhood encounter takes on special significance: itself a lesson, it reveals the machinery of social systems that are as formative as the machinery of the orphanage.[25] The scene of encounter here is not only psychologically formative, it is a site for condensed exploration of the formative power of enduring social systems.

The same life-or-death question haunts "That Evening Sun Go Down," and the story illustrates young Jason Compson protecting himself from it by developing a negatively defined whiteness. Narrated by an adult Quentin Compson recalling an episode that happened when he was nine, the story builds its tension upon the lacuna between the three Compson children's incomplete comprehension and the horrific adult reality they encounter. Nancy, the Black woman whom the Compsons have hired temporarily, is paralyzed by the very real fear that her husband will kill her. Her keening repetition—"I ain't nothing but a n[-----]"—is a sickening explanation for the violence she experiences: unpaid prostitution, blood and teeth kicked out of her face in public and with impunity by a white man, attempted suicide, her vulnerability highlighted by repeated nakedness (see 259–61). Jason's childish attempts to orient himself in what he's witnessing appear as a fugue in Nancy's ordeal, the urgent conversation between Nancy and Dilsey punctuated by Jason's growing violent mastery of the social order:

"How do you know he's back?" Dilsey said. "You ain't seen him."
　"Jubah is a n[-----]," Jason said.
　"I can feel him," Nancy said. "I can feel him laying yonder in the ditch."
　"Tonight?" Dilsey said. "Is he there to-night?"
　"Dilsey's a n[-----] too," Jason said.
　"You try to eat something," Dilsey said.
　"I don't want nothing," Nancy said.
　"I ain't a n[-----]," Jason said. (261)

Like Joe Christmas, Jason sees that whether or not one is a "n[-----]" is a matter of life or death.

Jason's engagement with the word is an iterative process.[26] Later in the story, he makes his pronouncement a second time, this time seeking assurance that the word's violence can't name him: "'I ain't a n[-----],' Jason said. 'Am I, Dilsey?'" (262). The scene with which I began this essay is actually the third time Jason makes his pronouncement. It comes at the very end of the story, as Mr. Compson leads the children away from Nancy's house, across the ditch that serves as a literal and figurative division between the Compsons and Nancy's life and problems:

> Then we had crossed the ditch, walking out of Nancy's life. Then her life was sitting there with the door open and the lamp lit, waiting, and the ditch between us and us going on, the white people going on, dividing the impinged lives of us and Nancy. (267)

The children go on into the future while Nancy recedes, unmoving, into their past. Yet that phrase, "*dividing* the *impinged* lives of us and Nancy" (emphasis added) connects the Compsons and Nancy as it divides them with "a ditch, a chasm," on opposite sides of a social order. That paradoxical dividing dependence echoes the structure of negative white self-definition, hearkening back to Baldwin's warning: "If you think I'm a n[-----], it means you need it." The division Jason will come to "know" depends on the impingement he learns to forget.

Caddy's childish response to Jason's final negative assertion of his whiteness and invulnerability—"You're worse.... [Y]ou are a tattletale. If something was to jump out, you'd be scairder than a n[-----]"—conflates telling and fear, yet points to Jason's very reasonable terror of Nancy's position. In highlighting the contrast between adult horrors and uncomprehending witnesses, "That Evening Sun" relies on readers' associations between children and lessons. Absent a better model (Mr. Compson is no Atticus Finch), seven-year-old Caddy tries to figure out what the adults are talking about; nine-year-old Quentin is concerned with how Nancy's potential death will affect him ("Who will do our washing now?"); and Jason, negatively defined both by his age (what he doesn't know) and by his whiteness ("I'm not a n[-----]"), unquestioningly accepts the fatal social machinery as he becomes a part of it.

The ditch metaphor in "That Evening Sun" recalls, of course, the one from *The Reivers* I brought in at the beginning of this essay.[27] It divides by race and class, separates childhood from adulthood, and—as with Quentin narrating this childhood story at twenty-four—it stands between the past and the present, adult memory and childhood encounter, dividing the reader and the text.[28] The ditch here is an invitation and a warning. Faulkner's use of the juvenile gaze holds out the possibility of crossing back over the ditch, to remember the encounter with ideology. Yet the footlog is gone, the ditch an unspannable chasm—like Quentin Compson and Lucius Priest, we project our adult understanding onto child characters: we can't unsee what we have seen. And while we can't go back to the past, it can come uncannily forward, distorting our perceptions of the present.[29]

Heeding Baldwin's warning—that "the future of the country depends on" understanding the instruments of white supremacy—requires letting go of another type of innocence, one he elsewhere called "monstrous": "People who shut their eyes to reality simply invite their own destruction, and anyone who insists on remaining in a state of innocence long after that innocence is dead turns himself into a monster."[30] Baldwin's concept of monstrous innocence exposes a central paradox that Faulkner explores through his child characters: what they come to know is to not know. Successful assimilation into a monstrous system requires trading one type of innocence for another. As temporal palimpsests who are repositories for old stories *and* the means for those stories to continue, as receptacles for "old blood" *and* those who will pass it on, and as carriers of history, Faulkner's children—both within families and outside them—are illustrations and warnings for those whose learning ironically blinds them to the violence all around them. At once nostalgic and doomed, they paradoxically give, through their particular brand of innocence, insight into the social machinery of fate in Faulkner's fiction.

NOTES

For valuable suggestions about this essay, I would like to thank Ben Anderson-Nathe, Miriam Abelson, David Wolf, and Jonathan Walker.

1. William Faulkner, "That Evening Sun Go Down," *American Mercury*, March 1931, 267. This older version of the story later published as "That Evening Sun" has a richer treatment of the ditch that I discuss later in this essay. Hereafter cited parenthetically.

2. William Faulkner, *Light in August*, rev. ed. (1932; repr., New York: Vintage International, 1990), 384. Hereafter cited parenthetically.

3. Koritha Mitchell, "Belief and Performance, Morrison and Me," in *Toni Morrison: Forty Years in the Clearing*, ed. Carmen R. Gillespie (Lewisburg, PA: Bucknell University Press), 245–61.

4. Wallis H. Tinnie, "Jefferson vs. Grierson: Feuding Families and the Lynching of Homer Barron in 'A Rose for Emily'" (paper presentation, University of Mississippi, Oxford, MS, July 23, 2019).

5. See Leslie A. Fiedler, *Love and Death in the American Novel* (Champaign, IL: Dalkey Archive Press, 2003), 142–44; Bill Brown, "Reification, Reanimation, and the American Uncanny," *Critical Inquiry* 32, no. 2 (2006): 198–200; Hershini Bhana Young, "Black 'Like Me':

(Mis) Recognition, the Racial Gothic, and the Post-1967 Mixed-Race Movement in Danzy Senna's *Symptomatic*," *African American Review* 42, no. 2 (2008): 290-91.

6. See Robin Bernstein, *Racial Innocence: Performing American Childhood from Slavery to Civil Rights* (New York: New York University Press, 2011), 22-24; Clémentine Beauvais, *The Mighty Child: Time and Power in Children's Literature* (Philadelphia: John Benjamins, 2015), 18-20.

7. "'My Childhood Is Ruined!': Harper Lee and Racial Innocence," *American Literature* 88, no. 3 (September 2016): 597. Readers can't project racial innocence onto these child characters precisely because their innocence is a not-(yet) knowing. We see them in the process of learning the rules of cultural violence, briefly revealing those rules and learning to accept them.

8. William Faulkner, "Barn Burning," in *Collected Stories* (1950; repr., New York: Vintage International, 1995), 7-9. Hereafter cited parenthetically.

9. "Then he was moving, running, outside the house, toward the stable: this the old habit, the old blood which he had not been permitted to choose for himself, which had been bequeathed him willy nilly and which had run for so long (and who knew where, battening on what of outrage and savagery and lust) before it came to him" (Faulkner, "Barn Burning," 21).

10. As with Joe Christmas and Jason Compson, the figure of the "n[-----]" is the instrument of Sarty's self-identification. Jennie Joiner demonstrates that young Sarty comes to occupy the position of "the n[-----]" in "Barn Burning" (Jennie J. Joiner, "Constructing Black Sons: William Faulkner's 'Barn Burning' and Flannery O'Connor's 'The Artificial N[-----],'" *Flannery O'Connor Review* 8 (2010): 31. In the makeshift court where his father is first accused, he is asked to testify in the position of the "strange n[-----]" who warned Harris against Ab (Faulkner, "Barn Burning," 4); in deciding to run to Major de Spain's house, he puts *himself* in that position ("Ain't you going to even send a n[-----]?" [21]). It is this second iteration that underscores Sarty's growing awareness of his social position. Like Joe and Jason, Sarty measures himself against a haunted and haunting construct. What Sarty apprehends reflects the unspoken rules of the world he is beginning to understand. Kirstine Taylor demonstrates that the period in which "Barn Burning" (as well as "That Evening Sun Go Down," *Absalom, Absalom!*, and *Light in August*) was produced is the period of "white trash's movement from racial contaminant to guilty white" ("Untimely Subjects: White Trash and the Making of Racial Innocence in the Postwar South," *American Quarterly* 67, no. 1 [March 2015]: 57). This particular form of abjection, Taylor shows, is the condition of possibility for patrician racial innocence.

11. William Faulkner, *As I Lay Dying*, rev. ed. (1930; New York: Vintage International, 1990), 66.

12. William Faulkner, "A Justice," *Collected Stories* (1950; repr., New York: Vintage International, 1995), 360.

13. William Faulkner, *The Reivers*, rev. ed. (1962; repr., New York: Vintage International, 2011), 5.

14. Patricia Yaeger, *Dirt and Desire: Reconstructing Southern Women's Writing, 1930-1990* (Chicago: University of Chicago Press, 2000), especially chapter 4, "Race and the Cloud of Unknowing" (88-112).

15. Beverly Tatum, *Why Are All the Black Kids Sitting Together in the Cafeteria?* (New York: Basic Books, 2003), 55.

16. James Baldwin, interviewed by Kenneth Clark, *The Negro and the American Promise*, WGBH Boston, 1963, *American Experience | Citizen King*, Public Broadcasting Service, http://www.shoppbs.pbs.org/wgbh/amex/mlk/sfeature/sf_video_pop_04c_tr_qt.html, accessed November 7, 2019.

17. Notably, their moments of encounter send Faulkner's characters in profoundly different directions from child characters created by contemporaneous African American authors

(Du Bois, Johnson, Harper, Hurston, and dozens of others), who solidify their self-concepts in reaction to moments of encounter that produce them as integrated, if racialized, subjects.

18. Hortense Spillers, "The Family, Our Beloved Crisis: Faulkner's Version" (paper presentation, University of Mississippi, Oxford, MS, July 21, 2019).

19. William Faulkner, *Absalom, Absalom!*, rev. ed. (1936; repr., New York: Vintage International, 1990), 179. Hereafter cited parenthetically.

20. Patricia Yaeger, "Ghosts and Shattered Bodies, or What Does It Mean to Still Be Haunted by Southern Literature?," *South Central Review* 22, no. 1 (March 2005): 90.

21. Yaeger describes "the almost invisible force of *everyday haunting*, the trauma of living neither in the epic nor the extraordinary but in the everyday South" ("Ghosts," 97).

22. While Eupheus Hines, our source for the scene between Joe and the janitor, is an unreliable narrator, the striking similarity between this scene and young Jason Compson's racial musings in "That Evening Sun" invites exploration.

23. Richard Godden, "Call Me N[-----]! Race and Speech in Faulkner's *Light in August*," *American Studies* 14, no. 2 (August 1980): 238.

24. Tatum, *Why Are All the Black Kids*, 59–65.

25. In her conference paper on *Light in August*, Maite Urcaregui described the process of racialization within the novel despite white supremacy's dependence on concealing that process from view ("Materializing Race through Lena's Maternal Body in *Light in August*," paper presentation, University of Mississippi, Oxford, MS, July 22, 2019). I contend that the child is Faulkner's primary mechanism for revealing its shadow.

26. In an essay that centers on the same moment in a later version of Faulkner's short story, Ellen Bonds notes that "each time that Jason repeats "I ain't a n[-----]" represents a progression in the development of his racism" ("An 'Other' Look at William Faulkner's 'That Evening Sun,'" *Studies in Short Fiction* 37, no. 1 [Winter 2012]: 65). While this is certainly true, the particular development of Jason's iterative process is reflective of the lessons he is learning, moving from encounter with Nancy's terror and the word that perversely blames her and leaves her vulnerable, to seeking assurance that the violence can't name him ("am I, Dilsey?"), to self-assurance in his own literal and figurative separation from the relentless potential violence expressed by the word *n[-----]*.

27. The ditch is an incredibly rich metaphor in "That Evening Sun," appearing twenty times in the story: in addition to connecting and separating the Compsons and Nancy, it is the place whose profusion of weeds reflects Caddy's confusion about events, the ditch the queen must cross in Nancy's story, and the place where Nancy believes Jubah is lying in wait. It belongs with a network of other ditches or chasms in Faulkner's writing, recalling the ditch Joe Christmas hides in as well as the chasm that divides another type of innocence and experience—the chasm of virginity to which Jennie J. Joiner alluded in her July 23, 2019, presentation ("What Sutpen Discovered in New Orleans": Marriage and Plaçage in *Absalom Absalom!*), that "chasm which could be crossed but one time and in but one direction" (Faulkner, *Absalom, Absalom!*, 87).

28. The ditch may also be seen as a metaphysical divide, since Quentin narrates "That Evening Sun" in 1915, five years after his death in *The Sound and the Fury*.

29. Like Byron Bunch's stunted adult relationships, those "still shapes like discarded and fragmentary toys of childhood piled indiscriminate and gathering quiet dust in a forgotten closet" (Faulkner, *Light in August*, 439–40).

30. James Baldwin, "Stranger in the Village" (1953), in *The Price of the Ticket: Collected Nonfiction, 1948–1985* (New York: Macmillan, 1985), 89.

Faulkner's Future Americans

REBECCA NISETICH

In Faulkner's Yoknapatawpha, families like the Compsons, McCaslins, Beauchamps, and Sutpens span generations, and folks adhere to a one-drop definition of race. In novels like *Light in August* (1932), *Absalom, Absalom!* (1936), and *Go Down, Moses* (1942), racial definition precipitates death.[1] For example, defined as "Black" in the wake of Joanna Burden's murder, Joe Christmas is lynched in Reverend Hightower's kitchen. When Charles Bon is outed as "Black" by his father, Thomas Sutpen, Bon is shot and killed by his brother, Henry, at the front gate of the Sutpen plantation. Their deaths suggest that it is impossible to forge and embrace a viable identity outside of the confines of the American racial structure.

But Faulkner also peoples the margins of these texts with a younger generation of racially indeterminate individuals: Bon's grandson, Jim Bond, and the nameless babies in *Light in August* and *Go Down, Moses*. These marginal characters' existence, their ability to leave Yoknapatawpha, their *survival* points towards new possibilities. I call these individuals "Faulkner's future Americans," drawing on Charles W. Chesnutt's controversial theory from his *Boston Evening Transcript* article, "The Future American" (1900). As we will see, Faulkner's future Americans are not reductively defined by "blood" or appearance or ancestry; instead, they are defined subjectively and contextually. For these characters, indeterminacy, ambiguity, and anonymity enable the elision of racial definition. Like their predecessors, they do not know their family histories or racial ancestries; however, their identities are not fundamentally shaped by their racial indeterminacy, and their lives are not destroyed by it.

This essay explores Faulkner's portrayal of future American figures in *Absalom, Absalom!*, *Light in August*, and *Go Down, Moses*. As I will demonstrate, these characters exemplify Faulkner's gesture towards imagining a postracial future. For the past thirty years, scholars of Faulkner have productively explored race and identity in his work.[2] I further this conversation by exploring Faulkner's engagement with the concept of postracialism, a theory this essay explicitly critiques.

I. "Future Americans"

In Faulkner's world, the only way to escape racial definition is to erase knowledge of ancestry and "blood." Such an erasure, Faulkner implicitly suggests, will lead individuals away from regional particularism and towards an identity that is decoupled from race and ancestry. At first blush, postracialism in Faulkner's oeuvre seems remarkable, but fantasies about curing America's "race problem" through miscegenation and assimilation have existed since at least the turn of the twentieth century. In fact, they remain present today: both *Time* magazine and *National Geographic* have posited racial mixture as the basis for a racially homogenous society *in the future*. For example, *Time* magazine's 1993 cover story, "The Future Face of America" presents a computer-generated image of a woman with the caption, "How immigrants are shaping the world's first multicultural society." Similarly, *National Geographic*'s 2013 story "The Changing Face of America" prints (and fetishizes) images of mixed-race individuals and suggests that they provide us with "an opportunity" to challenge normative assumptions about race: "If we can't slot people into familiar categories, perhaps we'll be forced to reconsider existing definitions of race and identity, presumptions about who is us and who is them."[3] This is highly problematic because, in this framing, when "they" become "us," they become *white*. As Houston A. Baker Jr. and K. Merinda Simmons contend in *The Trouble with Post-Blackness*, the theory of postracialism exhibits "the impulse to treat race as a necessary signifier of difference while leaving whiteness alone as a cohesive whole."[4] The supposed elimination of difference and the elision of "us" and "them" does not make America postracial; it makes America *white*.

The assumption that racial mixture can alleviate and might possibly eliminate race differences has percolated in American popular discourse for over a century. In "The Future American" (1900), Charles W. Chesnutt articulates the desire for racial assimilation with the goal of attaining a postracial future. Chesnutt boldly describes Americans as not only heterogeneous but miscegenated: racial mixture, he writes, is "an historical fact that only an ostrich-like prejudice could deny."[5] Despite legal and social efforts to the contrary, Chesnutt predicts that Americans will inevitably become "a composite and homogeneous people" (126). And he argues that homogeneity itself will solve racial prejudice precisely because the elimination of the visual signifiers of "race" will correspondingly eliminate the concept of "race." When Americans became physically indistinct, he writes, cultural and legal distinctions will "lose their importance" as well (135).

Ignoring the structural elements of race and racism and focusing on its social construction, "The Future American" exemplifies the problem with the theory of postracialism. As Dean McWilliams observes, "Chesnutt tries conceptually to move immediately from a society saturated by race to one from which race is absent. Put differently, he tries to move from racial essentialism to racial subjectivism, without adequately understanding the power, and potential value, of racial constructions."[6] Chesnutt posits assimilation as a way to eliminate the cultural and economic differences that are used to socially construct "race," but he does not recognize the power dynamics that create and maintain the distinction. Put simply, "race" is a concept that privileges and benefits white people at the expense of everyone else. Chesnutt's argument seems odd, given his experiences of race prejudice documented in his journals. As he knew from personal experience, one can "look white" and still experience race prejudice.[7]

Published in 1900, Chesnutt's article appeared at a moment when the public discourse on race had become increasingly virulent. As George M. Frederickson writes, during this period racist propaganda "spewed forth in unprecedented volume" (*Racism* 256).[8] For example, in 1900 Paul Barringer published *The American Negro: His Past and Future*, which in Frederickson's words argued that the "Negro race" was so "degraded" that its own "savagery" would ensure its extinction.[9] In 1901, William Hannibal Thomas published the racist treatise, *The American Negro*. These and other major publications demonstrate the extent to which anti-Black racism permeated American culture.[10] This veritable onslaught of pseudoscientific propaganda paved the way for works like Madison Grant's *The Passing of the Great Race* (1916), Lothrop Stoddard's *The Rising Tide of Color* (1921), and Charles Gould's *America: A Family Matter* (1922).

Chesnutt underscores the subjective nature of racial definition and explores theories of assimilation and postracialism in essay and fiction. For example, in *The House Behind the Cedars* (1900), he dramatizes the effects of assimilation through the Walden siblings, Rena and John.[11] Rena believes that her slight African ancestry makes her "Negro." Conversely, John treats his racial identity pragmatically: because he can legally define himself as "white" in South Carolina, he simply moves there and embraces his new identity and privileges.

John's decision to live as white necessitates that he conceal his ancestry. Although the law in South Carolina enables him to define himself based on his white appearance, social practices follow the one-drop rule. Because of this, John's son, Albert, is sheltered from the emotional burden that his father must bear, daily and alone. His silence ensures that his son will have no reason to think of himself as anything but a white man. Baby Albert can grow up to be a white southern gentleman without the psychological burden of racial passing. John's decision enables Albert to unquestioningly embrace a white racial identity. Because of the choices his father makes, the son has a degree of agency that both John and Rena lack.

Albert is a prototypical "Future American." In the article, Chesnutt writes about living in Reconstruction-era North Carolina, where he knew of many people of mixed ancestry whose children are, like baby Albert, "wholly unaware of their origin" (*Essays*, 127). Chesnutt's novel is set at a time when people could legally move from Black to white by simply crossing a state line, but in the turn-of-the-century milieu in which it was written and published, the legal and social boundaries between Black and white had become increasingly rigid. By the time Faulkner was writing *Light in August*, *Absalom, Absalom!*, and *Go Down, Moses*, the flexibility to which Chesnutt alludes in *The House Behind the Cedars* and "The Future American" had been largely eliminated, and the one-drop rule pervaded American legislative and popular discourses on racial identity.[12] But balanced against this racial essentialism, there was also an emerging progressive movement *against* it. Indeed, the word "racism" itself came into popular usage in the 1930s, the same period when Faulkner penned *Light in August* and *Absalom, Absalom!*[13]

Swedish economist Gunnar Myrdal's *An American Dilemma* (1944) is an example of the era's emerging socially progressive racial discourse. Published two years after *Go Down, Moses*, Myrdal's study portrays race prejudice as *individual* and *personal* choices to discriminate, and neglects to elucidate the structures and systems that create and uphold racism in America. As Ian Haney López writes, "Building on the view that race reduced to phenotype and nothing more, Myrdal attributed racially harmful actions to the persistence of the irrational belief that race said something meaningful about individual capacity" (999).[14] Ibram Kendi categorizes Myrdal's approach as "assimilationist": "assimilationists constantly encourage Black adoption of White cultural traits and/ or physical ideals."[15] Indeed, Myrdal writes, "It is to the advantage of American Negroes as individuals and as a group to become assimilated into American culture, to acquire the traits held in esteem by the dominant white Americans."[16] In this, Myrdal aligns with Chesnutt, who wrote in his journal forty years earlier that "the steady progress of the colored race in wealth and culture and social efficiency will, in the course of time, materially soften the asperities of racial prejudice and permit them to approach the whites more closely, until, in time, the prejudice against intermarriage shall be overcome" (*Essays* 133). In *The House Behind the Cedars*, Chesnutt dramatizes this process: Rena and John are not only accepted into white society, they are admitted into its upper echelons: Rena is crowned "The Queen of Love and Beauty" in her society debut;

John marries a rich white woman shortly after arriving in South Carolina. Chesnutt's project is an explicit exploration of the possibility of a postracial future; Faulkner's dabbling in postracialism is implicit and perhaps even subconscious. Nevertheless, like Chesnutt, he tries on a kind of postracialism in his portrayals of marginal characters, which I explore and critique in the sections that follow.

II. Faulkner's Future Americans

Who are Faulkner's "Future Americans" and why do they matter? There are two major defining traits that these marginal characters exhibit. First, they do not know their racial ancestry. It is precisely this lack of knowledge which accounts for their survival. For example, in *Absalom, Absalom!* Shreve imagines that Jim Bond, grandson of Charles Bon, "not only would not have known [his ancestry], he wouldn't have cared" (174). In "Delta Autumn" the Beauchamp-Edmonds baby sleeps through the entire exchange between his mother and Ike McCaslin, an exchange that reveals his ancestry to be tainted not only by miscegenation but by incest as well. Sleep shelters the child from being reductively defined and thus breaks the McCaslin family legacy's cycle of racial definition via ancestry. Finally, within the text of *Light in August*, the racial identity and paternity of Lena's baby is never questioned; however, as we will see, Faulkner's narrative implicitly hints at his racial indeterminacy and posits several men as potential father figures. In all of these instances, racial indeterminacy, ambiguity, and anonymity suggest a new freedom of self-definition

Second, unlike their predecessors, these marginal characters survive because they *escape* the physical space of Yoknapatawpha: at the conclusion of *Absalom, Absalom!*, Jim Bond exists in some liminal space where he quite literally can't be "caught"; Lena and her baby together leave Jefferson and move northward to Jackson, Tennessee. Similarly, in *Go Down, Moses,* the nameless mother and child leave the Big Woods of Mississippi. For these marginal figures, Faulkner seems to suggest that new geographies hold the possibility that their racial identities might be granted a greater degree of fluidity. Faulkner's marginal characters implicitly demonstrate that it is the erasure of racial and ancestral knowledge that enables individuals to survive. The presence of this new generation of characters at the margins of each text suggests that binary and one-drop definitions of Blackness might lose their defining power. When the criteria used to establish and maintain the Black-white binary no longer exist, perhaps "race" ceases to exist, as well.

However, the survival of these marginal figures is problematic because it necessitates that they fade not into *racelessness* but into *whiteness*. In making this distinction, I follow critics like Henry Louis Gates Jr., who points out that "in a system where whiteness is the default, racelessness is never a possibility. You cannot opt out; you can only opt in."[17] Similarly, Baker and Simmons observe that "the discourse on post-blackness keeps up and running an untroubled category of whiteness against which it demarcates itself" (*Post-Blackness*, 3).

As we will see, for Faulkner's future Americans, survival is contingent on leaving Yoknapatawpha for some other place where, ostensibly, one's racial identity (or the lack of knowledge regarding it) no longer determines one's fate. For all three characters, leaving Jefferson means losing their connection to their families, to their ancestries, and to the past more broadly. The survival of Faulkner's marginal characters demonstrates that Yoknapatawpha itself is unchanging: the area remains hostile towards racially indeterminate individuals.

Absalom, Absalom!

Almost no one in *Absalom, Absalom!* escapes unscathed, but there is one notable survivor: Jim Bond. As "the scion, the heir, the apparent (though not obvious)," Bond, at least as portrayed, doesn't suggest a future that is particularly bright (296). In Quentin and Shreve's reimagination, the "slack-mouthed idiot" epitomizes the eugenic nightmare of miscegenation. While conarrators Shreve and Quentin define Bond in this way, Faulkner subtly undermines their portrayal of Bond by emphasizing the inherently subjective nature of family history and legacy. The stories we hear in *Absalom, Absalom!* are in fact mediated through the voices of characters who are generationally, situationally, and physically removed from the action. Quentin, Shreve, and Mr. Compson are not contemporaries of Sutpen; indeed, Sutpen is long dead by the time Quentin shares his story with Shreve. Although she lived for a time at Sutpen's Hundred, Rosa Coldfield witnesses the downfall of the Sutpen clan primarily from a distance. Although technically "family" by marriage, she is not a Sutpen, and most of the time she recounts events and interactions that she has observed but which she does not understand.

In fact, the only "objective" (i.e., unmediated by the four character-narrators) information we have about Jim Bond appears in the novel's appendix, where he is described simply as "Son of Charles Etienne de Saint Valery Bon. Born, Sutpen's Hundred, 1882. Disappeared from Sutpen's Hundred, 1910. Whereabouts unknown" (309). There is no mention of Bond's supposed mental handicap here, and this is significant because other appendix descriptions are much more colorful.[18] Bond's description exemplifies a purposeful omission on Faulkner's part and underscores the subjective and partial sense we have of his character, as presented to us through the imaginings of Quentin and Shreve.

Quentin is haunted by Bond's survival: as Shreve intuits, "You still hear him at night sometimes. Dont you?" To which Quentin replies, simply, "Yes" (302). Representing the specter of miscegenation, Bond's continued presence is a disturbing reminder of the ramifications of racial mixing. Eric Dussere underscores the economic implications of Bond's survival: "In his haunting presence, Jim Bond is an eternal reminder to the South that it owes a debt which cannot be paid—and which is still owed to and from the 'heirs' of the initial bond—that the books will always remain uneven, that it will never cancel its checks and leave the past behind" (*Balancing the Books*, 56). Seen in this way, Jim Bond is the embodied reminder of southern guilt who continues to haunt Quentin

At the novel's close, Bond's liminal existence makes definitive closure impossible; as Shreve puts it, "You've got one n[-----] left. One n[-----] Sutpen left. Of course you cant catch him and you dont even always see him and you never will be able to use him. But you've got him there still" (302). His description highlights a defining characteristic of Faulkner's marginal characters: whereas the present generation is eventually "caught" (i.e., defined racially), the future generation escapes, both geographically and metaphysically.

Bond's name has significant legal resonance: As Luster understands, "Dat's a lawyer word. Whut dey puts you under when de Law ketches you" (174). But Jim Bond can't be caught in this way; as Shreve imagines, "They could hear him; he didn't seem to ever get any further away but they couldn't get any nearer and maybe in time they could not even locate the direction of the howling anymore" (300–301). Bond exists outside of the control of community and law. Unlike his predecessors, he cannot be "caught" and thus he cannot be killed off. This is why Quentin is still haunted by Jim Bond: everyone else has been accounted for, defined; their stories have been racially made sense of.

Light in August

In *Absalom, Absalom!* Jim Bond is at once a literal figure and a haunting presence. In *Light in August*, Faulkner shows how racialized hysteria makes violence inevitable, and Joe Christmas's death suggests the impossibility of maintaining an identity outside of the racial binary. *Light in August* throws into relief the fatal consequences of not knowing your racial ancestry: at the center of this novel, a man is hunted and killed; but at its margins, a child is born. While Christmas's death demonstrates the fatal consequences of racial indeterminacy, Lena's baby exhibits the full range of possibilities for Faulkner's marginal characters. In the text of the novel, this baby is presumptively white, but Faulkner subtly undermines this assumption by connecting a cast of paternal figures to Lena's baby: Lucas Burch, Joe Christmas, Reverend Hightower, and Byron Bunch. Faulkner suggests not simply that this baby's racial identity is ambiguous and indeterminate but also that it is hybrid and communal.

The narrative is sprinkled with little clues that destabilize both the paternity and the racial identity of the child. For example, Reverend Hightower envisions both himself and Byron Bunch as potential father figures: after delivering the baby single-handedly, he imagines that Lena might name the baby in his honor, until he remembers, *"there is Byron. Byron of course will take the pas of me"* (Faulkner, *Light in August*, 406. Byron Bunch, unrequited lover of Lena, is the man responsible for setting her up in a slave cabin on the Burden plantation and haphazardly procuring Hightower and a doctor to help when she goes into labor.[19] At the novel's close, Byron remains on the road with Lena and her baby, still trying to find a way into her heart (and her bed).

After delivering Lena's baby, Hightower returns to his home in town, where he reflects on this momentous event. Here, his conception of present and past becomes blurred: "It seems to him that he can see, feel, about him the ghosts of rich fields, and of the rich fecund black life of the quarters, the mellow shouts, the presence of fecund women, the prolific naked children in the dust before the doors; and the big house again, noisy, loud with the treble shouts of the generations" (407). On Joanna Burden's barren plantation and in its ruined slave cabin, Lena's giving birth suggests revitalization. In Hightower's vision, the birth of this baby powerfully unites past and future. Lena's fecundity also unites white with Black by connecting her to the slaves who once inhabited the Burden plantation: "More of them. Many more. That will be her life, her destiny. The good stock peopling in tranquil obedience to it the good earth; from these hearty loins without hurry or haste descending mother and daughter. But by Byron engendered next" (406; emphasis removed). Hightower's vision gives us a glimpse of a new kind of communal family with different paternal and racial elements. Here, Lena appears at the center of a much bigger cycle, the births figured in Hightower's fantasy.

Along with Byron and Hightower, two other significant paternal figures for Lena's baby are Lucas Burch and Joe Christmas. As I have demonstrated elsewhere, Lucas Burch's racial identity is—like Christmas's—unstable and ambiguous. While the townspeople in Jefferson do not question Lucas's self-identification as a white man, Faulkner subtly undermines it.[20]

The connection between Lucas and Christmas intensifies their relationship to Lena's baby and is made visible through the eyes of Christmas's grandmother, Mrs. Hines. The chaos of the birth has confused both grandmother Hines and Lena. In fact, no one seems able to keep the family ties straight. Even the doctor thinks that Lena and her baby are somehow related to Doc and Mrs. Hines: arriving at the birth too late, the doctor says, "Byron must have been excited. He never told me the whole family would be on hand, grandpa and grandma too" (397). All of this confusion makes Lena confused, too. As she tells Hightower, Mrs. Hines "keeps on talking about [the baby] like his pa was that—the one in jail, that Mr Christmas. She keeps on, and then I get mixed up and it's like sometimes I cant—like I am mixed up too and I think that his pa is that Mr—Mr Christmas too" (409). As Mrs. Hines witnesses the birth of Lena's baby, she relives the birth of her grandson; afterwards, she repeatedly calls the baby "Joey" and even refers to Lena as "Milly," her deceased daughter (397, 398). Here, the orphan Joe Christmas is reconfigured as both father and son. Through the confusions of Mrs. Hines, Lena, the doctor, Hightower, and the others, the family becomes inclusive, even communal.

For Lena, this connection to Joe Christmas is deeply disturbing; but for readers, such a connection also points towards a future where a more broadly defined conception of the family might take the place of the current blood-based conceptions. Here the ties that bind the members together might not be "blood" in the traditional sense, though they are, as Jay Watson contends, shaped by the trope of blood. As Watson observes, Lena's birthing and Joe's castration mirror each other: "It may even be that in the violent opening of Joe's loins, and the sudden emergence of their precious contents onto a scene dramatically altered by that arrival, we are meant to recognize a visual echo of . . . the image of a woman in birth."[21] Watson emphasizes the difference between these twinned births, and argues that Faulkner purposefully "minimizes the material presence of blood in the novel's scenes of birth, menstruation, and sexualized violence in order to appropriate their power for Joe's death scene." Indeed, in the text, these events are literally juxtaposed (occurring in chapters 17 and 18); temporally, they occur on the very same day. In the context of the racialized discourse on blood—in which blood carries racial essence and threatens contagion when spilled or commingled—this twinned flowing of bloods signifies a mixture that fundamentally affects Lena's baby and the family he is at the center of.

Go Down, Moses

In *Light in August*, the family is expansive and inclusive. In "Delta Autumn" the family we see is exclusive and redundant—McCaslin twice over. This baby's ancestry is the opposite of communal: he is the offspring of a relationship that is not only miscegenous but incestuous too. However, Faulkner makes clear that this nameless woman and her infant son will break the cycle of interracial incest that has haunted the McCaslin clan for generations.

For the McCaslins, generations of miscegenation and incest have made it hard to know who is who, and kinship lines have become hopelessly entangled. In his effort to break the cycle of interracial incest, Ike McCaslin has renounced his marriage and his family's land. But as he realizes in his dank tent in the Mississippi Delta, these efforts have been in vain: his cousin Roth Edmonds and his mixed-race cousin from the Beauchamp side of the family have together produced another miscegenated McCaslin heir. The child is inextricably connected to his family's legacy, as Ike notes "harshly," "It's a boy, I reckon. They usually are, except that one that was its own mother too" (345). Although Ike appears gruff, this encounter shakes him to the core; after his niece and her infant son leave the tent, he lies in bed, "rigid save for the shaking" (347). Ike can only see the existence of this child as further punishment for his family's original sin: Carothers McCaslin's rape of his mixed-race and enslaved daughter, Tomasina.

In contrast, the unnamed mother and child of "Delta Autumn" are not destroyed by their familial past, and their survival suggests the possibility of hybrid and communal family structures. While this woman and her child are descendants of the McCaslin family history, they will not be destroyed by it. This woman's portrayal underscores her agency and self-determination in several ways. First, she has a more complete understanding of the McCaslin family tree than either Ike or Roth. She sees Ike's renunciation for what it is, a largely symbolic and wholly futile gesture: as she tells him, "You gave to [Roth's] grandfather that land which didn't belong to him, not even half of it by will or even law" (343). When she suspects that Roth has abandoned her, she travels to the Delta to get an answer from him, and she refuses the money he offers as compensation for his abandonment. Instead, she leaves, which enables her to maintain her power of self-definition. The decision to leave also shields her child from the provincial identity formation system, one that conceals interracial kinship ties and preserves a power structure that enables white men to abuse Black women. This is the structure that fostered and continues to foster the perpetuation of the McCaslin fate.

Faulkner makes clear that the cycle of interracial incest will be broken not by the white Ike McCaslin but by this Beauchamp cousin and her infant son. As I noted earlier, because the infant sleeps through the exchange between his mother and Ike, he is untouched by the legacy of his ancestry. His familial history does not define him even though he is shaped by it. It is significant that throughout this exchange, his mother purposefully maintains a physical distance between her child and his "Uncle Ike": "Just for an instant her free hand moved as though she were about to lift the edge of the raincoat away from the child's face. But she did not" (345). Her decision to shelter her baby from physical contact with his ancestor is significant: it is only when Ike touches the hand of his kinswoman that he can recognize her as such: "the gnarled, bloodless, bone-light bone-dry old man's fingers touching for a second the smooth young flesh where the strong old blood ran after its long lost journey back to home" (345). When Ike touches this woman's hand and realizes who she is, he defines her *but not her child*, although he sees them both: "Now he understood what it was she brought into the tent with her.... He cried, not loud, in a voice of amazement, pity, and outrage: '*You're* a n[-----]!'" (344; emphasis added). Although the McCaslin blood is still strong enough to define them both, Ike's verbal definition does not extend to the child.

Faulkner deploys both antimiscegenation *and* postracialism rhetoric in these novels. For example, *Go Down, Moses* is set in the liminal space somewhere between town and wilderness, as well as in the wilderness of the Big Woods, and in the town of Jefferson. The novel explores both the past and the future. The central figure of this novel, Ike McCaslin, is an elderly man who sees the world around him changing, modernizing, and slowly rendering his old ways of life obsolete. Ike laments a world where men are destroying the purity of their land, and he sees this destruction as fundamentally connected to the racial mixture of men: "Chinese and African and Aryan and Jew, all breed and spawn together until no man has time to say which one is which nor cares" (347; emphasis removed). In his mind, this mixture is man's punishment for his crime of the destruction of the forest: "No wonder the ruined woods I used to know dont cry for retribution! he thought: The people who have destroyed it will accomplish its revenge." This dystopian vision of the future recalls Shreve's understanding of the inevitability of race mixture: for both men, the possibility of hybrid and communal identity is degenerative.

As the narrative makes clear, Ike's nostalgia is inextricably connected to the McCaslin legacy, because it relies on identity structures that are blood-based and exclusive. Ike sees this baby, like his predecessors, as likewise trapped by this legacy that the McCaslin men cannot seem to escape, and his reaction is of its time and place: "Maybe in a thousand or two thousand years in America.... But not now! Not now!" (344; emphasis removed). His solution is provincial—he tells his Beauchamp cousin to "Go back North. Marry: a man in your own race. That's the only salvation for you" (346). The solution to reentrench racial boundaries is not only reductive; it doesn't work.

Similarly, by the end of *Absalom, Absalom!* Shreve and Quentin have reconfigured Bond into a horrific miscegenated forefather. In their hysterical fantasy, the consequences of racial mixing have global implications: as Shreve tells Quentin, "I think that in time the Jim Bonds are going to conquer the western hemisphere . . . and so in a few thousand years, I who regard you will also have sprung from the loins of African kings" (302). Shreve's prediction follows Chesnutt's in "The Future American" in this respect: they both suggest that eventually—and inevitably—racial mixture will be the rule, and not the exception. But Shreve's dystopian vision aligns with early twentieth-century eugenic fears about the insidious and degenerative effects of racial miscegenation, whereas Chesnutt suggests that universal mixture will ensure that racial distinction no longer plays a role in defining identity.

At the center of these texts, racial miscegenation seems inextricably linked to death and destruction. At the margins, the survival of these young, racially liminal figures imbues what are otherwise tragic conclusions with a kind of tentative optimism—an optimism that is specifically *postracial*. Freed from the destructive identity patterns that defined and destroyed their forbears, these marginal characters live on. Their survival suggests that, removed from Yoknapatawpha, understanding and representing oneself might become a matter of choice. Elsewhere and somewhere in the future, Faulkner suggests, Americans will disentangle the messy connections between "blood" and identity. In this future America, perhaps individuals will be able to honor all aspects of their identities, to entirely disregard "race" as fundamental to identity, or to chart some other path for themselves.

III. The Problem with Postracialism

As Baker and Simmons point out, postracialism is itself not *post*racial at all—it is post-*Black*, and that is highly problematic. Post-Blackness does not, in fact, move us *beyond* race, it implicity upholds whiteness as the norm against which all other differences are defined (*Post-Blackness*, 2–3). Critics have recognized this flaw regarding Chesnutt's "Future American" series. For example, William Ramsey points out that "such an argument would seem to entail, if not encourage—the loss of distinctive black ethnicity through the flow of dark blood toward white."[22] Similarly, as SallyAnn Ferguson writes, "Chesnutt . . . is essentially a social and literary accommodationist who pointedly and repeatedly confines his reformist impulses to 'the colored people'—a term that he almost always applies to color-line blacks or those of mixed race."[23]

Chesnutt's understanding of "race" as a legal and social invention—and not a visible, physical entity—anticipates critical race theory by nearly a century. However, the fact that this field of scholarship exists today shows that Chesnutt's theory in "The Future American"—that race mixing will eliminate the concept of "race" entirely—has yet to solve America's "race problem." The one-drop rule continues implicitly to shape American conceptions of race, and when a single drop of "blood" defines "Blackness," then "race" need not be visible to be real. Today, race exists because the majority of Americans continue to accept three salient and related beliefs: first, that race is real; second, that it is definable by blood, ancestry, appearance, behavior, etc.; and third, that racial identity fundamentally matters. These beliefs are thrown into relief when we look at our country's pronounced racial disparities in education, wealth, incarceration rates, life expectancy, etc.

Even my own formulation of marginal and central characters is arguably problematic, for as Kimberlé Crenshaw and her fellow editors of the recent *Seeing Race Again* collection point out, "The humanities falsely aggregated all of humanity into a disembodied universalism said to be the only alternative to parochial particularisms. This legacy has structured the study of difference largely on axes of margins and centers rather than axes of domination and oppression, leaving the humanities ill-suited in respect to race to discern which differences make a difference and why."[24] This critique resonates specifically with my argument here: shifting the focus to domination and oppression exposes an important power differential. Faulkner's Future Americans aren't postracial at all, they've simply become white. Their marginality or centrality isn't the point: they aren't moving out of the system, rather, they are moving into positions of power *within* the system.

NOTES

1. William Faulkner, *Absalom, Absalom!*, rev. ed. (1936; repr., New York: Vintage International, 1990); *Go Down, Moses*, rev. ed. (1942; repr., New York: Vintage International, 1990); *Light in August*, rev. ed. (1932; repr., New York: Vintage International, 1990). Hereafter cited parenthetically. Faulkner's portrayals of Joe Christmas, Charles Bon, and other victims of southern racism align with Ruth Wilson Gilmore's definition of racism as "the state-sanctioned or extralegal production and exploitation of group-differentiated vulnerability to premature death" (Ruth Wilson Gilmore, *Golden Gulag: Prisons, Surplus, Crisis, and Opposition in Globalizing California* [Berkeley: University of California Press, 2007], 28).

2. Seminal book-length studies include Thadious M. Davis, *Faulkner's Negro: Art and the Southern Context* (Baton Rouge: Louisiana State University Press, 1983); Eric J. Sundquist,

Faulkner: The House Divided (Baltimore: Johns Hopkins University Press, 1985); Theresa M. Towner, *Faulkner on the Color Line: The Later Novels* (Jackson: University of Mississippi Press, 2000); Erik Dussere, *Balancing the Books: Faulkner, Morrison, and the Economies of Slavery* (New York: Routledge, 2003); John N. Duvall, *Race and White Identity in Southern Fiction: From Faulkner to Morrison* (New York: Palgrave MacMillan, 2008); Joel Williamson, *William Faulkner and Southern History* (Oxford, UK: Oxford University Press, 1993); Jay Watson, ed., *Faulkner and Whiteness* (Jackson: University Press of Mississippi, 2011); and John T. Matthews, ed., *William Faulkner in Context* (Cambridge, UK: Cambridge University Press, 2015).

    3. Lise Funderburg, "The Changing Face of America," *National Geographic*, October 2013, https://www.nationalgeographic.com/magazine/2013/10/changing-face-america/. See also Ted Thai, "The New Face of America," *Time*, November 18, 1993, http://content.time.com/time/covers/0,16641,19931118,00.html.

    4. Houston A. Baker Jr. and K. Merinda Simmons, *The Trouble with Post-Blackness* (New York: Columbia University Press, 2015), 3. Hereafter cited parenthetically.

    5. Charles W. Chesnutt, *Essays and Speeches*, ed. Joseph R. McElrath, Robert C. Leitz, and Jesse S. Crisler (Stanford, CA: Stanford University Press, 1999), 125. Hereafter cited parenthetically.

    6. Dean McWilliams, *Charles W. Chesnutt and the Fictions of Race* (Athens: University of Georgia Press, 2002), 55. Hereafter cited parenthetically.

    7. Chesnutt recognized his liminal position, as he describes in his journal: "I am neither fish[,] flesh, nor fowl—neither 'n[-----],' poor white, nor 'buckrah.' Too 'stuck up' for the colored folks, and, of course, not recognized by the whites" (in *The Journals of Charles W. Chesnutt*, ed. Richard Brodhead [Durham, NC: Duke University Press, 1993], 157–58). His liminal position on the color line gave him intimate experience with the ways that race is socially constructed and maintained.

    8. George M. Frederickson, *Racism: A Short History* (Princeton, NJ: Princeton University Press, 2002), 256. Hereafter cited parenthetically.

    9. George M. Frederickson, *The Black Image in the White Mind: The Debate on Afro-American Character and Destiny, 1817–1914* (New York: Harper and Row, 1971), 253.

    10. Thomas's book was published by a major press, the MacMillan Company, and it was favorably reviewed by *The Boston Evening Transcript*, which also published Chesnutt's "The Future American."

    11. Charles W. Chesnutt, *The House behind the Cedars* (Boston: Houghton Mifflin, 1900). Hereafter cited parenthetically.

    12. A lawyer by training, Chesnutt explores the legal construction of race in his novels, as well as articles including "The Future American." For another example, see Charles W. Chesnutt, "What Is a White Man?," *Independent* 41 (May 30, 1889): 5–6.

    13. As Frederickson writes, "The word 'racism' first came into common usage in the 1930s when a new word was required to describe the theories on which the Nazis based their persecution of the Jews" (*Racism*, 5).

    14. Ian F. Haney López, "'A Nation of Minorities': Race, Ethnicity, and Reactionary Colorblindness," *Stanford Law Review* 59 (2007): 999. Hereafter cited parenthetically.

    15. Ibram X. Kendi, *Stamped from the Beginning: The Definitive History of Racist Ideas in America* (New York: Nation Books, 2016), 3. Hereafter cited parenthetically.

    16. Gunnar Myrdal, *The Negro Problem and Modern Democracy*, vol. 2 of *An American Dilemma* (New Brunswick, NJ: Transaction Publishers, 1996), 928–29. Hereafter cited parenthetically.

    17. Henry Louis Gates Jr., *Thirteen Ways of Looking at a Black Man* (New York: Vintage, 1997), 207.

    18. For example, Wash Jones is described as a "hanger-on of Sutpen" (308).

19. The facts surrounding the birth destabilize Lena's racial identity: she delivers her child in the Burden plantation's slave cabin, and it is Hightower who delivers her baby (recall that he previously delivered a stillborn Negro child).

20. Rebecca Nisetich, "When Difference Becomes Dangerous: Intersectional Identity Formation and the Protective Cover of Whiteness in Faulkner's *Light in August*," *Faulkner Journal* 31, no. 1 (Spring 2019): 43–66.

21. Jay Watson, *Reading for the Body: The Recalcitrant Materiality of Southern Fiction, 1893–1985* (Athens: University of Georgia Press, 2012), 155.

22. William M. Ramsey, "Family Matters in the Fiction of Charles W. Chesnutt," *Southern Literary Journal* 33, no. 2 (2001): 32.

23. SallyAnn Ferguson, "Chesnutt's Genuine Black and Future Americans," *MELUS* 15, no. 3 (1988): 109. Other critics, such as Walter Benn Michaels, posit instead that adherence to a conception of "blackness" as determined by "blood" is itself reductive. As Michaels points out, those who wish to "respect and preserve" rather than abolish the concept of race "remain, in fact, committed to racial essentialism" (Walter Benn Michaels, "Autobiography of an Ex-White Man: Why Race Is Not a Social Construction," *Transition* 73 (1997): 128). What Michaels neglects here is the way the white racial frame operates to conceal structural racism. Race is real: it was created and is maintained through law and culture. Michaels is right to affirm the concept of race as a social construct, but this fact doesn't mean that race isn't *real*, or that "race" isn't still foundational to the ways we order our society.

24. Kimberlé Williams Crenshaw, Luke Charles Harris, Daniel Martinez HoSang, and George Lipsitz, introduction to *Seeing Race Again: Countering Colorblindness across the Disciplines*, ed. Crenshaw, Harris, HoSang, and Lipsitz (Berkeley: University of California Press, 2019), 8.

"It Takes Two People to Make You"

Brotherhood and Loss in *As I Lay Dying*

JOSEPHINE ADAMS

In his 1984 study *Reading for the Plot*, Peter Brooks distinguishes between plot and plotting, the latter, in its gerund form, implying the "dynamic aspect of narrative—that which makes a plot 'move forward' and makes us read forward."[1] What fuels this momentum, Brooks tells us, is desire: the reader's desire for meaning, the thematic desire within the narrative, and the desire of the narrative itself, functioning as a "self-contained motor" running on its own internal energies (41). If we think about *As I Lay Dying* as shaped by this kind of libidinal economy, we could say that Addie's desire to be buried in Jefferson is responsible for the narrative's momentum, its temporal and spatial thrust toward resolution. "It was her wish," Anse explains.[2] "I promised my word me and the boys would get her there quick as mules could walk it, so she could rest quiet." And yet when we reach the narrative's end—what should be "the realization of a blocked and resisted desire" (Brooks, *Reading*, 12) the site of "significant discharge" (101)—Addie's burial is all but hidden from us, buried itself in a dependent clause—"when we got it filled and covered" (Faulkner, *As I Lay Dying*, 237)—halfway through Cash's penultimate monologue, implying that this would-be culminating event, even to the son who so painstakingly built the coffin, is less important than the subject of the main clause, which in this case is Darl's arrest.

There's something off balance here; more than just an act of grammatical subordination, Cash's narration of Addie's burial seems to have changed the terms of the narrative itself. According to Brooks's model, thematic desire and the reader's "passion of (for) meaning," running on the same narrative track, should eventually and ideally find themselves in the same moment(s) of realization, each coming to an end with and by way of the other (37). So why are we robbed of the very event toward which we, and the Bundren family, have been moving all along? Of course, to some extent we have been aware throughout that there are other desires that allow for, or generate, an identical momentum—that is, desires for which Jefferson is the site of potential realization: Anse wants a new set of teeth, Dewey Dell is after an abortion, Vardaman can't stop thinking about the toy trains on display in shop windows. But *As I Lay Dying*'s denouement suggests that the myriad reasons for going to Jefferson, ostensibly justified by the burial journey, are not only *other* desires but also *competing* desires. To rebalance the narrative thus means to reevaluate the source of its trajectory: in retrospect, these wants have been fighting for the same narrative space, circling in and out with the monologues. It seems impossible to name only one desire, let alone Addie's, responsible for creating and sustaining narrative movement, especially in light of a finale that appears to upend the very meaning of everything that precedes it: "Meet Mrs Bundren" (261). Have we simply been moving toward Anse's remarriage all along? It seems more likely that, in a narrative made up of fifty-nine monologues and fifteen narrators, the reservoir of fuel is in fact *reservoirs*: at any point in the narrative, the momentum comes from a different person, a different desire.

What's more, Addie can't possibly be a source of the thematic desire that helps turn plot into plotting, not least because placing a (dead) woman at the center of Brooks's androcentric model necessarily generates significant issues.[3] But my goal is not to perform a Brooksian reading of *As I Lay Dying*; rather, I simply find it useful to open this essay through the lens of narrative desire because it forces us to confront the idea that Addie, in all her forms—alive, dead, somewhere in between—and despite apparent evidence to the contrary, is not necessarily the narrative's determining force. So what if, like the desire, the grief in *As I Lay Dying* has multiple sources? So often in the critical conversation, Addie's death is treated as the central, or only, loss. As Irving Howe put it nearly seventy years ago, "the theme is death, death as it shapes life."[4] Or, in Diane Blaine's more recent words, "Addie smears death all over the narrative, making it impossible to discern presence from absence in any cogent way."[5] It seems to me that this apparent smearing also makes it difficult to discern one absence from another—to see losses instead of loss. There can be no doubt that *As I Lay Dying* is a kind of cubistic piecing together of coping mechanisms and the ramifications of Addie's death, but I want to look beyond Addie in the hope of demonstrating that Vardaman's ten interior monologues are haunted by a different absence: Darl's. While Vardaman may be consciously and conspicuously narrating the family's burial journey, his monologues are also a subconscious series of attempts to name and to fill the void that Darl, his now-institutionalized brother, has left behind.

There's an obvious reason why Vardaman's monologues haven't been read in this way before: Darl isn't institutionalized until the very end of the narrative, and most critics, following André Bleikasten, assume that there is little to no distance between the time of narration and the time of the narrated. Faulkner's deliberate choice to open with and (in)consistently use the present tense, Bleikasten explains, should signal our access to an "immediate, moment-by-moment transcription" of reality.[6] And if that's the case, then Vardaman can't possibly experience grief over Darl's departure until his final monologue, the only one of his ten that occurs after Darl has been arrested and sent to the asylum in Jackson. But we know that Faulkner was hardly consistent with his tenses in *As I Lay Dying*: the present, that supposed sign of immediacy, soon gives way to the past, and the two bump up against one another for the majority of the narrative, often sharing space within a single monologue. Stephen Ross, in an attempt to prove that Faulkner's tense shifts were choices rather than hasty mistakes, has suggested that they are meant to mimic the nonlinear experience of time within consciousness: their irregularity, in other words, mirrors the "infinite variability of human awareness," which perhaps cannot be patterned but surely can be represented.[7] To Ross, tense allows psychological distance to manifest as temporal distance. But Ross intentionally limits his study of time in *As I Lay Dying* to fictive experience rather than narrative structure, choosing to address the "psychological implications" of tense shifts rather than how they order events.[8] In the (long) wake of Ross, I find that a return to order is, in fact, in order. The apt question seems to be, how do the characters' internal experiences of time, reflected in these irregular tenses, affect or reveal a narrative structure?[9]

No matter how we look at it, any instance of first-person, past-tense narration in *As I Lay Dying* creates a division between utterance and statement: the "I" becomes an implicit "we," now signifying both character and narrator, each of whom occupies a distinct temporal space. Ross, of course, sees this as a psychological division rather than a structural one, exemplified in monologue thirty-three, in which Tull's past-tense narration of the event at hand—his choice to cross the submerged bridge with Anse, Dewey Dell, and Vardaman—is also an explicit mental detachment, not only from the experience but also from the version of himself who lived that experience: "Like it couldn't be me here [on the other bank]," Tull narrates, "because I'd have had better sense than to done what I just done" (138-39). While I agree that tense implies a specific mental distance, it seems unreasonable to assume that every instance of past-tense narration that isn't a clear, controlled analepsis is also a present-moment division of self, that all narrators feel, like Tull, a kind of out-of-body experience each time they narrate what "is" as what "was." Instead, it is likely that these are two different Tulls, separated by time: the Tull who narrates and the Tull who crosses the bridge. This is simply a reorganization of Ross's model: it is memory that generates the past tense—splits the self into selves—and it is *re*experience, not experience, that generates an *evocative* present tense. It is my understanding, then, that by the time Darl's first monologue commences the narrative, he has already been sent to Jackson, Addie has already been buried, and Anse has already taken a new wife. What we are dealing with, in other words, is a kind of retrospective narration, formally masked by the prominence of the narrative's present tense. Perhaps it is useful to think of time in the narrative as Faulkner thought of time: "There is only the present moment in which I include both the past and the future, and that is eternity."[10] *As I Lay Dying* is this alloy of past, present, and future, at once a fragment of and *all* of eternity. Time, singular, has happened and is happening.

As a bonus, this perspective allows us to rid ourselves of the idea that Darl is somehow clairvoyant, a commonplace belief held by readers and critics alike that imbues the narrative with what I see as an unnecessary paranormal element.[11] Darl's ability to narrate events for which he is (was) absent, such as his mother's death, now suggests a kind of community endeavor: a telling and retelling. These scenes of would-be clairvoyance remain imaginative, but the accuracy of Darl's imagination—he perfectly reproduces, for instance, Addie's dying words: "'You, Cash,' she shouts, her voice harsh, strong, and unimpaired. 'You, Cash!'" (48)—suggests that they are also products of a kind of collective memory: part Darl's, part his family's, the filtering of another's past reality through Darl's narrative poeticism. And Darl's use of the present tense here, if we take Ross's conception of thematic time to be true, suggests that while he may have been physically absent from Addie's side at the moment of her death, he is able to feel and (re)experience her final moments along with those who witness them.[12]

If *As I Lay Dying* is a collection of rememberings (of the past) and reexperiencings (as the present)—if we allow the end to be always-already present in the beginning—the narrative and the narrators are now haunted not only by Addie's death—the loss that we can readily anticipate from page 5—but by so many other, later losses: Cash loses the use of his leg, Jewel loses his horse, Dewey Dell loses her abortion, Darl loses his sanity, and the entire family loses Darl. Of course, most members of the Bundren family don't see Darl's institutionalization as a loss. Anse, for instance, is more than willing to sacrifice his son for the family's financial security: "It was either send [Darl] to Jackson," Cash explains, "or have Gillespie sue us" (232). Cash, though unsure that his own logic—"I dont reckon nothing excuses setting fire to a man's barn and endangering his stock and destroying his property" (233)—gives him the right to call Darl crazy, nonetheless sees the asylum as a good thing for his brother: "Down there it'll be quiet," he tells Darl. "It'll be better for you" (238). And both Jewel and Dewey Dell, wrapped up in an intense hatred for the brother who knows too much about who and what they are—Jewel, a bastard; Dewey Dell, pregnant—are desperate to send Darl away. It is only Vardaman who experiences the loss of Darl *as* a loss, which is to say, as an absence that produces grief and longing.

Grief and longing: perhaps the two defining attributes of Vardaman's monologues no matter how—or in what direction—we choose to read them. His narration begins at the moment of Addie's death, and the resulting trauma manifests in a series of angry (setting loose Peabody's team of horses in an act of misplaced revenge) and desperate (boring holes in Addie's coffin and disfiguring her face) acts. By Vardaman's third monologue—"My mother is a fish" (84)—he is in complete denial. There are many excellent readings of Vardaman's famous declaration, but I am less interested in the specific belief—that his mother is *fish*—and more interested in the fact that, in the act of believing, Vardaman in effect gives himself a new identity: he is now the *son* of a fish.[13] It makes sense, then, that he struggles to reconcile this new version of himself—not motherless, but Addie-less—with his understanding of what family is:

"Jewel's mother is a horse," Darl said.
"Then mine can be a fish, cant it, Darl?" I said.
Jewel is my brother.
"Then mine will have to be a horse, too," I said.
"Why?" Darl said. "If pa is your pa, why does your ma have to be a horse just because Jewel's is?"
"Why does it?" I said. "Why does it, Darl?"
Darl is my brother.
"Then what is your ma, Darl?" I said.
"I haven't got ere one," Darl said. "Because if I had one, it is *was*. And if it is *was*, it cant be *is*. Can it?" (101)

At first, Vardaman tries to work through something like a familial transitive property, but Darl allows him to reconfigure, or perhaps loosen, the demanding logic of blood-ties: "If pa is your pa, why does your ma have to be a horse just because Jewel's is?" In effect, Darl tells Vardaman that it is possible for brothers to have different mothers—for Vardaman's to be a fish, for Jewel's to be a horse, and for his own to be *was*. The attention Darl pays to Vardaman here is performative: he recognizes Vardaman's belief and, in doing so, he validates Vardaman's identity. Far from a cruel joke or a callous dismissal, this is an act of love, one that Darl continually reperforms throughout the narrative.[14] We can infer, for instance, that the anguish Vardaman goes through after Darl "loses" his mother in the river—the coffin is retrieved; the "fish," escaping through the holes Vardaman bore, is not—is later quelled with a simple reassurance: "Darl says that when we come to the water again I might see her" (196; emphasis removed). Over and over again, Darl does for Vardaman what his other family members either cannot or will not do, which is acknowledge, and therefore sustain, the metaphorical (re)birth of his mother: "My mother is not in the box. My mother does not smell like that. My mother is a fish" (196; emphasis removed).

In many ways, Vardaman's narration is the story of his relationship with Darl, almost an unwitting ode to his brother's care in the wake of Addie's death. And because of the double movement of the narrative—it is, in a sense, told both forward and backward—we are able to witness the development of a bond forged in metaphor, *as well as* the result of that development. In other words, the "I" of Vardaman's monologues, split as it is along the character-narrator seam, necessarily harbors within it, even while it is working toward, a new kind of brotherhood: by the story's end—that is, at the moment of the discourse's beginning—Darl and Vardaman have become so woven together that they slip into each other's monologues.

According to Dorrit Cohn, the language of interior monologues, as transcriptions of self-address, "will appear valid only if it is 'in character': if it accords with [the narrator's] time, his place, his social station, level of intelligence, [and] states of mind."[15] Faulkner certainly took liberties in this regard—Darl, for instance, presents as more of a poet than he could possibly be—but for the most part his narrators' styles are, if not properly accordant, at the very least consistent. ("Valid" is perhaps in the eye of the beholder.) At the end of Vardaman's first monologue, however, just as we are getting comfortable with his style—Vardaman's mind works as we might expect a child's to work: more jumbled, less coherent—he develops a voice that is not only already conspicuously un-Vardaman—the sentences are noticeably elegant, the vocabulary unexpectedly sophisticated—but also already conspicuously *Darl*-esque. Broadly speaking, Darl's monologues have two distinct narrative features: first, his language is poetic and complex, and, second, that language is often used to express ontological concerns. Darl repeatedly questions presence and being— what *is* and what is *is-not*. With that in mind, consider this aforementioned out-of-place and out-of-character passage from Vardaman's monologue and a passage from Darl's next monologue side by side, respectively:

It is as though the dark were resolving him out of his integrity, into an unrelated scattering of components—snuffings and stampings; smells of cooling flesh and ammoniac hair; an illusion of a coordinated whole of splotched hide and strong bones within which, detached and secret and familiar, an *is* different from my *is*. I see him dissolve—legs, a rolling eye, a gaudy splotching like cold flames—and float upon the dark in fading solution; all one yet neither; all either yet none. I can see hearing coil toward him, caressing, shaping his hard shape—fetlock, hip, shoulder and head; smell and sound. I am not afraid. (56–57)[16]

Beyond the unlamped wall I can hear the rain shaping the wagon that is ours, the load that is no longer theirs that felled and sawed it nor yet theirs that bought it and which is not ours either, lie on our wagon though it does, since only the wind and the rain shape it only to Jewel and me, that are not asleep. And since sleep is is-not and rain and wind are *was*, it is not. (80)

You can *hear* and *see* the similarities between the passages. They share an intensity, a rhythm, a kind of finesse. They also share a unique preoccupation with what and how it means to be.[17] There are, of course, other moments in the text when Darl seems able to verbally or mentally connect with his siblings, most often with Dewey Dell. In those instances, Darl and Dewey Dell do share the same language—at one point, for example, Darl imagines Dewey Dell's internal pleading with Peabody ("*You could do so much for me if you just would. If you just knew*" [51]), which, apart from the pronouns, mirrors Dewey Dell's own, later narration ("He could do so much for me if he just would" [58])—but that language does not distinctly "belong" to either one of them. The similarity between their words is apparent only by way of those words' repetition. Furthermore, Darl prepares us for this change in language, brings us into his vision of Dewey Dell's mind with him. In the passage from Vardaman's monologue, on the other hand, Darl's words appear without warning; Vardaman does not consciously imagine them so much as subconsciously let them in.

Indeed, this kind of appropriation is more startling because it appears right after Vardaman empties himself *of* himself: "I am not crying now. I am not anything. Dewey Dell comes to the hill and calls me. Vardaman. I am not anything. I am quiet" (56). But which "I" is quiet? Which "I" is "not anything"? After all, Vardaman the character continues to "cry quiet," even speaks: "'Then hit want. Hit hadn't happened then. Hit was a-layin right there on the ground. And now she's gittin ready to cook hit'" (56). Vardaman the narrator, however—the "I" of the end, responsible for the beginning—does go quiet: he is out of language and therefore out of *being* Vardaman. Emptying himself of self, Vardaman rejects presence altogether, and it is in that self-vacuum—a kind of opening up of linguistic and ontological space—that Darl's words slip in. Ross has suggested that *As I Lay Dying*'s narrators, *as narrators*, "[are their] voice[s] and nothing more," and, as a result, "this isn't the voice of Vardaman; this voice *is* Vardaman, all there is of him."[18] Far from mere appropriation, then, this Darl-like passage in Vardaman's monologue is not, in fact, Darl-like, nor is it even just Darl's voice. It *is* Darl, all there is of him. By temporally splitting Vardaman into character and narrator, we can see the extent to which Darl has become not only responsible for sustaining, but also a *part of* Vardaman's after-Addie identity. This is, in Howe's words, "death as it shapes life," but it is also death as it shapes loss, for when Darl goes to Jackson, Vardaman not only suffers the loss of his brother, he also feels the loss of a piece of himself. So while we may be witnessing throughout Vardaman's monologues most apparently the grief born of his mother's death, we are also privy to a grief that lies *underneath* that telling. It might be helpful to think of this in a Lacanian way: that Vardaman's narration, his chain of signifiers, simultaneously creates and rests on a bar of repression, one that necessarily disallows those signifiers from ever reaching their signified, the object of Vardaman's unconscious desire: Darl. Vardaman's narration, in other words, despite what it is saying, is always pushing toward Darl, *insisting* on Darl, even while it does not, or cannot, speak that desire.

This is where Vardaman's italics come in: as I understand them, these graphic intrusions are the *symptoms* of this unconscious desire to bring Darl back. I mentioned earlier that Ross understands the narrative's tense system as a means of conveying psychological distance. In my own remodeling of his interpretation, the present tense marks the moment(s) when remembering becomes reexperiencing: the intrusion of the past on the present. Within this structure of retrospective narration, though, the past (as a temporal site, not a tense) necessarily dominates: the gaze is always-already backward, even while the narrative moves (for the most part) chronologically forward. No verb tense—no shift—seems equipped to perform the reverse of what the present tense performs: to bring the present—the moment of narrating—into the past, allowing it to interrupt. By using italics, however—by visually altering the narrative—Faulkner can communicate a temporal shift that is distinct from the back-and-forth movement of remembering and reexperiencing. As narrator interruptions, then, the italics convey what the present tense structurally cannot: immediacy, or unmediated access to the (nonnarrative) present. And if we are attentive to Vardaman's italics—when they appear, what they say—we can see that, as a narrator, he *is* distinctly preoccupied with Darl.[19] Moreover, the closer his narration gets, chronologically speaking, to Darl's departure, the more prevalent this preoccupation becomes, and the closer Vardaman gets to articulating the loss that haunts him throughout.

It makes sense, then, that the majority of Vardaman's italicized portions of text—eleven of twenty—occurs in his final monologue. The narrative present of this monologue is Vardaman's trip to the pharmacist with Dewey Dell, but the frequency of the italics almost splits the monologue in two as Vardaman's thoughts continually interrupt his narration:

> The moon is not dark too. Not very dark. *Darl he went to Jackson is my brother Darl is my brother* Only it was over that way, shining on the track. (249)

> "You'll have to wait till then, when he brings it back."
> *Darl went to Jackson. Lots of people didn't go to Jackson. Darl is my brother. My brother is going to Jackson.* (250)

> They have all gone home to bed except me and Dewey Dell.
> *Going on the train to Jackson. My brother.* (250)

We witness Vardaman trying to comprehend Darl's absence and, in comprehending it, to accept that absence. There's a distinct *lack* of acceptance here, though, for the italics emerge over and over again; indeed, it seems as though these words are at once the illustration and cause of his struggle. In other words, Vardaman's italics are simultaneously the symptom of his unconscious desire *and* the method by which he is trying to realize that desire: he is attempting to recreate Darl with language, to bring him back—and thereby to make *himself* whole again. But as Addie tells us in her strange, posthumous monologue, "Words are no good; [they] dont ever fit even what they are trying to say at" (171). In the same way that Derrida conceived of language adding itself to presence, supplanting it and therefore deferring it, each time Vardaman names "Darl," the name itself at once contains traces of Vardaman's lost brother and inevitably stands *in* for Darl, creating a space in which Darl is necessarily absent.[20] The fragments of italics littered throughout Vardaman's monologues are a never-ending series of fillings that, in the very act of attempting to fill, never cease to unfill: in the hope of generating presence, Vardaman generates absence. When Vardaman's narration comes to a close, then, he is left not with a resolution, but with a fragment of his brother: "*He had to get on the train to go to Jackson. I have not been on the train, but Darl has been on the train. Darl. Darl is my brother. Darl. Darl*" (252). "*Darl*," italicized and stripped of a concluding period, is the final word of Vardaman's final monologue. This is the perpetual deferral of Darl: "just a shape to fill a lack" (172).

If we think about *As I Lay Dying* itself as structured like a language, then Vardaman's monologue is *his* because it is not anyone else's: difference itself allows each monologue—and each collection of monologues under a single narrator—to exist, to have value, to *mean*. And yet that difference seems to fail here, for Darl's final monologue begins just as Vardaman's ends—a kind of continuation of voice across textual (and geographic) space: "Darl has gone to Jackson. They put him on the train, laughing, down the long car laughing, the heads turning like the heads of owls when he passed" (253). In a poignantly circular fashion, Darl once again slips into the empty space that Vardaman creates for him, this time with Darl's at once ended and endless name. But this is a kind of reverse mirroring of that first slipping-into, for Darl appropriates Vardaman's voice this time, a voice that emerges in and by the sporadic use, which is also a continuation, of the name "Darl"—that heavy-handed third-person narration that distinguishes Darl's final monologue from all his others. The care and love that Darl offered Vardaman, the rebuilding and affirming of his younger brother's identity in the wake of Addie's death, were mutually affecting: by the narrative's chronological end—the point at which character becomes narrator—Vardaman is as much a part of Darl as Darl is a part of Vardaman.

Repeated throughout this monologue is a series of questions asked by some equivocal I: "'What are you laughing at?' I said. . . . 'Is it the pistols you're laughing at?' I said. 'Why do you laugh?' I said. 'Is it because you hate the sound of laughing?' . . . 'Is that why you are laughing, Darl?'" (253-54). This "I," which remains without an antecedent, seems to consist of both Vardaman *and* Darl, a linguistic moment in which, to use Darl's language, "are" has become "is": a fleeting moment of unity. But the answer we get to these questions is "Yes yes yes yes yes yes yes yes" (254), a series of repeated affirmatives, quoted as though dialogue but without any speaker at all, as if both brothers have now retreated, leaving only words, but no voice, in their wake. If the "I" is a moment of unity, now behind, then this speakerless series of "yeses" is the disintegration of that unity: a self split into now-distant, now-gone selves. It is telling, then, that this "yes" series ends Darl's monologue and thus ends both his and Vardaman's presences in the narrative; while they are bound up with one another, connected by the story they tell and the identities they've built, Darl is nonetheless now alone, far from Vardaman, "in a cage in Jackson" (254). This is, of course, the very separation that led to the grief and longing present throughout Vardaman's narration: the brothers do not, nor can they, coexist outside the narrative.

I want to end, though, on a more hopeful note, with the empty space that exists *between* their two final monologues. This space is, perhaps, the moment Addie once longed for, what she called "the right time" when "you wouldn't need a word" (172). The union of the brothers, though born of language, is here a kind of temporal space: the moment just before their words come together. Darl and Vardaman harness a sense of fragmentation, using one another to partially fill the inevitable spaces that language generates—a duet of alternating voices. Perhaps, then, their relationship can teach us something about how we cope with loss, with absence: it is not so much about filling the void as it is about sharing it and, in the process, bridging it. Indeed, if we think about Addie's death in these terms, her absence is the end of one idea of family and the beginning of another: by validating and sustaining Vardaman's new sense of the world, Darl generates not only a new identity for his younger brother, but also a new *kind* of brotherhood, one in which the sharing of blood means less than the sharing of language.

NOTES

1. Peter Brooks, *Reading for the Plot: Design and Intention in Narrative* (New York: Vintage Books, 1985), xiii. Hereafter cited parenthetically.

2. William Faulkner, *As I Lay Dying*, rev. ed. (1930; repr., New York: Vintage International, 1990), 19. Hereafter cited parenthetically.

3. According to Brooks, this kind of narrative desire is usually found in the *male* plot of ambition. Furthermore, due mostly to his dependence on Freud, the language Brooks uses to describe narrative movement—"the arousal that creates the narratable as a condition of tumescence," "forepleasure" of delay, the danger of "premature discharge"—is grounded in male heterosexual satisfaction (*Reading for the Plot*, 103, 109). The linear, teleological movement of narrative he points to is necessarily associated with masculinity, is generated by and expresses male desire, which is reflected at once in the narrative's male hero and in the male (or cross-dressing) reader.

4. Irving Howe, *William Faulkner: A Critical Study* (Chicago: University of Chicago Press, 1951), 176.

5. Diane Blaine, "The Abjection of Addie and Other Myths of the Maternal," in *William Faulkner: Six Decades of Criticism*, ed. Linda Wagner-Martin (East Lansing: Michigan State University Press, 2002), 86. Blaine draws attention to the fact that much of the criticism on *As I Lay Dying* forgoes an analysis of Addie's death in favor of considering the "heroism, humor, and aesthetics" of the narrative, and her own essay is a deliberately feminist attempt to return the critical gaze to Addie and her dying, and then decaying, body. In effect, Blaine wants us to focus on the "I" of the title rather than the "as"; my goal here, though, is to look *beyond* the title.

6. André Bleikasten, *Faulkner's* As I Lay Dying, trans. Roger Little (Bloomington: Indiana University Press, 1973), 52.

7. Stephen M. Ross, "Shapes of Time and Consciousness in *As I Lay Dying*," *Texas Studies in Language and Literature* 16, no. 4 (1975): 726.

8. Ross, "Shapes of Time and Consciousness," 725.

9. Joshua Kavaloski has pointed out the same tendency in Faulkner scholarship to focus on psychological time rather than formal time, and in response he puts forward his own

compelling theory of the narrative's temporal structure: to Kavaloski, *As I Lay Dying* refuses linearity, or "unidirectionality," in favor of a more complex, chiasmic structure. See Joshua Kavaloski, "Chiasms in William Faulkner's *As I Lay Dying*," in *High Modernism: Aestheticism and Performativity in Literature of the 1920s* (Rochester, NY: Camden House, 2014), 167–84.

10. James B. Meriwether and Michael Millgate, *Lion in the Garden: Interviews with William Faulkner, 1926–1962* (New York: Random House, 1968), 70.

11. Both Kavaloski and Charles Pallisner reject Darl's clairvoyance as well, though for different reasons. Kavaloski sees Darl's ability as evidence for *As I Lay Dying*'s nonlinear structure, while Palliser claims it is simply "the result of guesswork based on his knowledge of the past." See Kavaloski, "Chiasms," 178, and Charles Pallisner, "Fate and Madness: The Determinist Vision of Darl Bundren," *American Literature* 49, no. 4 (1978): 623. Neither of these readings, however, successfully accounts for other moments of problematic knowledge: Cora, for example, is capable of chastising Anse for "carting [Addie] forty miles away to bury her" when "she was not [yet] cold in the coffin" (22), despite the fact that Addie, in the narrative present, is not dead. And Cash calls the home from which Anse borrows the shovels to bury Addie "Mrs Bundren's" (235) but does so twenty-five pages before Anse returns to marry the woman inside. However we choose to read Darl, we should be willing and able to read Cora and Cash in the same way.

12. Ross also reads this as Darl's mental presence at Addie's deathbed but sees it as the result of his "clairvoyant imagination" ("Shapes of Time," 734).

13. See, for instance, Mark Boren, "The Southern Super Collider: William Faulkner Smashes Language into Reality in *As I Lay Dying*," *Southern Quarterly* 40, no. 4 (2002): 21–38; Doreen Fowler, *Faulkner: The Return of the Repressed* (Charlottesville: University of Virginia Press, 1997), 54–55; and Christopher White, "The Modern Magnetic Animal: *As I Lay Dying* and the Uncanny Zoology of Modernism," *Journal of Modern Literature* 31, no. 3 (2008): 95–111.

14. Judith Lockyer and Laurel Bollinger both read Vardaman in this conversation as Darl's victim. Lockyer calls him "the unwitting straight man in Darl's linguistic joke," while Bollinger claims that this is Darl's direct "refusal to offer the comfort Vardaman so badly needs." See Judith Lockyer, *Ordered by Words: Language and Narration in the Novels of William Faulkner* (Carbondale: Southern Illinois University Press, 1991), 77; and Laurel Bollinger, "'*Are* is too many for one woman to foal': Embodied Cognition in *As I Lay Dying*," *Texas Studies in Literature and Language* 57, no. 4 (2015): 433.

15. Dorrit Cohn, *Transparent Minds: Narrative Modes for Presenting Consciousness* (Princeton, NJ: Princeton University Press, 1978), 89. Worth noting is that Cohn finds it troublesome to attach the moniker "interior monologue" to all of *As I Lay Dying*'s monologues, especially Addie's (which she calls an autobiographical monologue) and Darl's (182, 205–6).

16. Kavaloski also draws attention to this passage of Vardaman's, but he attributes its out-of-character language to "a narrative agency that operates on a level above that of the characters" ("Chiasms" 174).

17. These ontological preoccupations are noticeably different from the concerns with being Vardaman expresses in his social interactions with others. The conversation between Vardaman and Darl that I cited earlier—when Vardaman tries to understand how he, Jewel, and Darl can have different mothers—continues as follows:

"Then I am not," Darl said. "Am I?"

"No," I said.

I am. Darl is my brother.

"But you *are*, Darl," I said.

"I know it," Darl said "That's why I am not *is*. *Are* is too many for one woman to foal." (101)

"*Are*" here divides the brothers: Vardaman pays attention to the reality "are" calls into existence—"you *are*, Darl," i.e., you exist, you're here—while Darl plays with what "are" itself—that is, stripped of a subject—signifies. This is the difference, in other words, between what it means to be and what "to be" means.

18. Stephen M. Ross, "'Voice' in Narrative Texts: The Example of *As I Lay Dying*," *PMLA* 94, no. 2 (1979): 303.

19. There are twenty sets of italics dispersed throughout Vardaman's ten monologues: one set in the fifth monologue, four in the sixth, two in the eighth, two in the ninth, and eleven in the tenth. The content of the eight sets that aren't analyzed in this essay can be traced, without much effort, back to Darl: in his fifth monologue, Vardaman uses the italics when Darl comes out of the river without his mother (the fish); in his sixth, he uses them when grappling with Darl's metaphor, "Jewel's mother is horse"; and in his eighth and ninth, he uses them for his account of seeing Darl set fire to Gillespie's barn and Dewey Dell's subsequent warning not to tell anyone. The preoccupation is apparent. Its intensity is matched only by Darl's clear obsession with Jewel, though the latter doesn't manifest exclusively in Darl's use of italics, which often, but do not always, feature Jewel. Still, these preoccupations suggest a shared governing force: a deep tie between brotherhood and a sense of identity. As Elizabeth Hayes has suggested, Jewel's relationship with Addie—coupled with Addie's rejection of Darl—serves as a kind of "central signifier" in Darl's own crisis of being: "if [Darl] can discover the nature" of Jewel's bond with Addie "and its effect upon Jewel's unquestioning sureness, perhaps he will see how he can achieve existential certainty" (Elizabeth Hayes, "Tension between Jewel and Darl," *Southern Literary Journal* 24, no. 2 [1992]: 57).

20. Hortense Spillers has noted that Faulkner "'told' us a great deal about the workings of language and discursive regimes long before the protocols of structuralism and poststructuralism has given us names for them" ("Faulkner Adds Up: Reading *Absalom, Absalom!* and *The Sound and the* Fury," in *Black, White, and in Color* [Chicago: University of Chicago Press, 2003], 339). In a similar vein, I find that reading Addie's monologue demands, at least to a certain extent, the use of certain poststructuralist thinkers. This does not mean, however, that I believe a poststructuralist reading of the text necessary, or even helpful; rather, thinkers like Derrida and Lacan simply offer us a specific language to talk about, and therefore anchor, the ideas Addie espouses. For the alternative—a reading that pushes against Addie's role as "a spokesperson for post-structural narrative futility"—see Kathryn Olsen, "Raveling Out Like a Looping String: *As I Lay Dying* and Regenerative Language," *Journal of Modern Literature* 33, no. 4 (2010): 96 and passim.

Undutiful Daughters

Women, Kinship, and Monument beyond Family in *Absalom, Absalom!*

JULIE BETH NAPOLIN

Daughters have their own agenda....[1]
—HORTENSE SPILLERS

During a recent Faulkner and Yoknapatawpha conference, while on the walking tour of Faulkner's Oxford, we passed by his mother's home, and I learned that Faulkner's brother, Dean, had died in an aviation accident in the plane that Faulkner had given to him, a fraternal gift. Devastated by loss and guilt, Faulkner set to work on *Absalom, Absalom!*, returning to the hearth of his maternal home to compose the novel at his mother's kitchen table. It was profoundly clarifying to learn that Faulkner's greatest novel of slavery is also a book of mourning and lost kin, though I had sensed this fact from the moment I encountered it.

In this, Faulkner's project extends to the ancients. There were two bans on public mourning that defined the Athenian polis in the fifth century, Herodotus becoming the historian of the first.[2] In *Mothers in Mourning*, French classicist Nicole Loraux describes a situation not so distinct from Faulkner's moment and our own. At the beginning of the century, the state banned theatrical depictions that might remind the civic body of its traumatic vanquishing; by the end of the century, the ban had been internalized, enacted within the civic self through the oath *ou mnesikakeso*, or "I shall not recall the misfortunes."[3] Institutional memory obliterates "those chapters of civic history that the city fears time itself is powerless to transform into past events."[4] Faulkner wrote in a moment that would seem to be defined by relentless memorialization, "a material remaking of the Southern landscape" in the image of a memorial myth.[5] *The Sound and the Fury* concludes with the image of a Confederate statue, one with centrifugal, organizing power in Jefferson, and it demands of its denizens a familiar route through civic space. This route—a counterclockwise motion—is violated by a young Black boy, Luster, who forces his wagon in a forward, clockwise direction, as if thrusting himself away from institutional memory toward an indeterminate future. This unsanctioned motion arouses the agonizing cry of Benjy Compson, an autistic white man whose extreme capacity for sensual recollection leaves him without words to name it. The heavy sensuality of the mythic past evacuates from the novel most signs of a horizon.[6] Such a horizon, were it not lost to the novel's characters, would otherwise promise incorporation in the psychical sense, or recognizing loss as loss such that it may be named, laid to rest, and futurity opened.

We learn in the statue's empty gaze over the town of the paradoxical power of monumentality. It coerces not memory but forgetting. Benjy's cry becomes in the novel the sound of civic memory's obliteration. Issued "with scarce interval for breath,"[7] it is a haunting fore-echo of a more recent cry issued against the oath *ou mnesikakeso* that clings to the edifice of social memory today: "I can't breathe."[8] This phrase is a memorial watchword of the totalizing and authoritarian power of the state.

Confederate monuments, the same that are so fiercely contested today, were erected decades after the Civil War, between the 1890s and 1950s: an era of African American advancement violently suppressed by segregationist backlash. Such monuments to the "Lost Cause" were, in the Freudian lexicon, a "screen memory," for they "superimposed" one story over another.[9] As collective markers, they carry a double address and define the two faces of monumentality, from the Greek *mnenosynon* and from the Latin *monēre*: "to remind," "to advise," or "to warn."[10] Where one might look upon a Confederate monument and be reminded of the legitimated power of their civic self (which often goes under the name "heritage"), another might look upon that same monument and see a warning. Of course, these monuments were not in all cases mandated by the state, but today they continue to be protected by it.[11] The hegemonic boundaries of civic life, as an appendage of the state, depend on damming the force of memory and mourning, if not through law, then through monuments and nonlegalistic decrees that set out to punish defiant acts that might embody an alternative or counter-monumentality. Such defiant acts are designed—in a nearly theatrical action—to stimulate public memory where it has otherwise been foreclosed.[12] They take place along the tenuous border of the civic "we," making visible and audible the seams of the inside and outside. In these moments, the state must confront the fact that it is powerless to transmute civic injuries into past events.

Our moment today, as it was for Faulkner, is a crisis in public mourning. To mourn publicly is to protest, to insist that the state not cast its shadow on memory, on the tie that binds "not only the old dead ones but all the living ones."[13]

With *Absalom, Absalom!* Faulkner takes the body of the brother, and through this corpse as medium, he writes an otherwise banned civic history. He tells a familial, domestic story—also a civic story, a story on the borders of private and public life—that spans several generations. A Civil War-era narrative preoccupies the novel's many narrators. A young biracial man born in Haiti, Charles Bon, was long ago rejected by his white father, never to have been granted the paternal name or a natal place in Sutpen's Hundred, the dynastic plantation erected by his father, Thomas Sutpen. Upon returning to Sutpen's Hundred after the war, where Bon intends to wed his own half sister, Judith Sutpen, a defiant attempt to seize his birthright through incest, Bon is murdered by his half brother, Henry Sutpen, at the threshold. Bon is one of many lives that have been excommunicated, and his demand is nothing short of a demand for repatriation, the borders of Sutpen's Hundred being national in their significance.[14] Later, we learn that Sutpen erected the plantation in his own effort to preserve differently the memory of a traumatic childhood event, when he first learned of the limitations of paternal authority. It was a violent ejection from the private order of the family into the public order of civic life, the boy learning of its race and class hierarchies. This trauma, like Bon's, takes on an expatriating proportion, forcing a young Sutpen to flee not only the natal home, but the nation itself, for the West Indies, whose revolutionary history of slave uprising will later return to haunt Sutpen's design.[15] He returns, in a kind of tabula rasa, as someone who has sworn to forget. He builds his own dynasty as if on a "soundless Nothing" (Faulkner, *Absalom*, 4). When Bon, the rejected son, returns to the threshold of the home and is murdered by Henry, the legitimate son acts in the father's name. Henry acts, to some extent, not simply as son but as citizen, and though his act has been sanctioned by the father, he disappears to escape the law. But the father is not coterminous with the sovereign, and the novel continually restages their split, the differential space that opens between the familial—as "blood kinship"—and the civic (181).

In the moment of traumatic recognition, a "monument" arises with Sutpen to his "innocence" (192). Sutpen's Hundred is such a monument, a monument to the time before an injury transpired, before the traumatic severing of the self. The trauma is nothing short of the private self being thrust into the public when the boy must confront himself as deracinated and no longer rooted in the family. The monument is erected at the sharp division between public and private. Though his plantation originates as a counter-monument, in a desire to mark a space open to the kind of boy he once was, Sutpen's Hundred does not invite memory, but its opposite: it is an obstruction that prevents the self from seeing the injury that gave rise to it. Lapsing from counter-monument into monument, it curses the self to repeat the injury on another. Bon's corpse that lay beyond a closed door becomes the novel's most charged image prohibited from depiction. It is the image that would expose the Sutpen dynasty to the failure of its founding purpose: to undo the original injury.[16] The novel's visual economy—like Sutpen's monument—is a product of an institutional oath. This economy circulates a *Bilderverbot*, one akin to the Judaic prohibition of the divine image, that the narrative struggles to overcome.

According to Athenian doctrine, it is only in leaving kin and the *oikos*, or the household (from *oikinomia*, or economics and the management of house affairs), that a boy discovers himself as a citizen who obeys the laws of the state. Women are never traumatically severed from the natal home; they are never to become citizens. In *Absalom, Absalom!*, these two orders confront one other, the one masculine—defined by forgetting—and the second feminine—defined by the insistence on remembering. Together they produce a double narrative economy. Rosa Coldfield, a member of a different clan that becomes tied to Sutpen through marriage, is the novel's principal bearer of feminine memory. Yet she herself is afflicted by several repressive dicta that prevent her from knowing, or recognizing and incorporating, the fraternal identity of Bon. She recalls approaching the door concealing the corpse of Bon before being blocked at its threshold. This foreclosure doubles the scene of the traumatic instantiation of Sutpen's adult self when, in the revelation of class consciousness, he was rejected at the door of the plantation by an enslaved man while bearing a message from his father to the planter. It is as if the door, a screen in its own right, conceals some knowledge or memory that would destroy the fabric of her identity. Such a memory, had it been recognized, would have propelled her toward the political as it is nonsynonymous with the state. We will find that such memory and its political propulsion are instead recognized and embodied by Rosa's spiritual twin, one whom she refuses to recognize as kin: Clytie, Sutpen's enslaved daughter.

If critical consciousness is first inscribed in the insurgent will not to forget, and such a will, like the political itself, is anarchic and changeful, then it can never be reduced to or become continuous with the state power it petitions for redress. State power is essentially conservative in mandating what shall be remembered and forgotten. In this moment of approaching the threshold that conceals Bon's body, Faulkner makes it startlingly clear that "a rejected memory . . . [is] still a memory,"[17] for even if the novel's psychic economy bans the profane image of the lost brother, Faulkner discovers in *Absalom, Absalom!* that such an image is more perfectly conjured through negation. The missing image of lost kin in Faulkner defies the institutionalizing edict and its related linguistic power of renaming.[18] His aesthetic of depiction by negation is a counter-memorializing technique, Faulkner engaging in a seditious act of political memory. He shares in the motive of Lost Cause memorialization in its original, post-Reconstruction purpose (sedition), though the two projects are ultimately antithetical, the second becoming aligned with the post-Reconstruction southern state.

In his literary act, which reanimates not only lost bodies but suppressed desires, Faulkner insists on kinship between the living and the dead to exceed the discourses of blood that organize bodies along the immutable axis of race. The unbreakable tie between the living and the dead summons a political and ethical possibility not easily subsumed by the state, the law, and their coercive oaths. Faulkner's literary monument is a feminine order,[19] defined not by the son but by the daughter and sister whose forbidden sorrow becomes wrath.

Faulkner's Antigone

Sophocles's Electra is a "perfect incarnation of living memory" against a forgetful Orestes.[20] In thinking of a forgetful Jefferson, one is reminded of another daughter of the house of Oedipus: Antigone and her suicidal claim to the mourning of kin. Recall that she has lost both of her brothers, Polynices (a "returned exile") and Eteocles ("this city's champion"), who feud bitterly to ascend to the throne after Oedipus's self-banishment. Sophocles's play begins in medias res, the two brothers already dead and Antigone encountering her sister, Ismene, just before what is to be her defiant act of separation from the decree of the new king, Creon, Antigone's father-in-law to be. Antigone says:

> Yes, indeed; for those two brothers of ours, in burial
> has not Creon honored the one, dishonored the other?
> Eteocles, they say he has used justly
> with lawful rites and hid him in the earth
> to have his honor among the dead men there.
> But the unhappy corpse of Polynices
> he has proclaimed to all the citizens,
> they say, no man may hide
> in a grave nor mourn in funeral,
> but leave unwept, unburied . . .[21]

Among Creon's first declarations is to ban Polynices from proper burial, mandating that his corpse be kept above ground, food for the animals. He makes this decree not as kin but as sovereign. For the Athenians, it was the special purview of women to mourn; it was they who wept, lamented, and conducted burial rites. Across ancient Athenian texts, both poetic and philosophic, we find the conjunction of women and mourning. The "surrender to grief and lamentation [are] among the feminine forms of behavior that are not to be imitated," women's grief also posing a threat to civic order.[22] But such grief could not be fully excised, underscored not only by Athenian tragedy, which represents it over and over again, but by the religious fact that, until feminine rites had taken place, the unburied corpse had not the right to be called dead. Psychically speaking, Creon commands melancholy and failed incorporation amongst citizens, and this burden is to be carried especially by women, or noncitizens. In forbidding Polynices from being mourned, he silences feminine memory so as to speak as sovereign, both dynastic father and king. Precisely where the feminine lament and speech-rite expires, the king's voice emerges in its sovereignty, the two gestures, silencing and voicing, being one. By that same token, precisely where lament becomes audible, we can expect the sovereign to dissolve. (It is as if all dialogue in *Absalom, Absalom!* teeters on this edge.)

The resuscitation of politically suppressed speech, the kind of speech Michel Foucault might call "fearless," is foundational to Faulkner's novel as a work of mourning.[23] In it, the recurring question of burial, of both Bon and Henry, and the numerous invocations of tombstones, are the first indications of its feminine principle of lamentation as civic protest. Antigone insists on burying Polynices. "I shall be a criminal," she says, "but a religious one."[24] Not only does she insist that Ismene shout aloud her sister's crime, but even when Polynices is exhumed by citizens in obedience to Creon's law, Antigone commits her act again. She then commits it a third time, philosopher Judith Butler observes, for, when questioned by Creon, Antigone refuses to deny her act, reclaiming it once again in language. Turning to Antigone's acts and performative speech acts, Butler describes a failure of the history of philosophy to recognize the full meaning of her insurgency for the meaning of kinship. From Hegel to Lacan, Antigone emblematizes woman's prepolitical and presymbolic status, the symbolic being the special purview of the Law of the Father. She chooses blood and family over the state and the Law (the symbolic order of language). The Athenian woman, like the enslaved person, can never fully transcend the household to engage in the bonds of political and ethical action. For Hegel, Antigone's suicidal act—defying the state edict and preferring to join her brother in premature death—sublates a familial bond that must die so that the state and its ethical bond might become possible. Creon's edict is exemplary of the beginnings of the modern state that sheds its dependency on blood ties. From this point forward, the family is enlisted by the state "in the service of its own militarization," the family dissolving into the state.[25]

Hortense Spillers makes plain in her keynote for "Faulkner's Families," "Our Beloved Crisis: The Family," that we are living through nativist times in which the state attempts to coopt the logic of family in its rage to identity, a "tribal effect," "unreason summoning its own."[26] As unreason, this logic must suppress what in the family is not in the service of reproducing the state. Butler reclaims Antigone as a queer figure who not only steals the modes of speech proper to the father but, in insisting on burying her exiled brother, is guided by forms of desire that cannot be normatively framed. In this vision, the family is not the locus through which the citizen comes into existence but a locus of counterinsurgencies that may be returned to over and against the state. In the face of Creon's decree, which she hears and hears well, Antigone turns to and insists on bonds of kinship and love in order to relocate alternative potentials, even though they will end in certain death.

It has never been more important to return to *Absalom, Absalom!* and glean its *politics of family*, long an oxymoron to philosophy but nonetheless foundational to the antebellum plantation whose direct extension was the southern economy as well as the southern state. For the Athenians, there was a spatial separation between *oikos* and *polis*, household matters being economic ones that, conducted in private, could not be brought to bear on the citizen speaking out loud in the sanctioned sphere of the agora. By contrast, in the antebellum South, the domestic and the political were intimately enmeshed.[27] The transgressive intimacies of kinship (incestuous blood ties) are a deconstructive locus in Sophocles, the southern plantation being particularly vulnerable to their insurgencies. The plantation is home, as it were, both to the feminine noncitizen (of the *oikos*) and the Law of the Father (of the *polis*). As we will find, the climactic ending of the novel's saga in conflagration stages their violent coincidence.

Faulkner's Antigone—embodied variously by Rosa, Judith, and, above all, by Clytie, Judith's half sister and daughter to an unnamed enslaved Haitian woman—is a figure who represents what in the family is insurgent and never identical to itself: a feminine principle that refuses institutional edict and insists on memory and mourning. Clytie is both of and other from these women, the Black feminine being "marked," Spillers suggests, by "layers of attenuated meanings" ("Mama's Baby," 65). Like Antigone, Clytie mourns two brothers, one of whom had also been the rightful heir to the plantation and its property, including its captives. Polynices and Eteocles feud over ascendance to the throne, and to the extent that a woman, like an enslaved person, is noncitizen, she exists in equally ambiguous relation to these would-be kings. In Sophocles' vision, however, it is clearer which brother is exiled and treasonous to mourn, and which brother is embraced by the state. In *Absalom, Absalom!*, the special historico-political circumstances of the plantation mandate that these two images collide such that Sutpen's exiled son becomes an uncanny double of the acknowledged son. In Henry's act of murder, the would-be king becomes an exile and convict. Though Judith will also depart from her assigned position, it is Clytie who is the emblem of a politically transformative kinship.

In Faulkner, family and kinship are host not only to prepolitical violence but to static and immutable bonds. Natal bonds do not simply attach one to others but also strangle and coerce. Particularly for white male characters, it takes a suicidal or homicidal act to locate a line of flight. But this line of flight does not lead unidirectionally towards the state, particularly when it involves women. Rather, as for Antigone in relation to her bereaved brother, the line of flight is to be found somewhere *within* the family, in the interstices of family as a structure. If structure involves seemingly immutable "positions" (mother, father, son, and daughter), then the interstices of the family and its positions are particularly visible or operative in the case of the antebellum plantation as both prepolitical household and civic "domain" ("the Domain," Rosa calls the Sutpen estate [290]). It exposes what Spillers, in another context, calls "the not-quite spaces of an American domesticity" ("Mama's Baby," 77). These interstices make the family fundamentally vulnerable to what would seem to be outside of it. In other words, there is a "beyond" of the principle of the family in Faulkner—and the plantation is precisely where we might expect to find it.

Across Yoknapatawpha, a sustained site of this imagining of alternative bonds is not the brother but the undutiful daughter, a phrase I borrow from *King Lear*. If the son becomes both father and citizen, then the transition from daughter to wife and mother is no less mandated, which is immortalized in Benjamin Franklin's adage drawn from *Lear*: "An undutiful daughter will prove an unmanageable wife."[29] This oft-quoted phrase discloses the transcendental logic on which the reproduction of normative family bonds depends. The husband occupies the paternal position so that the first family is not only training for a second family but an essential origin, daughter becoming wife, as if bud to flower. But what of the women like Antigone who, in Faulkner's imaginary, are daughters who never becomes wives and mothers?

To be sure, Faulkner's white female characters frequently move outside of and flee the family for erotic fulfillment and other kinds of "unspeakable" because nonreproductive intimacy.[30] Consider, for example, Rosa's clandestine vocal intimacy with Quentin Compson, a young man half her age; the two figures sit cloistered in her office, where the aging Rosa is continually described as existing both prior to and after sex. Yet she seduces the young man with the erotics of her voice. These lines of flight connect characters beyond the confines of acceptable attachment; they are often secreted within the echoes of names across different families (such as Addie and Caddie, two women who turned outside of the matrix of family to express desire). Severe social punishment often follows on the heels of such expression in Faulkner, who understood the normative demands that women leave their kin in marriage and replace those bonds with children. However, Faulkner made space for erotic attachments for and between his unmarried and nonreproductive women.

This being caught between daughter and wife is in Faulkner so predominant as to be a temporality in its own right, one not easily contained by existing positions shaped by the Oedipal complex.[31] This psychic complex is thought to mandate, structurally, that sons desire to supplant their father. The so-called "Electra-complex" is the reverse in the case of the girl, the desire to supplant the mother, but it was an afterthought in Freud's thinking. Women's sexuality is what he once called, in reference to the eponymous nineteenth-century imperial travelogue, the "dark continent," that is, a theoretical hinterland not to be fully broached by thought.[32] In a question that, routed through Faulkner, has profound bearing on Freud's suppression not only of the feminine but of the Black feminine, Butler asks, "What would happen if psychoanalysis were to have taken Antigone rather than Oedipus as its point of departure?" (*Antigone's Claim*, 57). Antigone is, Butler continues, "caught in a web of relations that produce no coherent position within kinship."

It is through the catastrophe wrought upon Black kinship described by Spillers in her seminal essay, "Mama's Baby, Papa's Maybe: An American Grammar Book," that Clytie becomes Faulkner's Antigone: she demands that we rethink the dilemma of the daughter through the analytic of what Spillers calls the *flesh*, where to be enslaved is not simply to be property and atomized into vulnerable matter, but to be "kinless," ripped apart spiritually and physically from mothers, fathers, children, and siblings (74). Spillers concludes her essay with a dialectical thought about the possibilities of this horror: though the African American female is the one for whom "motherhood as female blood-rite is outraged, is denied, [she is] at the very same time . . . the founding term of a human and social enactment" (80). Without her, the New World would not be. For Spillers, this "enactment" goes by several names in the New World, including "ethnicity" and "the Family," seemingly fixed, timeless, and immobile terms that, in their discursive ossification as *structure*, blind us to their own dynamism and violent reinstantiation (a kind of forgetting). The subject must not be reinvented again and again (as the American mythos would have it) but "'murdered' over and over again by the passions of bloodless and anonymous archaism" (68). Among the most bloodless of these archaisms is the sociological term "white family," with its fiction of gender integrity, and "Negro family," with its fiction of the castrating mother standing in the place of an immoral, absent father. Ripped apart in this way, the African American woman is nonetheless "the insurgent ground" of "a radically different text for female empowerment" (80).

If Antigone, in resisting marriage and procreation, becomes a queer figure, then Clytie experiences what Spillers describes as the violent "ungendered" life of female flesh under slavery ("Mama's Baby," 68). Quentin muses that she is "*a little dried-up woman not much bigger than a monkey and who might have been any age up to ten thousand years, in faded voluminous skirts*" (173).[33] That Clytie is a "she" is itself ambiguous to the phenomenology of perception through which her body is seen. Her femininity is unintelligible to and negated by the narrative. "This was one of the supreme ironies of slavery," Angela Davis writes: "in order to approach its strategic goal—to extract the greatest possible surplus from the labor of the slaves—the black woman had to be released from the chains of the myth of femininity."[34] Yet this "deformed equality ... could unharness an immense potential in the black woman," namely, her "ability to transform things."[35]

Antigone dies as neither mother nor wife, names which the slave woman was barred from inheriting, except in cases of determining the legal status of her children (*partus sequitur ventrem*, from Roman law, where the status of the mother determines that of the child). There is something of the outraged and denied flesh, then, that echoes from the far distance, between Antigone and the captive. This reverberation finds its "final clap-to" in the figure of Clytie (Faulkner, *Absalom*, 127). With her father Oedipus and mother Jocasta already in the grave, Antigone is also no longer daughter, a position that Clytie never occupied, or only ever occupied ambiguously and monstrously, enough to be legally a slave. The first two formations, being mother and wife, involve us in the subjunctive temporality of what Rosa calls "*a might-have-been*" (115)—for, had Antigone obeyed Creon, she could have joined Haemon, Creon's son, in marriage and gone on to reproduce motherhood. With mother and father in the grave, we confront another formation, one that involves us in the temporality of what Rosa calls "*Once there was*" (115). Antigone once had a mother and father, and yet. Among Sophocles's most negating yet potentiating claims—releasing Antigone from normative life, according to Butler—is that it would be better to have never been born, a call to undo the present. There is a third kinship relation irreducible to these: it is under the insignia of the *sibling* that Antigone undertakes her greatest act of defiance.

For Clytie, this act must be understood as the radical clearing out of the plantation-monument, also a forced opening of the many closed doors that began in Sutpen's Virginia childhood. She sets fire to Sutpen's Hundred in a suicidal conflagration—a politically transformative act—that also buries Henry, such that the two perish together in what becomes a marital tomb. To clear out is *"to make a place* for this different social subject," the subject that, in the culmination of her essay, captures Spillers's imagination of the potentials of living in the absence of motherhood ("Mama's Baby," 80; emphasis added). For "if her actions are not politically survivable ones," Butler writes of Antigone, then "her death [is] precisely a limit that requires to be read as that operation of political power that forecloses what forms of kinship will be intelligible, what kinds of lives can be countenanced as living" (*Antigone's Claim*, 28–29). In setting fire—the radical, suicidal clearing out—Clytie announces herself as living and as kin: a Haitian daughter and sister of the revolution.

Family by Other Means

In August of 2019, the most powerful hurricane in the recorded history of the Atlantic Ocean ravaged the Bahamas. In its ecological devastation, Dorian was compounded by a human indifference of the law to kin, which we have found to be in ontological opposition in the nation-state. Many survivors of Hurricane Dorian were deported to Haiti, while others, those without legal documents, experienced fates equally undocumented. They lived and died amongst other "unclaimed bodies," writes Bahamian poet and activist Angelique V. Nixon, not to be officially enumerated; these and other questions "haunt" the months after the storm.[36] Climate crisis is also migration crisis, and Dorian was a "boundary event."[37] Single narratives nonetheless escape the failure of enumeration and, in September 2019, the *Miami Herald* reported on a twelve-year-old Bahamian girl who fled the disaster with her godmother. United States Customs and Border Protection separated the two from each other in a South Florida airport, transferring them to Miami International before sending Kaytora Paul to a "shelter for abused and abandoned children."[38] The two were separated because the godmother was not her biological parent, the girl being counted amongst the "unaccompanied minors" because there was, in the lexicon of US

Customs, "no identifiable familial relationship" between them. Such a phrase underscores the life-and-death stakes of the static, state-imposed meaning of "family," but also its weaponization against Black kin.

Does not a sustaining web of caring relations threaten to escape normative kinship and its Law of the Father? "And this question," Butler writes, "which seems so hard to ask when it comes to kinship, is so quickly suppressed by those who seek to make normative versions of kinship essential to the work of culture, . . . without then ever asking, what happened to the heirs of Oedipus?" (*Antigone's Claim*, 24–25). It is a question that Faulkner poses with an equally profound political weight, confronting subjects whose familial relationships are unnamable and unrecognizable. The question answered by Clytie's final act might be phrased, "what happened to the heirs of Saint-Domingue?" Butler wrote in 1998: "I ask this question, of course, during a time in which the family is . . . idealized in nostalgic ways within various cultural forms. . . , where to become human, for some, requires participation in the family in its normative sense" (22). Migration, exile, refugee status, and "global displacements of various kinds," she continues, are not easily organized by positions. Instead, they involve a "move from one family to another, [a] move from a family to no family" and can also involve those who "live, psychically, at the crossroads of the family, or in multiply layered family situations" that may include one woman, more than one woman, one man or more than one man, no mother or no father, half-siblings. In other words, Butler concludes, "This is a time in which kinship has become fragile, porous, and expansive."

Yet as Faulkner understood of the world-constituting displacement that is the Middle Passage, it has never not been this time. Spillers has shown how, to the extent that Black women under slavery and within its reverberating afterlife do not reproduce "motherhood" in the traditional sense, then the daughter and son, too, occupy equally precarious places in relation to the American grammar of declension: they are "mama's baby, papa's maybe," a formation that cannot be said to be a "position" in the structural sense of the term. Spillers makes it clear that, from the moment the first slave ship set sail, the symbolic in its transcendental stasis has never held. The fictions of subject positions—the overbearing mother, the absent father—as they structure the imaginary of the "white" and "Negro" family in binary opposition "in effect transports us to a common historical ground, the socio-political order of the New World" ("Mama's Baby," 67). This fact is continually translated, transferred, and transported (a different kind of iteration than genealogy and chronology).

This relationship between the critique of psychoanalysis to be found in Butler and Spillers brings me back to Clytie as an undutiful daughter not easily theorized through traditional accounts of family structure. Again, she is Faulkner's Antigone. Judith is, too, "caught in a web of relations that produce no coherent position within kinship. . . . Her situation can be understood, but only with a certain amount of horror" (Butler, *Antigone's Claim*, 57). But the horror, in Clytie's case, is tied to what Spillers names "monstrosity": ungendering and the revelation of her origins in rape and miscegenation.

We learn from Mr. Compson—one of the many fathers who demand control of the narrative in Faulkner's novel—that two Black women accompanied Sutpen's first arrival in town with captive life. Clytie's mama, I wrote in another context, "is a doubled maybe; she could be one of two women," and for all we know, both of these women cared for her, or perhaps they were sold and never could care for her at all.[39] It is a story that the novel does not compass, existing outside of its laws of chronology, genealogy, and cartography, in the interstices of Yoknapatawpha as structure. In thinking of the unnamed and substitutable enslaved woman or women, we confront the unnarratable origins of the Sutpen genealogy and with it, the novel's linguistic and symbolic claim to discourse, its zero degree of narratability.

Clytie's first name and surname are recorded together only once in text, which is after the novel proper ends, in the genealogy that appears in the endpapers of the text, just after the chronology. Genealogy and chronology: these are two hallmarks of patrilineage. If the surname is the locus of family in recording patrilineage, then the first name holds potentials for self-remaking. It is difficult to know by what authority Clytie is given the surname "Sutpen"—has she received the name as daughter or as property? "Under conditions of captivity," Spillers writes, "the offspring of the female does not 'belong' to the Mother, nor is s/he 'related' to the owner, though the latter 'possesses' it" ("Mama's Baby," 74). The two identities, the one a psychic position, the second its limn, are confounded, she being, in any case, Sutpen's Clytie. The surname is genitive: she belongs to Sutpen's Hundred. The slave appellation is, then, a "blank space" without a proper name (76). The surname appears in text attached to Clytie, but never is there the moment of conjoining, an ascription and inscription of the full name in all of its significance. It is linguistic, but it fails to attain to the symbolic. Instead, we learn of her origins metonymically through what Rosa calls the "*Sutpen coffee-colored face*" (Faulkner, *Absalom*, 109). Such moments are akin to depiction through negation, utterance through silence (silence: another name, Spillers argues, for "distortion" ["Mama's Baby," 73]). Such distortion places a burden of remembering on the reader, bringing us back to what I claimed at the beginning of this essay to be Faulkner's aesthetic technique of negative political memory.

Rosa repeats this phrase in chapter five, which exists in the interstices of the story as told paternalistically by the Compson men. Chapter 5, uttered in a lyric, unheard-of voice that approaches song, does not obey the logic of declension. Its events have the floating quality of having happened and not yet having happened; it is both cyclical and aleatory. It is there that we learn of the feminine time that once enveloped Sutpen's Hundred when the men, away at war, leave only Rosa, Judith, and Clytie. Writing of lesbian desire in *Absalom, Absalom!*, Jaime Harker suggests that this space is more properly "Judith's Hundred," defined by her forms of desire, giving, and love (48). In their time living together, these three become what we might call in Faulkner's negative lexicon, not-sisters and not-daughters. What are they if not daughters, what are they if not sisters? Rosa of course is not sister to Judith but her aunt. Yet as Rosa repeats across the novel, she was born too late: age situates Rosa in proximity to Judith, less an aunt than a sibling (and one who, Harker persuasively argues, incestuously desires both to be and to be with Judith, Clytie's intimacy with Judith interrupting that desire). Rosa is already in between positions by virtue of chronology.

They wait for Supten to return. Waiting is an interstitial time. In waiting, contingency bears heavily on them. As they wait, there is a suspension of what had previously appeared to the daughters as necessity in all of its structural inevitability. "*No. We did not need him, not even vicariously . . . . Perhaps it was because we did not believe it could be done,*" Rosa recalls (Faulkner, *Absalom*, 124). They share a time and way of living that is, by structural definition, impossible, and that impossibility lends this space and its actions a political charge. For in that impossibility, Rosa describes a situation of being like the earth itself "*which dreams after no flower's stalk nor bud.*" In essence, it is a time that is not simply uncreative but ungenerative and antigenerative. According to Butler, Antigone in the Greek means "instead of mother," from *gone*, or she who generates (Butler, *Antigone's Claim*, 22).

Recall that Antigone commits suicide in her marital chamber, joining her brother in death. For Butler, this act links her to precarious life, a kind of plea for another way of living beyond normative value, a radical refusal that prefers death. This interstitial time during war is a time that bears no fruit, that does not propel towards a future structured by reproduction. At stake is the very definition of the human as it is tied up with the family. Rosa, Judith, and Clytie live not as "*three women,*" Rosa says, nor as "*two white women and a negress,*" but merely as "*three creatures*" (Faulkner, *Absalom*, 125). The creaturely language of Rosa's chapter is premised on a feminine linguistic order observed by Minrose Gwin in her seminal account of Faulkner. But the feminine in Faulkner is, in its very temporality, subaltern: it extends far beyond the white women Gwin centralizes in her study. In being both aleatory and interruptive, feminist theorist Emanuela Bianchi argues, feminine temporality also subverts the "monumental" time of patriarchy, opening up the stasis of metaphysics itself to contingency and, with it, "the temporal texture of other kinds of lives—women's lives, queer lives, non-Western lives, black lives, subaltern lives, trans lives, disabled lives, or even lives beyond the human or animal—[that] are often suppressed and rendered invisible."[40] Women are often situated outside of history and politics, Bianchi argues, trapped in a double bind where they must "shake off" ties to the cyclical in order to join linear, masculine time. In the process, "a rather different and submerged dimension of temporality . . . has accrued to the side of women and the queer": an "interruptive time" that is neither cyclical nor linear.[41] This temporality is redoubled in Clytie, a subaltern and anticolonial figure whose destructive, antireproductive action, though much delayed, is a continuation of an interruptive (Black) feminine time, neither line nor cycle.

Clytie and Judith are not able to live fully as sisters, and in that suppression of the sibling bond, some other kind of bond surfaces that, while structured by the master-slave relation, cannot be totally subsumed by it. It is thus in the memory of this interstitial time that another memory comes back to Rosa, that of hearing Ellen describe finding Clytie, as a young girl, on the pallet next to Judith's bed or in bed with her. This image, for Harker, is above all an image of erotic, same-sex intimacy. The pallet, across Faulkner's Yoknapatawpha, is an emblem of racial separation and ordering: it recurs again in the novel in relation to Bon's descendant, Valery Bon, who is the son of the disavowed son. Though his full name is often elided by the initial "V." in the text, it will ultimately be monumentalized when, in chapter six, the full name appears on a headstone—and this appearance despite the fact that Valery, too, is the child of a slave mother. This single appearance suggests that Clytie's gender bears heavily on the elision of her full name from the narrative. Valery Bon is taken on by Judith and Clytie as a "son," even though he is, by blood, a nephew, such that Judith and Clytie become, to some extent, queer mothers through their (asymmetrical) deviance as undutiful daughters.

It is thus that, without right, Clytie claims for herself the discourse of the father, to speak in his name, when she says, "*Dont you go up there, Rosa*" (Faulkner, *Absalom*, 111), at the door that bars the image of Bon's corpse. This voice, in Quentin's memory, issues commands in ways that he describes as proper to a white woman, making her biracial articulation also somewhere between the masculine and feminine. Antigone, according to Butler, co-opts and perverts the sovereign voice of Creon when she says, "Yes, I confess: I do not deny it."[42] For Butler, Antigone's claim exists in a grammatical interstices, one that bears the political weight of possessing her deed by "publishing" it. She does not so much affirm as refuse to deny (*Antigone's Claim*, 8). If the imperative grammar of Clytie's command is sovereign, its effect is ultimately decolonizing: to bring her and Rosa into the same social space, into an otherwise foreclosed intimacy by which, Rosa remembers, flesh touches with flesh. She takes possession of the outlines of Rosa's physical being and its external manifestation in voice. They speak and move as one vexed being.

In this intimacy, one that could only be wrought by the antebellum plantation where *oikos* and *polis* mingle, there are first names rather than surnames, the names of the Father. Women's psychology to some extent is passed on through the mother, and Rosa and Clytie are both motherless figures, Rosa's mother lost to childbirth and Clytie's mother more profoundly lost to the formations of slavery. Rosa's desire remains unexpressed, but it is at least given a name: "*all polymath love's androgynous advocate*" (117). We never experience Clytie's desire; she loses and perhaps never achieves sexual differentiation in ways that are structured not by the Oedipal complex but by slavery. She is, as Spillers might suggest, ungendered, but the violent dedifferentiation of the Black woman is, at the same time, "an amazing stroke of pansexual potential" ("Mama's Baby," 77).

In chapter five, Faulkner presents the image of Clytie as a young girl, desirous and pubescent, intimately entangled with Judith. In the floating phrase uttered by Rosa, "and you too, sister, sister?" (a phrase on which the unutterable circulation of same-sex desire turns for Harker), the referent is unclear in part because the structure that secures the positionality of the sister has become undone. In chapter five, we come to understand that Rosa's desire is mediated and that she herself is an intermediary—she is neither mother nor quite aunt because she is also not quite sister, like Antigone, who mourns the "unwept, unburied" kin. She is outside of or between both paternal and maternal transmission; she says what others cannot and will not say. If she is, to some extent, unsexed, it is because she was unparented in an absolute deprivation of care. Rosa's chapter brings us into a realm that is not presocial, but rather the social's desedimenting, its redynamizing. The structure that has mandated certain positions has become weak; it can no longer hold. If only in the moment of speech, new arrangements of kinship bloom in Rosa's language, and not only to the extent that they had been previously suppressed. These include Clytie's kinship with Judith and Henry, but also with Bon and Rosa. Crucially, Rosa is not blood to Bon and Clytie, but she is family by other means. What Rosa's experience and articulation of

Clytie's touch of flesh with flesh demonstrate, in essence, is the transcendental image of the totality of relation. At stake in chapter five, then, is not what separates Rosa and Clytie but what binds them.

Rosa ultimately fails to be propelled into the political and counter-monumentalizing act. Her vocalization reaches its limits in refusing to claim the paternal identity of Charles Bon. Recall that Rosa, at the same time that she pronounces her androgynous advocacy (from *voce*, or voice), struggles to name Charles Bon and remembers instead the gap where his name and voice should be: "*I had not even heard his name.... I had never even heard his voice, had only Ellen's word for it that there was such a person*" (117). Perhaps this word is a slur, or perhaps it is unutterable within the existing structure of family. There is no name for such a person, just as there is no name for such a person as Clytie. Bon's voice will never be inscribed in the novel except through the fantasies of Quentin and Shreve, or those who never heard it. In refusing to recognize and speak Bon's identity, Rosa never crosses the political threshold. It is Clytie who, in protecting the image of his corpse, crosses the threshold to co-occupy with Bon a nameless, unutterable space, the novel's zero degree of narratability. It is she who will recognize and ultimately act on behalf of Bon's refuted name to assert herself as sister.

We never learn what Black kin might have meant for Clytie, and that loss haunts her vexed attachments. But this missing name and image are the locus of the deconstructive potential of the Haitian daughter. We do know that it was Sutpen who named her, according to Mr. Compson, by mistake, confusing Cassandra with Clytemnestra, and thus sealing her fate. It is Clytemnestra who kills both Agamemnon and Cassandra, whom he had taken as his prize from the Trojan war. How are we to receive and interpret Clytie's final act of conflagration? As the state authority approaches Sutpen's Hundred, her act is, by one interpretation, an act of allegiance to the dynastic father and his acknowledged son. In protecting Henry from civic scrutiny, she protects him as the bearer of the family crime. She chooses the domestic over the civic and remains buried (quite literally) in the economy that defines her not as person but as slave. If we look only at the history of philosophy that positions Antigone as emblematic of women's prepolitical status, then Clytie can only be interpreted as failing in this moment to transcend the *oikos*. But this transcendence was never hers to have in the first place, and her action—like that of Antigone—is a deconstructive one. As such, her act of conflagration cannot be read univocally as the reinforcement of the family's boundaries of exclusion, the very boundaries that mandate she is not-daughter and not-sister and that Bon is not-son and not-brother. This act of defiance is perhaps the one act in the Compson saga committed with absolute freedom and without necessity (it exceeds, then, even Quentin's suicide in *The Sound and the Fury*). In being routed errantly through Haiti as a site of revolution and uprising, Clytie is both mama's and papa's baby: her ambiguous act insists on mourning Henry and Bon equally, a burning down the monument that refuses to deny.

Her name links her to the order of action, the etymology of Clytemnestra essentially meaning "famous plotter," from *médomai*, to plan or to be cunning. In its origin, the name links her to Supten himself, his plan, and the "plot" out of which critic Peter Brooks has made so much.[43] If Rosa is without a right to speak in the novel, it is because everything she knows she learned by listening in clandestinely at closed doors. But her plot is limited, intended to expose Henry as the embodiment of Sutpen. As the living embodiment of contradiction, Clytie is more subversive in her potential. Her act is, like Antigone's, an act of public mourning. For, in burying Henry Sutpen, she names him as kin; in destroying Sutpen's Hundred, she names Charles Bon as kin. These acts give the name of kinship that the social denies; they insist that the state not cast its shadow on intimacy and memory.

NOTES

1. Hortense Spillers, "Mama's Baby, Papa's Maybe: An American Grammar Book," *Diacritics* 17, no. 2 (July 1987): 66. Hereafter cited parenthetically.

2. Nicole Loraux, *Mothers in Mourning*, trans. Corinne Pache (Ithaca, NY: Cornell University Press, 1998), 84. Herodotus describes the banning of Phyrnichus's traumatic depictions of Persian conquest in the *Capture of Miletus*, after which "the whole theater broke into tears" (Herodotus, quoted in Loraux, 85). Phyrnichus was fined by the Assembly "for having reminded them of their own misfortunes," and the Assembly declared that the play should never be seen again.

3. Loraux, *Mothers in Mourning*, 86.

4. Loraux, *Mothers in Mourning*, 83.

5. Jaime Harker, "'And you too, sister, sister?': Lesbian Sexuality, *Absalom, Absalom!*, and the Reconstruction of the Southern Family," in *Faulkner's Sexualities: Faulkner and Yoknapatawpha, 2007*, ed. Annette Trefzer and Ann J. Abadie (Jackson: University of Mississippi Press, 2010), 49.

6. In the phenomenological lexicon, a "horizon" is an opening of what is towards an alternative. In an existential vein, philosopher Jean-Paul Sartre comments that in *The Sound and the Fury*, everything has already happened. See Sartre, "On *The Sound and the Fury*: Time in the Work of Faulkner" (1939), in *The Sound and the Fury*, ed. Michael Gorra, 3rd ed. (New York: Norton, 2014), 316–23.

7. William Faulkner, *The Sound and the Fury*, rev. ed. (1929; repr., New York: Vintage International, 1990), 320.

8. These were the last words of Eric Garner, a Black man placed in a murderous chokehold in 2014 by a white NYPD officer, Daniel Pantaleo. Garner uttered this phrase eleven times before succumbing to asphyxiation. They were also among the last words of George Floyd, a Black man asphyxiated in 2020 by Derek Chauvin, a white police officer in

Minneapolis, Minnesota. Both events were recorded on video and circulated widely on the internet. These last words can be seen on t-shirts and facemasks internationally at Black Lives Matter protests against police brutality.

9. Harker, "'And you too,'" 49.

10. In the press release for "American Monument," a sound and video installation that engages recordings of police brutality, the artist lauren woods describes this etymology of "monument." The installation never formally opened in its planned venue for California State University, Long Beach, however, after woods closed it in protest over the museum's firing of a curator. One is left imagining its sound and look. https://www.csulb.edu/university-art-museum/article/american-monument.

11. President Trump vowed on the social media website Twitter to jail those who topple monuments. Consider, too, that the Black woman who climbed the Statue of Liberty to protest the US's immigration ban was arrested and tried. Such defiance is global, or testimony to imperial interconnectedness: in June of 2020, acting in solidarity with protests against police brutality an ocean away, protestors in Bristol toppled the statue of Edward Colston, who acquired his wealth by trading enslaved people, builders of the city. The protestors gave the statue a watery grave, tossing it into the same waters where Colston's ships once docked and replacing it with cardboard mementos to lives lost to police brutality on the other side of the Atlantic.

12. Consider, for example, what it meant for the American football player Colin Kaepernick to "take a knee," kneeling during the national anthem in order to stimulate the memory of gratuitous police violence against Black men, women, and children. Though there was no state law against Kaepernick's act, the governing body of the NFL deputized and disclosed itself as an arm of the state when it decreed that no player was allowed to take a knee during the anthem, the nationalist song that acts as a connective tissue between the American government and American playing fields.

13. William Faulkner, *Absalom, Absalom!*, rev. ed. (1936; repr., New York: Vintage International, 1990), 178. Hereafter cited parenthetically.

14. For example, Barry Hudek points out that the District of Columbia, like Sutpen's estate, is also 100 square miles in area. See Hudek, "Mississippi on the Potomac: Sutpen's Hundred as Washington D.C.," in *Faulkner and Hemingway*, ed. Andrew B. Leiter and Christopher Rieger (Cape Girardeau: Southeast Missouri State University Press, 2018), 179–98.

15. For a discussion of the place of the Saint-Domingue revolution in Faulkner's fiction, see Chris Bongie, *Islands and Exiles: The Creole Identities of Post/Colonial Literature* (Stanford, CA: Stanford University Press, 1998), 189–261.

16. Thank you to Jay Watson whose editorial remarks helped me to work through these thoughts. One could argue that Sutpen fails because he desires to undo the past, rather than to heal it. John Irwin touches on this point when he argues, in a Nietzschean vein, that the novel's psychic economy is motivated by a revenge against the "so it was" of time. See John Irwin, *Doubling and Incest / Repetition and Revenge: A Speculative Reading of Faulkner*, rev. ed. (1975; repr., Baltimore: Johns Hopkins University Press, 1996).

17. Loraux, *Mothers in Mourning*, 84.

18. I do not only mean to invoke contemporary acts of removing Confederate names from public places renamed after progressive figures. I also mean the kind of euphemism that populates colonial memory. For example, Hazel Carby recalls family stories of a "housekeeper" and a planter. "It was as if language itself was being cleansed of history. Just a planter and a housekeeper. No relationship, no language of enslavement, of brutality, of force, of sexual abuse." See Saidiya Hartman, "Errant Daughters: A Conversation between Saidiya Hartman and Hazel Carby," *Paris Review*, January 21, 2020, https://www.theparis

review.org/blog/2020/01/21/errant-daughters-a-conversation-between-saidiya-hartman-and-hazel-carby/. Accessed August 18, 2020.

19. This concept is one extension of claims to be found in the seminal work of Minrose Gwin, who argues that Faulkner's mind is essentially of two sexes. See Minrose Gwin, *The Feminine and Faulkner: Reading beyond (Sexual) Difference* (Knoxville: University of Tennessee Press, 1990). According to Harker ("'And you, too,'" 41), this concept is also to be found in the work of Frann Michel who, Harker describes, argues that Faulkner was writing in a lesbian tradition, identifying not only with women but with queer women.

20. Loraux, *Mothers in Mourning*, 97.

21. Sophocles, "Antigone," in *Oedipus the King, Oedipus at Colonus, Antigone*, 2nd ed., trans. David Grene (Chicago: University of Chicago Press, 1991 [1942]), 162 (lines 25–34).

22. Loraux, *Mothers in Mourning*, 11.

23. Fearless speech, or *parrhesia* in ancient Greek, is akin to "free speech," but it is also connected to the right to speak in the *polis*. The noncitizen role of women, children, slaves, and aliens prevented them from accessing *parrhesia*. See Michel Foucault, *Fearless Speech*, ed. Joseph Pearson (Los Angeles: Semiotext[e], 2001), 12n4. "The *parrhesiastes* [fearless speaker] is always less powerful than the one with whom he speaks. The *parrhesia* comes from 'below,' as it were, and is directed towards 'above'" (18). It is an act of dangerous criticism that puts one at risk. One could argue that among Antigone's transgressions is accessing fearless speech.

24. Sophocles, *Antigone*, 164 (line 85).

25. Judith Butler, *Antigone's Claim: Kinship Beyond Life and Death* (New York: Columbia University Press, 2000), 36. Hereafter cited parenthetically. Consider, for example, the way that Mississippi Governor Tate Reeves mobilized the word "family" when his spokesperson said that the state flag should only be changed through conversation with "our Mississippi family." See https://twitter.com/GeraldHarrisTV/status/1275494665257660416. Accessed June 24, 2020.

26. Hortense J. Spillers, "The Family, Our Beloved Crisis: Faulkner's Version" (lecture, University of Mississippi, Oxford, MS, July 21, 2019).

27. See Elizabeth Fox-Genovese, *Within the Plantation Household: Black and White Women of the Old South* (Chapel Hill: University of North Carolina Press, 1988).

28. Loraux, *Mothers in Mourning*, 11.

29. Lois Kerschen, *American Proverbs about Women: A Reference Guide* (Westport, CT: Greenwood Press, 1998), 58.

30. Such intimacy has been explored by John N. Duvall in *Faulkner's Marginal Couple: Invisible, Outlaw, and Unspeakable Communities* (Austin: University of Texas Press, 1990). Also see Harker, "'And you, too,'" which argues for the pronounced centrality of lesbian desire in Jefferson.

31. For a discussion of "queer temporality" in Faulkner, see John T. Matthews, "Faulkner's Untimely Fiction," in *The Cambridge History of the Literature of the US South*, ed. Harilaos Stecopoulos (New York: Cambridge University Press, forthcoming). Thank you to Matthews for sharing this essay with me.

32. Sigmund Freud, *The Question of Lay Analysis*, trans. James Strachey (New York: Norton, 1990), 38.

33. Harker writes of this passage, "Clytie is beyond any known categories—no age, no discernable gender," she occupying what is, for Harker, a "queer space" ("'And you, too,'" 46). Drawing from the Black feminist framework of Spillers and Angela Davis, however, we might say that the queering of Clytie does not derive from the same locus as that of the novel's other female characters. She has been ungendered by slavery, and the homophobia though which Rosa perceives her is fundamentally racialized.

34. Angela Davis, "The Black Woman's Role in the Community of Slaves," *Black Scholar*, December 1971, 5. https://www.freedomarchives.org/Documents/Finder/DOC46 _scans/46.RoleBlackWomenSlavery.pdf. Accessed July 12, 2020.

35. Davis, "The Black Woman's Role," 6.

36. Angelique V. Nixon, January 6, 2020. https://twitter.com/sistellablack/status/12143201 30701877250. Here, Nixon is quoting her blog, "Missing, Deported, Uncounted: Who Matters after Dorian?" *In the Diaspora*, January 6, 2020, http://web.archive.org/web/20200209141654 /https://www.stabroeknews.com/2020/01/06/features/in-the-diaspora/missing-deported-or -uncounted-who-matters-after-dorian/. Accessed July 12, 2020.

37. I borrow this phrase from Trinh T. Minh-ha, *Elsewhere, Within Here: Immigration, Refugeeism and the Boundary Event* (New York: Routledge, 2011).

38. Monique O. Madean, "12-Year-Old Bahamian Girl Separated from Parents, Ends up in Miami Home for Migrant Kids," *Miami Herald*, September 10, 2019. https://www.miami herald.com/news/local/immigration/article234933792.html. Accessed August 18, 2020.

39. Julie Beth Napolin, "The Expropriated Voice: Sonority, Intertextuality, Flesh," in Jay Watson and James G. Thomas, Jr., eds., *Faulkner and Slavery: Faulkner and Yoknapatawpha, 2018* (Jackson: University of Mississippi Press, forthcoming 2021).

40. Emanuela Bianchi, "The Interruptive Feminine: Aleatory Time and Feminist Politics," in *Undutiful Daughters: New Directions in Feminist Thought and Practice*, ed. Henriette Gunkel, Chrysanthi Nigianni, and Fanny Söderbäck (New York: Palgrave, 2012), 35.

41. Bianchi, "The Interruptive Feminine," 36.

42. This translation is Butler's. Antigone's claim is made in response to Creon when he pressures her to confess (she says in Greek, *kai phemi drasai kouk aparnoumai to ne*). See Butler, *Antigone's Claim*, 8.

43. Peter Brooks, *Reading for the Plot: Design and Intention in Narrative* (New York: Alfred A. Knopf, 1984), 286–312.

White Noise/Black Codes

Inscription and Representation in *The Unvanquished*

JEFF ALLRED

It goes without saying that Faulkner's world features families bound together and sundered by *talk*, by modes of storytelling that are collective, embodied, and evanescent. This chapter explores the less-examined relationship between family and writing in Yoknapatawpha. Faulkner himself pointed to the salience of writing in southern culture, if deprecatingly, in a discussion with Virginia undergraduates in the 1950s: when asked the inevitable question about the South's cultural lag, Faulkner quipped, "Everyone in the South has no time for reading because they are all too busy writing."[1] In a more earnest register, I want to ask what writing means in Faulkner's world: how do Faulkner's families store their stories in durable form? Who has access to the "means of production" of writing in Faulkner's world, and how does his work thematize issues of gender, race, class, and sexuality through scenes of writing, drawing, and other forms of inscription? How are the media of these communicative acts, from letterhead and steel pens to repurposed wallpaper and pokeberry juice to telegraphs and chalkboards, related to their messages?

I will examine these issues via his understudied work *The Unvanquished*. This story cycle has been something of an ugly duckling in Faulkner studies, criticized for its formal simplicity and especially for its resonances with the nostalgia for the Old South that was so pronounced in Depression-era culture, most notably in the blockbuster novel and film *Gone with the Wind* (1936 and 1939, respectively). As several critics have noted in recent years, however, *The Unvanquished* seethes with tensions that exceed the boundaries of the moonlight-and-magnolias metanarrative, tensions that sabotage the expected cultural work of reuniting the national "family" by revising white supremacy and patriarchy to rise again in an ostensibly kinder, gentler form.[2] Like these revisionist readers, I will emphasize the importance of marginalized figures like Drusilla, Rosa, and Ringo, figures whose presence unsettles the seemingly comic closure of Bayard Sartoris's rebooting of patriarchy and white supremacy for the postbellum era. Prior work, however, has neglected the role of writing as a technology that helps marginal subjects imagine and, to some extent, enact alternatives to the social dominant embodied by the Sartoris patriarchs, old and new. In what follows, I argue that both the insurgents who want to liberate themselves from patriarchy and/or enslavement and the reactionaries who want to restore the status quo ante recognize the centrality of these nineteenth-century media to the struggle.

At the center of this battle over the meaning of "family" lie scenes of writing undertaken chiefly by subjects on the periphery of the Civil War-era South—enslaved people, white women and children, and the elderly—using stolen or improvised materials. I focus on the darkly funny gambit devised by the unlikely writing team of Rosa "Granny" Millard, elderly white matriarch of the Sartoris family, and Ringo, a young boy enslaved by the Sartorises, in which the duo hacks the communications systems of the Union Army in order to claw back some of the capital extracted from north Mississippi by the conquering troops. Beneath the superficial comedy of manners lies a focus on the material means by which messages are produced, disseminated, and consumed. We are accustomed to think of marginalized subjects as "silenced" or "invisible," metaphors that valorize, in turn, the recovery of "silenced" voices or the devising of new "lenses" capable of bringing heretofore invisible figures into clear view. *The Unvanquished* estranges these well-worn critical habits in several ways. First, it displaces the scene in which marginal subjects demand recognition. Rather than resorting to the Romantic-era trope of the voice as self-presence, one that demands recognition via self-celebration or aggressive assertion, or the related notion that one's corporeal self forces a recalibration of dominant ways of seeing, *The Unvanquished* features characters who assert themselves through the indeterminate and anonymous spaces of media networks. Second, in so doing, the text emphasizes the activity and agency available to users of modern media. In emphasizing subjects' capacity to write, and thus to be read, *The Unvanquished* foregrounds the capacity of subjects to fashion themselves. This dynamic differs fundamentally from that governing the dialectic of recognition that presumes vocal/visual interfaces and often situates marginal subjects in a frustratingly passive role, from Echo and Narcissus to Du Bois and his contemporaries who famously found him a "problem."[3] Third, *The Unvanquished* stages the politics of recognition, not as an ethical encounter between faces, but as a more complex sociopolitical battle over infrastructure. As we shall see, the battle over who gets full representation is waged, not between subjects speaking face-to-face in an idealized public sphere or hermetic domestic space, but over who controls the mechanisms through which individual and collective wills are alienated, abstracted, and reconfigured in modern, corporate forms of communication. These networks that enable communication are not neutral entities, but sites of struggle that can be used, adapted, hacked, and destroyed to both hegemonic and counterhegemonic ends. This struggle over access to inscription unfolds simultaneously at the minute scale of the individual family all the way up to the national scale of the "house divided" of Lincoln's discourse.[4]

My argument will be framed within two major contexts, one theoretical and one historiographic. The first derives from the work of German media theorist Friedrich Kittler, who elaborates a long history of "discourse networks" or "inscription systems" from 1800 to the present.[5] For Kittler, the central object of cultural analysis is not the text but the historically variable "network of technologies and institutions that allow a given culture to select, store, and process relevant data."[6] Much of Kittler's work consists of dense, synchronic analyses of the state of "discourse networks" at distinct moments conveniently (if somewhat reductively) located at the turn of a century. Thus "Discourse Network 1800" is organized around the trope of the "voice" immanent in printed forms like lyric poetry and the institutions and practices, from manuals teaching mothers how to teach children to read to new hermeneutic practices in higher education, that enabled print to bring this voice to life. "Discourse Network 1900" represents a near-total reorientation occasioned by the rise of what we now call analog media (e.g., the phonograph and cinema): these media pull apart the strands of voice, image, and word that are braided tightly in the lyric poem and reintegrate them in new, multimodal forms that break, Kittler argues, the "monopoly" print enjoyed for five hundred years and usher in an era dominated by analog media.[7] As we shall see, Faulkner's text explores a midpoint between these moments, a "Discourse Network 1850," if you will, characterized by an unstable mixture of "optical media" elements and the notion of the text as a container for a "voice" that arrives, intact, in the hands of readers of print.

The terms of this complex in-betweenness become clearer through a look at historiographic accounts of the rise of so-called "systematic management" and "business communications" in the nineteenth-century United States. As is often the case, Faulkner proves a canny social historian in *The Unvanquished*. He recognizes that the sophisticated regime of interoffice memos, graph-heavy corporate reports, and intricate filing systems that became dominant by the turn of the twentieth century have their origin in the communicative circuit that Rosa and Ringo exploit: the "orders" typical of military communications in the Civil War era. Beneath the surface-level comedy lampooning bureaucrats and their unlovely literary outputs lies a more serious point: that the very anonymity and abstraction of this emergent inscription system proves hospitable to marginalized subjects in ways that present a striking contrast to the oral modes of expression that convey the collective self-presence of the southern patriarchy. As many critics have noted, the plot arc of *The Unvanquished* forecloses a Whiggish reading of transracial sympathy or family feeling: by the end of the text, the South has largely "redeemed" itself under the aegis of a revised patriarchy.[8] My reading concedes this foreclosure but emphasizes, on the one hand, the unsettling presence of marginalized figures like Ringo and Loosh, who seem ill-disposed to remain "in their place" in the new dispensation and, on the other, the way the "redemption" of the South, even in its success, points to the strategic value of inscription systems that might be exploited by marginalized users in future struggles.

Before turning to the subplot of Rosa and Ringo's grift, we should note that *The Unvanquished* opens with an arresting focus on inscription. The first story, "Ambuscade," opens in 1863 with two boys, Bayard Sartoris, the scion of the Sartoris line, and Ringo, his enslaved sidekick, scrawling a detailed map of the ongoing siege of Vicksburg in the dirt. They then use this improvised text to anchor imaginative play, swapping between them the roles of the Confederate and Union generals. Their play, and their painstakingly etched map, are disrupted by Ringo's uncle Loosh, who truculently sweeps the slate clean and sets the boys straight: "There's your Vicksburg," he declares, following up with the insistence that both Vicksburg and Corinth have already been conquered in reality.[9] This revelation, catastrophic or liberating depending on perspective, leads to a twin realization on Bayard's part. First, he speculates that the enslaved Loosh knows things that he and perhaps his father don't. After anxiously asking Ringo, "Do you reckon Loosh knows anything that Father dont know?" he answers his own question in free indirect discourse, acknowledging to himself that "n[-----]s know, they know things" (6). Second, this vertiginous fact of African American knowledge that is unshackled from masters' control deracinates Bayard, rendering Ringo and himself as equals:

> Maybe he wasn't a n[-----] anymore or maybe I wasn't a white boy anymore, the two of us neither, not even people any longer: the two supreme undefeated like two moths, two feathers riding above a hurricane. (7)

The slippage between moths and feathers is striking: are the boys in passive flight, drawn unconsciously to the light that will abolish them, or are they figures of flight and inscription (via the implication of the quill pen), hovering above the disaster in ways that make them capable of not just surviving it but of comprehending it and fixing it in narrative form?

Like an overture, this scene compactly states a range of major themes that unfold throughout the text. First, we see an emphasis on the pleasure of writing and the importance of access to writing materials and spaces in order to forge a cognitive map of a rapidly shifting society under unimaginable strain. Second, we see how writing is not created from whole cloth but extends a fabric of prior knowledge. Here, Loosh's violent reaction expresses both his own desire to be an author (if negatively, like an erasure poet) and, also, his position in a network of enslaved subjects who constitute an unauthorized intelligence agency, a proto-WikiLeaks in a media-starved wartime landscape. Finally, noise emerges here as a last resort for white supremacy under siege. Struggling to understand how Loosh can know things he and his father can't, young Bayard notes that his response to Loosh "would have to be something louder ... than words to do any good" (6), so he grabs handfuls of the dust that has been his expressive medium for his and Ringo's maps and flings it in the air, accompanied by the "rebel yell," rendered as a repeated "Yaaay! Yaay!" (7). This strategy of responding to Black knowledge, not with counterargument but with noise, with a strategic overloading of the circuitry that makes messages possible, recurs in the text as central to the reestablishment of white supremacy in the war's aftermath.

These themes return in the subsequent stories, "Raid" and "Riposte in Tertio," in a subplot in which Sartoris matriarch Rosa Millard, outraged by the seizure of Sartoris property by Union troops, follows the Union Army into Alabama and petitions an officer for restitution. On its face, the episode unfolds as a comedy of manners, in which stereotypical Yankee officiousness and bureaucracy collide with the more locally colored and improvisatory mode of the South. The comedy hinges on the infelicities that plague Rosa's oral petition as it is translated into the form of the written military "order" that enacts restitution. Rosa asks one Colonel Dick for "the chest of silver tied with hemp rope.... Two darkies, Loosh and Philadelphy. The mules, Old Hundred and Tinney" (109), yet the orderly tasked with jotting the utterance and writing up the order mishears Rosa's drawl and renders it thus:

> Ten (10) chests tied with hemp rope and containing silver. One hundred ten (110) mules captured loose near Philadelphia in Mississippi. One hundred ten (110) negroes of both sexes ... [and] necessary food and forage. (112)

Meanwhile, the Colonel leaves in search of the General's blessing, while the Lieutenant and Sergeant parse the order: like the old screwing-in-a-lightbulb jokes, it takes an entire chain of command to garble a simple request so fully.

The joke would seem to flatter white southerners, whose orality eludes the routinization of modern communication in ways that reveal the vulnerability of military intelligence to what Donald Rumsfeld once called "unknown unknowns," a vulnerability that works in the favor of the local yokels.[10] But the rest of the subplot works against the grain of this interpretation, as the southerners move from radical exteriority from the inscription system to radical interiority, entering the circuit that produces and disseminates "orders" and manipulating it masterfully. The initial stage in this movement takes place on the way home from the Union encampment. After Rosa piously attributes the unasked-for bounty of mules and enslaved people to "the hand of God" (112), the group encounters a troop of Union cavalry on the way home. The officer confronts them, seizes the order, and "began to swear" (113), asking them, "How many do you lack?" Ringo blurts out, "We like fifty," a request the officer obliges to the letter of the order, leading Ringo to retort, once they are out of earshot, "Hah. . . . Whose hand was that?" (114). The slippage between the hand of God and a hand more Satanic, and between "like" and "lack" (the southern "like" being a near-homophone for the Northern "lack"), point to a feature of the inscription system that Ringo and Rosa quickly learn to exploit. The system is designed to translate evanescent utterances from the chain of command into fixed forms that are portable, authenticated, and auditable. That is, the hand of the General (if not quite God) is enabled through the unseen agency of an extensive division of labor, from the workers who produce the letterhead to the orderlies who transcribe the orders to the couriers who carry messages up and down the chain of command. This ubiquity and performative force, however, in its very pretension to omniscience and impersonality, lacks awareness of "unknown unknowns," especially those embedded in the *différance* of language.[11] Thus what Ringo likes—not just livestock but the ability to speak with performative force—fills what he lacks, and this intoxicating experience becomes a template for further experimentation.

Inspired by the unexpected and unsought surplus from the military, Ringo and Rosa stop speaking *at* the media apparatus as petitioners and instead *occupy* it as users: under orders from Rosa, Ringo sneaks behind enemy lines and steals a hundred pages of letterhead, a steel pen, and ink (127). The pair then concoct a plot in which they forge orders for mules and distribute them—plus the cash they generate from selling some back to clueless Union officers—throughout the community, in a mix of grifting and primitive socialism (138–39). In their division of labor, Rosa is the CEO and Ringo is middle management, forging orders, reconnoitering, and doing data entry. It is Ringo's skill, not his position of servitude, that has him occupy the position of writer and forger, a position that threatens to usurp Bayard's role in the family. Bayard anxiously notes that Ringo "was smarter than me" (125) for having taught himself to draw and, thus, to forge, and he notes further that Ringo "had got to treating me like Granny did—like he and Granny were the same age instead of him and me" (126).[12] In sum, the one-trick pony of duping the Yankees (if accidentally) by speaking a nonstandard dialect that jams their inscription system gives way, in the text, to a more sophisticated ruse that reorganizes the slaveholding family as a little corporation, a corporation located in the humble space of the slave quarters and exhibiting liberal policies regarding the age and race of its workers.

In concocting this neo-Robin Hood narrative enabled by complex inscription systems, Faulkner gestures at a real historical emergence, one that social historians call the rise of "systematic management." Above all, systematic management, which emerged in the mid-nineteenth century in the military and in nascent railroad corporations, depends on the recording, circulation, and orderly storage of writing. These systems were stabilized by standardized genres (e.g., memos, orders, and charts), hierarchical orchestrations of far-flung and asynchronous acts of data collection into coherent reports, and the development of new technologies of duplication and filing to render these written documents accessible.[13] The mule scheme underscores, above all, the impersonality of the "inscription system" that systematic management entails: unlike participants in conversations or letter exchanges, inscribers of these messages are invisible to recipients, hidden under the abstraction of the authorizing agent in the hierarchy. Users of the network take it for granted that the "voice" of the order is a representation of an officer's will that is processed through the work of orderlies and deliverers and relies on the visual technology of letterpress for its authority. The performative force of a military order inheres not in the particulars of the message but in the way that message is inscribed on scarce printed letterhead and secured by the supposedly unique trace of the commanding officer's bodily presence in his signature. This combination of emergent (letterhead) and residual (manuscript signature) elements, the latter conveying the "voice" of authority intact to readers and the former its ubiquitous power and near-anonymity, signals the in-betweenness of this midcentury discourse network. In an order, the particulars of the message pale in comparison to what Roman Jakobson calls the "phatic" dimension of language, its embeddedness in communicative networks: every order says, before it commands the reader to remit payment for mules or stipulates how many buttons a chaplain's coat must have, "I issue from the chain of command and you must obey me." And this phatic aspect is grounded in the visual "look" of the document more than its "content."[14]

In other words, the very anonymity that is supposed to guarantee the stability of this network and the hierarchy it was designed to serve makes it more accessible to different kinds of subjects: just as in the words of the famous *New Yorker* cartoon, "On the Internet, nobody knows you're a dog," nobody knows you're enslaved or a grandmother in a military order, or in the writing spaces of "systematic management" more broadly.[15] Faulkner's text emphasizes that this system is vulnerable to what we now call hacking in cybernetic contexts. From the implausible site of the slave quarters that, after the burning of the "big house" by Union troops, house both the Sartorises and their slaves, Rosa and Ringo turn the logic of systematic management against itself: they steal the letterhead and forge the handwriting that guarantee authenticity, and they thus assume the voice of military authority, a voice that rings with performative force and, ultimately, with economic power.

Rosa and Ringo also employ a second aspect of "systematic management": the use of emergent techniques of data collection and visualization, coupled with the orderly movement of data and analysis up and down the organization's hierarchy. Although it may seem strange to use such language for a "corporation" of four (counting Bayard and Ab Snopes, who contribute modestly to the enterprise), the text's depiction of Ringo and Rosa's meticulous tabulation of the flow of troops, mules, and money exemplifies the everyday functioning of the new systematic management. A central feature of systematic management was its combination of "bottom-up" reporting—the work of low-level employees' tabulating inventories, sales, locations, etc.—and "top-down" communications—the work of executives' broadcasting policies and instructions, along the lines of the military order discussed above, via circulars or orders to the rank and file.[16] Here we find Rosa and Ringo engaging in this new model, if on a modest scale: they fashion a "map" from a "window shade" in the slave cabin (124); Ringo sketches in the locations of towns; and Granny, "in her neat spidery hand like she wrote in the cookbook with" (125), completes the data visualization by filling in names of officers and numbers of mules in their corresponding locations in homemade pokeberry juice ink, noting which transactions are "*Complete*." Thus the techniques of the new systematic management pop up in this unlikely space, staffed with female, enslaved, and/or unlettered and uncredentialed subjects, using the humblest imaginable media to run a remarkably sophisticated, cutting-edge operation. The compensatory pleasures of Ringo and Bayard's childlike "dramatic play" from the text's opening pages are transformed at this moment into a much more serious form of play, one that possesses a remarkable potency in the "real world" of adults.

Beyond the pragmatic aspects of this hustle, which generates thousands of dollars and a large barren of mules for the starving community, Faulkner emphasizes the pleasure of this mode of writing for Rosa and especially for the enslaved Ringo. From his first dim notion of wielding power through the agency of the letter on the way home from the Union encampment, Ringo clearly relishes the opportunity to view his mind and body as a site of the satisfaction not of others' desires but of his own. The text, however, emphasizes pleasures that move beyond this primal desire for power: part of the forgery entails inventing names for the fictional petitioners demanding their seized property, and Ringo relishes the pure linguistic freedom, creating an algorithm that would make Nabokov or the OULIPO collective feel right at home. The series runs through the alphabet, featuring surnames from "A" on down, and Ringo emphasizes the ludic limitlessness inherent in this random approach: "I reckon when we run out of letters, maybe we can start in on numbers. We will have nine hundred and ninety-nine before we have to worry, then" (128). The final pseudonym in the series is the rather Joycean "Plurella Harris" (131): when the Union officers finally catch Rosa and Ringo and break up the grift, they identify Rosa as "Plurella" in a tacit recognition that the hackers have shed their skins and become plural and deracinated to their own pleasure and profit, marginalized members of the republican "pluribus" that has learned to speak, if under cover, in the voice of the "unum," endowed with plenary power.

There's much more to say about Faulkner's examination of the distinctive network that Rosa and Ringo exploit here, but given space constraints, I want to sketch out, however briefly, how this episode fits into the text's broader exploration of inscription systems. One might examine this dynamic in various sites in the text, from the feminine circuit of letter exchanges using cut-up wallpaper, home-brewed pokeberry juice ink, and hand delivery, to the looming presence of the railroad, which Faulkner represents as a kind of inscription on the very landscape by corporate and military power.[17] I will emphasize instead the unsettling subplot involving voting, arguably the most fundamental inscriptive practice in a democratic society. The episode unfolds within a comic frame, hammering both the individual southern family and the collective southern society back into a white supremacist and patriarchal shape. But the resolution is haunted by loose ends and elements of the grotesque that resist easy closure.

"Skirmish at Sartoris," the penultimate story in the cycle, encompasses in twenty-three pages and a few days of fictional time the turbulent period of the so-called "Redemption" of the South from federal control. In Faulkner's text this gradual, violent, and uneven process resolves neatly by condensing two events: on the one hand, the marriage of Drusilla Hawk and John Sartoris, which restores the gender-bending Drusilla to proper white southern femininity, and on the other, the disenfranchisement of the region's emancipated African Americans, which restores white men to sociopolitical supremacy. Critics such as Patricia Yaeger and Deborah Clarke have written extensively about the gender dynamics of the text via the unsettling/liberating figure of Drusilla; here, I want to emphasize the way the text brings together race and inscription in its depiction of struggle over the franchise.[18]

The double plot, joining marriage and voting, is activated by the alarm on the part of whites at learning that Cassius "Cash" Benbow, emancipated slave of the genteel Benbow family, has been made "Acting Marshal" of Jefferson and currently stands unopposed for election as marshal, aided by federal officials and a robust "get out the vote" campaign among African Americans (199). Benbow's threat to the status quo inheres not just in his race, but in his relationship to the related inscription systems of paper money and voting. His very name, "Cash," links him to currency, the paradigmatic site in capitalist societies where the sensuous particularities of objects and their transformations through labor are translated into abstract, exchangeable quantities stored and circulated via the highly optical medium of the paper bill, whose authenticity and value is guaranteed by its having issued from a monopolized printing process under State control. The text emphasizes the significance of this linkage by having Ringo introduce Cash to readers in striking terms:

> "Do you know what I aint" he said.
> "What?" I said.
> "I aint a n[-----] anymore. I done been abolished." Then I asked him what he was, if he wasn't a n[-----] anymore and he showed me what he had in his hand. It was a new scrip dollar; it was drawn on the United States Resident Treasurer, Yoknapatawpha County, Mississippi, and signed "Cassius Q. Benbow, Acting Marshal" in a neat clerk's hand, with a big, sprawling X under it. (199)

What one *is* and what one *ain't* here depend utterly, not on one's body and mind in real time, but on the alienation of the self in and through inscription systems. Ringo has been emancipated by a circular whose force extends into Mississippi's boundaries and supersedes its sovereignty.

Cash is both guarantor of the system of currency, whose "sprawling X" represents a zero degree of inscription, and something like a piece of money itself, having entered a mode of subjectivity in which he is no longer bound to a particular master and territory but one in which he is, at least in theory, equal and abstract, a citizen like any other in the eyes of the law. Here we see the implied analogy to the system of voting: as in the system of money, which resolves particularities into easily comparable quantities, voting channels, in effect, the very noisy and unruly entity of the democratic "general will" and pulls out a signal that is quantifiable and clear.[19] From the standpoint of the individual user, one reduces the untidy bundle of one's political demands and desires to a legible mark, hanging chads and hacked machines notwithstanding, an anonymized quantum of data that becomes legible in the aggregate as the expression of an ideal "general will."

The plot confronts the prospect of an abstract, race-dissolving citizenship with brutal economy, having John Sartoris and Drusilla Hawk take an unannounced detour on the way to their wedding to murder the Federal officials overseeing the polls. This depiction of masculine sovereignty asserting itself through extralegal violence in the service of what Sartoris calls, without a hint of irony, "law and order," is unsurprising to the point of cliché, in light of the history of the postbellum South, with the rise of spectacle lynchings and the Ku Klux Klan, for example (208). What is more surprising is the way the text quickly passes over this moment, emphasizing instead the more abstract assault on voting procedures in the aftermath of the killing. In a tacit recognition of the threat, not just of federal oversight of political procedure, but of emancipated slaves like Cassius and women like Rosa leaving legible marks within the inscription systems that govern everyday life, Sartoris and the remnant of his troop stage a dramatic assault not just on the individuals who would assert their will in political life, but on the networks through which that will manifests. Race and gender coalesce in this assault, such that people of color and women are not merely excluded from voting; rather, voting itself is reconfigured to seal off entry points of the kind that Rosa and Ringo and Cassius have previously exploited to gain access to the means of cultural inscription.

Sartoris's initial plan involves a displacement of voting procedure: having preserved the veneer of "peace through law and order" by turning himself in to the sheriff and making bail for the killing, he, Drusilla, and the troop carry the ballot box and blank ballots to the Sartoris plantation, where the wedding party has assembled (208). Drusilla is deputized as acting Voting Commissioner, and the election is thereby displaced from the neutral public space of Jefferson's town square to the private space of Sartoris's home, and thus subject to plantocratic control (207–8). This plan, however, collides with the assembly of matriarchs, who are furious at the attempt to elevate civic over domestic duties and the decision to permit Drusilla to breach her "separate sphere" by serving as a public official. In dramatic fashion Aunt Louisa "snatch[es] the polling box from Drusilla and fling[s] it across the yard" (209). In an extraordinarily condensed half page, order is restored by carefully putting each potential threat to the patriarchal order in its place: as the women watch the proceedings from inside, Ringo is dispatched to bring pokeberry juice and a window shade, Sartoris instructs the men to vote "yes" or "no" on Benbow's candidacy on the cut-up pieces, and Sartoris's *consigliere*, Wyatt, offers to "do the writing and save some more time," using his saddle as a desk (210). Even this feeble gesture at voting procedure dissolves, as Wyatt claims, "You needn't bother to count them. . . . They all voted No." The story ends with the sound of the troop's affirmation—of the election results, the wedding, and, in some sense, themselves as hegemons of a restored South—as they shout "Yaaaaay, Drusilla! . . . Yaaaaaay, John Sartoris! Yaaaaaaay!"

Each element of this ostensibly comic resolution demands unpacking. The use, not of the printed ballots but of the window shades and pokeberry ink, at once integrates the "feminine" circuit of inscription into voting and excludes actual women from using it, since Wyatt does the writing on the ultramasculine surface of the saddle. Moreover, the substitution of these improvised materials for the printed ballots signals a broader rejection of inscription systems, like military orders and scrip money, that rely for authority on standardized graphical elements and official signatures, an implication that is deeply underscored by having Ringo, the former pokeberry ink scribe, present Wyatt with the inscriptive media, only to watch in silence as Cassius's candidacy is annulled. Even more striking, however, is the weaponization of noise at the end of this episode.

It is not enough, it seems, to wrest control of the voting apparatus by violence, to displace the site of voting from neutral, public space to private, plantocratic space, to dispense with the secret ballot and pressure voters to vote unanimously, and to eschew tabulating and recording procedures in the assumption of a unanimity that would make a twentieth-century totalitarian dictator blush. The end of the story blots out this entire devolution of voting procedure in a Dionysian, protofascist wash of pure unanimous noise. As we have seen above, in the scene of Bayard's rebel yell in response to Loosh, this "yaaay" is not a humane, unmediated "spontaneous overflow of powerful feeling" or "barbaric yawp" that exists outside of the modern communications circuits used by Ringo and Rosa in the text. Rather, it's a countertechnology, one deployed with tactical precision to disable systems more hospitable to users with nonmale, nonwhite bodies. Faulkner emphasizes the technological and instrumental aspect of this white noise machine immediately after the murders of the election overseers: the troop shouts "Yaaaaa—" only to be precipitously cut off by Sartoris: "Father raised his hand and they stopped. Then you couldn't hear anything" (207). If the more deafening shout celebrating the election and the nuptials at story's end outstrips Sartoris's control—Bayard tells us that "even Father could not have stopped them" (210)—the text emphasizes the way "the Sartoris," which is to say the plantocracy, will keep his hands on the knob of this powerful, synthetic voice in order to wash out signals that threaten to introduce inconvenient differences into the family, the region, or the nation.[20]

The Unvanquished unleashes social and cultural possibilities that occasion, in the words of John T. Matthews, a collective "panic attack": an incomplete list would include a "don't ask/don't tell" military, literate and tech-savvy slaves, cohabitation of black and white families in slave quarters, women-led families, free, unfettered movement of the black masses, and black signatures guaranteeing the value of greenbacks.[21] The final item of the list, perhaps, should be "men who pack heat but refuse to shoot," and it would be redundant to dig into the way "An Odor of Verbena" closes the cycle by promoting Bayard Sartoris as the New Man at the helm of a New South and thus restoring southern patriarchy and white supremacy in a kinder, gentler form. What makes *The Unvanquished* worth reading today, despite its shameless shunting aside of black and female agency, is its close attention to the particular ways mid-nineteenth century media form identities, individual and collective. Surprisingly, in *The Unvanquished*, communications circuits grounded in corporate and military spaces and practices emerge as a model for thinking about postpatriarchal and/or transracial families in this text, an especially unexpected discovery, given the habitual way we associate southernness, especially among interwar figures like the Fugitive group and Zora Neale Hurston, with oral form and antibureaucratic pastoralism.[22] From this perspective, we can read *The Unvanquished*, not as a period piece venerating the Old South, but as a forward-looking exercise in thinking about creative occupation of media infrastructure. In this way, Faulkner's text anticipates Ellison's Invisible Man, who exploits vulnerabilities in Monopolated Power and Light and slips his voice into the "lower frequencies"; the Freedom Riders, who turned interstate bus networks into televised political theater; and users of "Black Twitter," who occupy Silicon Valley's infrastructure, created overwhelmingly by and for white men, in order to create new modes of familial belonging and political speech across space and time.[23]

NOTES

1. M. Thomas Inge, ed., *Conversations with William Faulkner* (Jackson: University Press of Mississippi, 1999), 166.

2. For surveys of the text's denigration and/or neglect, see Ted Atkinson, *Faulkner and the Great Depression: Aesthetics, Ideology, and Cultural Politics* (Athens: University of Georgia Press, 2005), 221-22; and Austin Graham, "Reconstructions: Faulkner and Du Bois on the Civil War," in *Faulkner and the Black Literatures of the Americas*, ed. Jay Watson and James G. Thomas, Jr. (Jackson: University Press of Mississippi, 2016), 119-20. Graham's and Atkinson's essays also exemplify recent attempts to recover *The Unvanquished* and reveal its complexities: the former argues that the text provides a "metacommentary" on the vogue for Lost Cause narratives in the 1930s (228), and the latter argues that Faulkner was the rare white author who joined Du Bois and other writers of color in arguing for the centrality of slavery to the Civil War. Other significant efforts to reanimate this text include the feminist readings of Yaeger and Clarke from the 1990s, which focus on the figure of Drusilla, and Barbara Ladd's reading, which centers seemingly marginal characters like Ringo, Loosh, and the unnamed masses of camp-following enslaved people depicted in "Raid." See Patricia Yaeger, "Faulkner's 'Greek Amphora Priestess': Verbena and Violence in *The Unvanquished*," in *Faulkner and Gender: Faulkner and Yoknapatawpha, 1994*, ed. Donald M. Kartiganer and Ann J. Abadie (Jackson: University of Mississippi Press, 1994), 197-227; Barbara Ladd, "Race as Fact and Fiction in William Faulkner," in *A Companion to William Faulkner*, ed. Richard C. Moreland (Malden, MA: Blackwell, 2007), 133-47; Deborah Clarke, "Gender, War, and Cross-Dressing," in *Faulkner and Gender: Faulkner and Yoknapatawpha, 1994*, ed. Donald M. Kartiganer and Ann J. Abadie (Jackson: University of Mississippi Press, 1994), 228-51.

3. In Greek myth, Echo's unrequited love for the self-regarding Narcissus dooms her to become a mere voice, one that eternally finds no answer beyond its own resonance. For Du Bois's somewhat analogous position as a black man in a white supremacist society, see W. E. B. Du Bois, *The Souls of Black Folk* (1903; repr., New York: Penguin Books, 1996), 3-4.

4. Abraham Lincoln, "'House Divided' Speech at Springfield, Illinois, June 16th 1858," in *Lincoln: Speeches and Writings 1832-1858*, ed. Don E. Fehrenbacher (New York: Library of America, 1989), 426-34.

5. Kittler's term *Aufschreibesysteme* has been generally translated as "discourse networks" in English. I prefer the more literal "inscription systems" here, both for its fidelity to the German (*aufschreiben* means "to inscribe" or "to write on") and its emphasis on the materiality of writing, which is central to my argument.

6. Friedrich Kittler, *Discourse Networks 1800/1900*, trans. Michael Metteer (Stanford, CA: Stanford University Press, 1990), 369.

7. Friedrich A. Kittler, *Gramophone, Film, Typewriter*, trans. Geoffrey Winthrop-Young and Michael Wutz (Stanford, CA: Stanford University Press, 1999), 4-7.

8. See, for example, Yaeger's argument that Bayard's mastery of "new moral norms" comes alongside an erasure of the "egalitarian community" Bayard himself dimly imagines at the text's beginning. See Yaeger, "Faulkner's 'Greek Amphora Priestess,'" 224-25.

9. William Faulkner, *The Unvanquished*, rev. ed. (1938; repr., New York: Vintage International, 1991), 5. Hereafter cited parenthetically.

10. Rumsfeld's notorious discussion of epistemology occurred at a February 2002 press conference. See "Defense.gov Transcript: DoD News Briefing—Secretary Rumsfeld and Gen. Myers," February 12, 2002, https://archive.defense.gov/Transcripts/Transcript.aspx?TranscriptID=2636 (accessed October 1, 2020).

11. "Différance" is Jacques Derrida's term to describe the way language simultaneously generates "difference" via semantic indeterminacy and "deferral" of meaning. See Jacques Derrida, *Margins of Philosophy*, trans. Alan Bass (Chicago: University of Chicago Press, 1985), 5.

12. The text repeats the theme of Ringo's superiority to Bayard obsessively, leading some readers to surmise that Bayard and Ringo are brothers, an implication that nicely literalizes the figurative interracial "family" that coalesces around this "corporation" located in a slave cabin. For an elaboration of this reading, see Graham, "Reconstructions," 123.

13. JoAnne Yates, *Control through Communication: The Rise of System in American Management* (Baltimore: Johns Hopkins University Press, 1993), 1–20.

14. Roman Jakobson, *Language in Literature*, ed., Stephen Rudy and Krystyna Pomorska (Cambridge, MA: Belknap Press, 1987), 68–69.

15. Peter Steiner, "On the Internet, Nobody Knows You're a Dog," *New Yorker*, July 5, 1993, 61.

16. Yates, *Control through Communication*, 5–9, 13–14.

17. For a depiction of the railroad as inscription of the landscape, see Bayard's description of "the straightest thing I ever saw" (87); for a depiction of the feminine circuit of letter writing, see, for example, 188–89.

18. See Yaeger, "Faulkner's 'Greek Amphora Priestess'"; and Clarke, "Gender, War, and Cross-Dressing."

19. For Rousseau's discussion of the emergence of "societies of the general will" and the complex representational issues this emergence entails, see Jean-Jacques Rousseau, *Of the Social Contract and Other Political Writings*, ed., Christopher Bertram, trans. Quintin Hoare (New York: Penguin, 2012), especially book 4, chapters 1–2.

20. Jay Watson suggested to me the intriguing connection between this "rebel yell" and the noise of the whistles of Sartoris's trains. Both technologies feature high-amplitude sources of noise subject to the control of a general or CEO and point out the way that "the Sartoris" functions as a transitional figure for the postbellum South.

21. John T. Matthews, *William Faulkner: Seeing through the South* (Malden, MA: Wiley-Blackwell, 2009), 221.

22. The introduction to *I'll Take My Stand*, the 1930 collection of essays primarily written by the Fugitives, a group of early twentieth-century poets and writers, presents southern "manners, conversation, hospitality, [and] sympathy" as an antidote to the dominant "industrial civilization"; in her novel *Their Eyes Were Watching God*, Hurston has her protagonist, Janie, declare "mah tongue is in mah friend's mouf" as a similar defense of orality and face-to-face communication. See Zora Neale Hurston, *Their Eyes Were Watching God* (1937; repr., New York: Harper Collins, 2010), 7; Twelve Southerners, *I'll Take My Stand: The South and the Agrarian Tradition* (1930; repr., Baton Rouge: Louisiana State University Press, 1977), xliii.

23. Ralph Ellison, *Invisible Man* (1952; repr., New York: Vintage International, 1995), 581.

When Will We Be Extinct?

Faulknerian Cosmopolitanism and the Family Network

ROBERT JACKSON

> *This approach of a powerful man was like a sudden jolt which had shocked her body out of its slumber. All the instincts of a highly strung woman now burst to the fore with incomparable violence, as her mother's blood, that African blood which burned in her veins, began to pulse furiously through her slight, still almost virginal body.*
> —EMILE ZOLA, *Thérèse Raquin* (1868)

A Mild Shock

The early 1940s left William Faulkner brooding over the many ways in which his world was coming apart, and brooding over how to hold it together. His correspondence with his publishers was suffused with worries about financial solvency; indeed, after more than a decade of his most prolific and brilliant literary production, he found himself in such straits that he was driven to write to his agent Harold Ober, regarding a draft of "The Bear," in November 1941: "Please sell it for something as soon as you can. I am in a situation where I will take almost anything for it or almost anything else I have or can write."[1] The origins of *Go Down, Moses* (1942), much of this correspondence reveals, can be traced to Faulkner's desire to produce an entire book from the fragments of sold and unsold short fiction of recent years, following the model, as he observed, of *The Unvanquished* (1938).

But Faulkner's correspondence from this period goes far beyond his fear of financial ruin in detailing the threats to his world's order. On January 21, 1942, in the same letter in which he sent the famous and controversial dedication of *Go Down, Moses* ("TO MAMMY / CAROLINE BARR

/ Mississippi / [1840-1940] . . . ") to Robert Haas at Random House, he alluded to Japan's bombing of Pearl Harbor and his early thoughts about volunteering for military service. "This world is bitched proper this time, isn't it?" he began. "I'd like to be dictator now."[2] If not a dictator in the strict sense, Faulkner remained, of course, "sole owner and proprietor" of his vast fictional world, and the impulse to produce a kind of order that triumphs over the centrifugal and annihilating forces of capitalism, race, war, and time itself is everywhere present in *Go Down, Moses*.[3] The book constitutes a radical experiment even in the context of Faulkner's prior fiction. With major and minor episodes seeming to diverge from one another to such a degree that critics (following the lead of Faulkner's publisher, who released the first edition as *Go Down, Moses and Other Stories*) questioned the nature of their relations with one another in a single volume, the book's revision of earlier stories and its development into a coherent whole provided Faulkner the opportunity to imagine and work towards their deeply interconnected familiarity, to generate a kinship in constant tension with itself. "Moses [*sic*] is indeed a novel," Faulkner insisted to Haas as late as 1949, amid their discussion of the book's reissue. "Indeed, if you will permit me to say so at this late date, nobody but Random House seemed to labor under the impression that GO DOWN, MOSES should be titled 'and other stories.' I remember the shock (mild) I got when I saw the printed title page. I say, reprint it, call it simply GO DOWN, MOSES, which was the way I sent it in to you 8 years ago."[4]

Go Down, Moses is, like many of Faulkner's greatest works, a novel about family and genealogy. It dramatizes the struggle, and perhaps the impossibility, of keeping families intact, not just in the face of the hard facts of history, but also in the closer context of a genealogy that contains and reproduces its own trauma. From Tomey's Turl's scheming to live with his girlfriend Tennie, and the McCaslin brothers' attempt to retrieve him, their half brother and runaway slave, in "Was," to Rider's suicidal longing for communion with his deceased wife Mannie in "Pantaloon in Black," to Gavin Stevens's effort to return Samuel Beauchamp's body, at the request of the young man's grandmother Mollie Beauchamp in "Go Down, Moses," this struggle runs through many of the stories, including those whose connection to the book's major episodes—Lucas Beauchamp's effort to consolidate his property in "The Fire and the Hearth," Ike McCaslin's coming of age in "The Old People" and "The Bear"—has been questioned by many critics.[5] Stevens's realization, in the closing lines of the novel, that Mollie Beauchamp "doesn't care" how her grandson, executed by the State of Illinois after a murder conviction, died, but that "she just wanted him home," emphasizes the universality of this struggle, which continues even after death.[6] The eternal question of *Go Down, Moses*'s classification as a novel or a collection might well be reframed as a question about genealogy, with Faulkner's revision of the disparate stories a radical attempt to unify a number of wayward relations and their unwieldy, sometimes even unspeakable, histories. Here I suggest that family estrangement provides the tools—and more precisely, the media—with which Faulkner questions the model of the heteronormative, genealogically blood-obsessed family that he, with a reluctance comparable to that of Ike McCaslin himself, had inherited as the dominant template of his civilization.

The Family Network

Would Ike McCaslin have developed his intense connection to the forests and animals if he'd come from a better family? Better, that is, in the sense of not including the tainted domestic history passed on by his grandfather Lucius Quintus Carothers McCaslin? Better, also, in consisting of two parents who'd lived beyond his early childhood and perhaps given him some siblings? But *better*, a veiled euphemism for *normative*, obscures alternative possibilities, and may not be an entirely relevant category. Ike's mother Sophonsiba remains a caricature, almost a nonperson, even in the mind of her own son, who twice refers to her in "The Bear" not as his mother but as "his Uncle Hubert's sister" (287, 295). A figure whose comic fixation on family origins is expressed by her insistence that her brother "was probably the true earl" of a "place in England," Sophonsiba constitutes yet another illustration in Faulkner's work of the impossible, inhumane expectations placed on southern white womanhood (5). At the same time, Ike has four highly nonnormative fathers, if we count the twins Theophilus and Amodeus McCaslin, as well as Cass Edmonds—"rather his father than either" brother or cousin, Faulkner writes (4)—and Sam Fathers, himself of complex origins, who becomes the most influential of the four because it is his sacred history, rather than the profane history of Ike's birth family, that Ike adopts and embodies: "And as he talked about those old times and those dead and vanished men of another race from either that the boy knew, gradually to the boy those old times would cease to be old times and would become a part of the boy's present, not only as if they had happened yesterday but as if they were still happening, the men who walked through them actually walking in breath and air and casting an actual shadow on the earth they had not quitted" (165). There is something queer not just in Sam's conjuring of "those dead and vanished men of another race," but in the overall movement of Ike's development through these all-male spaces and networks, a groping towards viable, if temporary and experimental, alternatives. Even decades later, near the end of his life, when "his companions were the sons and even the grandsons" of the hunters whom he had known as a young man, Ike reflects on the fact that a canvas tent in the woods, rather than his small house in Jefferson, was his home and "these men . . . were more his kin than any" (335). What is it in Faulkner that leads to the creation of Ike McCaslin and his ilk, young men whose development is shaped—or twisted—by such an unconventional family history, and who diverge from the traditional *bildungsroman* protagonist (especially its European model, a young man who finally ascends to his appropriate position in the social and civil orders) precisely in their dawning knowledge that history itself—and certainly *family* history— has reached its end? For Ike, "the old people" are the *extinct* people, even as they live on in Sam's storytelling and in Ike's phenomenological experience of the present, and even as Ike renounces the position handed down to him—"weakly relinquishing" it, as Faulkner puts it (via Lucas Beauchamp's free indirect discourse) in a none-too-discreet critique of Ike's malformed manhood (39).

In much of the European and American literature of the nineteenth century, Jobst Welge writes in *Genealogical Fictions* (2015), "the notions of family and pedigree have served as powerful images for the discourse of nationhood, the emergence or transformation of collective identities and communities, especially during those moments when the continuity of succession came under threat."[7] Welge identifies a Darwinian strain in this nineteenth-century literature: with its "chronological retrospections and the search for origins, antecedents, predecessors, or archetypes," genealogical narratives are "necessarily developmental in nature, they are oriented toward both the past and the future" (2). Faulkner's families, by contrast, beginning at least as early as the Sartoris and Compson novels of the late 1920s, seem to point not just to deeply problematic origins but also, and simultaneously, to the prospect of their own extinction in the near future. It is not just Ike's beloved wilderness that is endangered in *Go Down, Moses*; it is also a certain model of the family itself.

Faulkner took extinction very seriously, and did so in ways that seem more evident as we contemplate the dire consequences of climate change in the era of the Anthropocene. Thomas L. McHaney notes, in an article collected in *Faulkner and the Ecology of the South* (which emerged from the 2003 Faulkner and Yoknapatawpha conference), "In the context of the current ecological crisis, Ike may look even better" to contemporary readers—McHaney has his own students in mind—than his passive conservationist politics and residual segregationist ideology might seem to warrant.[8] More recently, in 2015, Susan Scott Parrish drew attention to Faulkner's relevance to an emerging ecocritical consciousness and noted his articulation of "how much environmental degradation and ensuing disasters were crucial to the period [of American modernism]—its sense of altered embodiment, perception, strategies of representation, and even ontology"; while Ramon Saldivar and Sylvan Goldberg, considering the implications of human agency as a geological force in the Anthropocene, likewise have identified Faulkner as an early model of this awareness: "Visible only at a temporal scale in which earth-systems data can be tracked across millennia, this newly visible form of agency can be told through neither a purely natural nor a purely human history, necessitating the type of hybrid historical knowledge we have seen in Faulkner's understanding of modernity."[9]

Indeed, Faulkner may be even more immanently relevant in this era of ecological crisis than these scholars have suggested. As one of the greatest of all writers of disavowal, Faulkner devoted much of his best work to exploring the consciousness of individuals whose sheer quantity of things to say is matched only by their genius for talking around and away from fundamental truths they would rather not acknowledge. Who better than Faulkner, then, to look to for insights into the elaborate social, psychological, and rhetorical strategies of climate-change denialism so pervasive today, as well as into the processes by which a few individuals struggle heroically, and at enormous personal cost, against this disavowal? Ike McCaslin's relinquishment of the exploited land and people of his inheritance constitutes a rejection of what Judith Butler calls, in *Precarious Life* (2004), "a national melancholia, understood as a disavowed mourning," which "follows upon the erasure from public representations of the names, images and narratives" of victims of state violence.[10] Queerly, Ike *avows* mourning, his final recorded words—"It was a doe"—a valedictory summation of his life's work of bearing witness to so much that has been violently eradicated from the official memory of his civilization (348). Tom McHaney's students are right: Ike should "look even better" these days, because he accepts the devastating social consequences that come with his acknowledgement of the truth of the sacredness of the wilderness as it is desecrated and destroyed by capitalism.

To apprehend the underlying truth of this soon-to-be-achieved extinction as it concerns Faulkner's families, we must return to the genealogies—not just of the McCaslins, but of Faulkner's other families: the Sartorises, Compsons, Bundrens, Sutpens, and Snopeses—and view them as media forms themselves. These are, in the useful terms of Lisa Gitelman's definition of media, "socially realized structures of communication," with discrete histories and infrastructures of their own and unique modes of mapping the transmission of important information and data from one point to another, across points not separated just by space, as in a live radio or television broadcast, but also by time.[11] Friedrich A. Kittler's "discourse network" also provides some guidance here, particularly in its association of media with data storage—consider, for example, the recurrent efforts of characters in *Go Down, Moses* and *Flags in the Dust* (1929) to record genealogical data, and Faulkner's own compiling of the Compson Appendix (1946) and the genealogical data in the endpapers of *Absalom, Absalom!* (1936)—and its emphasis on the technological limits placed on media by their historical contexts.[12] These historicizing concepts invite new attention to Faulkner's genealogies, especially in light of Gitelman's insistence that media history, in addition to attending to technological forms, "must be social and cultural" (7), as well as Kittler's somewhat more deterministic vision of historical progress and the future. And the work of American cultural historians has made it clear that this media theory has ready applications in genealogical terms, suggesting that Faulkner is largely repurposing rather than inventing this longstanding blood discourse. Russ Castronovo, for example, speaks of the "ancestral paths" of early American bloodlines across generations in *Fathering the Nation* (1995), while Shawn Salvant, discussing the "one-drop rule" of the Jim Crow era in *Blood Work* (2015), writes: "A drop of black blood was no longer regarded only as the presence of a deterministic biological essence but also as a reference to an irrepressible historical and cultural narrative."[13] The ancestral path, the irrepressible historical narrative: these terms go some way to describing what we ought to understand in the more particular terms of media, means of transmission, broadcast, and communication, with an emphasis on mobility and movement. Faulkner's powerfully genealogical work does, however, invite the creation of a new term here: the *family network*.

Faulkner goes to extraordinary lengths to map the genealogies of his fictional families, with the mediatory function of the genealogy itself hiding in plain sight. So the question for understanding Faulkner's larger design then becomes: what is transmitted through this medium? The most direct answer is *blood*, which courses from one end of a Faulkner genealogy to the other. But this way of framing the question is misleading in itself, not least because Faulkner's genealogies do not map strictly linear and progressive routes. Indeed, here we might entertain the proposition that Faulkner's rejection of linear narrative, and his experiments with other temporalities especially in his genealogical novels, are simply consequences of the fact that the genealogy, in which little, if anything, is straightforward, is his preferred medium of expression. Blood is also difficult to assess because it plays so many roles, some of them more concrete than others. For Faulkner, of course, blood is inescapable, yet across his writings it is so overdetermined that it may seem impossible to define in any straightforward way. Blood in Faulkner is not just many things at many times and places; it can also be many things at once: a physical property, a biological necessity, a consciousness, a voice, a home, a foreign place, a site of conflict and struggle, an inescapable, iron law from deep history, an explosive source of rupture and change, a vision of the future that declares its own agency and freedom from the past, an impenetrable mystery, and on and on.

Of all Faulkner's genealogical novels, blood is perhaps most omnipresent in *Go Down, Moses*. Its physical and biological matter is emphasized at many inflection points in the novel, including during hunting episodes and rituals such as young Ike's initiation in "The Old People": "The boy did that—drew the head back and the throat taut and drew Sam Fathers' knife across the throat and Sam stooped and dipped his hands in the hot smoking blood and wiped them back and forth across the boy's face" (158). This buck's blood is sacred. Elsewhere, and quite frequently, blood has deep knowledge and memory of its own. Cass Edmonds invokes this element in his rationalization for Sam Fathers's—and all the Natives'—looming extinction: "He was a wild man. When he was born, all his blood on both sides, except the little white part, knew things that had been tamed out of our blood so long ago that we have not only forgotten them, we have to live together in herds to protect ourselves from our own sources. He was the direct son not only of a warrior but of a chief. Then he grew up and began to learn things, and all of a sudden one day he found out that he had been betrayed, the blood of the warriors and chiefs had been betrayed" (161-62). Likewise, Lucas Beauchamp credits the blood of his grandfather as he reflects on the moment of his greatest trial in "The Fire and the Hearth": "*So I reckon I aint got old Carothers' blood for nothing, after all. Old Carothers,* he thought. *I needed him and he come and spoke for me*" (57). Lucas is, indeed, one of the most blood-obsessed characters in all of Faulkner's work, the sheer complexity of his identity revealed in the many different ways in which he experiences and contemplates his own blood:

> Yet it was not that Lucas made capital of his white or even his McCaslin blood, but the contrary. It was as if he were not only impervious to that blood, he was indifferent to it. He didn't even need to strive with it. He didn't even have to bother to defy it. He resisted it simply by being the composite of the two races which made him, simply by possessing it. Instead of being at once the battleground and victim of the two strains, he was a vessel, durable, ancestryless, nonconductive, in which the toxin and its anti stalemated one another, seetheless, unrumored in the outside air. (101)

Here, invoking "capital," Faulkner suggests one mediatory role—that of money itself—available for blood in the novel, even as the "durable, ancestryless, nonconductive" Lucas constitutes an end in himself. The paradox of blood—as simultaneously a means and an end—follows Gitelman's observation that any medium is simultaneously a physical object as well as an abstract process, requiring a delicate balance between technological determinism and antideterminism. "At certain levels" she writes, "media are very influential, and their material properties do (literally and figuratively) *matter*, determining some of the local conditions of communication amid the broader circulations that at once express and constitute social relations" (10).

Ike McCaslin suggests another such mediatory role for blood in "The Bear," proposing that God has used the blood of the South's white settlers to "accomplish His purpose" of expiating the curse of man's exploitation and corruption of the land itself:

> —when He used the blood which had brought in the evil to destroy the evil as doctors use fever to burn up fever, poison to slay poison. Maybe He chose Grandfather out of all of them He might have picked. Maybe He knew that Grandfather himself would not serve His purpose because Grandfather was born too soon too, but that Grandfather would have descendants, the right descendants; maybe He had foreseen already the descendants Grandfather would have, maybe He saw already in Grandfather the seed progenitive of the three generations He saw it would take to set at least some of His lowly people free— (248)

This vision of blood's mediation—its liberatory power—motivates Ike to renounce his inheritance of his family's land, and thereby to justify his estrangement from his past, present, and future relations on the basis of setting "at least some of His lowly people free." These monumental forces of blood and freedom finally reach an impasse at the end of "Delta Autumn," when the elderly Ike has no choice but to confront the young mixed-race woman who has had a child with Roth Edmonds. Yet the most Ike can do at this critical moment is defer its implications into the distant future; for this child's blood, he considers, is not necessarily *wrong*, but certainly a millennium or two *too early*: "*Maybe in a thousand or two thousand years in America,* he thought. *But not now! Not now!*" (344).

The place where these two things—the mobile, irrepressible blood of the genealogy and the biological prospect of extinction—converge, for Faulkner, is the family itself. And this, I suggest, is why Faulkner's families are so terrible. Incest, of course, is a violation of the genealogy's greatest taboo, and just as fundamentally a circling back of the blood that in any normative family would be moving progressively through time. Miscegenation represents a slightly different kind of taboo in the Jim Crow South, though one that, in texts like *Absalom, Absalom!* and *Go Down, Moses*, overlaps with the incest taboo in complex ways. But even in many of Faulkner's families where incest and miscegenation aren't present, doom seems to be just over the horizon. These families are full of suicides and mental breakdowns and addictions and self-hate and self-destructiveness, and full of people who just can't get along with each other. A castrated brother here, a disavowed mixed-race descendant there, a daughter who becomes an accomplice to her father's murder and then helps the killer escape there, and so on. Considering the sheer familial and temporal chaos of Faulkner's genealogies, *As I Lay Dying* (1930) is atypical in this tradition, its comedy arising from the fact that this family, despite burying one member and sending another one to a mental institution, stays intact—and even replaces the lost members with a couple of new, more adaptable ones along the way. The Bundrens, with their unlettered origins and lack of social pretension, have a comparatively compact genealogy as well as a more streamlined embrace of the possibilities and demands of the future. Cleanth Brooks, marveling at the indestructibility of Anse Bundren, expresses "baffled admiration for the stubborn vitality which like that of some low order of organism allows him to fatten on what would starve nobler creatures and survive blasts that would kill more sensitive organisms."[14] Extinction is not the Bundrens' destiny; this family, rare among those of Faulkner, will remain together well into the future.

More typically, though, the estrangement of family members from one another is Faulkner's signal that extinction is coming, transforming the genealogy into a medium that foretells its own demise. Dilsey's prophecy, at the end of a novel in which she's borne witness to generations of domestic warfare and estrangement, might well express the general rule: "I seed de beginning, en now I sees de endin."[15] The dwindling of the Sutpen lines—Black and white—and the conflagration of the family's mansion, which might have been avoided if a father had simply acknowledged his own son, are likewise acknowledged: "Jim Bond, the scion, the last of his race, seeing it too now and howling with human reason now since now even he could have known what he was howling about."[16] These are well known expressions of what many scholars have categorized broadly as Faulkner's "tragic vision," but Ike McCaslin's life in *Go Down, Moses* may provide Faulkner's fullest exploration of estrangement as a historical process.

The first chapter, "Was," comes off initially as a comic, even nostalgic, treatment of slavery, featuring a slave who ensnares his owner in an elaborate plot and achieves not quite freedom but a real measure of agency in his own life: Tomey's Turl engineers his owner Theophilus McCaslin's purchase of Tennie from a nearby plantation so that he can start a family with her—a family, we learn later, that will include Lucas Beauchamp, who along with Ike is the most important character in the entire novel. But "Was" is also the narrative record of the sheer unlikelihood of Ike's existence, a story of how he should never have been born, and it speaks indirectly—genealogically, we might say—to the horrors of slavery: Ike's father Theophilus (Uncle Buck) courted his mother with deep reluctance, and married her towards the end of his life at least partially as an act of capitulation and resignation; and more disturbingly, the slaves and slavers are family members themselves—Tomey's Turl described as "that damn white half-McCaslin" by Ike's future uncle (a moment that is jarring because truth is spoken amid a haze of lies and evasions)—each playing a distinct role in this family game of authority, transgression, and disavowal (6). Here we see some of the precedents to Ike's estrangement from his own wife, from the descendants he fails to produce and those he disavows, and from the extended family history he attempts to abandon by rejecting his inheritance.

Towards the end of the novel, in "Delta Autumn," Ike's bluff is called, his visions of extinction challenged in the person of Roth Edmonds's estranged lover. This young woman of two races, a distant blood relative of Ike's and Roth's—the familial link an evocation of the incest/miscegenation precedent generated by Ike's grandfather, as well as another case of nonlinear genealogical development—is not only *not* in danger of extinction despite her "face's dead and toneless pallor," but is, to the contrary, "ineradicably alive" (343). Here at the novel's unfulfilling climax—in which Ike does not commit an act of love but receives a lecture on love—his reluctance to recognize his own blood when faced with a future not of his own design does not necessarily presage the extinction of the entire human race (although Faulkner of course had World War II on his mind, even to the extent of staging a debate between Ike and Roth on Hitler's threat to the free world). Instead, it suggests, in a kind of Darwinian way, a lack of adaptability that renders Ike, in his segregationist ideology, the last of a species as ripe for extinction as Sam Fathers, the old people, Old Ben, and their beloved wilderness. Jim Crow, it seems, is the most estranging figure of all.

Bitched Proper

If *Go Down, Moses* represents, on one level, Faulkner's grieving for a model of heteronormative and dynastic family relations that, he rightly recognizes, must go, can we articulate an alternative, or set of alternatives, to replace it? The question transforms Faulkner's critique of the Jim Crow South into something no longer, or no longer merely, a regional concern, but instead a search for constructive, sustainable models of human community. This may bring us into the realm of what several thinkers have termed *cosmopolitan*, an effort, in the terms of W. E. B. Du Bois—whose own contexts for Jim Crow were international rather than regional—to embrace "higher and broader and more varied human culture" as the "main end of democracy."[17] Judith Butler, with gender as well as race in mind, likewise envisions a diverse network of voices: "We could have several engaged intellectual debates going on at the same time and find ourselves joined in the fight against violence, without having to agree on many epistemological issues" (48). Butler articulates a cosmopolitan ideal around the all-too-human experiences of vulnerability, precarity, and endangerment that invites comparison to Faulkner's intimations of mortality; the sheer range of human culture, she argues, necessitates "a coalition that affirms the thinking of activists and the activism of thinkers and refuses to put them into distinctive categories that deny the actual complexity of the lives in question."

The Ghanaian-English philosopher Kwame Anthony Appiah begins *In My Father's House* (1992) by reflecting on his own family genealogy (with sources from Botswana, Norway, the United States [Black and white], Lebanon, France, Kenya, Thailand, and Nigeria) as a way of "seeing the world as a network of points of affinity."[18] Like Faulkner, Appiah privileges the concept of genealogy-as-medium—the family network—in the imagination of new opportunities and alternative futures. Along with this genealogical awareness that both grounds and liberates his ethic of cosmopolitanism, Appiah advocates "the idea that we have obligations to others, obligations that stretch beyond those to whom we are related by the ties of kith and kind, or even more formal ties of a shared citizenship."[19] These obligations, he makes clear, extend to those who will come in the future, and thus, at the very least, require us to maintain the capacity to imagine their existence and to avoid our own extinction. I suggest that Faulkner's failed family genealogies are designed to force us into the position of apprehending something very much like Appiah's foresight, just as they force Ike McCaslin to recognize that the future—one he only strains to imagine and, reflexively, violently defers to a time not yet present—belongs to Roth's spurned lover and her child rather than to himself. In this way, what we might label Faulkner's cosmopolitan regionalism constitutes a far more complex literary model than prominent strains of Faulkner criticism, running from the Nashville Agrarians and early New Critics through much of the Cold War consensus regarding Faulkner's exemplary "southern" identity, ever recognized: in revealing the dead end of such inward-looking models of regionalism, Faulkner points instead to a cosmopolitan ideal that has more in common with Appiah's radically outward-looking one.[20]

Faulkner's families, in failing, in modeling extinction, remind us to look beyond the family, the plantation-as-corporation, the closed society, the nostalgic blind alley, the incestuous and self-negating genre. Other affiliations beckon—if we can just imagine them, if we can bind them together. Appiah's frequent returns to considerations of the influence of homosexuality—his own and others'—in the development of cosmopolitanism also suggests the profound paradox at the heart of Faulkner's pessimism about the future of any strict heteronormative line of descent.[21] For what Ike McCaslin—like a number of doomed young men in Faulkner's other novels, including Quentin Compson, Darl Bundren, Henry Sutpen, and others—carves out in *Go Down, Moses* is a space of dogged resistance to heteronormative reproduction of many destructive kinds. Imagining, instead, queer family models, Faulkner seems to be suggesting, is not just an aesthetic preference or orientation, but an essential act for passing a viable civilization on to those who are not yet with us. Indeed, in these unsettled days of the Anthropocene, our survival may depend on it.

NOTES

My thanks to Pardis Dabashi and Mike Zeitlin for a series of productive conversations before and during the 2019 Faulkner and Yoknapatawpha Conference, and to Sarah Gleeson-White, Jack Matthews, and Don James McLaughlin for perceptive readings of an earlier draft of this piece.

1. Joseph Blotner, ed., *Selected Letters of William Faulkner* (New York: Random House, 1977), 144.

2. Blotner, *Selected Letters of William Faulkner*, 148.

3. For the "sole owner and proprietor" designation, see the map of Yoknapatawpha County in the endpapers of William Faulkner, *Absalom, Absalom!*, rev. ed. (1936; repr., New York: Vintage International, 1990).

4. Blotner, *Selected Letters of William Faulkner*, 284–85.

5. See, for example, Dirk Kuyk Jr., *Threads Cable-Strong: William Faulkner's* Go Down, Moses (Lewisberg, PA: Bucknell University Press, 1983).

6. William Faulkner, *Go Down, Moses*, rev. ed. (1942; repr., New York: Vintage International, 1990), 365; emphasis removed. Hereafter cited parenthetically.

7. Jobst Welge, *Genealogical Fictions: Cultural Periphery and Historical Change in the Modern Novel* (Baltimore: Johns Hopkins University Press, 2015), 2. Hereafter cited parenthetically.

8. Thomas L. McHaney, "The Ecology of Uncle Ike: Teaching *Go Down, Moses* with Janisse Ray's *Ecology of a Cracker Childhood*," in Joseph R. Urgo and Ann J. Abadie, eds., *Faulkner and the Ecology of the South: Faulkner and Yoknapatawpha, 2003* (Jackson: University Press of Mississippi), 99.

9. Susan Scott Parrish, "*As I Lay Dying* and the Modern Aesthetics of Ecological Crisis," in John T. Matthews, ed., *The New Cambridge Companion to William Faulkner* (New York: Cambridge University Press, 2015), 78; Ramon Saldivar and Sylvan Goldberg, "The Faulknerian

Anthropocene: Scales of Time and History in *The Wild Palms* and *Go Down, Moses*," in Matthews, *The New Cambridge Companion to William Faulkner*, 199. See also Parrish, *The Flood Year 1927: A Cultural History* (Princeton, NJ: Princeton University Press, 2017), esp. chapter 6, for more on Faulkner and these environmental concerns.

10. Judith Butler, *Precarious Life: The Powers of Mourning and Violence* (London: Verso, 2004), xiv. Hereafter cited parenthetically.

11. Lisa Gitelman, *Always Already New: Media, History, and the Data of Culture* (Cambridge, MA: MIT Press, 2006), 7. Hereafter cited parenthetically.

12. Friedrich A. Kittler, *Discourse Networks, 1800/1900* (1985), trans. Michael Metteer (Palo Alto: Stanford University Press, 1990).

13. Russ Castronovo, *Fathering the Nation: American Genealogies of Slavery and Freedom* (Berkeley: University of California Press, 1996), 15-16; Shawn Salvant, *Blood Work: Imagining Race in American Literature, 1890-1940* (Baton Rouge: Louisiana State University Press, 2015), 11, 14.

14. Cleanth Brooks, *William Faulkner: The Yoknapatawpha Country* (1963; Baton Rouge: Louisiana State University Press, 1990), 155.

15. William Faulkner, *The Sound and the Fury*, rev. ed. (1929; repr., New York: Vintage International, 1990), 297.

16. Faulkner, *Absalom, Absalom!*, 300.

17. W. E. B. Du Bois, *Writings*, ed. Nathan Huggins (New York: Library of America, 1996), 1063-64. For more on Du Bois's cosmopolitanism, see Ross Posnock, *Color and Culture: Black Writers and the Making of the Modern Intellectual* (Cambridge, MA: Harvard University Press, 1998), 2-4, and chapters 3-5; and Tania Friedel, *Racial Discourse and Cosmopolitanism in Twentieth-Century African American Writing* (New York: Routledge, 2010), 1-19.

18. Kwame Anthony Appiah, *In My Father's House: Africa in the Philosophy of Culture* (New York: Oxford University Press, 1992), viii.

19. Kwame Anthony Appiah, *Cosmopolitanism: Ethics in a World of Strangers* (New York: W. W. Norton, 2006), xv.

20. For more on Faulkner's complex relationship to inherited models of American regionalism, see Robert Jackson, *Seeking the Region in American Literature and Culture: Modernity, Dissidence, Innovation* (Baton Rouge: Louisiana State University Press, 2005), chapter 2. For a treatment of Faulkner as a major figure in world literature mediated not by American regional contexts but by a more network-oriented global literary economy (albeit one in which Paris enjoys a highly privileged position), see Pascale Casanova, *The World Republic of Letters* (1999), trans. M. B. DeBevoise (Cambridge, MA: Harvard University Press, 2007), 130-31, 336-45. For a related attempt to "reclaim Faulkner as a 'regional' writer: but regional in a new sense, embracing a new set of geographical coordinates, and a new set of historical references," see Wai Chee Dimock, "Faulkner Networked: Indigenous, Regional, Trans-Pacific," in Jay Watson and James G. Thomas, Jr., eds., *Faulkner and History: Faulkner and Yoknapatawpha, 2014* (Jackson: University Press of Mississippi, 2017), 3-20. Dimock's "networked regionalism" has the most potential, she argues, "when it is oriented outward, imagined as a principle of connectivity extending beyond Mississippi, a basis for reaching out to other localities with not much else in common" (3).

As scholars including Casanova and Welge have made clear, Faulkner's heirs in world literature seem to have gotten the blood-soaked message. His imprint on the great genealogical novelists from Fuentes, Márquez, and Lins do Rego in Latin America to Tomasi di Lampedusa, Benet, and Thomas Bernhard in Europe reveals, as Welge writes, that Faulkner "was enormously important for enabling literary innovation in backward or culturally dominated areas throughout the twentieth century" (197). Bernhard's 1986 novel *Auslöchung*—a term (with connotations of extinction, eradication, obliteration) that "bears strong associations with the Holocaust, [and] goes to show that the narrator's project to extricate himself from the familial and national continuity is strongly affected by what it seeks to negate" (Welge 202)—offers an apt comparison to *Go Down, Moses*, its central struggle closely resembling that of Ike McCaslin.

21. See, for example, Appiah, *Cosmopolitanism*, 2, 77–78, 80–81; for a more autobiographically grounded discussion, see Appiah, "Ghanaians Like Sex Too Much to Be Homophobic," http://bigthink.com/videos/ghanaians-like-sex-too-much-to-be-homophobic (accessed January 15, 2020).

Faulkner's Subversive Genealogies

GEORGE PORTER THOMAS

"The Bear," in *Go Down, Moses*, ends with an image that structures Faulkner's greatest period in retrospect, as genealogy does: Boon Hogganbeck, sitting in that clearing, beneath the gum tree "alive with frantic squirrels," in the last stretch of Major de Spain's soon-to-be-logged forest, with his "streaming walnut face," his impotent, dismembered gun, his "hoarse strangled voice" yelling "They're mine!"[1] What does it mean to claim the last tree in the last clearing?

In this great novel of genealogy, Boon's tree represents both the ownership of nature and the ownership of time; it is a family tree. The cursed "mine" of the fathers is reborn as the "mine" of the debased and degraded progeny. It is an image that connects the abiding tragedies of race and dynasty to the sin of ownership itself, which destroys the very things—and people, and nature—it seeks to possess. Patrimony becomes not an extension, but a declension: in a final irony, it is whittled down to the single tree that had been its symbol and summation. And yet, when I teach Faulkner, I must nevertheless always have in front of me my own set of family trees, marked "Compsons," "Gibsons," or "McCaslins." I tell my students about the great mystery game of Faulkner's fiction, how it teaches us to learn to piece together these trees, to fill them in, to discover their revelations, their harrowing content. But what if the tree itself, its form, is part of the crime? Are we so sure we see what Boon does not?

What makes family trees pernicious? First of all, they should probably be bushes, or perhaps webs—in which we are caught. But trees are what we usually get, and that should tell us something. Whether we imagine them stemming from a particular ancestor or leading to a particular descendent (us), they are always abridged—the putatively natural tree shape is of our own making. We imagine that trees make lineages traceable, transparent, and trackable—but they also tell the story of a past figured as *ours*. None of this is innocent. Indeed, the kinds of familial bonds drawn in actual, professional genealogies are often, at best, suspect. As any reader of Faulkner knows, the issues come thick and fast: incomplete records, naming mistakes, hidden paternities. If these problems are considered across several generations, they can quickly render the kinds of genetic claims we make on the past highly dubious, if not preposterous. How much do you really know about your sixteen great-great-grandparents? Does your irascibility—or your race—really come from one of them? When we add into the mix that historical records are irretrievably biased (the records of slaveowners will always exceed and erase those of slaves), we start getting into politically murky territory, as well—yet another problem familiar in Yoknapatawpha. Nobody's shadow family from slavery times shows up on ancestry websites—not even Faulkner's. I do not have a family tree for Joe Christmas in my lecture notes.

And yet Faulkner returns us, again and again, to family trees. Indeed, he keeps enlisting us in filling them in. I suspect some irony here. What if he is trying to tell us something, not just about the shocking family trees of the Sutpens and McCaslins, but also about the idea of genealogy itself? What if what needs reconsidering is not just the pasts of these families, but also the way that we tend to view the past in familial terms?

For all that we recognize Faulkner as a great writer of southern families, we have not always attended to a structuring contradiction in his fiction: even as he forces us to become genealogists to read him, the genealogies we learn to follow always fail. Each author, of course, must create his own readers—and few change us more than Faulkner. Yet even as we learn to reconstruct his family trees, we discover their rotten roots, and the human manure in which they have thrived and swollen, as they break under their own weight. It is as if he meant to set us against ourselves; to make us learn to trace bloodlines into the past knowing full well his final purpose was to force us to see the folly, and indeed, the terror of the bloodline in all its pernicious extent. Yoknapatawpha, finally, becomes a kind of genealogy of genealogy, and we are left with the paralyzing realization that the horror of it all lies not only in the origins we uncover but in the very ways we have come to think about origins—and therefore about ourselves.

For my title I have stolen from Michael Rogin's book on Herman Melville the phrase he stole from Judith Shklar—"subversive genealogy"—in order to emphasize her point that all genealogies begin with a crime.[2] Genealogy, for Shklar, depends on the idea of the bloodline cutting through the fog of history: a hereditary principle that justifies power and explains us to ourselves. It involves claims of evidence, precedence, and authority—a recognition of change but also an insistence on constancy and belonging. Shklar's contention is as simple as it is unsettling: she argues that genealogies, in the political arena originally a form of dynastic claiming that was intended to imbue power with legitimacy through descent, actually, almost necessarily, have the opposite effect. They subvert themselves, revealing through their backwards tracings not the organic legitimacy of bloodline descent but instead the brutal origins and fictive pedigrees of the ruling class.[3] I want to emphasize two aspects of this provocative thesis. First, that genealogy's own origins are dynastic and aristocratic; in important senses, it is synonymous with patrimony.[4] Given the theoretical and political uses to which genealogical critique has been put over last several decades, this is a problem.[5] And second, that actually undertaken genealogies are ironically self-subverting: they reveal not only the brutality behind legitimacy but its arbitrariness.

Subversive genealogies are, I want to contend, one of the defining tropes of Yoknapatawpha. As readers, following along with Faulkner's protagonists, we turn to genealogy to discover some hidden truth in their family lines, and yet what we find are outrages and, perhaps worse, fictions. For example, in *Go Down, Moses*, we join in Ike's investigation of his family's past, most famously through our gradual realization—parallel to his own—of the miscegenation and incest committed by his grandfather Carothers McCaslin as recorded in the ledgers Ike finds in the plantation commissary. But Noel Polk and Richard Godden have pointed out the relatively scant critical attention paid to the Percival Brownlee episode that Ike finds in those same ledgers.[6] Their audacious explanation—that Ike's cathexis to his grandfather's sins is a result of his repression of his homosexual father's incestuous relationship with his uncle and miscegenous relationship with the slave Brownlee—is not ultimately convincing, but their painstaking rereading of one of the key moments of the text has the effect of unsettling the novel as a whole: the erstwhile historical truth at the core of the text, the concrete primary document, the very records on which any genealogy must be based, is constitutionally incomplete. The ledger must always remain, in part, illegible. Ledgers record not only credits, but debits, too.

The next step requires a little game. Which Faulkner text is this?

A young man of not exactly royal birth but with royal ambitions nonetheless appears suddenly in north Mississippi following seven sketchy years in New Orleans. There are scurrilous rumors of scandal and crime, of mixed-race brides and furious family members and gunplay. He arrives with a group of slaves, a Frenchman, and a grim plan. He tries to jumpstart a new dynasty by any means necessary, including both outright violence and the brutal disowning of his own mixed-race son. And yet his dark house will turn out to be cursed from the start—or so we are told. Because we learn his story not firsthand or even exactly secondhand, but through a kind of compound narration that is not just unreliable but in fact casts doubt on the entire enterprise of reliability itself, like a historiographic version of the children's game of telephone.

I am not describing Thomas Sutpen from *Absalom, Absalom!* Or, rather, I am not describing only Thomas Sutpen. The story is actually Ikkemotubbe's. More precisely, it is the story of how Ikkemotubbe became l'Homme and then Doom, the Indian chief who eventually sells the land that will make up the holdings of Yoknapatawpha's white dynasties, so that his names themselves turn out to be a kind of subversive genealogy-in-miniature. Faulkner tells this story more than once and never in quite the same way: in "The Old People" in *Go Down, Moses* (159-61), in the "Compson Appendix" to *The Sound and the Fury*, originally published in *The Portable Faulkner*, and in *Requiem for a Nun*.[7] But the story also appears in a series of complex short stories, two from over a decade before *Go Down, Moses*—"Red Leaves" and "A Justice"—and one written just afterwards, "A Courtship."[8] The chronology here is important, because these Indian texts would seem to bookend some of Faulkner's greatest work on race, time, and history between 1930 and 1948. And yet white characters are peripheral, because, fascinatingly, these texts are set during a time before white people have fully taken over.

Faulkner's representation of Mississippi Indians is vexed, at best. The laconic "yaos" ("Red Leaves," 313), the squatting figures repeating what sometimes sounds like dialogue lifted from Western films—it can all be hard to stomach. Accordingly, critical opinion has been divided into three occasionally overlapping schools: first, those who see Faulkner's Indians as entirely made up; second, those who think Faulkner deals in racist stereotypes; and third, those who argue that his Indians are either more historical or more complex than they might seem. In that order, here are a few representative examples: Elmo Howell argues that Faulkner's Indians are "pure fantasy" and that, "with his aversion to research, Faulkner makes no pretensions to accuracy in his treatment of Indian life."[9] Robbie Ethridge argues that Faulkner abides by the racist assumption that Indigenous people are essentially part of the natural world.[10] However, Patricia Galloway has offered a more measured evaluation—for her, these stories are not quite so ahistorical as they might at first seem.[11] Galloway, while granting the problems in Faulkner's representation of Indigenous history, nevertheless argues Faulkner has, as usual, done more research than he lets on. There is more going on here than might be apparent at first, and these stories bear important connections with Faulkner's more famous novels.

One such hidden aspect is that this cycle is about the origins of genealogy in Yoknapatawpha, the immediate prehistory of the white and Black family histories that suffuse *Absalom, Absalom!* and *Go Down, Moses*. These stories tell of how patrimony (like a forward-looking genealogy-in-the-present) came to Yoknapatawpha before the white families themselves did. These stories therefore become a sort of experimental control group; they allow us to examine some of the *form* of genealogy divorced, so to speak, from the more familiar *content* of the "white" houses of Yoknapatawpha. There is nothing nostalgic or close to nature about this version of Indian land becoming the South. Doom seizes power ruthlessly, imports European-American notions of gender and the ownership of land and people to Yoknapatawpha, and even kills puppies. He also, at least in the version of the story we get in "A Justice," kills his uncle and nephew—the classic dynastic atrocity. Yoknapatawpha begins with murder.

Yet it is not so simple as tracing the lines back to the primal crimes, because Doom's family tree is sketchy, or even variable. Faulkner seems to change his mind between texts. Not only do Doom's offspring change between "Red Leaves" and "A Justice," but in "The Old People" and "A Courtship," Faulkner moves Issetibbeha (who was originally Doom's son) to the other side of the family and back two generations, so that he becomes Doom's uncle. This, I want to suggest, is a purposeful sketchiness. When Faulkner plays fast and loose with dynastic practices, character genealogies, even historical plausibility, it can seem blasé, sloppy, or even colonial, but the effect is also to lend a certain opacity—and even contingency—to the past. The contrast with the (generally) watertight genealogy of the Compson family is palpable and reflects a changing attitude toward family history in Faulkner's fiction; this uncertainty had already become overpowering with the Sutpen past, and flagrant with the Snopes one. At a more local level, working within the sketchiness of Doom's family tree also makes us work to try to explain it, an errand which, as usual with Faulkner, itself points us toward certain intertextual themes, just one of which I want to explore here.

We also get in these stories Sam Fathers, who is crucial. "A Justice" pairs Doom's coup d'état with a paternity plot. Here Doom rules on the rival claims of two different men on an unnamed enslaved Black woman: her husband, an enslaved Black man, and her lover, the Indian Craw-ford, whom Sam believes to be his real father—he calls him "pappy" (345). At first blush, then, the origin story we get in "A Justice" can seem merely humorous. The Jerry Springer moment is when the Black husband becomes enraged when his supposed child (Sam Fathers) comes out mixed-race; he knows immediately that Craw-ford must be the real father. The titular "justice," then, is Doom's ruling: Craw-ford must build a tall fence around the Black man's cabin and hereafter respect the latter's "melon patch" (357). But as Faulkner remarked at Virginia, the humor of these Indian stories is a thin surface; they are really quite ominous.[12] For this is actually a political story, and the enclosure of land, we should note, is here coterminous with the enclosure of race and the bloodline.

Here is where things get complicated: in "The Old People" in *Go Down, Moses*, when Sam himself tells the story to Ike, the genealogy appears to have changed: now Sam is Doom's son. The later text is unambiguous about this: "Doom pronounced a marriage between the pregnant quadroon and one of the slave men which he had just inherited . . . and two years later sold the man and woman and the child who was his own son to his white neighbor, Carothers McCaslin" (160).[13] Now perhaps this is just Faulkner revising—or forgetting. However, another explanation is worth considering. In "A Justice," Doom's immediate reaction to hearing the news of Sam's birth is "I thought it was about that time" (357); he seems to know when this child would be born. It is at least plausible, then, that the child was always his from the start, and that he is using both Craw-ford and the unnamed enslaved husband to launder this paternity because he knows full well that he will need a son untainted by Black blood in order to carry on his dynasty. (The prospective bloodline matters because Doom's postcoup dynasty will adhere not to matrilineal and ambiguously racialized Chickasaw practices, but instead to the patrilineal and racialized order of what is becoming Mississippi.) Such an explanation would both bring the stories in line with *Go Down, Moses* in regard to Sam's paternity and help line up the texts thematically.[14] That is, Faulkner had already conceived of the hidden birth and dynastic abjuring of mixed-race children—central plot points in both *Absalom, Absalom!* and *Go Down, Moses*—as early as 1930. These genealogies were subversive from the start. In *Go Down, Moses*, Sam tells Ike his real name is "Had-Two-Fathers," but it is shortened to the less precise plural "Fathers" (160)—perhaps a wink from Faulkner at this complex patrimony, or indeed, from Doom himself, who in "A Justice" names the child (358). It is a cruel thought: when Doom says to Sam's Black adoptive Father, "You should be proud of a fine yellow man like this" (357), it is not the last bittersweet moment before racialism reaches this society but really the opposite: Doom cleverly deceives everyone so that, eventually, he can sell his own son into slavery. If that does not sound like Sutpen, I do not know what does. But maybe it would be better to say Sutpen will one day turn out a lot like Doom.

In *Faulkner, Mississippi*, the Martinican author and critic Éduoard Glissant has also contended that Ikkemotubbe was always Sam Father's father.[15] Glissant understands the intertextual episode through the familiar Francophone trope of the *"mise en abyme,"* and he argues that, in "A Justice," Doom's secret "victory," in fact, "really meant nothing to him" (76). On this account, patrimony itself, with its infinite false copies of the father, becomes a kind of abyss. For Glissant, Faulkner's form is shot through with this sense of irresolution, with "opacity" (65), "deferral" (20), and "vertigo" (139); it is a style of writing that never reveals what it suggests, that arrives at no final truth, realization, or origin, an "epic literature for which no 'resolution' could be conceived" (99). This understanding of Faulknerian poetics as implicitly poststructuralist, in turn, implies a postcolonial politics as well: Glissant situates Faulkner in the Caribbean world, emphasizing the "composite" (that is, mixed or hybrid) nature of New World cultures that resist the hierarchical and genetic notions of metaphysical truth Glissant associates with the European metropole (115). By interpreting Faulkner's fiction as inherently subversive of the origin narratives that sustain imperial meaning making, Glissant suggests fascinating directions for antigenealogical critique. "Faulkner writes in rhizomes," argues Glissant (177). These formal iterations of the horizontal networks of meaning that Deleuze and Guattari call "antigenealogies,"[16] plural antitheses to the unitary and vertical paradigm of trees and roots, become vectors for the potentially transnational and transracial politics Glissant finds in Yoknapatawpha.

Yet for all of the vital import of these ideas, I am not sure that Faulkner actually *is* opaque in the way Glissant wants him to be, nor am I sure that Faulkner lets us escape so easily into a rhizomatic Caribbean. For one of the ironies of Faulkner's families—given the notorious difficulty of his writing—is that we *do* tend to get a sense of their sordid geneses. There is no infinite deferral in what Ike finds in the ledgers, and while we cannot know for certain exactly what Doom or Sutpen did—mired as we are in layers of convoluted mediation—what we come to suspect qualifies as more than just a *mise en abyme*. In fact, these novels are indictments. And what they indict is not just the ancestral crimes themselves but the very regime in whose name the crimes were committed—a regime, we begin to suspect, that still reigns in us.

This is why, if you do enough genealogizing in Faulkner, you will always find both outrage and fiction. You will unearth dynasties that rend the reader in two directions: revealing illegitimacy even as they cruelly insist on inheritance and involvement, suggesting genealogies of genealogy that penetrate into the self. What we see in declension in "The Bear" and in microcosm in "A Justice" is also the pattern we see across the "Dark House" novels of the 1930s and early 1940s, which are filled with tropes of subversive genealogy—rotting or burning houses, castration, suicide, patricide, degeneration, miscegenation, racial passing, and uncontrollable female sexuality (even Caddy in the tree in *The Sound and the Fury*—that is a family tree, too).[17] All represent threats to the hereditary principle.[18] And yet all are also framed by inescapability—the sense that genealogy, though subverted, nevertheless suffuses how we see the past.

I do not mean to deem this pattern universal, to offer up the shape of these doomed dynasties as the synchronic or natural course of all genealogy. Instead, I mean to offer a particular historical conjecture stemming from the *arriviste* nature of would-be planter dynasties in antebellum Mississippi: because Faulkner's doomed scions can trace bloodlines to their sordid beginnings in the space of a few generations, we can get from their stories a sort of compound image of the shape that genealogy took in the nineteenth- and twentieth-century South.

And yet, if subversive genealogy were limited to the grotesque vestiges of the planter class in the Deep South in the decades following the Civil War, it would be self-limiting and so ultimately of limited importance. After all, even in Yoknapatawpha, the great families are eclipsed by the profligate and vulgar Snopeses, an irony Faulkner plays with for hundreds of pages with abundant relish. *The Hamlet* begins with the image of a ruined plantation house, built by the Frenchman (hence Frenchman's Bend) who might not have even been French and whom nobody remembers—an explicitly antidynastic image in which the literal name of the father is lost.[19] But Faulkner returns again to genealogy in *Go Down, Moses*, perhaps in his fullest treatment of the theme, just two years after *The Hamlet*. He will not let us off so easily, and the problem of genealogy turns out to be very much not self-limiting. People have thought about the past in family terms for a very long time; we can hardly just cut ourselves out, even if we would like to, as both Quentin Compson and Ike find out to their dismay.

Furthermore, Faulkner traps *us* in his family trees; he trees us, just like Boon's squirrels. We recognize that we have become (or perhaps already were) genealogical *readers*. There is then this double irony in Faulkner's families: the genealogies we trace subvert themselves, and yet in the very act of tracing them we come to recognize and participate in their further extension. His fiction therefore forces us to confront just how invested we remain in bloodlines, even as we struggle against them in our work on race, gender, sexuality, or the environment. Because here is the most subversive question of all: if we *think* in bloodlines, can we ever get out? It is almost as if we cannot imagine a past not shaped by descent and inheritance. Could we ever approach an *un*familiar past? Could we ever recover its radical alterity? Could we recover not only our lost ancestors but those hazy generations who did not lead to us at all?[20] I often fixate on what Ike inherits from Sam as some alternative legacy, some vestigial past made of radical difference, something before race or some ancient ecology before patriarchy even—a distaff genealogy, "an inheritance incorruptible, and undefiled, and that fadeth not away."[21] But then I remember that Ike sounds a lot like Ikkemotubbe. Given his painful origins, are we so sure Sam Fathers has passed on something good? Faulkner's fiction helps us to see the manmade shape of a past we so often assume to be natural, but he leaves us with the haunting suspicion that we are ourselves made of such brutal fictions.

What we must confront is how the constitutively patriarchal, dynastic, and racialist ideas that inhere in genealogy have persisted into the ways we still think about the past. In our favored metaphor of the family tree (or in the related trope of roots), we still imagine a past shaped by lines of ownership, power, and belonging, and there is perhaps no better place to see the problems inherent in that paradigm than in Faulkner's representation of the US South. We fall into a genealogical fallacy: we run the lines we trace to the past through the needs of present-day politics, so that the political lineages we seek in historical interpretation—almost always lineages of resistance, subversion, and solidarity figured in terms of content—become paradoxically dynastic and patriarchal in terms of form. The fallacy ultimately stems from the idea that what matters most about the past are the ways it led to us. We forget that genealogy is always also about disclaiming pasts we want to disown, and in ignoring such erasures we come to retain a certain vicious sense of the self-evidence of what survives to be remembered—a literal bloodline in places like Mississippi. We feel deeply that the sine qua non of history is a family relation, structured by continuity, inheritance, and transmission. What if what we really need is the opposite? Not descent, but difference. Could we find a way to see the past without claiming it as ours?

NOTES

1. William Faulkner, *Go Down, Moses*, rev. ed. (1942; repr., New York: Vintage International, 1990), 315. Hereafter cited parenthetically.

2. Michael Paul Rogin, *Subversive Genealogy: The Politics and Art of Herman Melville* (1979; repr., Berkeley: University of California Press, 1985); Judith Shklar, "Subversive Genealogies," *Daedalus* 101, no. 1 (1972): 129-54.

3. At the core of Shklar's argument is a powerful revision of how we think about family relationships in Western political culture: in emphasizing Hesiod's pessimistic portrait of Zeus over the Adamic myth, she explores the possibility of an original sin that inheres not in the son, but in the father, replacing the Fall with the idea that the original order is itself tainted with the crimes undertaken to establish it. Sin, in short, is located in patrimony itself—and it is that sin we pass on.

4. George Handley, in *Postslavery Literatures of the Americas: Family Portraits in Black and White* (Charlottesville: University of Virginia Press, 2000), explores genealogy as a key aspect of the ideology of planter classes in the Americas, a transnational reading that also brings into focus the imperial entanglements of genealogy in American literatures.

5. I have in mind here the genealogical method of Friedrich Nietzsche and especially Michel Foucault, whose replacement of history with genealogy set the terms for the widely

influential poststructuralist break with ideas of transcendental truth in everything from madness to sexuality to gender. This break inspired the New Historicism in American literary criticism, whose method, largely still regnant if usually unnamed, seeks in literary history resistances and subversions to forms of political power that pretend to be natural or metaphysical, a critical task undertaken in the retrospective interest of contemporary political struggles. There is not room here for an extended discussion of theory, but I do mean to ask if genealogical critique itself, as a form, might retain aspects of the very patriarchal and racial power we often imagine it to resist or oppose.

6. Richard Godden and Noel Polk, "Reading the Ledgers," *Mississippi Quarterly* 55, no. 3 (2002): 301-59.

7. William Faulkner, *The Portable Faulkner*, ed. Malcolm Cowley (1946; repr., New York: Penguin, 2003), 258; and *Requiem for a Nun* (1951; repr. New York: Vintage, 1975), 185-87.

8. William Faulkner, "Red Leaves" (1930), "A Justice" (1931), and "A Courtship" (1948), all in *Collected Stories* (1950; repr., New York: Vintage, 1977), respectively 313-41, 343-60, and 361-80. Hereafter cited parenthetically. "A Courtship" was written in 1942, shortly after the publication of *Go Down, Moses*. See Theresa M. Towner and Stephen Railton, "A Courtship (Text Key 4674)," Digital Yoknapatawpha, University of Virginia, 2016. http://faulkner.drupal.shanti.virginia.edu/content/courtship. I have not included "Lo!" (originally published in 1934 and also included in *Collected Stories*) here because it does not involve Ikkemotubbe and his rise to power. The story does, however, give some evidence of Faulkner's sympathy towards Indians and provides another instance of the political complexities that he explored through his nominally humorous Indian stories.

9. Elmo Howell, "Faulkner and the Indians," *Georgia Review* 21, no. 3 (1967): 386-87. See also Lewis Dabney, *The Indians of Yoknapatawpha: A Study in Literature and History* (Baton Rouge: Louisiana State University Press, 1974) and Howard C. Horsford, "Faulkner's (Mostly) Unreal Indians in Early Mississippi History," *American Literature* 64 (June 1992): 311-30.

10. Robbie Ethridge, "Sam Fathers as Ecological Indian," in *Faulkner and the Native South: Faulkner and Yoknapatawpha, 2016*, ed. Annette Trefzer, Jay Watson, and James G. Thomas, Jr. (Jackson: University Press of Mississippi, 2016), 135-47.

11. Patricia Galloway, "The Construction of Faulkner's Indians," *Faulkner Journal* 18, no. 1-2 (Fall 2002-Spring 2003): 9-31. To give some examples of this surprising historicity, Galloway posits that the red moccasins from *Requiem for a Nun* actually *were* a noble signifier in Choctaw and Chickasaw cultures; several historical chiefs are identified by the name "Red Shoes" in texts that were available to Faulkner (23). Moreover, Issetibbeha was a historical figure; he is recorded in treaty documents as the last "King" of the Chickasaws (Galloway, 17). The historical succession was, indeed, matrilineal, but even here there is a strange accuracy: Ikkemotubbe, as the son of the sister of "The Man," *would* have been next in line to be "King" (Galloway, 17).

12. On May 2, 1958, Faulkner, answering a question about "Red Leaves," told a Virginia class that "the picture of—of those lazy people that didn't want to do that having to—to catch that Negro, to me, was funny. But the result, the purpose of it, was anything but funny." Stephen Railton, "Faulkner at Virginia," University of Virginia, 2019, https://faulkner.lib.virginia.edu/display/wfaudio26_2#wfaudio26_2.15, accessed May 25, 2020.

13. We have then two different versions of transmission: in "A Justice," Sam tells Quentin Compson the story as he heard it from Herman Basket. In "The Old People," however, the narrator paraphrases what Sam tells Ike.

14. There might be only one person in "A Justice" who already believes in the fictions of race and its potential threat to the line: Doom himself. For this is a political drama about the attempted foundation of a dynasty, although this dimension is obscured by the imagined Indian vernacular and its double narration through Herman Basket and Sam Fathers—itself

a hypothetical, a native-infused Mississippi vernacular that must have existed, though whether it looked and sounded like this is unknowable. I do not think this second point is incidental: Faulkner's reliance on the trope of the vanishing Indian has been rightly criticized by Ethridge and others, but here we should recognize that such accounts of disappearance are, necessarily, the other side of the genealogical coin. Genealogy does not merely trace or recover; it erases, too.

15. Édouard Glissant, *Faulkner, Mississippi*, trans. Barbara Lewis and Thomas Spear (Chicago: University of Chicago Press, 1996), 75–80. Hereafter cited parenthetically.

16. Gilles Deleuze and Félix Guattari, *A Thousand Plateaus*, trans. Brian Massumi (Minneapolis: University of Minnesota Press, 1987), 11.

17. William Faulkner, *The Sound and the Fury*, rev. ed. (1929; repr., New York: Vintage, 1990), 39.

18. Incidentally, incest in and of itself does *not* represent such a threat, because it involves a consolidation of dynastic blood.

19. William Faulkner, *The Hamlet*, rev. ed. (New York: Vintage International, 1991), 3

20. Cf. David Lloyd, "Specters of Irish Hunger," *Representations* 92, no. 1 (Fall 2005): 152–85.

21. 1 Peter 1:4 (Authorized Version).

Beasts in the Mississippi Jungle

Ike McCaslin's Queer Animal Kinship

JOHN N. DUVALL

> *There was a man and a dog too this time. Two beasts, counting Old Ben, the bear, and two men, counting Boon Hogganbeck, in whom some of the same blood ran which ran in Sam Fathers, even though Boon's was a plebeian strain of it and only Sam and Old Ben and the mongrel Lion were taintless and incorruptible.*
> —WILLIAM FAULKNER, "The Bear"

What does Ike McCaslin know with more certainty than anything in the world? He is positive that his grandfather was a very bad man. Reading the cryptic McCaslin family ledgers, Ike decides that Old Carothers committed incestuous miscegenation. Ike imagines in great detail what led to his grandfather's sexual abuse of his Black daughter, Thomasina, and his subsequent failure to acknowledge his Black son, Terrel. Clearly, then, Ike also knows he shares a blood heritage with former McCaslin slaves. His grandfather's sexual misdeeds cause Ike to believe his male bloodline is corrupt. As a result, he chooses to identify with an alternative father figure, Sam Fathers, who is racially other and celibate. Claiming this racially other father figure allows Ike to repudiate his descent from someone who failed to acknowledge his Black children in favor of being descended, figuratively at least, from someone who was similarly denied acknowledgement: because he was part Black, Sam was sold to the McCaslin family by his father, the Chickasaw chief Ikkemotubbe. Having at age sixteen recognized his kinship with African Americans and chosen a former McCaslin slave as his spiritual father, Ike goes on to defy a southern racial prohibition by proudly claiming and openly socializing with his Black relatives.

Wait, what? My opening paragraph was giving a fairly straightforward account of Ike's narrative trajectory in *Go Down, Moses*, one that I hope most readers would find recognizable, until I got to the final sentence, which suddenly veered off into crazy talk. Clearly, my last characterization of Ike's response to his knowledge of the McCaslin shadow family and his relation to Sam Fathers bears no relation to the book Faulkner published in 1942. Ike's thinking about kinship relations that cross the color line, rather than leading him to acknowledge Black family members, makes him a kind of limit case of the fetishization of whiteness.

Indeed, whiteness's relationship to the open secret that was the mixture of the races in Faulkner's South can be thought of as a fetish, if we recall Slavoj Žižek's articulation of the formula of the fetish: "I know very well, but still . . ."[1] This formula underscores the disconnect between what one knows (one isn't stupid, after all) and how the fetish overwhelms knowing and shapes both the imaginary and one's relation to the social real. Žižek reminds us of the Freudian fetish: "I know very well that Mother has not got a phallus, but still . . . [I believe she does]." Žižek then turns to the Marxian fetish: "I know very well that money is just a commodity, but still . . . [it is as if it were made of a special substance over which time has no power]." In the context of racial and familial relations for a white southerner of Faulkner's time, a racial fetish might be articulated as follows: I know very well that I share a blood heritage with these particular Black people, but still . . . [they are not my kin]. Even more than "they are not my kin," we might add the following: but still . . . [my whiteness is contingent on not acknowledging my Black relatives].

Because of the South's fetishization of whiteness, rather than embrace his Black kin, Ike in his old age ends up privileging an impossible all-male kinship, that of the hunting camp. In "Delta Autumn," while lying in his tent on the first night of the annual hunt, Ike thinks of his issueless marriage and his house in Jefferson:

> it was still kept for him by his dead wife's widowed niece and her children and he was comfortable in it, his wants and needs and even the small trying harmless crochets of an old man *looked after by blood.* . . . But he spent the time within those walls waiting for November, because even this tent with its muddy floor and the bed which was not wide enough nor soft enough nor even warm enough, was his home and *these men*, some of whom he only saw during these two November weeks and not one of whom even bore any name he used to know—De Spain and Compson and Ewell and Hogganbeck—*were more his kin than any.*[2]

This nonbiological homosocial kinship appears to devalue blood as the basis of understanding family. But in fact, this male kinship is based on a logic of "loving the life [one] spills" (175) that informs the bloody business of hunting. This logic is central to Ike's fantasy of Indianness, which maintains that before Ikkemotubbe, who became corrupted by white ideas that the land and people could be property, the Chickasaws practiced a kind of primitive communism in which the hunting grounds were a commons used by all. That's why Ike sees this younger generation of hunters as his kin: because, to the extent that he can imagine them partaking in the true spirit of the hunt, they may all be white, but they've transcended race and gone native, or Native American, if only for a couple of weeks each fall.

When Ike reaches his majority and refuses his patrimony, the property that is his legal inheritance, he simultaneously disavows his McCaslin identity; nevertheless, he tries to preserve a normative white identity through the racial fantasy of Sam Father's Indianness. Ike's construction of Sam Fathers as the quintessential Indian is no mean feat because to the larger southern community, Sam is no Indian. He wears the clothes of a Black man; he consorts with other Blacks, he goes to the Black church; and he is, after all, part Black, which by the South's one-drop rule means that he is one thing and one thing only—an embodiment of the Negro. But Ike needs to bracket Sam's Black racial identity and foreground Sam's Indianness as a bulwark against the sexual violations he discovers in the plantation ledgers if he is to construct a usable alternative genealogy.

Indeed, Ike's fantasy of Sam's Indianness creates not one but two alternative genealogies—Native American and animal.[3] Such alternative forms of genealogy allow Ike to fashion himself as Indian and animal but still white, much like Boon Hogganbeck, who has Chickasaw blood (and is certainly figured as an animal) yet retains his whiteness. Ike would like to keep human-animal kinship safely in the realm of the spiritual, but Faulkner's novel insists on materializing the interspecies relationship, most particularly in what might be the most marginal couple in all of Faulkner—Lion and Boon.[4] I want to use Lion and Boon's coupling to create a different purchase on Ike's polymorphous senses of kinship, senses that lead him ultimately to locate his truest idea of family outside of human sexual reproduction. Ike wishes to practice safe homosociality (safe because it is asexual), but this kinship is always shadowed by recurring intimations of same-sex desire.

In what follows, I draw on the work of Michael Lundblad, whose book *The Birth of a Jungle: Animality in Progressive-Era US Literature and Culture* looks at the emergence of what he identifies as a Darwinist-Freudian cultural synthesis that, in the early twentieth century, constructs the epistemology of the jungle, one that is contemporaneous with what Eve Kosofsky Sedgwick has identified as the epistemology of the closet. Both

Darwin and Freud limit the possibilities of human exceptionalism by placing the human within the realm of the animal. Such a move means that the relation of the human animal to the violent and instinctual realm of the jungle becomes a key cultural issue, and we might note in passing that in several places in *Go Down, Moses*, Faulkner identifies the big woods in which the white hunters test themselves and their dogs as a jungle.[5] From Darwin comes the notion that the unself-conscious instinctual behavior of nonhuman animals strives to perpetuate their species: "Fight for your mate and pass on your genes."[6] Freud subsequently links human instinct "with human sexuality in a broader cultural sense."[7] Despite his position that homosexuality wasn't necessarily pathological, Freud, for Lundblad, participates in two assumptions about animality that are central to the "discourse of the jungle: First, animals are instinctively heterosexual; and second, representations of animals are legible signifiers of human sexuality."[8] (On this second matter, think no further than Freud's Wolf-Man and Rat-Man case studies.) *Go Down, Moses*, however, calls into question even as it invokes jungle law and violent animal instinct. Exploring animality in *Go Down, Moses* raises a series of interrelated issues involving race, sexuality, and the nature of southern kinship.[9]

The racism of the South that helped shape Faulkner's world picture when the novelist was coming of age needs to be mapped onto the larger field of racialized discourse in the United States during the same period that Darwin and Freud were being popularized. The first two decades of the twentieth century saw a rapidly changing relationship between the animal and the human. Drawing on shared claims in Darwin's *Descent of Man* and Freud's *Totem and Taboo*, Lundblad argues that, precisely because lower orders of animals evolved into the human prior to humanity's separation into distinct races, it became easier for whites (in order to retain a belief in their racial supremacy) to admit their evolutionary kinship to animals than to see themselves as related to supposedly savage races. In other words, for whites, it was more excusable in the heat of passion to act on "natural" (read "violent") animal instincts than to act with the cruelty of the racially other jungle savage, who had yet to become civilized enough to repress violent impulses.[10] McCaslin Edmonds essentially draws on the latter half of this formulation when he tries to explain to a young Ike the nature of Sam Fathers: "When he was born, all his blood on both sides, except the little white part, knew things that had been tamed out of our blood so long ago that we have not only forgotten them, we have to live together in herds to protect ourselves from our own sources" (161). Although McCaslin's words animalize white society (identifying it as a herd) and seem to romanticize Sam's untamed blood knowledge, ultimately they underscore the key claim of the Freud-Darwin synthesis in the popular imagination: savagery mediates animality and humanity, even as it bolsters whiteness as the civilized master race. By this logic, animals are instinctively violent; Blacks are also instinctively violent but have a greater intelligence that enables savage violence; and whites alone have transcended savagery, even if they retain animal instinct. This mediation is why Ike needs Sam (and why he needs Sam to be Indian, not African American). For Ike, the fantasy of Indian-inspired animal kinship is preferable, finally, to acknowledging his actual blood kinship with African Americans. But at the same time, animal kinship more broadly construed in *Go Down, Moses* troubles Ike's sense of McCaslin heteronormativity. The beasts in the Mississippi jungle, it seems, simply won't conform to an instinctive heterosexuality. And they're not just gender fluid; they're well-nigh anatomical shape-shifters.

A key step in the long process of becoming Sam's son occurs when the twelve-year-old Ike kills his first buck, a moment that serves as a perverse commentary on Ab Snopes's sense of the centrality of blood kinship in "Barn Burning" and the lesson he imparts to his son Sarty: "You got to learn to stick to your own blood or you ain't going to have any blood to stick to you."[11] *Go Down, Moses*, after all, literalizes Abner's metaphor of blood: after shooting his first buck, Ike slits the deer's throat with Sam's knife (sometimes a knife is just a knife; we're not going to go there, at least not just yet). What happens then? "Sam stooped and dipped his hands in the hot smoking blood and wiped them back and forth across the boy's face" (156). But if animal blood quite literally sticks to Ike, he then turns animal blood back into the blood of kinship. In "Delta Autumn," Ike thinks about killing his first deer and the way Sam knew "the buck would pass exactly there because there was something running in Sam Fathers' veins which ran in the veins of the buck too" (334). Ike appears to be extrapolating this impossible blood kinship between animal and human from the moment he takes to be Sam's showing him the spirit of the Great Buck in "The Old People." Sam's address to the spirit buck, "Oleh, Chief. . . . Grandfather" (177), claims the familial both of tribe and kinship.

While killing a buck represents a step toward Ike's becoming Sam's son, the hunt for and death of Old Ben moves this process much closer to completion. But this literal hunt is tied to a textual hunt, Ike's reading of the ledgers in which he fixes the sexual crimes of his grandfather. These two hunts occur in such close temporal proximity that they are essentially one intertwined event, something signaled by the formal placement of Ike's reading of the ledgers within "The Bear." There is a key difference, however, between Ike's reading the signs of nature and those of the ledgers. Throughout his life, Ike keeps open the possibilities of the hunt in the big woods as a kind of Book of Nature, a space that can teach white men something about their Indian-animal spiritual genealogy if only they learn to read the multivalent signifiers; however, he turns the ledgers and their signifiers into a sealed book of revelation. The reason, I believe, that Ike must refuse ever to look at the ledgers again (once he has decided on their meaning) is that if he continued to try to read between the lines of the cryptic communication between Buck and Buddy, he might find that his sense of the manly hunt and of jungle law would implode.

Here I want to follow Richard Godden and Noel Polk in their reading that challenges Ike's reading of the McCaslin ledgers. Through intense close reading of a select few entries, Ike sees only the tragedy of unchecked male heterosexual desire in his grandfather's transgressions; however, he registers but fails to interrogate several other entries that preface those about his grandfather, Eunice, and Thomasina. These largely unexamined entries, focusing on Buck's purchase of Percival Brownlee, an apparently worthless slave, are of interest because we see such a tiny fraction of the totality of the ledgers. What Godden and Polk suggest is history's farcical repetition of a very southern tragedy of sexual exploitation but this time embodied through male homosexual desire: Buck and Buddy's parodic inversion of the plantation hierarchy (housing their slaves in the unfinished mansion and living themselves in a small one-room cabin that they built without the labor of enslaved people) hints at another possible inversion, a homosexual relationship that turns into a love triangle and a breach of their relationship when Buck buys the effeminate, light-skinned Brownlee for perhaps the same reason Old Carothers purchased Eunice—for his sexual pleasure.[12] This brief summary doesn't do justice to Godden and Polk's long and complex argument, in which they are careful to point out that "any inference of homosexual incest" between Buck and Buddy "remains no more and no less than inferential."[13] Still, with that caveat, they proceed with their hermeneutic of suspicion to read the cryptic written exchanges between the twin brothers regarding Brownlee as evidence of something close to a lovers' quarrel. But interracial same-sex sexual exploitation is a possibility Ike forecloses when he vows never to look at the ledgers again. And a good thing he doesn't look again, because if he did, he might have to do so through the lens of the savage world of the Mississippi jungle, an animal world that, in its refusal to conform to instinctive heterosexuality, could complicate his tragedy of incestuous miscegenation. Let me hasten to acknowledge the problematic tendency of readings such as Godden and Polk's that take an absence of sexuality (here Buck and Buddy's many long years of bachelorhood) as "'evidence' of same-sex sexuality."[14] And so as not simply to point a finger at Godden and Polk, let me also admit my own implication in an arguably paranoid reading strategy. I am trying to understand Ike's sense of kinship relationally through epistemologies of the jungle, the closet, and miscegenation. If the epistemology of the closet is the epistemology of the open secret, what other open secrets are incompletely covered over in Ike's construction of alternative Indian and animal kinship?[15]

The hunt for Old Ben adds another layer to Ike's animal genealogy. This bear, Sam tells Ike, is "the head bear. He's the man" (190), which, as we know, links Ben to Ikkemotubbe, Sam's biological father, who was known as Doom, a corruption of the French "du homme" (loosely, "the man"). If the spirit buck is Sam's grandfather, the material (but anthropomorphized and mythologized) bear is Sam's father. The bear's masculinity and instinctive heterosexuality appear secure. But something odd happens to Old Ben in his relationship to Ike. The bear is not simply Ike's grandfather in some Indian-spirit animal genealogical line. Rather, in terms of Ike's education into the ways of the hunter, "The old male bear itself, so long unwifed and childless as to have become its own ungendered progenitor, was [Ike's] alma mater" (201-2). Although meditated through a third-person narrator, the narrative focalizes our perceptions here through Ike. Ike seems to read an animal sexuality that is nonheteronormative in its rejection of the instinctive desire to reproduce and that points us back to his father figure Sam Fathers. Like Sam, the bear has neither wife nor children. Both choose the nonheteronormative path of celibacy (and thus foreshadow Ike's own celibate future). Perhaps even what makes Old Ben taintless is that (in Ike's imagination, anyway) this bear does not have sex with female bears. The notion that the bear is its own "ungendered progenitor" pushes us toward androgyny, but the final figure suggests intersexuality (what Faulkner understood as hermaphroditism)—the bear as Ike's "alma mater." While the appearance of the Latin phrase would seem to suggest its figurative meaning—that the bear completes Ike's education as if the animal were the boy's college—earlier in the quoted sentence, the wilderness itself is identified as Ike's college. At the very least, then, the literal meaning of alma mater as "nurturing mother" or "nursing mother" comes into play. If this meaning obtains, the male bear becomes or is simultaneously a female (fore)bear. As Godden has elsewhere argued, if we recall Uncle Buck's accidentally entering the figurative bear's den that is the bedroom of Ike's future mother, Sophonsiba, then Ike's mother and Old Ben merge into "Sophonsib[e]a[r]."[16]

In order to kill Old Ben in a way that honors their code of hunting, Sam and Ike know they first have to find "the" dog (208). And the dog they find is at times described as the very figure of unself-conscious animal instinct and jungle law, possessing "the will and desire to endure beyond all imaginable limits of flesh in order to overtake and slay" (227). When General Compson hears that one of Major DeSpain's colts has been killed, he immediately says "It's a panther" (204), the same animal that earlier killed a doe and fawn: "the doe's throat torn out, and the beast had run down the helpless fawn and killed it too." From Ike's discussion with the men in the hunting camp in "Delta Autumn," we know that killing does and fawns is something a civilized human hunter should never do, but a disregard for a female and its offspring is excusable for the jungle beast.[17] Major DeSpain, however, knows that a mountain lion wouldn't have risked injury from the mare to kill the colt and assumes that it was Old Ben.[18] But when the hunters see the animal's tracks, the beast morphs again: "Good God, what a wolf!" (205). Panther-bear-wolf turns out, of course, to be a wild dog, one that Sam captures and ... enslaves? Is this word possible with the animal other?[19] A family trauma seems to be played out via this animal-human interaction. Sam imprisons and starves the dog to teach it that he is its master and that it is subject to his will. And Sam's will is harsh and perhaps even inhumane. In its passage from wild beast to hunting dog par excellence, this animal suffers horribly from Sam's starvation training technique. Christened "Lion" (perhaps a nod to the dog's being misidentified as a mountain lion, but more obviously the name of an animal indigenous to Africa), how could this dog with its "strange color like a blued gun-barrel" (206) not suggest the condition of slavery? Not a bluegum but a blue dog, and how did Lion get to be so black and blue?[20] It's not just because of the Airedale that is part of its genetics. Like *the* bear, Old Ben, *the* dog, Lion, participates in Sam Fathers's animal genealogy because through this dog, Sam, a former slave, effectively reenacts the central trauma of his relationship with his father. Doom fathers Sam, but then sells him, and Sam, like so many of Faulkner's wounded sons, repeats the insult. Having created Lion, Sam essentially gives away his animal son to Boon.[21]

Encountering Lion walking beside Sam is for Boon love at first sight, and not just puppy love: "Jesus. Jesus.—Will he let me touch him?" (211), Boon asks Sam. Donna Haraway opens her book *When Species Meet* with a question: "Whom and what do I touch when I touch my dog?"[22] This is a question we might modify for our purposes to "Whom and what does Boon touch when he touches Sam Fathers's dog?" Although an important question, Ike's role as focalizer constantly deflects our ability to answer it fully and asks us instead to respond to a very different question, one that forces us into Ike's symbolizing world of animal genealogy: "What does Ike think it means when Boon touches Lion?" Sam claims there is nothing but beast in Lion: "You can touch him. ... He dont care. He dont care about nothing or nobody" (211). But is that true? Is there only instinct in Lion or is there also response? Lion will not be denied his companionship with Boon, nor will Boon be denied Lion. There is mutual, interspecies pleasure in Boon's touching Lion. It is the most important relationship in Boon's life. After their final encounter with Old Ben, when both man and dog have been severely wounded, Boon insists that the doctor treat Lion's injuries first. Boon values Lion's life more than his own. But this until-death-do-us-part loving companionship is strangely gendered because of Ike's world picture that radically devalues female kinship and sees almost every relationship between men as a zero-sum game of masculinity: one male is more masculine than the other, leaving the other either implicitly or explicitly feminized. To Ike, Boon is less manly than Sam because Boon's Indianness comes through a female line of descent while Sam's aristocratic Indianness derives from the male line.[23] A similar dynamic holds true of Boon's relation to Lion. Ike watches the moment of first contact and his understanding of Boon's touching Lion shapes our understanding of these interspecies companions:

> Boon touched Lion's head and then knelt beside him, feeling the bones and muscles, the power. It was as if Lion were a woman—or perhaps Boon was the woman. That was more like it—the big, grave, sleepy-seeming dog . . . and the violent, insensitive, hard-faced man with his touch of remote Indian blood, and the mind almost of a child. (211)

One of these males must play the female role. What again was the final misrecognition of Lion's beastliness? The dog was identified as a wolf. If we recall George Chauncey on the making of the gay male world from the 1890s to the 1940s, a certain type of male sexual predator was known as a wolf. The wolf might have sex with a woman, or in the absence of women, the wolf would happily engage in homosex without any aspersions cast on his manhood because the wolf always assumed the "masculine" role.[24] OK, Boon, Lion—who do you think is hungry like the wolf? That question aside, let me be clear: I'm not claiming that Lion is doing Boon doggie style, but the act of sleeping together, as we have seen in Ike's postsexual marriage, is marked by the text as a form of blood kinship. Moreover, Lion and Boon's sleeping together is something that the white patriarch, Major de Spain, forbids—humorously, to be sure, and for a perfectly understandable reason: Boon's odor might interfere with Lion's ability to track Old Ben. But in the larger racial context of the novel, Boon and Lion's defiance of this prohibition (they continue sleeping together for the next two years) seems parodically to figure the often-violated prohibition against miscegenation.

Certainly, Boon and Lion's close companionship is something about which Ike obsesses, and his obsession constantly transforms an interspecies relationship into a function of the intrahuman:

> *I wonder what Sam thinks. He could have Lion with him, even if Boon is a white man. He could ask Major or McCaslin either. And more than that. It was Sam's hand that touched Lion first and Lion knows it.* Then he became a man and he knew that too. It had been all right. That was the way it should have been. Sam was the chief, the prince; Boon, the plebeian, was his huntsman. Boon should have nursed the dogs. (213)

Ike is able to contain what is troubling about the Boon-Lion relationship when he places it within the fantasy of Sam's aristocratic Indianness. At the same time, however, the trouble reemerges from its very containment. Boon nursing the dogs? Of course, his job was to nurse (in the sense of "to care for") the hunting dogs, including Lion. But if we recall the maternal meaning that resides in Old Ben as Ike's alma mater, then there's another meaning of "to nurse" that creates a vivid visceral image of Boon's relation to dogs that, once you visualize it, I don't think you'll be able to unsee it.

Any way you look at it, Boon is Lion's bitch.

Oddly, though, the more one looks at this relationship, the more difficult it is to maintain that it is completely interspecies, because in appearance and temperament, Boon and Lion are doubles. When Boon is first introduced as a foil to Sam Fathers's true Indianness, what is the central metaphor? "Boon was a mastiff, absolutely faithful" to Major de Spain and Cass Edmonds (164). If Boon is racially mixed, what is Lion? A mixed-breed dog, primarily mastiff and Airedale. Boon is a big man with a big head; Lion is a big dog with a big head. Boon has "little hard shoe-button eyes without depth or meanness or generosity or viciousness or gentleness or anything else" (218) and Ike notes that Lion's "yellow eyes" are "as depthless as Boon's, as free as Boon's of meanness or generosity or gentleness or viciousness" (227-28).[25] Well, I'll be dogged. The relationship between Boon and Lion: *Canis lupus familiaris*, indeed! They are male twins who sleep together. This intimate relationship helps us understand why Ike needs the ledgers to be a sealed book, its meaning clear and so heterosexually sure, because if Ike were ever to read his Book of Nature and the McCaslin ledgers intertextually, the sexuality of another set of twins—his father and his uncle, Buck and Buddy—might well become fodder for Ike's novelistic imagination that lovingly fleshes out the motives of his grandfather's unchecked heterosexual desire.

When the coupling of Lion and Boon turns into a male three-way with Old Ben, the (homo)eroticized scene of death becomes the *mise en abyme* that destabilizes Ike's understanding of his white, his Indian, and his animal blood, which in turn sheds light on his sense that his truest kinship lies within the male homosociality of the hunters.[26] Killing Ben almost seems like the primal scene of Ike's animal family romance. As Lion leaps at the bear,

> It *caught the dog in both arms, almost loverlike,* and *they both went down*. . . . [Ike] could see Lion still clinging to the bear's throat and *he saw the bear, half erect,* . . . *rising and rising as though it would never stop, stand erect* again and begin to rake at Lion's belly with its forepaws. Then Boon was running. The boy saw the gleam of the blade in his hand and watched him . . . fling himself astride the bear . . . , his legs locked around the bear's belly, his left arm under the bear's throat where Lion clung, and the glint of the *knife as it rose and fell*.
>
> It fell just once. For an instant they almost resembled a piece of statuary: the clinging dog, the bear, the man stride its back, working and probing the buried blade. Then *they went down*, pulled over backward by Boon's weight, Boon underneath. It was the bear's back which reappeared first but at once Boon was astride it again. . . . [T]hen the bear *surged erect* . . . (228, emphasis added)

Critics have certainly seen homoerotic figuration elsewhere in *Go Down, Moses*, but here? And yet Ben's loverlike embrace of Lion, Lion's passionately rough mouth on the bear's neck, the bear's standing figured as an erection (first half erect before rising to become fully erect), the repetition of "they went down" (when "to go down" had had its contemporary sexual connotation since the turn of the twentieth century), and Boon's thrusting penetrations of the bear with his knife, all work together to suggest a sexual subtext. Highlighting the sexualized language of this passage is really not that different than John T. Matthews's well-known and oft-cited essay on *Sanctuary* in which he reads the repetition of the phrase "standing erect" in reference to Judge Drake and his sons in the courtroom following Temple's testimony as a sign of transgressive incestuous desire that resides within the heteronormative family and as underscoring the way the moment is a kind of repetition of Temple's violation at the Old Frenchman place.[27] If this kind of figurative reading is available for positing transgressive heterosexual desire, why not for nonheteronormative desire as well, even if the agents are less recognizably family? But what exactly might be imaged forth in this all-male scene of multiple embraces and penetrations? It is Boon who kills the bear, but he doesn't do so as a true hunter would. After all, Boon simply can't appropriately handle the hunter's manly tool, a gun, and so is reduced to the much smaller tool of his knife (ok, so here maybe the knife is more than a knife). And given the outcome, apparently size doesn't matter.

To the extent that the twinned bedmates Lion and Boon stand in for the twins Buck and Buddy, is the bear a figure of Brownlee, with Boon as Buddy, the jealous and jilted plantation "wife"? Or, possibly the bear, if we accept Godden's Sophonsib[e]a[r] premise, stands in for the threat that Ike's mother represents to the woman-free bachelor bliss the twins enjoyed for thirty years, with Boon again suggesting Buddy but now the Buddy who rushes to the Beauchamp plantation to save his twin from succumbing to the female. Whether Black homosexual man or white heterosexual woman, the threat is the same—one male's loss of his twin to a sexual rival. Again, sealed ledgers mean that the possibility of alternative McCaslin sexuality remains illegible.

If we grant the possibility that McCaslin family matters are being mirrored in Old Ben's death, then it is a symbolic drama played in animal blackface. Old Ben is an American black bear. Lion's coloration is the blue-black of the Airedale. But what of Boon and his ostensible whiteness? We know he is as faithful as a dog and a "slave to all the appetites" (164). This seem to turn Boon into slave dog, a figure we might then place in the context of Ike's conversation with Cass Edmonds in which Ike renounces his patrimony. There's a moment when Ike argues for the superiority of Blacks over whites, extolling African American "pity and tolerance and forbearance and fidelity and love of children," to which Cass responds, "So have dogs" (282). In a novel in which Blacks are so often dehumanized by whites who negatively associate them with animals (think, for example, of the deputy in "Pantaloon in Black" who compares Blacks to "wild buffaloes" [150]), in Boon we have a man who, despite all his cognitive limitations and Indian blood, is still culturally white, yet who is similarly animalized. And in his animalization, Boon blackens up.

This erotically triangulated scene of black (miscegenated and interspecies) animal death and desire, however, refuses to point exclusively to Ike's McCaslin genealogy and reinscribes itself in Ike's alternative animal and Indian genealogies. Another all-male trio, Sam, Boon, and Ike, echoes that of Old Ben, Boon, and Lion. The consummation of Ike's transition from being McCaslin to becoming Sam's ideological son operates by the true hunter's logic of loving the blood you spill. In the climactic hunt of part three of "The Bear," Old Ben (Sam's animal father) and Lion (Sam's animal son) both die, and the dog's sacrifice is the penultimate step to the full emergence of Ike as Sam's racially transformed human son. Ben's death is something that Sam and Ike have anticipated. Sam knows the bear will be killed one day and Ike says that it must be one of them that kills the bear "when even he dont want it to last any longer" (204). Killing Old Ben, for Ike, is effectively a form of honoring the bear's wishes through a form of assisted suicide, effected by its human kin. Ike's wrong, of course, since Boon kills the bear, but Ike has already cast Boon as Sam's huntsman, so in that sense, it's still all in the family. Imagining Ben's choosing when to die cannot but point to Sam's decision following the bear's death that he has nothing left for which to live. Although nothing is physically wrong with Sam, he, like the bear, "dont want it to last any longer," and Ike is clearly implicated in Sam's leaving this world even if Boon actually kills Sam. If the process of Ike's refiliation begins in a moment of Sam's smearing buck's blood onto the boy's face, then its completion is Boon and Ike's euthanizing Sam Fathers. Sam's death, in other words, becomes the blood on Ike's hands that cements his fantasized Indian kinship more surely than any animal blood that sticks to Ike.

Becoming Sam's son means that Ike wants to walk the path of the "taintless and incorruptible" but what does that mean for women? In other words, if Ike's Indian and animal kinship is something that happens strictly between males and leads to his sense in his old age that his truest kinship resides in the homosociality of the hunting camp, what role can actual women play for Ike in forming the most enduring family bonds? Yes, Ike marries and briefly performs as a heterosexual but in the text he never once thinks of the name of his wife, a woman who married Ike (as he comes to believe) not out of love but out of desire for the wealth and position that the McCaslin farm represented. The one time he sees his wife naked leads to one of the most unfulfilling representations of the heterosexual sex act in twentieth-century fiction. Small wonder Ike seems relieved to retire into celibacy for the rest of his life following this coupling. And the one time in "The Bear" when Ike thinks of his mother, Sophonsiba, she is twice identified in a way that reduces her importance within the structures of family by subordinating her within the context of male kinship: she becomes merely his "Uncle Hubert's sister."[28]

The death of Old Ben and Lion continues to resonate in ways that underscore the devaluation of women and the privileging of purely masculine kinship relations. Returning to the woods a couple of summers after Ben's and Lion's deaths, Ike comes upon the dog's gravesite while looking for Boon. Just prior to this discovery, Ike thinks of the unchanging progress of the season and his thoughts turn to an even more generalized sense of his family circle, one that moves beyond spirit animal kinship into the pantheistic:

> summer, and fall, and snow, and wet and saprife spring in their ordered immortal sequence, the deathless and immemorial phases of the mother who had shaped him if any had toward the man he almost was, mother and father both to the old man born of a Negro slave and a Chickasaw chief who had

been his spirit's father if any had, whom he had revered and harkened to and loved and lost and grieved . . . (311)

Who is Ike's truest mother? Rather than Sophonsiba, it's Mother Nature. But that same nature is "mother and father both" to Sam Fathers, whom Ike here identifies as his spirit's father. And Sam's truest kinship is neither to the part-Black woman who gave birth to him, nor to his father, Ikkemotubbe, but rather to that same nature that is Ike's true mother. Only in Sam's case, nature (not unlike Old Ben) is androgynous if not intersexual, since it is both mother and father to him. This move on Ike's part allows Sam not only to transcend any link to racial Blackness but to be doubly taintless sexually: Sam doesn't have sex with women and the woman who gave birth to him wasn't really his mother. But to the extent that nature is also Sam's mother and Sam then spiritually fathers Ike, it seems as though the problem of incest that Ike identifies in his white genealogy returns in his attempt to exclude women from his Indian ancestry.

Even Ike isn't exempt from committing figurative incest. Noting the trees and their marks, Ike takes his hunting knife and penetrates Mother Nature's most basic element, the earth itself: "almost the first thrust of the hunting knife finding . . . the round tin box manufactured for axle-grease and containing now Old Ben's dried mutilated paw, resting above Lion's bones" (312). The thrusting phallic knife; the receptive grease box. In this moment, the climactic hunt, that male three-way, is replayed now as quiet ritual. Ike, however, must enact Boon's role now because Boon effectively has sold his birthright of Indianness by becoming the town-marshal at Hoke's after Major de Spain leases the hunting camp and surrounding woods to a lumber company. An agent now of the law and property rights, Boon is co-opted by the white ideology of possession. At the end of "The Bear," Boon comes to see nature and animals as things to be owned. Sitting beneath a gum tree teeming with squirrels, Boon shouts a warning to the approaching Ike, whom Boon has not recognized and fears might be another hunter: "Get out of here! Dont touch them! Dont touch a one of them! They're mine!" (315). From this point on, although racially white, Ike truly stands as the last of the Chickasaws for he now figuratively has united patrilineal (Sam Fathers's) and matrilineal (Boon's) native descent.

After assuming Boon's role in a ritual repetition of the bear's death, Ike moves close to Sam Fathers's grave and feels certain that Sam's spirit is nearby. At this moment, Ike nearly steps on an enormous rattlesnake— "the old one, the ancient and accursed about the earth" (314). Given Ike's familiarity with the Bible, it's impossible to discount the serpent tempter of Genesis. Yet in relation to a homoerotic rendering of Old Ben's death, the rattlesnake's presence turns into another sexualized animal figuration, this time a barely concealed depiction of the aroused male sex organ: "At last it moved. Not the head. The elevation of the head did not change as it began to glide away from him, moving erect yet off the perpendicular as if the head and that elevated third were complete and all." When Ike is close to this animate phallus, the snake inspires fear (it might kill him) and loathing (its "sick smell of rotting cucumbers and something else which had no name"). Animality here seems to suggest Ike's troubled relation to his own sexuality. Only when this phallic snake moves away from him may Ike venerate it. And when he does, he uses Sam's words of address to the spirit buck: "Chief. . . . Grandfather." It is difficult finally not to hear these words as addressed to Sam's spirit, which is now so diffused throughout nature that it can manifest itself in any animal form. Ike's clearest proclamation of animal kinship, then, simultaneously affirms his identification with the logos (and the ethos) of the (celibate, alternative Indian) father. To be loyal to that father, Ike in his adult life may only have true passion for the big woods, the Mississippi jungle, which becomes "his mistress and his wife" (311).

During his long dialogue with Cass Edmonds in part four of "The Bear," Ike may claim that African Americans are better than whites, but by embracing Sam Fathers—not as the Black jungle savage but rather as the Noble Savage with his spirit animals—Ike merely finds a more creative way than other white Americans of the late-nineteenth and early twentieth century to privilege an animal kinship over any possible relation to African Americans. For this reason, then, Ike's fantasy of Indianness centrally participates in what makes *Go Down, Moses* tragic—namely, the failure of whites to acknowledge the open secret of their Black kin.

There are only two moments in *Go Down, Moses* where kinship between Blacks and whites is openly expressed. In both instances, it is a northern African American who speaks of this kinship. The first is in "The Bear," when an educated Black man comes to McCaslin Edmonds to inform the white man of his intention to marry Fonsiba. In doing so, the Black man identifies a Black woman as "a female member of the family of which [McCaslin is] the head" (263). After all, the stranger notes, "No man of honor could do less" than "notify" the "chief of her family" of these forthcoming nuptials. As a witness to this exchange, Ike must surely again hear in the word "chief" the kinship of family and tribe. McCaslin doesn't take kindly to these words, telling the stranger, "That's enough . . . Be off this place by full dark" (264) because this Black man has named the unnamable of the white fetish: hey, white man, you have Black kin.

The other moment of explicitly named Black-white kinship happens in "Delta Autumn" when the extremely light-skinned African American woman, whose infant son was fathered by Roth Edmonds, comes to the hunting camp in search of her lover. Taken to Ike's tent, she addresses him as kin, "You're Uncle Isaac," even though he fails to recognize her address (341). He might have noticed that she didn't say, "You're Uncle Ike," which is how he's universally known in Yoknapatawpha County. He definitely should have been struck by how well versed she was in McCaslin and Beauchamp genealogy. But when he does finally figure out that she's Black by the one-drop rule of the South, he experiences a moment of full-on racial panic: *"Maybe in a thousand or two thousand years in America*, he thought. *But not now! Not now!* He cried, not loud, in a voice of amazement, pity, and outrage: 'You're a n[-----]!'" (344).

As I've argued elsewhere, this moment serves as the culmination of a textual logic that makes Ike the novel's secret Black man, someone whose role we'd have no trouble understanding if he were racially Black.[29] The misrecognitions arise because Ike, though white, essentially performs the narrative arc of a Black male. In renouncing the McCaslin property, Ike simultaneously renounces his proper white identity (the father he claims, after all, is Black), so that like a Black man, who is denied the minimal respect of being addressed as "mister," Ike is never "Mr. Isaac." Rather he's identified as boy and only in his old age (like the pliant elderly African American male) is he granted the honorific "Uncle." In this reading, Ike's use of the racial epithet is self-reflexive: looking into the mirroring eyes of a kinswoman, Uncle Isaac momentarily glimpses with horror that Uncle Ike is Black, too. For me, Ike's act of racial identification underscores why his fantasy of Indian and animal kinship cannot provide a stable ground for his whiteness.

Every time I come to this scene, though, I hope that it might turn out differently, that Ike, who knows very well, indeed knows better than anyone, of the fraught mixture of the Black and the white races, will overcome the "but-still" fetishization of his whiteness. This time surely, I think, Ike will not panic but instead respond to the woman's clear articulation of their kinship with a different n-word, one that confirms family: "You're my niece." But, no. Ike, again retreating to the safe harbor of his imagined Indianness and animality, cannot claim his kinship with African Americans. He repeats the very insult (material compensation rather than recognition) that he perceives in his grandfather's $1000 legacy to his unacknowledged Black son when passing along Roth's envelope of cash to the woman and gifting her infant son with General Compson's hunting horn "covered with the unbroken skin from a buck's shank" (346). If his grandfather's legacy *"was cheaper than saying My son to"* an African American (258), then Ike's, which hints at animal kinship via the buckskin that covers the horn, is cheaper than saying, "My nephew" to his racially mixed kinsman. Moreover, Ike can only offer a faux acknowledgement of the shared blood that runs in his and the unnamed woman's veins when he figures her as a doe, also casting her obliquely into his animal kinship even as he excludes her from his human family.[30] The displacement? They share McCaslin blood, but Ike only hints at a different shared blood: if Ike's being marked by the blood of his first buck creates animal kinship and these African Americans are metaphorically deer, then animality, not humanity, represents both the basis and the limit of their family ties. This figurative move allows Ike to absolve himself from his implication in repeating the McCaslin disavowal of Black kinship by placing the blame squarely and exclusively on Roth Edmonds. Roth has failed the code of the true hunter by killing a doe. Once again, Ike sees only the beastliness of unchecked male heterosexual desire. His remorse as he exits *Go Down, Moses* is neither for any moral failing on his part nor for any understanding of what his fantasy of Indianness has papered over, but only that, unlike Sam Fathers, he will have no spiritual heir to sustain his queerly conceived notion of animal kinship.

NOTES

My thanks to Jay Watson and the program committee for inviting me to present and to all of the conference participants who asked me questions or offered comments about my paper that have helped me in revising. These people include (but are certainly not limited to) Jay, Peter Lurie, Robert Jackson, John Matthews, Sarah Gleeson-White, and Michael Zeitlin.

1. Slavoj Žižek, *The Sublime Object of Ideology* (London: Verso, 1989), 18.

2. William Faulkner, *Go Down, Moses* (New York: Vintage International, 1990), 335, emphasis added. Hereafter cited parenthetically.

3. In *William Faulkner: Lives and Legacies* (New York: Oxford University Press, 2007), Carolyn Porter speaks of two genealogies that serve as "alternatives to the white patriarchal one that Ike so ardently and finally fails to disavow" (160), but for her these alternatives are, first, the white female line that creates the Edmondses and, second, the Beauchamp line, which she sees as carrying the force of the matrilineal.

4. I nod here to my first book, *Faulkner's Marginal Couple: Invisible, Outlaw, and Unspeakable Communities* (Austin: University of Texas Press, 1990), with a recognition of that study's limitations. At that time, my sense of marginal couples and alternative community was limited to men and women (and occasionally two men) at the margins of the southern community whose relationships called into question its gender and sexual politics. I did not see the possibility of marginal communion between human and nonhuman animals. The relationship between Boon and Lion came into focus after I read Michael Lundblad's "Becoming-Wolf" section of Chapter 2, "Between Species: Queering the Wolf in Jack London," in which he examines the relationship between White Fang and Weedon Scott in *White Fang* and Buck and John Thornton in *The Call of the Wild*. See Lundblad, *The Birth of a Jungle: Animality in Progressive-Era US Literature and Culture* (Oxford, UK: Oxford University Press, 2013), 62–74.

5. Here are two examples of the Delta forest figured as a jungle: In "The Bear," when McCaslin and Major de Spain return to the woods to pick up Ike, who has stayed by the ailing Sam Fathers, "they drove the thirty mile in the dark of that night and at daybreak on

Sunday morning they ... rode out of the jungle and onto the low ridge where they had buried Lion" (241). In "Delta Autumn" Ike notes recent changes to the land as he thinks of "cabin, clearing, the small and irregular fields which a year ago were jungle and in which the skeleton stalks of this year's cotton stood almost as tall and rank as the old cane had stood" (326).

 6. Lundblad, *The Birth of a Jungle*, 33.

 7. Lundblad, *The Birth of a Jungle*, 34.

 8. Lundblad, *The Birth of a Jungle*, 41.

 9. Although at times I will draw on animal studies, this essay is not an attempt to work within a posthumanist tradition of animal studies in which thinking about nonhuman animals involves advocacy for those who are not human. Instead, my interest is in the historicized cultural studies work of what Lundblad calls animality studies: how did human thinking at a particular moment construct not only humanity but also animality and how are the two concepts mutually constitutive? To be clear: Lundblad is not advocating for the correctness of the ways in which Freud's and Darwin's ideas shaped thinking about animals. Instead, he wants to demonstrate how these theorists problematically "animalize animals" (*The Birth of a Jungle*, 11). Lundblad's literary analysis of such writers as Jack London, Frank Norris, and Upton Sinclair reads for "discursive resistance," instances where their texts provide "alternative constructions of what it means to be 'human' or 'animal' in relation to the growing hegemony of the Dawinist-Freudian jungle" (16) in the first quarter of the twentieth century. In particular, Lundblad's use of Sedgwick's notion of the epistemology of the closet seems simpatico with uses that queer ecologists have made. For example, Stacey Alaimo's "Eluding Capture: The Science, Culture, and Pleasure of 'Queer' Animals" in *Queer Ecologies: Sex, Nature, Politics, Desire*, ed. Catriona Mortimer-Sandilands and Bruce Erikson (Bloomington: Indiana University Press, 2010), 51–72, similarly draws on "Sedgwick's paradigm of the 'open secret'" to discuss the ways "nonhuman animals have been fixed within a zoological closet: many people have witnessed some sort of same-sex activity between animals and yet still imagine the natural world as unrelentingly straight" (56).

 10. See Lundblad, *The Birth of a Jungle*, 120–23.

 11. William Faulkner, "Barn Burning," *Collected Stories of William Faulkner* (1950; New York: Vintage International, 1995), 8.

 12. In "Reading the Ledgers: Textual Variants and Labor Variables," in Richard Godden's *William Faulkner: An Economy of Complex Words* (Princeton, NJ: Princeton University Press, 2007), 119–55, Godden and Noel Polk see Buck's possible sexual exploitation of Brownlee as problematic for Buddy because it interrupts the twins' "systematic inversion of their father's world," one that attempts to ameliorate the institution of slavery: "The twins substitute their own free labor for their father's bound labor in the matter of the cabin, thereby modifying the very substance of McCaslin property. They translate their father's white house into Black quarters, in the process parodying the practice of the master's mastery. By renouncing the totality of their control over the body of labor, the abrogate their own authority, potentially setting Black and white bodies in an altered state of intimacy, at least by night" (126–27). In other words, one method that Buck and Buddy use to free themselves from the dead father's will regarding plantation life (housing) may point to a libidinal form (homosexuality—whether incestuous or interracial) that also disrupts the plantation mythos.

 13. Godden and Polk, "Reading the Ledgers," 124.

 14. Benjamin Kahan warns us of this tendency in *Celibacies: American Modernism and Sexuality* (Durham, NC: Duke University Press, 2013), 3.

 15. In chapter 4 of *Touching Feeling: Affect, Pedagogy, Performativity* (Durham, NC: Duke University Press, 2003), 123–51, Sedgwick historicizes the ways in which queer studies "has had a distinctive intimacy with the paranoid imperative" (126), from Freud's seeing paranoia as the repression of same-sex desire to Guy Hocquenghem's reasoning that paranoia,

rather than illuminating homosexuality, instead reveals "the mechanisms of homophobic and heterosexist enforcement against it." Reflecting on her earlier work, Sedgwick notes that "paranoia is drawn toward and tends to construct symmetrical relations, in particular, symmetrical epistemologies" (and positing symmetrical epistemologies is the basis of this essay). As a result, because "paranoia seems to have a peculiarly intimate relation to the phobic dynamics around homosexuality, then, it may have been structurally inevitable that the reading practices that became most available and fruitful in antihomophobic work would often in turn have been paranoid ones" (127). Ike's closet may have nothing to do with homosexuality per se, but he constructs a closeted identify nevertheless, for Ike's secret is that he believes he has discovered the racial, sexual, and familial secret of the ledgers. But his ostensible discovery is the open secret of Ike's South—everyone knows that the races have been mixed, but one does not speak of it; as a result, white southerners share a communal closet that fetishizes whiteness.

16. Richard Godden, "Bear, Man, and Black: Hunting the Hidden in Faulkner's Big Woods," *Faulkner Journal* 23, no. 1 (2007): 15.

17. Ike's position is that God only blesses fighting done in the name of protecting "does and fawns" (332), where does and fawns serve as a metaphor for women and children. While he acknowledges that, in his youth, the abundance of game meant that hunters did at times kill does and fawns, his perspective late in life regarding the protection of does and fawns reflects an ethical concern rather than simply the conservationist perspective that another hunter expresses.

18. Christina M. Colvin, in "'His Guts Are All out of Him': Faulkner's Eruptive Animals" (*Journal of Modern Literature* 38, no. 1 (2014): 94–106), reads the extent to which de Spain's disappointment with Old Ben for supposedly breaking the rules of their hunt "presents an animal who is not simply anthropomorphized, but whose mythic status depends on its *not* acting like a bear" (100).

19. This fraught question, I believe, is one that Faulkner's text raises. In the contexts of Faulkner studies and of the history of slavery in the United States, saying that animals might have the status of enslaved people seems automatically to demean African Americans in a fashion parallel to the way whites in *Go Down, Moses* frequently reduce Blacks to animals. Such reductions are based on a racist sense that Blacks operate more by instinct than reason. However, if we follow Jacques Derrida in his 2003 essay "And Say the Animal Responded?" (Derrida, *The Animal That Therefore I Am*, ed. Marie-Louise Mallot, trans. David Wills [New York: Fordham University Press, 2008], 119–60), which replies to Jacques Lacan's Cartesian distinction between animal reaction (or instinct) and human response, the case for animals as enslaved beings becomes more tenable (in no small part because it also problematizes the white racist's attempt to reduce the Negro to the animal). In troubling "a line between reaction and response" (126), Derrida reminds us that the psychic determinism of the unconscious means that there is always already a decided element of reaction in any response. But the matter is more complicated as one considers the problem of attempting to draw a definitive line between the human and the nonhuman animal. As Derrida notes, "It is *not just* a matter of asking whether one has the right to refuse the animal such and such power (speech, reason, experience of death, mourning, culture, institutions, technics, clothing, lying, pretense of pretense, covering of tracks, gift, laughter, crying, respect, etc.— the list is necessarily without limit, and the most powerful philosophical tradition in which we live has denied the 'animal' *all of that*). It *also* means asking whether what calls itself human has the right rigorously to attribute to man, which means therefore to attribute to himself, what he refuses the animal, and whether he can ever possess the *pure, rigorous, indivisible* concept, as such, of that attribution" (135). Because the human animal cannot finally claim the ground of pure response, Derrida implies, the extent to which one can imagine

or recognize the nonhuman animal's response constitutes an ethical responsibility toward all animals. Some animal studies perspectives have more bluntly embraced the parallel between the treatment of animals and the institution of slavery. For example, in *Animal Rites: American Culture, the Discourse of Species, and Posthumanist Theory* (Chicago: University of Chicago Press, 2003), Cary Wolfe imagines a future in which we will look back at "factory farming, product testing, and much else that undeniably involves animal exploitation and suffering ... with much the same horror and disbelief with which we now regard slavery or the genocide of the Second World War" (190).

20. Faulkner uses the term bluegum in *The Sound and the Fury* when Roskus (Dilsey's husband) tells the Compson children a frightening story; the term refers to a Black person whose skin is so dark that the individual's gums look blue.

21. Sam's traumatic rejection by his biological father, Ikkemotubbe, and the origin of Sam's Chickasaw name "Had-Two-Fathers" (Faulkner, *Go Down, Moses*, 160), in fact underscores the canine element in Sam's animal family tree. Doom is only able to order the marriage of the enslaved woman he impregnated to another enslaved man after he becomes chief, something he accomplishes by using a white powder to kill puppies, which causes Doom's cousin, Moketubbe, who has seen his son suddenly die the same day, to recognize the implied threat and to abdicate his leadership.

22. Donna Haraway, *When Species Meet* (Minneapolis: University of Minnesota Press, 2008), 3.

23. This is at the very least a marker of Ike's fantasy of Indianness. As Patricia Galloway points out in "The Construction of Faulkner's Indians" (*Faulkner Journal* 18, no. 1-2 [2003]: 9-31), Faulkner gets this exactly backward. The actual nature of Chickasaw clans means that Boon's matrilineal descent would have made him more Indian than Sam. Faulkner incorrectly imposes "the same patriarchal social structures he gave his Anglos and Africans" on his Chickasaws (15).

24. See George Chauncey, *Gay New York: Gender, Urban Culture, and the Making of the Gay Male World, 1890–1940* (New York: Basic Books, 1995), 87–95.

25. Quoting from this same passage, Colvin argues that "the dog's distinctly animal reality disrupts Ike's narrative" because he "perceives no metaphoric or anthropomorphic significance in Lion's look" ("'His Guts Are All out of Him,'" 103). While such a reading seems to point us (finally) to a fully animal perspective, Colvin elides a portion of the passage, the explicit simile Ike uses to link Boon's eyes and Lion's; for Ike, Lion's eyes are like Boon's and suggest the two beings' similar minimal affect. It is precisely Ike's comparison that I see as helping create these two as doubles. Ike may recognize for a brief instance that the dog is not looking at him but only toward him, but I am not sure how much that disrupts the way Ike focalizes the reader's perception of Lion and Boon's relationship.

26. Godden briefly suggests a homoerotic subtext in the bear's death inasmuch as Boon uses his knife to kill the bear and the bear "surges erect," a situation that "yields interleaved phalloi" ("Bear, Man, and Black," 18).

27. John T. Matthews, "The Elliptical Nature of *Sanctuary*," *Novel* 17 (1984): 246–67.

28. "After his father's and his Uncle Hubert's sister's marriage they moved back into the big house" (287); a few pages later Ike again devalues Sophonsiba as his mother by referring to "Uncle Hubert and his Uncle Hubert's sister" (295).

29. John N. Duvall, *Race and White Identity in Southern Fiction* (New York: Palgrave Macmillan, 2008), 47–61.

30. The failure of whites to acknowledge their Black kin is central to Faulkner's greatest tragedies, *Absalom, Absalom!* and *Go Down, Moses*. One might wish to see Faulkner's final turn to comedy in *The Reivers* (New York: Vintage, 1962) as creating a hopeful moment in which whites at long last acknowledge their Black relatives: Lucius Priest tells his unnamed

grandchild that Ned McCaslin "was our family skeleton; we inherited him in turn, with his legend (which had no firmer supporter than Ned himself) that his mother had been the natural daughter of old Lucius Quintus Carothers himself and a Negro slave; never did Ned let any of us forget that he, along with Cousin Isaac, was an actual grandson to" old Carothers (30–31). But these words fall short of embracing Black kinship. Uncle Ned during his life may have insisted on this McCaslin kinship, but his white family did not openly acknowledge him as their blood kin. With Ned now safely dead for several decades, Lucius tells his grandchild about something that is merely "legend," a Black man whom the Priest family indulged by allowing him to claim that he was a true McCaslin.

The Jefferson Outbreak

An Epidemiological Reading of the Snopes Family

MAXWELL CASSITY

This chapter was developed from a talk given in the summer of 2019, months before the COVID-19/SARS-CoV-2 pandemic would inflict the exigency of the epidemiological reading method it theorizes. Epidemiological methodologies, including their contributions of data and visualization to narratives of and about public health, have since become commonplace in our COVID-19 lexicon and, accordingly, so has the importance of reading these data and their underlying narratives critically and in the context of the intersecting social forces that shape them. The maps, visualizations, and narrative contexts presented here give shape to racialized inflections of contagious metaphors that dovetail with discourses of eugenics, genetics, and immunity in Faulkner's work. However, this dynamic is not unique to Faulkner. Rather, it represents only a literary glimpse at a history of linkages between race and disease in American culture. As this essay suggests, *epidemic* events, such as the Snopeses' invasion of Yoknapatawpha's social body, often reveal and exacerbate *endemic* social conditions by abruptly, sometimes painfully, bringing unseen or ignored racial, sexual, and economic tensions into focus. In the United States, the COVID-19 pandemic has proven to be no exception to this history. It has exacerbated racial disparities in healthcare and housing access, labor precarity, and policing in the United States and globally, and while this essay is intended to exemplify how literary studies might employ epidemiological methods and frameworks in order to examine these disparities, it does so in a way that is inherently limited to the specific racial and historical dynamics of Faulkner's Yoknapatawpha.[1] As the following reading of the Snopes family suggests, in contemplating how narratives are constructed from and about epidemics, we should also think critically about how those narratives function and whether they reinforce and reproduce endemic conditions that accelerate the pain and trauma of epidemics or envision new, healthier, and more just social relations.

When the Snopes family—Faulkner's itinerant barn-burning clan of outsiders and horse traders—reemerges in the idyllic rural landscape of Will Varner's Frenchman's Bend in *The Hamlet* (1940), the village's heir apparent Jody Varner and traveling salesman V. K. Ratliff sense the family's arrival as an oncoming plague. In the novel's opening movement, Ratliff recounts to Varner rumors regarding the summer of 1895, when Ab Snopes and his elder son (Flem, the archvillain of the Snopes trilogy) set fire to their landlord Major De Spain's barn. This parochial history, related through Ratliff's reliable second-hand gossip and in Faulkner's "Barn Burning" (1939), indicates a spreading pattern of Snopes-associated monetary schemes and legal exploitations in the county that leads Varner to anticipate he and his father will become the family's next victims. Hoping to diagnose what he sees as a looming epidemic of Snopes in order to inoculate his father's rural fiefdom, Varner tells Ratliff, "Maybe I can recognize at least some of the symptoms in time."[2] Varner's coming plague of Snopeses, which begins with Flem's movement out of his father's tenant shack and into Varner's country store in *The Hamlet* and ends with his presidency of the Sartoris bank and his murder in *The Mansion*, traces a narrative in which the Snopes' social contagion operates as a metaphor for tensions of race and class mobility in the modernizing South.[3]

This essay explores the methodological possibilities of reading the Snopeses as deeply intertwined in a corpus-wide assemblage of Faulknerian texts, characters, genealogies, and geographies. Throughout these works, Faulkner often depicts the Snopeses as a corrupting force that abuses social norms, leverages economic needs, and exploits legal loopholes; consequently, his other characters read them as a threat to the community's social stability and economic health. Accordingly, this essay also attempts to diagnose the Snopes family through the lens of epidemiology, a methodological framework that brings together data analysis and close readings in order to synthesize the family's symbolic relevance to Faulkner's work. I argue that the narrative and moral arc of the Snopes trilogy traces the family's disruption of Jefferson society like an epidemic outbreak, and, by extending this epidemiological reading to Faulkner's entire corpus using the University of Virginia's Digital Yoknapatawpha project, I propose epidemic as a new framework for examining the family's influence throughout this body of texts.[4] Jefferson society understands and imagines the Snopeses through an epidemiological epistemology that frames the family as contagious "others," outsiders who, in their invasion of structures and hierarchies of upwardly mobile whiteness, defy and disrupt social norms.

Reading Epidemiologically: Using Digital Yoknapatawpha to Map the Snopes Epidemic

Epidemiology emerged at the end of the nineteenth century as a distinct branch of medical science that sought to study health- and morbidity-related events.[5] While epidemiological work mostly studies disease outbreaks, aspects of its methodology can translate to other health-related concerns within a given population. The Centers for Disease Control and Prevention (CDC) currently define epidemiology as "the study of the distribution and determinants of health-related states and events in specified populations and the application of this study to the control of health problems."[6] In *Epidemiology: A Very Short Introduction*, Rodolfo Sarraci expands this characterization to include "not only the description of how diseases and, more generally, health-related conditions occur in the population, but also searches for the factors, as a rule multiple, at their origin."[7] Epidemiologists collect, study, and interpret data of many types in order to analyze how health-related events occur within a population. From this data, they construct models that underpin narratives that help reveal not only the symptoms and lines of transmission of events like disease outbreaks but also their causes, cures, and underlying factors. Context is also important for interpreting epidemic events. J. N. Hays, a historian of disease, explains that epidemics are bound to particular historical and social contexts in that they are "temporary, affecting a particular place, and resulting in mortality/morbidity in excess of normal expectancy"; this situates epidemiology as a project of historicization as well as public health.[8] However, these data-fixed notions of "epidemic" are also in tension with the term's semantic flexibility in its common use as a metaphor, "frequently chosen to dramatize any problem, to convey notions of both severity and temporal emergency."[9] Epidemiological methodologies embrace this tension, constructing and interpreting narratives of epidemics in accordance with data and context, thereby making holistic predictions to combat and prevent outbreaks.

Using the data-driven tools of the Digital Yoknapatawpha project, I extend this methodology to readings of Faulkner. This digital humanities project visually renders the geographic and narrative landscapes of Faulkner's literary works, allowing scholars to use this data to augment traditional modes of literary analysis. By tracking and mapping plot development and character locations throughout Faulkner's corpus, Digital Yoknapatawpha (DY) makes it possible to examine family units across texts, providing an encompassing perspective of the shifting social networks and patterns permeating Faulkner's families. By using DY's character search to locate a single family, such as the Snopeses, users can view and manipulate a range of data points, including the family members' appearances in different texts, at varying narrative or historical points in time, and at specific locations in Yoknapatawpha County and beyond. The project's international team of Faulkner scholars and contributors provides supplemental notes that assist the user in contextualizing this data in relation to plot development, narrative activity, and key themes. By aggregating data through the "MapIt" function, users can extrapolate characters' narrative influence, pinpoint critical textual moments, and examine discrete data in relation to larger patterns in a single novel or throughout the corpus. As in a traditional epidemiological approach, data visualizations play a reciprocal role with traditional (con)textual analysis: they can support interpretive claims developed through close reading, which in turn provides the necessary context and detail to make an interpretive argument from the data. In my case, DY's data significantly supplements an epidemiological reading of the Snopes family because of how the project maps them across many texts. This epidemiological lens reflects the perspective that the townsfolk of Jefferson adopt concerning the Snopeses and provides a way to visualize the Snopeses' movements and influence. Like the views of characters such as Ratliff, Varner, and Gavin Stevens, this analytical approach specifically attends to the family's slippage between rural and urban spaces as well as class positions, charting their rise and fall in both number and narrative influence as these movements shape the trilogy's narrative trajectory.[10]

One point of acceleration for this Snopes "outbreak" in *The Hamlet* coincides with Ratliff's recovery from an unnamed illness; this link predisposes Ratliff, and therefore readers, to approach this moment symptomatically and epidemiologically. While it is unclear from what particular malady Ratliff was suffering, it is obvious that "he ha[s] been sick, and he show[s] it" (74) when he returns to Frenchman's Bend from his convalescence with his homemade shirt "quite loose upon him" (75) and his normally brown face "a few shades lighter." The sudden multiplication of Snopeses and their transmission from the rural periphery into the idle hamlet of Frenchman's Bend gets Ratliff's attention and he becomes preoccupied with their growing preponderance and impact on the community. Ratliff returns to the Bend to find that in his absence, one Snopes at Varner's store—Flem—has turned into multiple Snopeses infesting the village's businesses, the blacksmith shop, and the local school. Ratliff wryly captures how the Snopeses seem to appear out of thin air when he asks, "How many kinfolks has Flem Snopes brought in to date? Is it two more, or just three?" (76). He even exhibits physical symptoms in response to Flem and his cousins' use of their foothold in the Varner store as an upward step into Yoknapatawpha's middle class: he feels as if "something black blew in him, a suffocation, a sickness, nausea" (94). Ratliff's compromised health becomes synonymous with that of the community, and his symptoms register his view of the Snopes family as an emerging and increasingly severe danger to Yoknapatawpha's social health.

Ratliff's reaction to the Snopeses exemplifies how populations constitute social order through the use of metaphors of disease and epidemic—a strategy that Susan Sontag warns has been a hallmark of hegemony and structures of social control. In this framework, she argues, "epidemic diseases were a common figure for social disorder": by comparing "the polis to an organism," it became "plausible to compare civil disorder to an illness" that the social body would need to cure itself of or inoculate itself against.[11] Diagnosing the Snopeses as such an illness of social disorder, Ratliff performs the role of a clinical epidemiologist who "describes the natural course of a disease in a patient population and evaluates the effects of diagnostic procedures and of treatments."[12] By identifying the Snopeses as a disease on the social body of Yoknapatawpha, Ratliff hopes to identify factors of the Snopeses' influence that can be exploited in order to slow or cease their infection of county society and to reestablish the status quo.

Reading aspects of Faulkner's novels epidemiologically, like Ratliff's judgments of the Snopeses, suggests that the trilogy can be read as what Priscilla Wald calls an outbreak narrative, or "a formulaic plot that begins with the identification of an emerging infection, includes discussion of the global networks throughout which it travels, and chronicles the epidemiological work that ends with its containment."[13] Faulkner's outbreak narrative follows the Snopeses' movement into Jefferson, tracks Flem's rise to power, and catalogs the actions that characters like Ratliff and Stevens take to stop it. As the trilogy depicts the family as a metaphorical epidemic, it also shapes an understanding of both their position within the community and the inherent—or endemic—social tensions in Yoknapatawpha that lead to their rise. Wald argues that outbreak narratives such as these often use epidemiological frameworks to determine and reinforce structures of difference between groups in a population:

> When epidemiology turns an outbreak of communicable disease into a narrative, it makes the routes of transmission visible and helps epidemiologists anticipate and manage the course of the outbreak. In that transformational capacity, the epidemiological narrative is, like the microscope, a technology,

and it is among the epistemological technologies that delineate the membership and scale of a population.[14]

In Faulkner's outbreak narrative, the community members reinforce an epidemiological reading that sees the Snopeses' movement from the rural landscape to the largest institutions of the city, county, and country as a contagious pattern of infection, assimilation, and corruption. To them, this makes the Snopeses corrupting outsiders, markedly "other" from those in the community.

As Faulkner's epidemiological narrators demonstrate, in constructing lines of difference outbreak narratives can also reflect the epidemiologist's class and race position. The community's willingness to see the Snopeses as a metaphorical biological threat to social stability reveals prejudices against the family as examples of a type of racial othering taking place in Frenchman's Bend and Jefferson. Collectively, as they study the abject whiteness of the Snopes family, these townsfolk become what Theresa M. Towner has called "Snopes-Watchers": characters "who collect and share information on the hope of defending themselves" against the Snopeses.[15] Through these "Snopes-Watchers," the trilogy interpellates readers as participants in epidemiological Snopes-watching, encouraging them to draw connections between the many "transfigured" Snopes stories in Faulkner's corpus through the altered perspective of the trilogy.[16] Towner's argument suggests that Faulkner's reassembling of Snopes stories such as "Spotted Horses," "Centaur in Brass," and "Mule in the Yard" into the trilogy places these tales into a symptomatic relationship to the family's larger influence on Faulkner's literary body and Yoknapatawpha's population and frames the trilogy as a central site for understanding the family—the epicenter of the textual epidemic that extends throughout Faulkner's corpus.

The near obsession of characters such as Ratliff and Stevens with this family reveals the epidemiological Snopes-watchers' narrative bias, which threatens to distract from *en*demic issues in the community. In particular, as lower-class whites moving up in Jefferson society, the Snopeses embody what Towner calls "various permutations of the racialized self, white and nonwhite," and their mutability along racial and class-based lines creates tension in the community.[17] Likewise, the inability to pin Flem and his family down into a single containable category unsettles the county's class hierarchies, which are built on notions of hygienic and homeostatic whiteness. Thus, Varner and Ratliff's use of epidemiological language to frame the Snopes family speaks to an underlying logic of biological difference that underpins the family's threat to the social orders of Frenchman's Bend and Jefferson. Although the Snopeses are not racial others in the sense of a mixed heredity, they are nonetheless depicted as abject creatures that are biologically below or outside the categories occupied by the other Yoknapatawpha residents. White, but not quite white enough or white in the right ways, the Snopeses are an aggressive strain of what Nancy Isenberg calls "white trash," a "race" of poor southerners who in the late nineteenth and early twentieth centuries "conjured a special fear, that they would spread their unique contagion" by passing on "horrific traits" to the otherwise healthy population of properly raced and classed Americans.[18] In its employment of the language of disease and the fear of small-scale genetic changes going viral, Isenberg's eugenic metaphor of contagion encapsulates the imagined degenerative effects of class-mixture on the dominant racial category of whiteness by extending the implications of genetic transmission to the level of culture and population. As poor rural whites climbing the economic ladder in a post–Civil War South, Flem and the other Snopeses eschew social norms that have upheld elite and middle-class white superiority. Ab's destructive traits of carpetbagging and barn burning resurface in his son Flem's willingness to defy Yoknapatawpha's economic and social traditions. By lending money to the white *and* Black populations in Frenchman's Bend from behind the counter of Varner's store and manipulating his wife Eula Varner and her daughter Linda's sexuality in order to exploit the chivalric dispositions of men like the Varners and Gavin Stevens, Flem acts as the primary vehicle for the Snopeses' degenerative effects on the social body of Yoknapatawpha. In constructing poor whites as not only economic but also biological threats, the metaphorical "contagion" of "white trash" frames the turn-of-the-century intrusion of the poor rural white population into the economic and genetic pool of middle-class and elite whiteness as an epidemic of which the Snopeses are symptomatic.

Moving from the rural periphery to the town center, the Snopeses enliven fears of racial and social collapse through the language of contagion. In *Not Quite White*, Matt Wray describes how the term "white trash" reveals "structural antinomies" between the sacred and profane, purity and dirt, race and class and how, in "conjoining such primal opposites into a single category, white trash names a kind of disturbing liminality: a monstrous, transgressive identity ... a dangerous threshold state of being neither one nor the other."[19] The language and frameworks of early critical approaches to the Snopeses also engage with the biological undertones of divided whiteness through notions of disease, degeneration, and contagion. For example, in 1968 James Gray Watson described Flem Snopes as "a character so completely resistant to moral definition as to be literally inhuman," a reading that marks Flem's disruption of Yoknapatawpha society as disqualifying at the level of species.[20] A decade earlier,

Irving Howe had written that "no sooner did Faulkner come upon his central subject—how the corruption of the homeland, staining its best sons, left them without standards or defense—than Snopesism followed inexorably"; the Snopeses are, in his words, "the creatures that emerge from the devastation, with slime still upon their lips."[21] Howe's argument reflects the epidemiological perspective of the Snopeses that characters like Ratliff, Varner, Stevens, and the young Chick Mallison develop: as "slimy, emerging creatures" who defy the community's "standards and defenses," the Snopeses are constituted as biological threats, and Howe's emphasis on the "corruption, staining, and devastating" of the homeland echoes Faulkner's characters' metaphors of health and epidemic that link class, race, and contagion. By embodying both privilege and putridity, "white trash" like the Snopeses created a unique dilemma for southern society. Emerging from the dust of the post-Civil War tenant-farming economy in which "white trash remained undeveloped, evolutionarily stagnant creatures," families like the Snopeses threatened whiteness as a dominant racial category by demonstrating its abject degeneration.[22]

The rise of the Snopeses runs concordantly with the fragmentation of whiteness as a racial construct in the US. As Wray reminds us, by the 1890s, when the Snopeses land in Frenchman's Bend and begin their epidemic leap, "cutting-edge research no longer focused on differences between races, but instead on recognizing and delineating differences within races."[23] Wray argues that terms like "white trash" were used to "mar[k] both recent immigrants and feebleminded poor whites as inassimilable, as threatening outsiders-within to be excluded from the national body."[24] As "white trash," the Snopeses signify anxieties about unclean contact within Yoknapatawpha's white population, implying not only competition for economic and biological fitness but also the fear of contagion between competing classes of whites. In his introduction to *Faulkner and Whiteness*, Jay Watson writes that Faulkner's conceptions of whiteness reflect how racial definitions during Faulkner's time represented whiteness as a more "culturally contingent phenomenon, a matter of affiliation and practice."[25] The representation of the Snopeses as a "white trash" epidemic infecting the population of Yoknapatawpha replicates these metaphorical, biological, and economic registers through which a monolithic understanding of racial whiteness became divided. In a modernizing South, buttressing entrenched class hierarchies offered a potential substitute for racial hierarchies threatened by emancipation and reconstruction, but differences in economic class lacked the strong foundational logic of biological difference on which classical racism and chattel slavery depended. Disease and epidemic offered an epistemology through which a degenerative strain of whiteness could be brought into accord with a hierarchy of biological difference that kept rich, landowning whites at the top of the social ecology.

Symptomatic Snopeses: Reading outside the Trilogy

Although the Snopes trilogy is the group of texts with the highest density of Snopes characters and influence, the family's contagious patterns are transmissible to other Faulkner texts where they appear. Examining these moments in light of the Snopesian metaphor of epidemic reveals how small Snopes-related events have large impacts on Faulkner's literary body. Here again the Digital Yoknapatawpha project can be helpful. The project allows users to search in texts for characters sorted by family, a feature which illuminates the prolific number of Snopes characters throughout Faulkner's work and pinpoints where, geographically and narratively, they appear. Using DY to examine the Snopeses throughout Faulkner's works reveals that in addition to their epidemic rise in the Snopes trilogy, they are an endemic presence in his literary body of texts. Major and minor Snopeses appear in nine novels and thirteen short stories (including those that were later adapted into the Snopes trilogy).[26] In many of those stories, the Snopeses serve as minor villains and tricksters, gaming the community's social norms and values in order to make a few quick dollars before disappearing back into the narrative periphery. Viewed in the context of the family's development as a metaphorical social contagion in the trilogy, these minor occurrences gain increased symbolic and symptomatic relevance. This data enhances pre-DY readings like Joseph Gold's, who argues that "it is necessary to see Snopesism as a product of its environment in order to comprehend the full significance of the Snopes idea wherever it occurs in Faulkner's fiction" and notes that an analysis of Flem's "compeers" can provide a larger and more encompassing perspective on the family.[27] With DY's toolkit, and by reading the Snopeses epidemiologically, these smaller events become symptomatic of the larger picture of "Snopesism." Additionally, expanding this reading outside of the narrative framework of Ratliff, Stevens, and other Snopes-watchers may help in constructing a more comprehensive and less prejudiced perspective on the Snopeses' influence on Faulkner's work.

This method reveals that the Snopeses' effect on the population of Jefferson appears as the combined effect of many singular occurrences of infection. Like a viral particle binding to its host and penetrating the cell body to deposit its destructive genome, a male Snopes—whom Ratliff describes as "like the malaria-bearing mosquito"—often uses a devious financial transaction to gain internal access to an icon of significance in the community (Faulkner, *The Town* 145). The Snopes then trades on the

An Epidemiological Reading of the Snopes Family   177

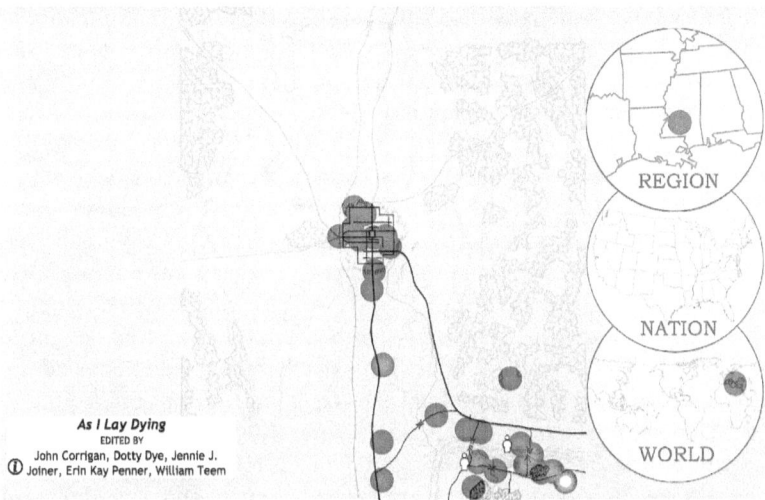

Figure 10.1. Spatial Heatmap, *As I Lay Dying*. In this visualization of narrative activity in *As I Lay Dying*, character-location figures place Snopes characters at a key point in the Bundrens' odyssey, near Frenchman's Bend. The two characters, the "unnamed Snopes cousin" and "Eustice Grimm," play key roles in the Snopes family's trade for Jewel's pony, which is a descendant of those whom Flem brings to Yoknapatawpha in "Spotted Horses" and *The Hamlet*. Image courtesy *Digital Yoknapatawpha*.

external appearance of the infected symbol and empties his victim's pockets, leaving them with only the empty shell of the item they held in high regard. While there are many examples of this throughout Faulkner's work, I turn here to two key examples: the trading of Jewel Bundren's prized horse in *As I Lay Dying* (1930) and Clarence Snopes's discovery and betrayal of Temple Drake's whereabouts in *Sanctuary* (1931). Together these scenes demonstrate how an epidemiological reading reinforces the Snopeses' disruption of narrative and social stability in Faulkner's pretrilogy works.

In *As I Lay Dying*, a Snopes plays a small but critical role in the narrative when they recover a descendent of the metaphorically contagious spotted horses that Flem releases into the Bend in *The Hamlet*. (See fig. 10.1.) The Bundren family faces a crucial obstacle to their pilgrimage to bury their slowly rotting mother in Jefferson when their wagon overturns attempting to ford the river near Frenchman's Bend. When the family's team of mules drowns in the crossing, Anse decides to trade Jewel's horse with an unnamed nephew of Flem's for a new team. The horse's spotted coat and its violent, untamable nature identify it as "a descendent of those Texas ponies Flem Snopes brought here"—an allusion to both "Spotted Horses" and *The Hamlet*.[28] The blotchy spotted coats of the horses signify their questionable heritage, their descent from inferior stock or degenerative cross-breeding, and, like the markings of measles and smallpox, the horses become symptomatic of Flem's chaotic and infectious impact on the community.

In *As I Lay Dying*, the fact that Jewel has been able to saddle and ride the wild pony, through a combination of deep affection and violent abuse, makes it an attractive and valuable commodity. To the savvy horse trader, the taming of the Snopes-related horse represents a symbolic victory over and domestication of the Snopeses: to tame the Snopes horse proves the contagion has a cure. Despite Armstid's halfhearted attempts to assure Anse that a "fellow that just beat Snopes in a trade ought to feel pretty good" (189), Anse's dealing with the unnamed Snopes cousin is disastrous for the Bundren family. In trade for a pair of broken mules that Darl says have been "fed ... on sawdust" (196), Anse offers Jewel's horse—one of the few of Flem's spotted horses to be brought under control—as well as a mortgage on some farm equipment and eight dollars of his son Cash's money. In the end, Jewel takes the horse to Snopes himself, saving his family the extra cost, since, as Eustice Grimm later remarks, "all [Snopes] liked was the horse" (192).[29] The tension of Jewel's secret heredity—and the mixture of anger and love which comes from it—is channeled into his relationship with the Snopes horse, inaugurating the Snopesian connection as a signifier for aberrant genetics and the debilitating effects of silence and secrecy under the name of respectability.

In *Sanctuary*, another minor Snopes dredges up allusions to disease through a brief but narratively critical trade, this time concerning information about Temple Drake's whereabouts in Miss Reba's "Memphis 'ho'- house."[30] (See fig. 10.2.) *Sanctuary*'s Clarence Snopes is a vicious, cigar-smoking racist and antisemite, as well as a state senator whose political influence is described as "a picture of stupid chicanery and petty corruption for stupid and petty ends, conducted primarily in hotel rooms" (175). Like many other Snopeses, Clarence gets his start terrorizing the community in Frenchman's Bend, where Will Varner makes him a local constable after he demonstrates a talent for biopolitical violence, "warring" against the Black population not "as representatives of a race which was alien because it was of a different appearance and therefore enemy *per se*, but ... because they were afraid of that alien race."[31] Once deputized, Clarence gains a reputation for beating black people "with a kind of detachment, as if he were using neither the man's black skin nor even his human flesh, but simply the man's present condition of legal vulnerability as testing-ground or sounding-board on which to prove ... just how far his ... official power and legal immunity actually went" (Faulkner, *The Mansion*, 330). Using racism as a means by which to

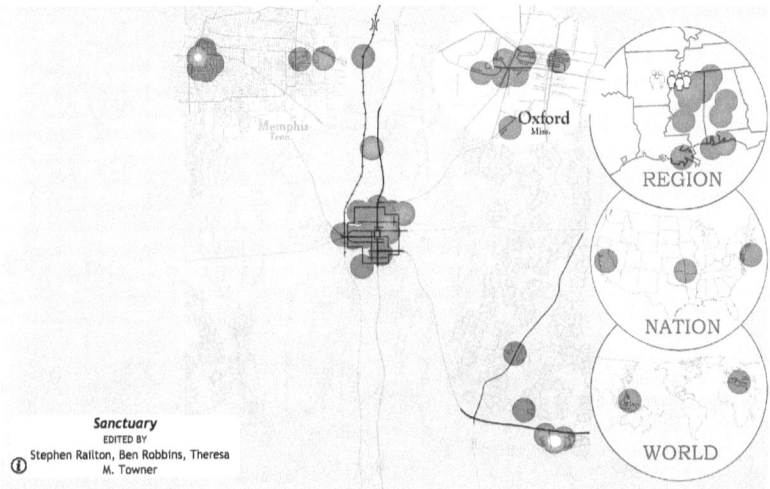

Figure 10.2. Spatial Heatmap, *Sanctuary*. In *Sanctuary*, the Memphis whorehouse where Clarence Snopes makes a regular appearance serves as a crucial intersection point. In chapter 21, Virgil Snopes and a companion take up residence in Reba's brothel, believing it to be a boarding house. Clarence discovers Temple Drake's location while visiting his younger cousin, whom he calls "the biggest fool this side of Jackson." Image courtesy *Digital Yoknapatawpha*.

experiment with the limits of his own immunity to law and social norms, Clarence demonstrates an aptitude for southern politics. Racist, but in a racially "objective" way that is flexible enough to accommodate both the Klan members and the southern moderates of his Yoknapatawpha constituency, Clarence rises to the corruption of his station.

In *Sanctuary*, Senator Snopes sells Temple's location not only to Horace Benbow but also to Temple's father, Judge Drake, and to Popeye's Memphis lawyer, a triple-cross fire sale which, as the notes in the DY analysis of the novel point out, critically links the Jefferson and Memphis sections of the novel. Benbow describes Clarence as having "a quality calculating and cunning and pregnant" (204), a description that resonates with the mosquito-linked viral mechanism of Snopesism that Ratliff invokes in *The Town*. Clarence's metaphorical pregnancy suggests that the qualities of eugenic degeneration carried by the Snopes genetic line are accompanied by an incipient threat of deceptions waiting to be born, a threat of emergent Snopesism that extends outwards into the social body of Yoknapatawpha through politics and economics as well as biology. In an epidemiological sense, Benbow recognizes that Clarence is "pregnant" with the Snopes contagion insofar as he senses that a Snopes's involvement in the affair will inevitably lead to chaos and

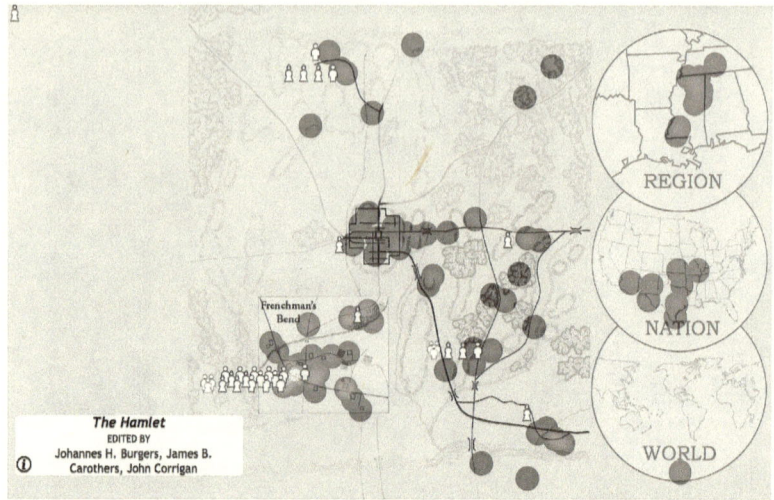

Figure 10.3. Spatial Heatmap, *The Hamlet*. Image courtesy *Digital Yoknapatawpha*.

violence, reinforcing the prevalence of an epidemiological reading of Snopes characters that further alludes to the family's contagious and degenerative influence throughout Faulkner's corpus.

The relationship between the Snopeses' roles in Faulkner's greater corpus and their figuration as a disease outbreak in the trilogy becomes further visible when we draw on mapping data made available by Digital Yoknapatawpha. Visualizing the Snopes trilogy using DY's heatmap function (which tracks narrative activity by location using lighter, hotter colors to indicate regions of increased narrative activity) in combination with the character-location feature (which marks the specific locations in Yoknapatawpha and Jefferson where characters participate in narrative events) renders the Snopes family's epidemic rise in a way that allows users to see their rapid growth and movements. For example, in the map for *The Hamlet*, the number of Snopes icons and the narrative heat increase rapidly as the family moves from the tenant farm to the village proper—a visualization that gives shape to the anxieties of characters like Ratliff and Varner.[32] (See fig. 10.3.)

The Snopes family's reputation is built in part on their role as horse traders, and both in the trilogy and in other texts the Snopeses' contaminating influence is symbolically linked to equestrian commerce. The outbreak of "Spotted Horses" in *The Hamlet* following Flem's return from Texas with his new bride Eula and her daughter Linda foreshadows the spread of his and other Snopeses' influence throughout the county. The horses' poxlike markings symptomatically represent their capacity for outbreaks of violence, a capacity described as a "contagion passing back through the herd from animal to animal" (303). The horses are a "kaleidoscope of inextricable and incredible violence" (318) with "a gaudy vomit of long wild faces and splotched chests" (333) moving with a "splotchy, sporadic surge and flow" (308) that "clotted and blended and shifted among themselves" (325) and which "seemed not to gallop but to flow, bodiless, without dimension" (305), descriptions infused with the language of unruly contagion. When the horses inevitably break out of the yard, Ratliff refers to the outbreak of spotted horses roaming the county as "that Texas disease Flem Snopes ... brought" (341) noting that by the time Flem was brought to court over the matter, "'that Texas sickness,' that spotted corruption of frantic and uncatchable horses, had spread as far as twenty and thirty miles" (356). Ratliff's epidemiological reading of the spotted horses as an outbreak prefigures the destructive, degenerating assemblage of Snopesism they represent and foreshadows Flem and the Snopes epidemic spread over the entire county and country in the Snopes trilogy.

Formally speaking, in the "Spotted Horses" set piece Flem does not operate as a contagion himself, but as a metaphor of a contagious vector—the medium through which the chaos and disaster of the ponies is passed on to the community. Although Flem attempts to use a Texan middleman to hide his involvement in the sale, the community is wary of the implications of Flem's apparent connection to the horses. When Flem shows up to the auction the other bidders establish a safe "social distance" from him, leaving "a space the width of three or four men on either side of him" (323). A comparative analysis of DY heatmaps of *The Hamlet* and *The Town* reveals how Flem enables the spread of his family's class position as he does that of his contagious spotted horses: by setting them loose in the community while maintaining his own immunity through distance (compare fig. 10.3 and fig. 10.4). As his class status rises throughout the novels, so too do the number and location of Snopeses on the DY maps. For example, in *The Town*, after Flem's salted gold mine scheme has tricked Ratliff out of his share of a Jefferson restaurant, he then moves into Jefferson proper and a trailing cloud of Snopes follows him. Flem becomes the vehicle by which his family infests the community: when one Snopes moves up in status, there is another one ready to fill the empty space left behind.

This mechanism exists in many of the Snopes interactions, but in the trilogy, Flem primarily embodies its contagious qualities. As Gavin Stevens, Ratliff's civilian epidemiologist counterpart, says, "when you say Snopes in Jefferson you mean Flem" (Faulkner, *The Town*, 34). However, according to Benjamin Child, this tendency to read Flem as

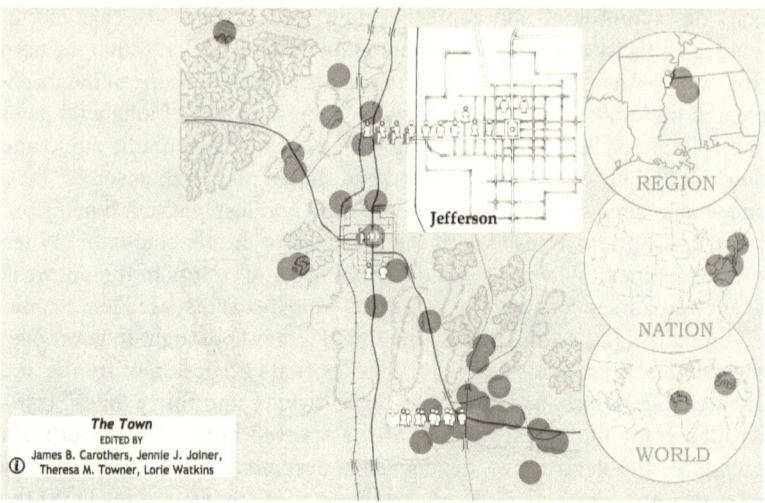

Figure 10.4. Spatial Heatmap, *The Town*. Image courtesy *Digital Yoknapatawpha*.

the sole embodiment of Snopesism is "symptomatic of the way that Faulkner often decollectivizes the energies that fuel social movements by assigning them to a rogue individual," so we should again be wary of the limits of Faulkner's narrators.[33] This wariness should also extend to ourselves, as Towner reminds us, since "a reader of the Snopes stories and novels participates in the evolution of Yoknapatawpha's folklore," joining the narrator-epidemiologists and Faulkner himself in using observations of the family not to discover inherent "truths" about the Snopes but rather "to organize the responses and behavior of his other characters."[34] Thus, Snopes-watching might reveal more about the Snopes-watchers (including Faulkner's participating reader) and their inherent biases and desires than it does about the Snopeses themselves. In fact, further close analysis of the data this epidemiological reading utilizes reveals how Flem is different from the other members of his clan in his drive for homeostasis as well as economic gain, a difference that necessarily differentiates his role as a vector of contagion from that of his kin.

The Jefferson Outbreak: Flem Snopes as a Cancer in the Body Politic in *The Town*

In *The Town*, Flem's power and the Snopes outbreak reach their peak. Reading the Snopeses through DY's narrative activity heatmaps and character-location markers reinforces the way *The Town*, the trilogy's second novel, and the town of Jefferson become the epicenter of the Snopes influence.[35] (See fig. 10.4.) Geographically speaking, Flem's move from Frenchman's Bend into Jefferson precipitates an explosion of Snopeses throughout the fictional county of Yoknapatawpha and into Mississippi more broadly, as well as Texas, Tennessee, and New York. Narratively speaking, *The Town* also sees Flem reach the peak of his power, becoming entrenched in the economic and social structures of Jefferson when he trades the knowledge of his wife Eula's affair for the presidency of the historic Sartoris bank. This symbolic act resounds as a powerful upheaval of the class hegemony of the town—the former tenant farmer now risen to inhabit one of the most powerful and symbolic seats of hierarchy. Together, these data points and narrative markers propel a reading that sutures the metaphors of outbreak and epidemic that accompany Flem's rise to power to the community's immunological response against it.

By the time Flem reaches the presidency of the Sartoris bank, the metaphorical vehicle of his social infection has mutated from a virus that moves quickly through the rural community of Frenchman's Bend into a cancer on the social body of Jefferson. Flem's belief, as described by Ratliff, that "money itself, cash dollars, possessed an inherent life of its mutual own like cells or disease" is reflected in the desire for respectability which, like his wealth and the bacterial sludge evoked by his first name, grows "by simple parasitic osmosis like a leech or goitre or cancer" (Faulkner, *The Town*, 279). Cancer is a particularly apt metaphor for Flem's influence because, like a tumor which may lie dormant for many years before finally becoming deadly, his manipulation of respectability allows him to hold the open secret of his wife Eula and Manfred De Spain's affair over Eula, her powerful father, Will Varner, De Spain, and the entire town—who have all been silently Snopes-watching the titillating affair develop for eighteen years. Knowing that everyone in the town knows about his wife's affair allows Flem to weaponize the threat of "discovering" the affair and throwing the social order of the town into disarray. Moreover, his ultimate revelation of the affair is accompanied by the arrival of polio in Jefferson, a symbolic resonance in which the twinned epidemic fears—polio and Snopesism—reflect the family's embodiment of contagion and disease.

The polio scare attunes the population of Jefferson to the potential for epidemic just as the epidemic of Snopeses that has been raging quietly in the community is set to reach its peak. As a result of the arrival of a highway engineer whose child is found to be sick with polio, the entire town is shut down "while they found out what to do next or what not to do or whatever it was while they tried to learn more about polio" (315). In the young Chick Mallison's description of the event, the potential polio outbreak and Flem's revelation about the affair bleed together into a consequential moment: "It was as if time, circumstance, geography, contained something which must, anyway was going to, happen and now was the moment and Jefferson, Mississippi was the place, and so the stage was cleared and set for it" (315). As Sontag reminds us, "Cancer is first of all a disease of the body's geography," a disease which is also "staged," in the language of diagnosis, "classifying it according to its gravity, determining how 'advanced' it is," but also through "a spatial notion: that the cancer advances through the body, traveling or migrating along predictable routes" (110). Much like in the epidemiological perspective of the DY map, "time, circumstance, and geography" operate to situate the Snopeses' influence on the community in space and time. By setting the stage for Flem's most deadly act, polio prefigures the epidemic import of Flem's deceit. Chick describes news of the affair and its impending fallout as a spreading contagion and a crisis of containment in the community. To him, the revelation of the affair is a social contagion that permeates "all the walls of Jefferson, the ground they stood on, the air they rose up in; all the walls and air in Jefferson that people moved and breathed and talked in" (316–17). When the Eula-Manfred affair is finally revealed, the community's Snopesian infection explodes out of its hidden domestic spaces and into the public domain to deadly effect; when it appears the affair will become public, Eula commits suicide in order to inoculate her daughter Linda with the respectability Eula has lost by becoming Flem's victim. By becoming a victim herself, Linda is immunized against Flem.

Like Ratliff, Chick sees the community's complicity in the secret as a factor in its virulence. He describes the town's acceptance of the open-secret affair as that of injury, illness, and trauma: "It was ours, we had lived with it and now it didn't even show a scar, like the nail driven into the tree.... [I]t dont go away; it just stops being so glaring in sight, barked over; there is a lump, a bump of course" (317–18). Reflecting back on these events through a narratorial hindsight not present in the perspective of other narrator characters like Ratliff and Stevens, Chick describes the "lump" that was the Eula-Manfred affair as not harmlessly incorporated into the social body as it may at first have seemed, but rather as a tumor merely lying dormant. This intertwining of cancer with secrecy reflects the twentieth-century American tradition of keeping cancer secret. This secrecy is an important part of the disease's metaphorization that, for Sontag, problematically reinforces the stigmatization of victims of the disease who—because of the detrimental effects of the disease on "one's love life, one's chance of promotion, even one's job"—lie and are lied to about the disease, not only because it is "a death sentence, but because it is felt to be obscene."[36] The victim's fear of losing respectability leads to cancer's insidious and dangerous absence from open public discourse. As with Flem and the community's secret knowledge of the affair, the social silence about cancer reflects a crisis of respectability; by remaining silent about the disease, doctors, patients, and communities hope to avoid the uncomfortable realties of pain and death, but in doing so they create favorable social conditions for the disease to propagate. Similarly, Flem's cancerous secret is "not buried, not healed or annealed into the tree but just cysted into it, alien and poison; not healed over but scabbed over with a scab which merely renewed itself, incapable of healing, like a signpost" (320). The Eula-Manfred affair here is rendered as a symptom and marker of the larger creeping force behind Flem's rise. Flem's willingness to let the affair continue and the town's unwillingness to break the social norm of respectable silence allows the secret—and its social stigma—to metastasize to deadly effect.

Epidemic and Immunity in *The Mansion*

Epidemic metaphor and epidemiological form in the early Snopes texts point to an immune response in the community that involves both enmity—the epidemiological perspective that marks the Snopeses as raced and classed others and sets society against them—and an assimilative aspect through which the population attempts to sort and incorporate certain Snopes characters into its social body while rejecting others. The discourse of immunity in Faulkner's work therefore imagines Yoknapatawpha's citizens, especially those who are white and middle-class, as a social body distinct from and worthy of defense against the Snopeses. As a result, townspeople like Stevens and Ratliff attempt, but largely fail, to produce a systemic reaction in the community against the family.[37] Interestingly, Flem's attempt to gain respectability and its accompanying social immunity leads him to take up a similarly epidemiological and immunological stance against his more virulent family members. In taking on the county's systems of immunity to further propagate his own rise, Flem embodies a type of autoimmunity, a state in which the (social) body's immune system is turned against the assemblage of systems that it usually acts to protect.[38] Flem's autoimmunity turns the town's structures of sexual propriety, class hierarchy, and racial anxiety against its population, as emblematized by his infiltration of symbolic markers such as Eula Varner, the De Spain manor, and the Sartoris bank to accelerate his unnatural defiance of established social norms.

Once he has achieved a stranglehold on the power structures of Yoknapatawpha, Flem installs his various cousins strategically throughout the social infrastructures of the town, county, and state; the stalwart epidemiological townsfolk such as Ratliff and Gavin Stevens cannot halt this part of the Snopes epidemic, which leads the majority of the population tacitly to accept the new social order of Snopesism. Sarcastically ventriloquizing his fellow citizens, Ratliff describes their mode of immunologically incorporating certain Snopeses into the social body so that the others' destructive pathogenesis might be averted.

> Realising that we would never defend Jefferson from Snopeses, let us then give, relinquish Jefferson to Snopeses, banker mayor aldermen church and all, so that, in defending themselves from Snopeses, Snopeses must of necessity defend and shield us, their vassels and chattels, too. (Faulkner, *The Town*, 45)

Ratliff's vision of a community committed to creating immunity through incorporating Snopesism is, of course, ironic and dystopian—an inverted world in which the dominant white class become the "chattels" of the Snopes. Having become immunologically symbiotic with the Snopes, Ratliff fears that neither he, nor Gavin, nor any other of the population can retain their freedom to live unfettered by Snopesism.

Flem's manipulation of social norms leads to a crisis of autoimmunity in the community. For Jacques Derrida, the notion of autoimmunity helped to theorize the ways that "colonization and decolonization were both autoimmune experiences wherein the violent imposition of a culture and a political language ... ended up producing the exact opposite of democracy."[39] In the Snopes trilogy, Faulkner turns this autoimmunity back on the "democratic" citizens of the town through Flem. As colonizers now facing their own colonization by insurgent Snopeses, the established epidemiological class of Yoknapatawpha has failed to protect its own boundaries and now can only watch or join in as its own systems and infrastructures are turned against it. In deploying the town's legal and social structures to further his rise to power, Flem's autoimmune maneuvers reflect Derrida's critique of the autoimmunity of (anti)democratic rule in which "the autoimmune topology always dictates that democracy be sent off elsewhere, that it be excluded or rejected, expelled under the pretext of protecting it on the inside by expelling, rejecting, or sending off to the outside the domestic enemies of democracy."[40] The topography of Flem's autoimmunity registers through the management of his infectious family's movements in and out of the social and economic assemblages of Yoknapatawpha society. Flem "sends off" Snopeses who threaten his own respectability, reifying the epidemiological frame that sought to remove him from the social body and doing so through an autoimmune exploitation of the infrastructures into which he originally emerged as

An Epidemiological Reading of the Snopes Family 187

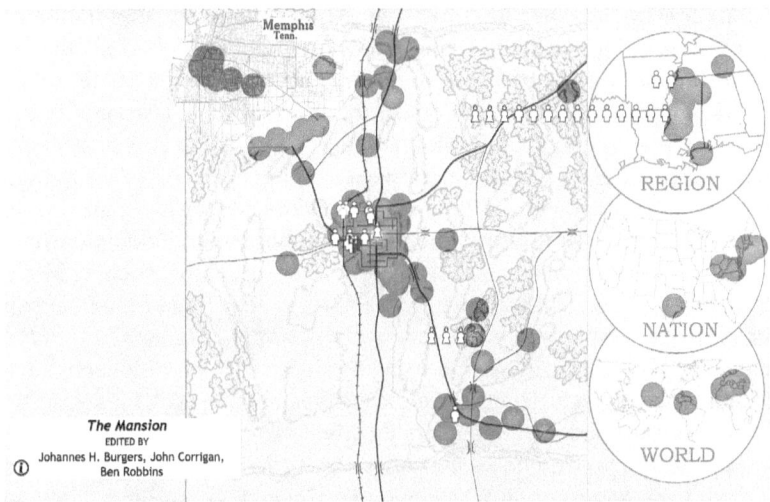

Figure 10.5. Spatial Heatmap, *The Mansion*. Figures 10.3, 10.4, and 10.5 are spatial heatmaps visualizing narrative activity in the mapped text with "hot" colors representing spatial areas with increased narrative activity. Areas that appear "hot" represent places and locations where large amounts of the narrative take place. Overlaid on the heatmap is "character-location" data for Snopes characters, who appear on the map as either white (racially white) or white/red (mixed-race) human figures that are distinguished by gender in the places and locations where they appear or are described in the mapped texts. Used in concert with the "epidemiological" readings proposed in this chapter, these maps reveal a number of important trends and themes below the surface of Faulkner's writing. For example, one can see the progression of narrative activity from the rural periphery of Frenchman's Bend in *The Hamlet* to the urban social center of Jefferson in *The Town* and *The Mansion*, with "hot" colors and the population of Snopes figures increasing over the trilogy. This visualizes a latent theme: characters like Ratliff and Stevens's stated concerns over the progressive advancing "invasion" and proliferation of Snopes throughout the trilogy, a movement that stands out in a comparison between *The Hamlet* and *The Town* heatmaps. This movement further reiterates *The Town* as the central peak of the "outbreak narrative" in terms of the epidemic reading of the trilogy, whereas in *The Mansion* both narrative activity and number of Snopes is decreased, although, notably, in the final text Snopeses have spread not only throughout the region but throughout the country and the world, indicating the possibility that the Snopes epidemic has pandemic potential. Images courtesy *Digital Yoknapatawpha*.

an infectious agent. When Flem's fellow Snopeses accede to his control, they are elevated to positions of social influence, but if they disrupt the matrix of Flem's power, he removes them to a safe distance where they cannot disrupt the hygiene of his constructed immune respectability.

Examining the movements of character-location markers and narrative activities of Snopeses between DY heatmaps of *The Town* and *The Mansion* reveals the autoimmunological dynamics of Flem's rise to power.

(Compare fig. 10.4 and fig. 10.5.) While in *The Town* the population of Snopes characters active in Jefferson reaches its peak, in *The Mansion* Flem begins to surgically cut Snopeses out of Jefferson society. The movement of some Snopeses out of Jefferson, such as Clarence to the statehouse in Memphis and Montgomery Ward to Los Angeles, where he is "engaged in some quite lucrative adjunct or correlant to the motion picture industry or anyway colony," suggest the intentional transmissive spread of Snopesism beyond the provincial borders of Yoknapatawpha (Faulkner, *The Mansion*, 404). However, other Snopeses, such as Mink, Byron, and Eck (sent off to Parchman prison, to Texas, and from Jefferson back to Frenchman's Bend, respectively), serve as examples of Flem's capacity for quarantining and excising Snopeses whom he sees as a threat to his metastasizing economic and social power.

Flem's autoimmune maneuvers disorient the epidemiological framework of Stevens, who notes that after this turn, "Something happened. The pattern went wrong" (Faulkner, *The Town*, 179); Ratliff is likewise stunned to find Flem no longer interested in only short-term gain. "Thishere new thing he has done found out it's nice to have, is different," Ratliff hypothesizes (184–85). "It's like keeping warm in winter or cool in summer, or peace or being free or content-ment.... It's got to be out in the open, where folks can see it, or their aint no such thing.... Call it civic virtue" (185). For Stevens and Ratliff, Flem's attempts to become a respectable citizen represent the greatest threat so far to civilized society as it brings him indistinguishably close to their own place as guardians of Yoknapatawpha's social health. Although the visible markers of Snopes activity in Jefferson are in decline in *The Mansion*, as the curve of the Snopes epidemic flattens, Flem's power becomes more, not less, entrenched.

Flem's downfall ultimately comes not through the efforts of the epidemiological townsfolk but through members of his own family who have themselves accrued an immunity to his influence. In *The Mansion*, Flem's adopted daughter Linda turns both his and Gavin's notions of respectability and immunity to her own motives—revenging the men who caused her mother's suicide and ending the pitched epidemiological battle which has been raging for decades in the community. When Linda returns to Jefferson deafened from fighting Fascists in the Spanish Civil War, Stevens notes that her immersion in silence only strengthens her "immunity" to the "dilemma of man's condition" (262). Linda's disability leaves her with an altered vocal timbre, but it also protects her from outside stimuli in a way that magnifies what Gavin sees as her already-developed immunity to the influences of both Flem and Jefferson's general population. In *The Mansion*, Gavin describes Linda as "the bride of quietude and silence striding inviolate in the isolation of unhearing, immune, walking still like she used to walk when she was fourteen and fifteen and sixteen years old" (254–55), believing that her communist and antiracist politics express her desire for and embodiment of immunity—a state she achieves by having lost her husband, Barton Kohl, and her mother, Eula.[41] Having been made immune to the impressions and pressures of the town by her devotion to causes of justice, Linda is able to act as a force for progressive change and resistance in the community.

Linda's immunity to Flem—her ability to navigate his environment safely due to her financial independence and genetic divergence—allows her to use the most virulent strain of the Snopes family, Mink, in order to destroy the most entrenched, Flem. As Ratliff explains, the murderous Mink "seems to be a different kind of Snopes like a cotton-mouth is a different kind of snake" (Faulkner, *The Hamlet*, 101), and by turning his embodiment of the family's stubborn and violent pride against itself, Linda successfully inoculates the town and ends the Snopes epidemic. Although the technology and study of the material systems of immunity and autoimmunity were only just being developed in Faulkner's time, Linda's exploitation of Mink reflects contemporary turns in experimental medical technology which use the structure of viral proteins to target autoimmune conditions such as cancer cells. For example, by emptying the viral structure of its dangerous material (RNA/DNA), immunologists and epidemiologists have "reprogrammed" viruses such as HIV, herpes, and measles to target human cancer cells instead of immune system cells.[42] Exploiting viral structures allows these treatments to take on diseases that otherwise hide within the body's own systems of immunity. Whereas Flem exploited the town's structures to gain power, Linda's mitigation of Snopesism in *The Mansion* presents an inversion of Flem's autoimmunity. By exploiting Mink's virulent vendetta against Flem, who refused to support his cousin during the former's trial for the murder of local farmer Jack Houston, Linda conscripts the structure of Mink's inevitable and violent revenge for the peace and health of Yoknapatawpha's social body.

Although the Snopeses are depicted predominantly as outsiders and adversaries to Yoknapatawpha's population, their significant place within Faulkner's larger corpus is reinforced by the final passage of *The Mansion*, in which Mink, having escaped Flem's murder scene, returns to his now dilapidated tenant-farming shack to rest. There, Mink has a vision of himself as transcending his physical body, his family, and his stigmatized "white-trash" identity and becoming part of the larger assemblage of Faulkner's world,

> all mixed up and jumbled up comfortable and easy so wouldn't nobody even know or even care who was which anymore, himself among them, equal to any, good as any, brave as any, being inextricable from, anonymous with all of them:

the beautiful, the splendid, the proud and the brave, right on up to the very top itself among the shining phantoms and dreams which are the milestones of the long human recording . . . (478)

In this final passage, Mink imagines and becomes a part of what Faulkner referred to in the opening note of *The Mansion* as a "living literature" that includes the characters and their author.[43] Faulkner uses Mink, Flem, Linda, and the other Snopeses directly and indirectly to approach his own corpus, its themes, its history, and even its mistakes, oversights, and internal tensions, thereby suggesting that his work's emergent truths lie not in single characters, or in an immunological defensiveness that would reject the interpenetration of history and progress, but in contagiously intersecting networks and the necessary susceptibility of self and other that accompanies healthy sociality.

Reading the Snopeses epidemiologically creates a metaphorical and methodological framework for reading them across and between texts, one that demonstrates an astounding level of formal congruency in how the family operates throughout Faulkner's work. Digital Yoknapatawpha's powerful set of tools, both creative and critical, are of great aid in this endeavor. The ability the project provides to map, track, and graphically situate critical approaches to Faulkner's texts offers a myriad of possibilities for reading the author's corpus in novel ways, of which this essay is only one small example. Imagining the Snopeses as a type of literary disease also brings into focus the ways that Faulkner constructed his work as an unruly literary body, with appendages and assemblages that shape a vast networked organism of literary works. In reading Faulkner epidemiologically, then, I also suggest that we might imagine his body of works as very much still alive and teeming with the possibilities of yet unseen contagious connections and novel interventions.

NOTES

This essay would not have been possible without the groundbreaking work of the scholars, contributors, and digital humanitarians of Digital Yoknapatawpha and the congenial atmosphere of the Faulkner and Yoknapatawpha conference. Special thanks to Jay Watson, Stephen Railton, Theresa M. Towner, Johannes Burgers, and Jenna Sciuto for encouragement in my collaborations with Digital Yoknapatawpha.

1. Centers for Disease Control and Prevention, "Covid-19 in Racial and Ethnic Minority Groups," CDC.gov, https://www.cdc.gov/coronavirus/2019-ncov/need-extra-precautions/racial-ethnic-minorities.html, accessed June 9, 2020.

2. William Faulkner, *The Hamlet* (New York: Vintage International, 1991), 16. Hereafter cited parenthetically.

3. For additional scholarship on class and race in the Snopes trilogy, see J. Warren Beck, *Man in Motion: Faulkner's Trilogy* (Madison: University of Wisconsin Press, 1961); Michael Wainwright, *Darwin and Faulkner's Novels: Evolution and Southern Fiction* (New York: Palgrave Macmillan, 2008); Sheldon S. Kohn, "'You're Like Me': Flem Snopes and the Dynamics of Citizenship in William Faulkner's *The Town*," *Mississippi Quarterly* 67, no. 3 (Summer 2014): 461-81; and Justin Millette, "'It aint nothing but jest another Snopes': White Trash in Faulkner's Snopes Trilogy," *Mississippi Quarterly* 70-71, no. 1 (Winter 2017-2018): 41-60.

4. Stephen Railton, Johannes Burger, Theresa M. Towner, et al., Digital Yoknapatawpha http://faulkner.iath.virginia.edu/index.html, accessed December 1, 2019. Hereafter cited internally. For more information on Digital Yoknapatawpha, see Stephen Railton et al., "Digital Yoknapatawpha: A Written Roundtable," *Mississippi Quarterly* 68, no. 3-4 (Summer-Fall 2015).

5. J. N. Hays, *The Burdens of Disease: Epidemics and Human Response in Western History* (New Brunswick, NJ: Rutgers University Press, 2009), 252.

6. US Department of Health and Human Services, Centers for Disease Control and Prevention, *Principles of Epidemiology in Public Health Practice*, 3rd ed. (Atlanta: CDC Office of Workforce and Career Development, 2012), 1-2.

7. Roldolfo Saracci, *Epidemiology: A Very Short Introduction* (Oxford, UK: Oxford University Press, 2010), 2.

8. Hays, *Burdens of Disease*, 4.

9. Hays, *Burdens of Disease*, 5.

10. Below, I examine how visualizations from Digital Yoknapatawpha visually reinforce the movement of Snopes characters in and out of Frenchman's Bend and Jefferson. See figs. 10.3-10.5.

11. Susan Sontag, *Illness as Metaphor and AIDS and Its Metaphors* (New York: Picador, 1990), 57, 76.

12. Sarraci, *Epidemiology*, 11.

13. Priscilla Wald, *Contagious: Cultures, Carriers, and the Outbreak Narrative* (Durham, NC: Duke University Press, 2008), 2.

14. Wald, *Contagious: Cultures, Carriers, and the Outbreak Narrative*, 19.

15. Theresa M. Towner, *Faulkner on the Color Line: The Later Novels* (Jackson: University Press of Mississippi, 2000), 76.

16. Towner, *Faulkner on the Color Line: The Later Novels*, 90.

17. Towner, *Faulkner on the Color Line: The Later Novels*, 77.

18. Nancy Isenberg, *White Trash: The 400-year Untold History of Class in America* (New York: Penguin, 2017), 283, 287, 284.

19. Matt Wray, *Not Quite White: White Trash and the Boundaries of Whiteness* (Durham, NC: Duke University Press, 2006), 2.

20. James Gray Watson, *The Snopes Dilemma: Faulkner's Trilogy* (Coral Gables, FL: University of Miami Press, 1968), 12.

21. Irving Howe, "Faulkner: End of a Road," *New Republic* 14, no. 23 (December 7, 1959), 19, 20.

22. Isenberg, *White Trash*, 373. Flem is often described as having eyes "the color of stagnant water" (Faulkner, *The Hamlet*, 24, 57), and his gaze is likewise described as "not really looking at you at all, like a pond of stagnant water is not looking at you" (William Faulkner, *The Town*, rev. ed. [1957; repr., New York: Vintage International, 2011], 175). *The Town* is hereafter cited parenthetically.

23. Wray, *Not Quite White*, 76.

24. Wray, *Not Quite White*, 94.

25. Jay Watson, "Introduction: Situating Whiteness in Faulkner Studies, Situating Faulkner in Whiteness Studies," *Faulkner and Whiteness*, ed. Watson (Jackson: University Press of Mississippi, 2011), x.

26. "Character search: Snopes," Digital Yoknapatawpha, http://faulkner.iath.virginia.edu/characters.html, accessed May 26, 2020.

27. Joseph Gold, "The Normality of Snopesism: Universal Themes in Faulkner's *The Hamlet*," *Wisconsin Studies in Contemporary Literature* 3, no. 1 (Winter, 1962): 25.

28. William Faulkner, *As I Lay Dying*, rev. ed. (1930; New York: Vintage International, 1990), 134. Hereafter cited parenthetically.

29. Near the conclusion of *The Hamlet*, Eustice Grimm is revealed to be a "secret" Snopes, as "Eustice's ma was Ab Snopes' youngest sister" (399). Foreshadowed by his role in *As I Lay Dying*, Grimm acts as Flem's accomplice in the salted goldmine scheme at the old Frenchman's place through which Flem seizes Ratliff's share in a Jefferson restaurant, a move which facilitates his epidemic leap into Jefferson.

30. William Faulkner, *Sanctuary*, rev. ed. (1931; repr., New York: Vintage International, 1993), 206. Hereafter cited parenthetically.

31. William Faulkner, *The Mansion*, rev. ed. (1959; repr., New York: Vintage International, 2011), 329. Hereafter cited parenthetically.

32. See figure 10.2, Johannes H. Burgers, et al., eds., "Character-Location Heatmap: Snopes, *The Hamlet*," Digital Yoknapatawpha, http://faulkner.iath.virginia.edu/index.html?search=Character&text=H&name_present=Snopes&name_mentioned=Snopes, accessed December 1, 2019. *The Hamlet* heatmap with character-location data from DY shows the large number of Snopes figures present in the novel and also clearly identifies Frenchman's Bend as the "hot" primary area of activity. Flem's trip to Texas with Eula and Linda also appears as darker or "cooler" narrative activity on the "nation" map.

33. Benjamin Child, "Astonishing Byblows: Rurality, Snopesism, and Populist Modernization in Faulkner's Frenchman's Bend," *Modern Fiction Studies* 64, no. 2 (Summer 2018): 293.

34. Towner, *Faulkner on the Color Line*, 77.

35. See fig. 10.3, James B. Carothers et al., eds., "Character-Location Heatmap: Snopes, *The Town*," Digital Yoknapatawpha, http://faulkner.iath.virginia.edu/index.html?search=Character&text=T&name_present=Snopes&name_mentioned=Snopes, accessed December 1, 2019. This visualization shows the epidemic movement and growth of the Snopes population both in Frenchman's Bend and in Jefferson, with the primary narrative activity taking place in the town. The figures of red and white indicate the "four Snopes Indians or Indian Snopes," which Flem exiles back to Texas (Faulkner, *The Town*, 381).

36. Sontag, *Illness as Metaphor*, 8, 9.

37. Inspired by a reading of Voltaire's *Candide*, Eula Biss suggests in *Immunity: An Inoculation* that immunity (and vaccination) is a way of "cultivating the world" in the way that Candide cultivates his garden—a way of dealing with the senseless cruelty of ours, "the best of all possible worlds." Biss writes, "Immunity is a shared space—a garden we tend together" (*Immunity: An Inoculation* [Minneapolis, MN: Graywolf Press, 2014], 200). For Ratliff, apparently also a reader of Voltaire, the most disturbing aspect of the Snopes outbreak is how little the local population seems to want to immunize against it. When the other locals brush off the sudden multitudinous appearance of Snopeses, Ratliff responds with exasperated sarcasm, asking, "What could be wrong with nothing nowhere nohow in this here best of all possible worlds?" (Faulkner, *The Hamlet*, 179). Ratliff sees the immunological garden-world of Yoknapatawpha as going dangerously untended, and the Snopeses embody the social contagion against which the community's weak immune system has failed to respond.

38. For more on the discourses of immunity and autoimmunity as both scientific and cultural objects and topics of study, see Warwick Anderson, *Intolerant Bodies: A Short History of Autoimmunity* (Baltimore: Johns Hopkins University Press, 2014); Ed Cohen, *A Body Worth Defending* (Durham, NC: Duke University Press, 2009); Donna Haraway, "The Biopolitics of Postmodern Bodies: Constitutions of Self in Immune System Discourse," in *Simians, Cyborgs, and Women: The Reinvention of Nature* (New York: Routledge, 1991), 203-30; Beth Ferri, "Metaphors of Contagion and the Autoimmune Body," *Feminist Formations* 30, no. 1 (Spring 2018): 1-20; and Biss, *Immunity*.

39. Jacques Derrida, *Rogues: Two Essays on Reason*, trans. Pascale Anne-Brault and Michael Naas (Palo Alto, CA: Stanford University Press, 2005), 34-35.

40. Derrida, *Rogues*, 36.

41. Linda's immunity is different in kind from her mother Eula's: "[Eula's] daughter didn't have whatever it was that she had" (Faulkner, *The Town*, 77) explains Chick, who calls Linda "frigid" (Faulkner, *The Mansion*, 389). Linda's immunity to Snopesism is explained in relation to her lack of Eula's appeal, which is rooted in her susceptibility, but "Linda didn't have that quality; that one was not transferable" (235): unlike Snopesism, Eula's tantalizing nonimmunity—her sexual and economic susceptibiulity—is apparently not genetically transmissible.

42. See Robert Cattaneo et al., "Reprogrammed Viruses as Cancer Therapeutics: Targeted, Armed and Shielded," *Nature Reviews Microbiology* 6 (2008): 529-40; Shanglong Liu et al., "Advances in Herpes Simplex for Cancer Treatment," *Sci China Life Sci* 4, no. 56 (April 2013): 298-305; and Daisuke Watanabe and Fumi Goshima, "Oncolytic Virotherapy by HSV," *Advanced Experimental Medicine and Biology* 1045 (December 2017): 63-84.

43. Also quoted in Joseph Blotner, ed., *Selected Letters of William Faulkner* (New York: Random House, 1977), 430.

"Faulkner Wasn't 'Our People'"

Faulkner's "Negroes," the McJunkinses' Faulkner, and Our Search for Greenfield Farm

GARRY BERTHOLF

In June 1963, WCKT, a Florida-based commercial radio station, conducted a studio interview in Miami with James Baldwin. During the interview, Baldwin was asked a question by a polite white woman who was sitting in the audience. "What," she asked, "is the role of the American Negro in literature today?"[1] Baldwin began his reply by explaining his resentment toward William Faulkner, whose "Negroes" (or Negro characters), according to Baldwin, "exist mainly for the comfort of whites," to "corroborate the American fantasy."[2] "For the first time in American history," explained Baldwin, "in the history of American literature—I, speaking now as a Negro, have been described by *you* for hundreds of years. Now *I* can describe *you*—and that's part of the panic!"[3] Of course we know well the so-called "Negroes" of Yoknapatawpha, but, after Baldwin, perhaps we should wonder how Faulkner's "Negroes" would have described *him*?[4] By "Faulkner's Negroes," then, I do not mean his fictional characters—I mean the real-life domestic servants and farmhands who toiled at Rowan Oak and Greenfield Farm.

Faulkner's home in Oxford, Rowan Oak, was built in 1844 and declared a National Historic Landmark in 1968. It stands on more than twenty-nine acres just south of the Oxford Square, while Greenfield Farm, which is located seventeen miles northeast of Oxford, was the name of Faulkner's 320-acre farm, which he purchased in 1938. Before we turn our attention to the oral history of Faulkner's Greenfield Farm, however, a bit of attention is due to the kinds of relationship Faulkner seems to have been at pains to project himself as having with his Black domestic servants and farmhands.

Perhaps nowhere is the ideology of southern white paternalism more egregiously captured than in the Ford Foundation's short film about William Faulkner. The episode, simply titled "William Faulkner," was produced by Robert Saudek and broadcast by CBS for its *Omnibus* program on December 28, 1952. While a single essay would scarcely suffice to unpack everything that is problematic with the painfully scripted scenes in Saudek's film, consider the following voice-overs, stills (see fig. 11.1 and 11.2), and conversation between Faulkner and farmworker Lawrence Arenza "Renzi" McJunkins:

> Narrator: Here in Oxford, Lafayette County, Mississippi, we have a citizen who refers to himself as a "farmer," a farmer who also writes. This is William Faulkner of Oxford, Mississippi. His family is "Old South," and he's never been gone from Lafayette County for long. Yet the name of William Faulkner is spread throughout the world as one of the greatest American writers of fiction today. His friends are the friends of his boyhood.... And what he writes about he has always known because it has been a part of his life.
>
> McJunkins: Mr. Bill! Step here—I can't leave the mules. Please, sir.
>
> Faulkner: What's on your mind, Renzi?
>
> McJunkins: Is it so, [that] folks all over the country read these books you write—those homemade books—and pay you big money for 'em?
>
> Faulkner: Sure is.
>
> McJunkins: If you ain't careful, your name is gonna be known further than your face!
>
> Faulkner: Ha ha! Well, when that happens, I'll just send them back here to get a recommend from you. Is that all right?
>
> McJunkins: That'll be good.
>
> Narrator: A lot of us talk about decency, about honor, about loyalty, about gratitude. Bill doesn't talk about these things; he lives them. If you are his friend and the mob should choose to crucify you, Bill would be there without summons. He would carry your cross up the hill for you.[5]

Throughout Suadek's film, the laureate-cum-farmer is seen attending to his horses, socializing with his Black farmhands, riding his tractor, and fastening chicken wire around a wooden fence post—all while joking about the global demands of the literary marketplace and the rising costs of prescription drugs, to name just a few of the topics that come up in conversation. While Faulkner wants us to believe that Black laborers are the fortunate objects of his paternal affection, what the film unwittingly exposes is how the white planter class appealed to the paternalistic rhetoric and logic of the "family" in order to mask unequal power relations.

Figure 11.1. Film still of William Faulkner (*left*) and Lawrence Arenza "Renzi" McJunkins (*right*) at Greenfield Farm. From the Ford Foundation's short film about William Faulkner, produced by Robert Saudek, broadcast by CBS (*Omnibus*), December 28, 1952. Courtesy of the David Susskind Estate.

Figure 11.2. Film still of William Faulkner riding a tractor at Greenfield Farm. From the Ford Foundation's film about William Faulkner, produced by Robert Saudek, broadcast by CBS (*Omnibus*), December 28, 1952. Courtesy of the David Susskind Estate.

Another important site for thinking about the fiction of southern paternalism is that which is perhaps the most intentional of Faulkner's writing acts—his last will and testament.[6] On March 27, 1940, William Faulkner executed a new will, revising the one he had previously prepared in 1934. His revisions included provisions for Ned Barnett—or "Uncle Ned," as the Faulkners put it. Barnett was, of course, not just the butler at Rowan Oak, but also a worker at Greenfield Farm.

Figure 11.3 is from the J. R. Cofield Collection at the University of Mississippi. It also appears in Thadious M. Davis's *Games of Property: Law, Race, Gender, and Faulkner's* Go Down, Moses (2003).[7] In the Cofield Collection, the photograph is titled "William Faulkner, Estelle, and Jill with group in costumes on the steps of Rowan Oak," while the accompanying description reads: "Hunt Club Breakfast. Marked '38 at home.'"[8] In *Games of Property*, Davis provides us with a much "thicker" description of this photograph, in words worth quoting at length:

> Faulkner role-playing as "lord of the manor" in formal riding gear and hosting a breakfast at Rowan Oak after a hunt, Sunday, 8 May 1938. Photographed with his wife, Estelle, and daughter, Jill, friends and servants, all dressed for the party. Ned Barrett [*sic*], serving as butler with a tray of shot glasses of bourbon, had been owned by Faulkner's great-grandfather, W. C. Falkner (the "Old Colonel"). [Barnett] remained with the Faulkner family after emancipation and was the model for Lucas Beauchamp in *Go Down, Moses* and *Intruder in the Dust*.[9]

Figure 11.3. "William Faulkner, Estelle, and Jill with group in costumes on the steps of Rowan Oak." May 8, 1938. Courtesy of the J. R. Cofield Collection, Archives and Special Collections, University of Mississippi Libraries.

The following excerpt from Faulkner's 1940 will, which is a part of the Louis Daniel Brodsky Collection at Southeast Missouri State University, appears in a 1979 article by Robert Hamblin:

> The above devise is made, with the understanding that Ned Barnett, colored, if he outlives me, is to have the house he now lives in, rent free, as long as he remains on this farm. If at my death the title to said farm is clear in my name, the said Barnett is to receive clear title to said house and the piece of ground on which it rests.... The said Ned Barnett is also to have rent free to cultivate a five-acre piece of ground ... until his death at which time all of said property will revert to my estate ... and the said Barnett is to have use of such livestock and tools as are on said farm and necessary to cultivate the land left to him.[10]

These provisions for Barnett were removed from subsequent iterations of Faulkner's will, however, due to the passing of Barnett in 1947.

No sooner had Barnett been removed from the will than Faulkner extended similar provisions to two of his Black farmhands: Payne Wilson and Lawrence Arenza McJunkins. In fact, a close reading of Faulkner's 1951 will reveals the names of several close friends and family members (in the order in which they appear): his wife, Estelle; his daughter, Jill; his brother Jack; his friend and mentor Phil Stone; his mother, Maude [*sic*];

his niece Dean; his brother John; his nephews, Jimmy and "Chooky"; his Black farmhands Wilson and McJunkins; his stepson, Malcolm; and his godson, Phillip.[11] And here the penultimate and final lines of "Item 11" of the 1951 will are worth quoting at length:

> This option is also subject to the right of Payne Wilson to use the land he is now using on said farm at a yearly rental of Fifty ... Dollars ($50.00) and the said Payne Wilson shall not be dispossessed from said property now being used by him as long as he pays said rent promptly each year. This option is also subject to the right of Lawrence Arenza McJunkin [sic] to remain upon said property as long as he chooses and without rent and, in the event, my said nephews shall exercise their option to buy said property it is my wish that they will continue to employ the said McJunkin [sic] as I now do.[12]

With few exceptions, Faulkner's 1954 will reveals the names of the same close friends and family members already mentioned (though his mother, Maud, is missing); in addition, three names are added: his editor, Saxe Commins, and Lawrence Arenza McJunkins's nephew and brother, Alvis and Charles respectively. In similar fashion to the February 1951 will, Faulkner's August 1954 will describes

> the right of Payne Wilson to use the land he is now using on said farm at a yearly rental of Fifty Dollars ($50.00) and the said Payne Wilson should not be dispossessed from said property now being used by him as long as he pays said rent promptly each year, either during the life of this option or as long as the title to said property shall remain in my daughter, Jill Faulkner. Even if said Payne Wilson fails to pay the rent, he shall not be dispossessed of the house in which he is living, but shall live in said house rent free; but my daughter, Jill Faulkner, may rent said land formerly used for farming by Payne Wilson if, in her opinion, this is practical or necessary. The above provisions of this paragraph are also subject to the right of Lawrence Arenza McJunkin [sic] to remain upon said property as long as he chooses, subject to the present arrangement with Charlie McJunkin [sic] as manager so long as my daughter, Jill Faulkner, shall keep said farm property, provided that said Lawrence Arenza McJunkin [sic], Alvis McJunkin [sic] and Charlie McJunkin [sic] meet any other competitive offer for profitable rent of said farm.[13]

Upon my discovery of these wills in January 2018, two basic questions preoccupied my initial research: "Who is Payne Wilson?" and "Who are the McJunkinses?" After days and days of scouring through the digital archives of the United States Federal Census Collection and Public Records Index, I finally discovered that the Wilsons and McJunkinses were Black farmers at Greenfield and that many of their descendants—and especially many of the McJunkinses—were still living in Lafayette County. I eventually learned that three of the McJunkinses were currently working for the University of Mississippi, and very shortly thereafter I made contact with LaTasha McJunkins, who referred me to her sister-in-law, Trudy (McJunkins) Young. Trudy, it turns out, is the daughter of Alvis McJunkins—the same Alvis McJunkins who appears in Faulkner's 1954 will. I first met Trudy and her husband, William, on July 24, 2018, on the eve of my presentation at the forty-fifth annual Faulkner and Yoknapatawpha Conference on "Faulkner and Slavery." That afternoon, a few hours before I met Trudy and William in person, I made the seventeen-mile trek by car from Rowan Oak to Faulkner's Greenfield farm.

For a little more than a dozen miles, I followed Mississippi Highway 30 east—the long stretch of road now designated "William Faulkner Memorial Highway"—until I turned north at the abandoned Philadelphia Country Bumpkin gas station. Less than a mile up county road 249, just on the other side of the creek, a farm lay buried in fields of soybeans. Turning left off the main road, I continued down a dirt path to the west, beyond the broken-down front gate, around acres and acres of soybean plants, to what appeared to be a literal and figurative dead end. To my dismay, I found no specific traces of either William Faulkner or the McJunkinses. With some time to spare before my meeting with Trudy, I hit the back roads of Holly Springs National Forest, wandering aimlessly north of Puskus Creek, for miles and miles, without a soul in sight. At one point in my journey, I happened on a small and unremarkable sign, pointing in the direction of the Bethlehem Christian Methodist Episcopal Church. And just down the road from the Bethlehem CME Church is a small and unkept cemetery, where the Wilson and McJunkins families are buried. Among those laid there to rest, then, is Lawrence Arenza "Renzi" McJunkins. (See fig. 11.4.)

According to the inscription on his headstone, Lawrence died on December 15, 1969. It turns out that he is buried just three and a half miles away from the main entrance to Faulkner's farm. It was in this moment that I think I felt something close to the frisson of uncanniness that frightened Alice Walker, back in the summer of 1973, when she discovered the unmarked grave of Zora Neale Hurston.[14]

Together with Trudy and William, I returned to the farm later that day. It was some little time before Trudy found her bearings, and she guided us deep into the woods. We turned off the beaten path and advanced uphill through the forested area, without any visible trace of her uncle's home that she remembered from her childhood. After what seemed like

Figure 11.4. Headstone of Lawrence Arenza McJunkins (1910–1969), Bethlehem CME Church Cemetery, Lafayette County, Mississippi, July 24, 2018. Photograph by Garry Bertholf.

Figure 11.5. Former home of Lawrence Arenza McJunkins, Greenfield Farm, Lafayette County, Mississippi, July 24, 2018. Photograph by Garry Bertholf.

an eternity, but what must in reality have been about fifteen minutes or so, we serendipitously spotted a building in the clearing (fig. 11.5).

According to Trudy, this is the former and now defunct home of her uncle, Lawrence Arenza McJunkins. Compare the façades pictured in figures 11.6 and 11.7.

As you can see above, the backdrop against which this familiar scene was filmed matches the façade of the abandoned house we found. Of course the two men featured in the still above are Lawrence McJunkins and William Faulkner.

Trudy also led William and me to the site of the house in which she was born—a home that, it turns out, originally belonged to Payne Wilson—and, despite being over a mile apart, both places, I have been told, are within the boundaries of Faulkner's Greenfield Farm. Later that night, the three of us had dinner with several other members of the McJunkins family, including Trudy's brother Charles, who shared with us his vivid childhood memories and oral history of Faulkner at Greenfield Farm.

I returned to Oxford the following year, in July 2019, for the forty-sixth annual Faulkner and Yoknapatawpha Conference on "Faulkner's Families." This time Charles and his cousin, Theron McJunkins, agreed to join me as I retraced some of the steps that I had taken with Trudy and William the summer before. In lieu of a more "disciplined" description of

Figure 11.6. Film still of Lawrence Arenza "Renzi" McJunkins (*above*) and William Faulkner (*below*) at Greenfield Farm. From the Ford Foundation's short film about William Faulkner, produced by Robert Saudek, broadcast by CBS (*Omnibus*), December 28, 1952. Courtesy of the David Susskind Estate.

Figure 11.7. Former home of Lawrence Arenza McJunkins, Greenfield Farm, Lafayette County, Mississippi, July 24, 2018. Photograph by Garry Bertholf.

what happened that day, I have chosen here to provide a partial transcription of my interview with Charles and Trudy, an interview that formed part of our 2019 panel titled "Faulkner's Black Families in Oxford and Lafayette County." I have sought in the following transcription to reproduce with as much fidelity as possible on the page the interview that I conducted with Trudy and Charles at the University of Mississippi's David H. Nutt Auditorium on July 22, 2019.

Garry Bertholf: Charles, I want to ask you about some of the family photographs you shared with me. When we met up with Theron on Suncrest Street, you shared a bunch of family photographs with me; and, as we agreed, I'm now going to share a couple of them with the audience.

Charles McJunkins: [The woman on the left is Sally McJunkins, who was born in 1864], and she lived pretty much through the Reconstruction era. And that's—on the right—is the first McJunkins relative that we have in this area. . . . He was born in 1862 . . . and he was a blacksmith and a horse doctor.

GB: How did you get this photograph, Charles?

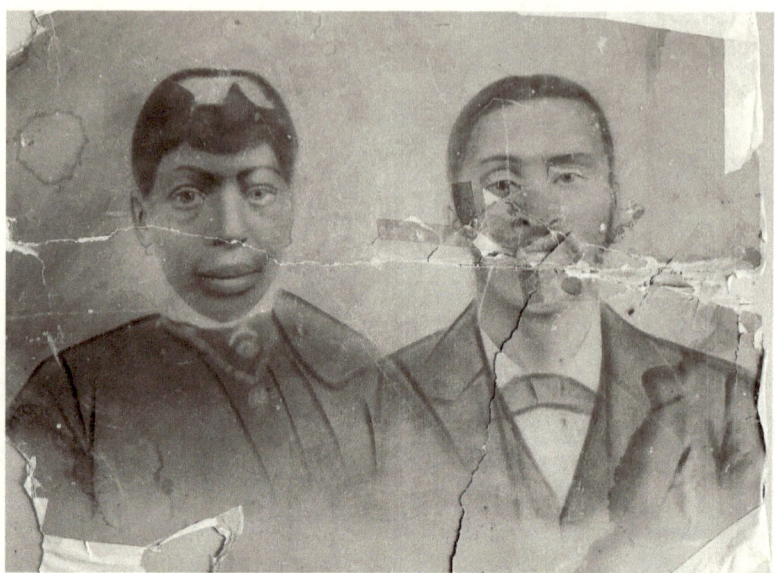

Figure 11.8. Family photograph of Sally (*left*) and Charles "Big Charlie" McJunkins (*right*)—great-grandparents of Trudy (McJunkins) Young and Charles McJunkins. Courtesy of the McJunkins family.

CM: This photograph came from my grandfather, Charlie—"Little" Charlie, not this Charlie—McJunkins, and it [was passed down to] my uncle, . . . and upon my aunt's passing, she passed it down to me.

GB: Okay, so there are a lot of Charlies—your great-grandfather, your grandfather, and [you]. So, here's another photograph that we talked about yesterday. Can you talk to us a little bit about this one?

CM: Yes, please don't be confused by all of the Charlies. These are the children of "Big" Charlie. This is "Little" Charlie McJunkins along with his sisters. . . . "Big" Charlie was a carpenter; he purchased his own property—he owned land north of what you call the Greenfield Farm.

GB: Do you know anything about his two sisters?

CM: His sisters married into the community. One went into the Williams family, which is another story. And the other. . . . I don't know much about them.

GB: Where did your grandfather live?

CM: My grandfather lived north of the Faulkner farm. He had a hundred-acre plat north of William Faulkner's farm, and he pretty much farmed that and lived [there]. Now he did work for Faulkner from time

Faulkner's "Negroes," the McJunkinses' Faulkner, Our Search for Greenfield Farm

Figure 11.9. Family photograph of Julie (*left*), Charles "Little Charlie" (*center*), and Barbara McJunkins (*right*)—the children of "Big Charlie" and Sally McJunkins. "Little Charlie" was Charles and Trudy's grandfather. Courtesy of the McJunkins family.

to time. . . . Him and William Faulkner were good friends; [he wasn't] necessarily an employee.

GB: So, he had a separate hundred-acre farm northwest of Greenfield?

CM: Yes, but that wasn't unusual because there were several plats of land that were owned by Black people.

GB: So, the McJunkinses had their own farm before Faulkner purchased Greenfield?

CM: Yes, absolutely!

GB: Trudy, here are a couple of family photographs that you shared with me. Can you talk to us about them?

Trudy (McJunkins) Young: This is my father, Alvis McJunkins, and my mother, Ardelia McJunkins. I didn't get to spend a lot of time with [my father]—I was eleven years old when he passed away—but he was kind; and when he told you something, he meant what he said. Back in those days he was somewhat strict, but he was kind. And in our community he was the barber; and I think he did electrical work and stuff around the community.

GB: Charles, earlier you said that you might want to add a couple of things here.

Figure 11.10 and 11.11. Family photographs of Alvis (*left*) and Ardelia McJunkins (*right*)—the parents of Trudy and Charles. Courtesy of the McJunkins family.

CM: My father had a seventh-grade education; but he could write, read, and spell almost any word in the dictionary—and I just couldn't understand that. People still can't do it! He did a lot of administrative work for William Faulkner—when William Faulkner wasn't around, he kind of kept things going smoothly. . . . After William Faulkner passed away, some gentleman picked him out somewhere and said, "I like you, and I think you're very sharply dressed. Come and work for me." And he spent his last five years working as a manager at a grocery store called Jitney Jungle.

GB: There's just one more photograph here. Who are these beautiful people?

TY: The lady in the blue is my mother, Ardelia McJunkins. . . . I'm in the middle. This is my sister, [Elmetria]. . . . And there is Charles. And this is my brother, [Sheldry]. My older brother, Dewayne, passed away. But this is Alvis Jr. He's next to the oldest. And in the white is my baby brother, [Ray]. And [my brother] Dana is on the very end.

CM: The brother that's missing is Dewayne McJunkins. I think the city of Oxford gives him credit for being the first Black firefighter in the city.

GB: And I promise you this is the last time that I'm going to make you watch some of this documentary. But I'm just going to pause here because in the montage that appears before the scene about Greenfield Farm, there's this image. Charles, who is this?

CM: That's my father, Alvis McJunkins.

GB: And now I'm going to show you just a minute or so from the film—I'm going to turn the sound down—and Charles has agreed to offer some real-time commentary. Yesterday, Charles, Theron, and I watched this together, and both of them were able to identify everyone in this video.

Figure 11.12. Family photograph of Ardelia McJunkins and her children (*counterclockwise from bottom left*): Ardelia, Trudy, Elmetria, Charles, Sheldry, Alvis Jr., Ray, and Dana. Courtesy of the McJunkins family.

Figure 11.13. Film still of Alvis McJunkins at Greenfield Farm. From the Ford Foundation's film about William Faulkner, produced by Robert Saudek, broadcast by CBS (*Omnibus*), December 28, 1952. Courtesy of the David Susskind Estate.

CM: The man you see here [fig. 11.1], to the left, is William Faulkner, and to the right is "Renzi" McJunkins.

GB: So, that's Renzi?

CM: That's Renzi.

GB: Okay.

CM: His name was Lawrence. They were friends. And he also worked for him. When William Faulkner wanted to come back to the farm and relax, this is the man he'd come and hang out with. I don't know what their conversation was about.

GB: Just a few more seconds. (See fig. 11.14.)

CM: Of course that's Renzi. And the man to his right is . . . a person that was adopted and placed in our family; his last name was Jones, and his first name is Tommy.

GB: So, you recognize this person [fig. 11.15] as well?

CM: That's Jim Buddy.

GB: Faulkner didn't live in that house [fig. 11.14]?

CM: No, Faulkner did not.

GB: Where did he stay?

CM: Faulkner did not live in the house. Faulkner had his own writing house or studio. . . . George McJunkins . . . was married to Bertha—they lived in that house.

GB: Okay, let's move on to another photograph [fig. 11.16]. Trudy, do you recognize this?

TY: That's an old tree. . . . My dad built a swing there. I'll never forget that tree. It was huge.

Figure 11.14. Film still of William Faulkner (*left*), Tommy Jones (*center*), and Lawrence Arenza "Renzi" McJunkins (*right*) at Greenfield Farm. From the Ford Foundation's film about William Faulkner, produced by Robert Saudek, broadcast by CBS (*Omnibus*), December 28, 1952. Courtesy of the David Susskind Estate.

Figure 11.15. Film still of Jim Buddy (*left*) and William Faulkner (*right*) at Greenfield Farm. From the Ford Foundation's film about William Faulkner, produced by Robert Saudek, broadcast by CBS (*Omnibus*), December 28, 1952. Courtesy of the David Susskind Estate.

GB: So, there used to be a house there, right?

TY: Our house was . . . a few feet from that tree.

GB: How far away was your grandfather's farm from this location? Because this is about a mile or so north from the entrance to Greenfield.

CM: The road we took, maybe a mile; but directly through the woods, along the power line, it would be right at a half mile.

GB: Do either of you want to say anything about the cemetery [fig. 11.17]?

CM: It goes all the way back to shortly after the Emancipation era. . . . The church itself was built by Charlie McJunkins.

GB: Trudy and Charles, what do you think about the fact that your father and grandfather and brother were all mentioned in Faulkner's last will? Do you have any thoughts about that?

CM: You know, Faulkner's [work] was both fiction and nonfiction, and I feel like the will is the same way.

GB: So, did your family know about the will?

CM: Well . . . we couldn't necessarily pin our lives on it. . . . My mother's mother had land near Oxford, and my father started working at the grocery store, and he was doing just fine—so, we took out an FHA Loan, and we moved up here in 1970, and I think my father passed away thirty days later.

GB: Do either of you have any thoughts on the theme of this year's conference, "Faulkner's Families"?

CM: We weren't necessarily "Faulkner's people," and Faulkner wasn't "our people." It was Etta, Mississippi. He came down there to find serenity and to be around us.

Figure 11.16. Childhood homesite of Trudy (McJunkins) Young and Charles McJunkins, Lafayette County, Mississippi, July 21, 2019. Photograph by Garry Bertholf.

Figure 11.17. Bethlehem C.M.E. Church Cemetery, Lafayette County, Mississippi, July 24, 2018. Photograph by Garry Bertholf.

GB: Trudy?

TY: Well, I guess I haven't given much thought about it. You know, I guess it's kind of cool in a way. You know what I'm saying? Because of who William Faulkner was and to know that my family was connected to him. I find it kind of cool. But at the same time, you know, I don't really take it seriously, if that makes any sense. Ever since I was a little girl, I always knew that we lived on William Faulkner's land. I never understood why, but I was always told that. And as I grow older.... It's kind of cool, but at the same time ... like I said....

From all this a more capacious history needs to be spun, the kind of deep history we seldom encounter in literary studies, one that privileges the collective labor of literary production rather than the creative genius of the individual writer. How often is the collective and antipaternalistic praxis of everyday laborers (blacksmiths, horse doctors, carpenters, farmers, barbers, electricians, grocery clerks, firefighters, and mothers) reduced to triviality or mentioned only in passing? At issue, it turns out, is a question about the political economy of Greenfield Farm and its racialized division of (invisible) labor. Lawrence Arenza "Renzi" McJunkins, for example, enters into the history (or at least Joseph Blotner's biography) of Faulkner through an anecdote in which some of the Nobel Prize winner's commercial success is, we are told, attributed to his Black farmhand, Renzi, whose responsibilities included "see[ing] that [Faulkner] returned to Oxford in condition to resume his unfinished work."[15] To be sure,

Blotner offers us a good point of entry, since there are (as we know) always already a multitude of historical actors involved in the creation of any literary work, fiction or otherwise. While our historiographical range usually extends to creative writers and their colonies, how often do literary scholars draw the line sharply at the "history that hurts," as Saidiya Hartman once put it: "the still-unfolding narrative of captivity, dispossession, and domination that engenders the black subject in the Americas."[16] A literary history that "hurts," so to speak, would necessarily entail a materialist approach to the history of the book. What might be taken up instead of questions like "where did this book come from?" and "how did it get here?" is a serious consideration of who built the actual writing space itself, not to mention the desk and the chair. Put another way: how often do we acknowledge the material foundations of canonical texts? How many conversations about American literature have been and continue to be predicated on the absence of the descendants of slaves? The fact that it has taken this long to investigate as an epistemological matter the lived experiences and oral histories of Faulkner's Black laborers and their descendants is a profound reflection of the problem.

The former home and final resting place of Lawrence Arenza McJunkins are both within seventeen miles of Bondurant Hall, the home of the English department at the University of Mississippi. Perhaps it is unsurprising that relatively little attention has been paid to McJunkins, other than a brief cameo appearance in that fourteen-minute film and passing mentions of him here and there. But in so far as the University of Mississippi was once serious about transforming Greenfield Farm into a "living history museum,"[17] it is surprising that there are still no historical markers at Greenfield; at least, none that I know of—and certainly none commemorating Faulkner's Black farmhands.

In a letter dated June 3, 1993, Don L. Fruge, former vice chancellor for university affairs at the University of Mississippi and former secretary of the university foundation, described what became known as the "Greenfield Farm Project": "It is our hope to develop Greenfield Farm into an outdoor historical museum which will illustrate and interpret everyday life in rural Mississippi during the late nineteenth and early twentieth centuries."[18] The University of Mississippi archive also contains an undated letter to Fruge from Jim Buck Ross, former Mississippi commissioner of agriculture, who endorsed the project: "It is a commendable project to try to depict this era of our heritage.... It is easy to predict that this proposed effort will be another mecca for those of us who appreciate our roots."[19] In order to "plan and implement" the Greenfield Farm Project, a committee of twenty-seven members was formed, including fifteen advisory board members, six ex officio members, and six steering committee members.[20]

Faulkner's "Negroes," the McJunkinses' Faulkner, Our Search for Greenfield Farm 209

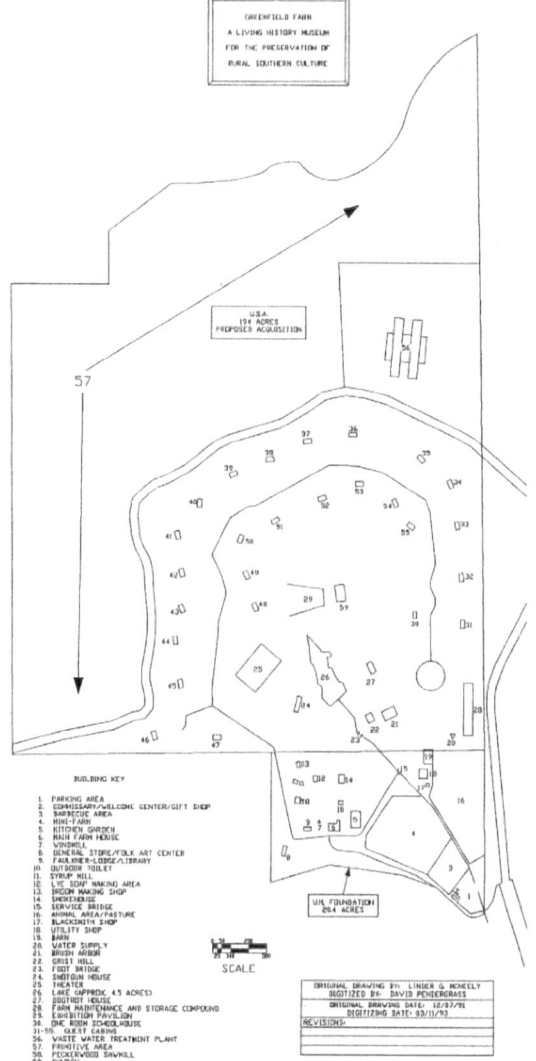

Figure 11.18. Blueprint for "Greenfield Farm: A Living History Museum for the Preservation of Rural Southern Culture." Digitized by David Pendergrass on March 11, 1993; originally drawn by Linder G. McNeeley on December 7, 1991. University of Mississippi Libraries, Archives and Special Collections [Box 28, Folder 2, William Faulkner "Small Manuscripts" Institutional Collections]. Reprinted with permission of the University of Mississippi Foundation.

The advisory board included former Oxford mayor John O. Leslie and former University of Mississippi chancellor R. Gerald Turner. The archives also reveal that the University of Mississippi foundation owned 20.4 acres of Faulkner's farm, while the federal government owned 194 acres at the time.[21] In addition to applying for grants to restore Faulkner's main farmhouse, lodge, and commissary, the committee also planned to fundraise for the creation of a number of functional period-specific amenities and activities—specific to 1938, that is.

On March 11, 1993, David Pendergrass digitized former steering committee chairman Linder G. McNeeley's hand-drawn blueprint from December 7, 1991. (See fig. 11.18.) For the sake of clarity, the "Building Key" above is easy enough to list: (1) Parking Area; (2) Commissary/Welcome Center/Gift Shop; (3) Barbecue Area; (4) Mini-Farm; (5) Kitchen Garden; (6) Main Farm House; (7) Windmill; (8) General Store/Folk Art Center; (9) Faulkner-Lodge/Library; (10) Outdoor Toilet; (11) Syrup Mill; (12) Lye Soap Making Area; (13) Broom Making Shop; (14) Smokehouse; (15) Service Bridge; (16) Animal Area/Pasture; (17) Blacksmith Shop; (18) Utility Shop; (19) Barn; (20) Water Supply; (21) Brush Arbor; (22) Grist Mill; (23) Foot Bridge; (24) Shotgun House; (25) Theater; (26) Lake (Approx. 4.5 Acres); (27) Dogtrot House; (28) Farm Maintenance and Storage Compound; (29) Exhibition Pavilion; (30) One Room Schoolhouse; (31–55) Guest Cabins; (56) Waste Water Treatment Plant; (57) Primitive Area; (58) Peckerwood Sawmill; and (59) Church.[22] Imagine, if you will, "Faulknerland." I should also mention that the steering committee's twenty-point plan called for "small plots" of crops such as cotton to be cultivated by "local workers ... knowledgeable in the old and authentic way" (by which they presumably meant the descendants of slaves).[23] In addition to these "authentic" workers, the plan called for the employment of "approximately twenty mildly handicapped persons."[24] While the Greenfield Farm Project was expected to yield an annual revenue of $3,750,000.00 ("25,000 Families at $150.00 per visit"),[25] it is no wonder that nothing more ever became of this, and we are better off without it. But it is also clear that, long before either the university or federal government took a vested interest in this property, Greenfield Farm had been a site of economic wheeling and dealing.

A close reading of the public land records of Lafayette County, Mississippi, reveals that William Faulkner's initial purchase involved a deed of trust with the Federal Land Bank of New Orleans, to whom he was indebted ($2,000.00 at an annual interest rate of 5%).[26] According to the chancery clerk's archives, Faulkner purchased the farm on March 9, 1938. Interestingly, on December 15, 1938, some nine months after the initial purchase, Faulkner granted one W. L. Stewart an "Oil and Gas Mining" lease "for the purpose of prospecting and drilling for and producing oil

131

LEASE CONTRACT

THE STATE OF MISSISSIPPI C. No.

Lafayette COUNTY

This lease contract made and entered into on this 8 day of October 19 49 by and between:
William Faulkner Lessor of Oxford, Miss.
and Lawrence A. McJunkins Lessee of Etta, Miss.

witnesseth:

1. That the said lessor has agreed and hereby does lease and let to the said lessee to occupy and use for agricultural purposes with full managerial control for a period of 4 year/s from and after the 1st day of November 19 the following described property, located in Lafayette County, State of Mississippi:

Section 28 Township 7 Range 1

and consisting of 20 acres more or less, together with all buildings and improvements thereon and all rights thereto appertaining.

2. That the lessee agrees and obligates himself to pay ~~1/4 of cotton and corn~~ to be delivered at (place) Mr. William Faulkner at time of marketing or as follows (time) ~~Time of marketing~~

OTHER CONDITIONS

IN WITNESS WHEREOF, the parties have signed this lease on the date first above written.

William Falkner (Lessor)

Lawrence A. McJunkins (Lessee)

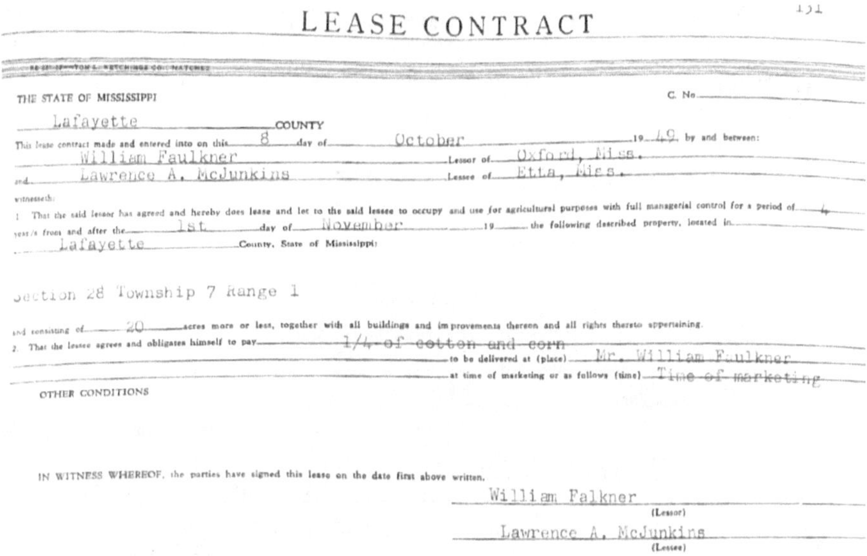

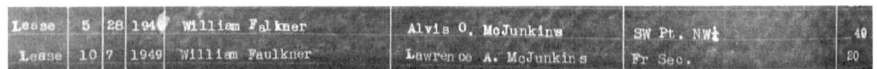

Figure 11.19. The lease contract between William Faulkner and Lawrence Arenza McJunkins, dated October 8, 1949, Deed Record 126, Public Land Records of the Chancery Clerk of Lafayette County, Mississippi, 131. Photograph by Garry Bertholf.

Lease	5	28	194[illegible]	William Falkner	Alvis O. McJunkins	SW Pt. NW¼	40
Lease	10	7	1949	William Faulkner	Lawrence A. McJunkins	Fr Sec.	20

Figure 11.20. "Sectional Index to Lands" (detail) featuring Faulkner's transactions with Alvis and Lawrence Arenza McJunkins, Public Land Records of the Chancery Clerk of Lafayette County, Mississippi, Section 21, Township 7-South, Range 1-West, 304. Photograph by Garry Bertholf.

and gas, and other minerals, laying pipe lines, building tanks, storing oil and building power stations, telephone lines and other structures thereon."[27] And according to the lease, the Federal Land Bank of New Orleans "reserved one half interest in and to all the minerals and mineral rights on [the] land."[28] In similar fashion to his deal with Stewart, moreover, Faulkner granted an "Oil and Gas Mining" lease to one Kennard Cook on July 25, 1942.[29] Of course it would make sense if Faulkner abandoned himself to the oil rush, since the late 1930s seem to have "marked the upward turning point in Mississippi's oil fortunes. . . . For the first time large companies had become interested in Mississippi. . . . Mississippi soon became a mecca for oilmen."[30] More important than his ostensible oil fever, however, is the fact that the public land records include Faulkner's official dealings with the McJunkinses.

On October 8, 1949, William Faulkner leased twenty acres to Lawrence Arenza McJunkins in exchange for 25 percent of the latter's "cotton and corn" (fig. 11.19).[31] The public land records of Lafayette County also reveal that, on May 25, 1949, Faulkner leased forty acres to Alvis McJunkins in exchange for a quarter of his crop (fig. 11.20).[32] These public records also prove Charles's important point above about the McJunkinses owning land in the area before Faulkner. The chancery clerk's "Sectional Index to Lands" indicates that George McJunkins, for example, was deeded one hundred acres on November 13, 1926.[33] One Starling O. McJunkins is also mentioned on several occasions involving various transactions that took place between 1953 and 1964.[34] Furthermore, the Sectional Index also contains a lease contract between "Charlie" McJunkins and one Buford W. McJunkins, dated September 24, 1949.[35]

In case it is not yet obvious, I have focused my hermeneutics on ephemeral archives—interviews, family photographs, transcriptions, blueprints, plans, films, stills, headstones, last wills, letters, public records, census data, deeds, contracts, memos, budget proposals, oral histories, maps, and more—in order to inspire some shifting of sights in the study of William Faulkner beyond, say, his narrative approach and authorial intent. Faulkner's literary achievements were created and constrained by the material and ideological foundations of his environment. His last will is not just a testament to the moral and economic debt his family incurred as slaveholders themselves; it is a part of the legal fiction of southern white paternalism—the same paternalism that is echoed in the memos of Don Fruge and Jim Buck Ross, and in the bullet points of Linder McNeely; and it is what marks Robert Saudek's film from beginning to end. But here I have already moved well beyond my original plan to simply track down some of the McJunkinses. This is the story of how I found Charles and Trudy. This is our story. This is the story of our search for Greenfield Farm.

NOTES

Earlier versions of this essay were presented at the forty-fifth and forty-sixth annual Faulkner and Yoknapatawpha Conferences at the University of Mississippi in Oxford, Mississippi, on July 25, 2018, and July 22, 2019, respectively, and before the African American Studies Department at Wesleyan University in Middletown, Connecticut, on February 12, 2019. Many thanks to Jay Watson for championing this project from the very beginning and then shepherding it to fruition, and to Hortense Spillers, Axelle Karera, Ren Ellis Neyra, Marina Bilbija, Lily Saint, Elizabeth McAlister, Khalil Anthony Johnson, and Sean McCann for their feedback. I am deeply indebted to Zoran Kuzmanovich for introducing me to the Brodsky Collection of Faulkner materials at Southeast Missouri State University and for his close readings of Faulkner's last will. Special thanks to

Jennifer Ford and Emily Oakes of the Department of Archives and Special Collections at the John D. Williams Library, University of Mississippi and to Gloria Nicks at the Chancery Clerk's Office of Lafayette County, Mississippi. I am especially grateful to my coconspirators in this essay—Charles McJunkins and Trudy (McJunkins) Young—for bringing me into their world and to William Young and Theron McJunkins for accompanying us on our journey. This essay is dedicated to the memory of Lawrence Arenza "Renzi" McJunkins (1910-1969), whose name shall long remain etched in the intellectual history of southern literature.

1. James Baldwin at the Florida Forum, moderated by Tom Miller, WCKT News, Channel 7, Miami, FL, June 28, 1963, Walter J. Brown Media Archives and Peabody Awards Collection, University of Georgia (63021 PST).

2. James Baldwin at the Florida Forum, June 28, 1963.

3. James Baldwin at the Florida Forum, June 28, 1963.

4. Together with Baldwin's 1963 WCKT interview, an Africana study of Faulkner might also compare the widely differing critical responses of Richard Wright, Ralph Ellison, Langston Hughes, W. E. B. Du Bois, Toni Morrison, and Édouard Glissant. A few important (if well-known) critiques in this reception history are particularly noteworthy: Wright's 1938 WNYC interview; Ellison's 1953 National Book Award acceptance speech; Baldwin's "Faulkner and Desegregation" (*Partisan Review*, 1956); Hughes's "Concerning a Great Mississippi Writer and the Southern Negro" (*Chicago Defender*, 1956); Du Bois's 1956 KROW interview and telegrammed public debate proposal; Morrison's *Playing in the Dark: Whiteness and the Literary Imagination* (1992) and "Mourning for Whiteness" (*New Yorker*, 2016); and Glissant's *Faulkner, Mississippi* (1996).

5. Robert Saudek, producer, "William Faulkner," *Omnibus*, Ford Foundation, CBS, (December 28, 1952).

6. I am indebted here to Robert Hamblin, founding director of the Center for Faulkner Studies at Southeast Missouri State University, where the Louis Daniel Brodsky Collection is housed. The wills cited in this essay are part of the Brodsky Collection, which is one of the four largest collections of Faulkner materials in the world.

7. Thadious M. Davis, *Games of Property: Law, Race, Gender, and Faulkner's* Go Down, Moses (Durham, NC: Duke University Press, 2003), 186.

8. "William Faulkner, Estelle, and Jill with group in costumes on the steps of Rowan Oak." May 8, 1938. J. R. Cofield Collection, Archives and Special Collections, University of Mississippi Libraries, accessed June 8, 2020, https://egrove.olemiss.edu/cofield/378/.

9. Davis, *Games of Property*, 186.

10. Robert Hamblin, "Lucas Beauchamp, Ned Barnett, and William Faulkner's 1940 Will," *Studies in Bibliography* 32 (1979): 282.

11. "Last Will and Testament of William Faulkner," February 1951, Louis Daniel Brodsky Collection, Southeast Missouri State University.

12. "Last Will and Testament of William Faulkner," February 1951.

13. "Last Will and Testament of William Faulkner," August 1954, Louis Daniel Brodsky Collection, Southeast Missouri State University.

14. Alice Walker, "Looking for Zora," *In Search of Our Mothers' Gardens: Womanist Prose* (New York: Harcourt, 1983).

15. Joseph Blotner, *Faulkner: A Biography*, 1 vol. ed., rev. ed. (1984; repr., Jackson: University Press of Mississippi, 2005), 432.

16. Saidiya Hartman, *Scenes of Subjection: Terror, Slavery, and Self-Making in Nineteenth-Century America* (New York: Oxford University Press, 1997), 51.

17. "Greenfield Farm: 'A Step Back in Time'" (Folder M.C.PS3511.A86Z78352 1993) and "Packet of information on making Faulkner's Greenfield farm an outdoor living museum"

(Folder 2), in "Faulkner Sites" (Box 28), William Faulkner "Small Manuscripts" Institutional Collections, Archives and Special Collections, University of Mississippi Libraries.

18. Fruge's letter appears in *both* the "Step Back in Time" and "Packet of Information" folders.

19. Again, Ross's letter appears in *both* the "Step Back in Time" and "Packet of Information" folders.

20. The document outlining committee membership appears in *both* the "Step Back in Time" and "Packet of Information" folders.

21. The relevant documents appear in *both* the "Step Back in Time" and "Packet of Information" folders.

22. The Building Key appears in *both* the "Step Back in Time" and "Packet of Information" folders.

23. The cited plan appears in *both* the "Step Back in Time" and "Packet of Information" folders.

24. The cited plan appears in *both* the "Step Back in Time" and "Packet of Information" folders.

25. "Packet of Information."

26. Deed of Trust between William Faulkner and the Federal Land Bank of New Orleans, March 9, 1938, Deed Record 111, Public Land Records of the Chancery Clerk of Lafayette County, Mississippi, 46–47; and Miscellaneous Trust Deeds 223, Public Land Records of the Chancery Clerk of Lafayette County, 154-55.

27. Oil and Gas Mining Lease between William Faulkner and W. L. Stewart, December 15, 1938, Miscellaneous Trust Deeds 230, Public Land Records of the Chancery Clerk of Lafayette County, 119-20.

28. Oil and Gas Mining Lease, 119.

29. Oil and Gas Mining Lease between William Faulkner and Kennard Cook, July 25, 1942, Sectional Index to Lands in Lafayette County, Mississippi, Section 21, Township 7-South, Range 1-West, 220.

30. John S. Ezell, "Mississippi's Search for Oil," *Journal of Southern History* 18, no. 3 (August 1952): 327-30.

31. Lease Contract between William Faulkner and Lawrence Arenza McJunkins, October 8, 1949, Deed Record 126, Public Land Records of the Chancery Clerk of Lafayette County, Mississippi, 131.

32. Lease Contract between William Faulkner and Alvis O. McJunkins, May 25, 1949, Deed Record 124, Public Land Records of the Chancery Clerk of Lafayette County, Mississippi, 419.

33. Deed of Trust between George McJunkins and D. A. Pritchard, November 13, 1926, Sectional Index to Lands in Lafayette County, Mississippi, Section 21, Township 7-South, Range 1-West, 228.

34. Oil and Gas Mining Lease as well as multiple Deeds of Trust for Starling McJunkins, 1953-1964, Sectional Index to Lands in Lafayette County, Mississippi, Section 21, Township 7-South, Range 1-West, 220.

35. Lease Contract between "Charlie" and Buford W. McJunkins, September 24, 1949, Sectional Index to Lands in Lafayette County, Mississippi, Section 21, Township 7-South, Range 1-West, 217.

"The Family of Man"

Willian Faulkner, Atomic Diplomacy, and US Visual Education in Post-Occupation Japan

YUKO YAMAMOTO

After its initial showing at the Museum of Modern Art (MoMA), New York, on January 25, 1955, *The Family of Man* toured thirty-eight countries on six continents between 1955 and 1962, curated by the celebrated photographer Edward Steichen and commissioned by the United States Information Agency (USIA). William Faulkner traveled to Latin America, Asia, and Europe between 1954 and 1961 under the auspices of the State Department and USIA. Faulkner arrived in Tokyo, Japan, on August 1, 1955. On this occasion, the Nobel laureate, increasingly known as a taciturn and private man, starred in the short documentary film *Impressions of Japan* (1955), produced by the United States Information Service (USIS) Tokyo, an overseas post of USIA. A week later, on August 8, Steichen arrived in Tokyo to make necessary arrangements for the Japanese version of *The Family of Man*. The exhibition opened on March 21, 1956, cosponsored by USIS.

Despite the growing interest in the role Faulkner played in the cultural Cold War, detailed research on his visit to Japan in 1955 is still very scarce.[1] Situating his visit and his appearance in a USIS film in the broader context of US public diplomacy towards Japan will shed new light on Faulkner's role as a cultural ambassador, adopting the motto of USIA, "telling America's story to the world." This essay considers the film *Impressions of Japan* and the exhibit *The Family of Man*, both USIS-sponsored cultural activities in Japan, in relation to the Atoms for Peace campaign of the mid-1950s. An analysis of the two "visual aids" in the context of atomic diplomacy reveals how deeply Faulkner had been implicated in the hidden agenda of US visual education in post-occupation

Japan. What emerges from juxtaposing the film and the exhibit in this context is that, in the postwar Cold War era, Faulkner himself became an official spokesperson and icon for "the Family of Man," the Cold War nuclear family of the Western Free World.

The Atoms for Peace Campaign in Japan, 1954-1955

When Dwight D. Eisenhower became president in January 1953, "psychological warfare" became of supreme importance to the implementation of US national and foreign policy. In 1952, in one presidential campaign speech drafted by C. D. Jackson, Eisenhower pledged to make it central to his administration. Eisenhower stated that the aim in the Cold War was not territorial or military conquest but "more subtle, more pervasive, more complete." It is the combat for "winning other people to your side." The psychological warfare he thus defines is "the struggle for the minds and wills of men." To triumph in this battle, he promised a strong central government in which federal agencies and bureaus cooperate "under a coordinated program" to "produce the maximum effect."[2] During his presidency, Eisenhower acted in accordance with his commitment to psychological warfare against Soviet-led communism.[3]

During the Eisenhower administration, USIA—created on August 1, 1953, as an independent agency in the Executive Branch under the Department of State's foreign policy guidance—was the major organization that overtly waged psychological warfare against the Soviet bloc. Although the Exchange of Persons Program remained in the Department of State, USIA carried out all overseas information services: broadcasting, staffing information centers, producing motion pictures and television programming, and overseeing press releases and other publications.[4] The mission of USIA, adopted by the National Security Council (NSC) and approved by Eisenhower on October 24, 1953, was "to submit evidence to peoples of other nations by means of communication techniques that the objectives and policies of the United States are in harmony with and will advance their legitimate aspirations for freedom, progress and peace."[5] Through books, radio programs, films, exhibitions, and cultural programs, USIA disseminated information and viewpoints that merited America's global hegemonic presence. If the word *propaganda* means, as the *Oxford English Dictionary* defines it, "the systematic dissemination of information, esp. in a biased or misleading way, in order to promote a political cause or point of view," then USIA surely was the agency that administered, coordinated, and supervised the US overseas propaganda efforts.[6] It promoted the American way of "freedom, progress and peace" and imbued "legitimate aspirations" in the minds of foreign audiences.

On December 8, 1953, Eisenhower made his "Atoms for Peace" speech to the plenary meeting of the United Nations General Assembly. He proposed that the world's nuclear powers, interpreted as the US and the Soviet Union, donate the same amount of fissionable materials to a proposed international agency so that they could be distributed to member countries for "the peaceful pursuits of mankind," such as electricity, agriculture, and medicine.[7] Arguably, by proposing this atomic pool plan, he gained "a win-win position: if [the Soviets] refused, it would be a victory of opinion for the USA; if they accepted, they would weaken their military potential to the US's advantage," since the US was believed to have a larger stockpile than the Soviet Union did.[8] In fact, this initiative was a clever measure to counter Soviet propaganda rather than to curtail its military power. Lewis L. Strauss, chairman of the Atomic Energy Commission, had initially responded to the idea cautiously, saying on September 17, 1953, that it is "novel and might have value for propaganda purposes" but "has doubtful value as a practical move."[9] The "Statement of Policy on Peaceful Uses of Atomic Energy," adopted by the NSC and approved by Eisenhower on March 12, 1955, explicitly states that the priority is in "military needs" and peaceful uses are for a counterpropaganda purpose: to "strengthen American world leadership and disprove the Communists' propaganda charges that the US is concerned solely with the destructive uses of the atom." "Atomic energy, which has become the foremost symbol of man's inventive capacities, can also become the symbol of a strong but peaceful and purposeful America." The president directed both Strauss and Secretary of State John Foster Dulles to implement the actions stated in the policy, "advising with" the Operations Coordinating Board (OCB), to "result in maximum psychological advantages to the United States."[10] The Atoms for Peace campaign, therefore, was more than a promotion of atomic energy; it was a well-coordinated program for establishing and expanding the nuclear world family in which the US would reign as the rightful patriarch.

Following Eisenhower's speech, USIA launched the massive Atoms for Peace campaign worldwide. USIA supported the *Atoms for Peace* exhibit, which toured Europe in 1954 and India and Pakistan in 1955.[11] Starting in Tokyo on November 1, 1955, the exhibit traveled to ten other locations in Japan over two years, attracting an estimated total of 2.6 million people.[12] By 1956, nineteen USIA atoms-for-peace films had been produced and distributed in seventy-nine countries; the soundtracks were available in thirty-two languages. In Japan, about four million had watched those films "during an intensive program that included 13,000 separate USIA film exhibitions"; about three million had watched one or more of the four televised films.[13] US visual education about atomic energy was a global, concerted project, carefully coordinated by USIA in Washington and tailored by each US Information Service office located in foreign countries.

The primary goal of the Atoms for Peace campaign in Japan was to make its citizens pronuclear and pro-America. Considering the Japanese public sentiment against atoms and America around 1955, it is quite surprising that USIS Tokyo achieved its goal within a year. The year 1955 was the tenth anniversary of the atomic bombings of Hiroshima and Nagasaki. It had been less than a year since twenty-three Japanese crewmen on the tuna fishing boat *Daigo Fukuryu Maru* (*Lucky Dragon No. 5*) were contaminated by the nuclear fallout from a US hydrogen-bomb test conducted at Bikini Atoll in the Marshall Islands on March 1, 1954. The *Yomiuri Shimbun*, which scored a scoop on the incident on March 16, reported the fear of "ashes of death."[14] Prompted by the extensive media coverage that followed, vigorous antinuclear movements and strong anti-American sentiment pervaded Japan. The Gensuibaku Kinshi Shomei Undo Zenkoku Kyogikai (National Council of Signature-Collecting Campaign to Ban Atomic and Hydrogen Bombs) was organized on August 8, and, within two months, twelve million people had signed the petition to ban nuclear bombs.[15] Meanwhile, Aikichi Kuboyama, chief radio operator, aged 40, lapsed into a coma on August 29, and since then, all major newspapers had been reporting his condition daily in both morning and evening editions. He died of radiation sickness on September 23. The *Mainichi Shimbun* issued an extra edition to report his death, and the headline read: "The First Human Victim of the US H-Bomb."[16] As several foreign affairs officers stationed in Japan would later recall, the years from 1954 to 1955 were a time when US-Japan relations were strained to the breaking point.[17]

The *Lucky Dragon* incident not only caused a tremendous uproar inside Japan but also attracted worldwide media attention. Both the State Department and the US Embassy in Japan were gravely worried about Japan's psychological state as well as the negative impact the incident had on the international community. On March 29, at 10:30 a.m., Dulles telephoned Strauss and cautioned him that the "wave of hysteria" was "driving our Allies away from us."[18] On April 15, John M. Allison, US ambassador to Japan, sent a telegram to the Department of State, informing them that the Embassy would now endeavor to "eliminate" the incident "as focus of international agitation" and "minimize its strain on US-Japanese relations."[19] On May 20, Allison further provided a detailed analysis of "emotionalism" that had taken over Japan. When the incident was added to Japan's already stressed mind, he explained, "government and people cracked," and a "period of uncontrolled masochism ensued, as nation ... seemed to revel in fancied martyrdom, and US-Japanese cooperation broke down." He counseled to bear in mind the "dangerous psychological vulnerability of Japanese"—the "depth of Japanese fear of nuclear weapons, their conviction of doom in event of war, and, as consequences their readiness to panic and their intense gullibility in nuclear matters."[20] On May 29, Robert Murphy, acting secretary of state and former ambassador to Japan, in a memorandum to Eisenhower, diagnosed Japan's condition: "The Japanese are pathologically sensitive about nuclear weapons. They feel they are the chosen victims of such weapons."[21] On December 31, an abridged memo by Hidetoshi Shibata, an informant of the Central Intelligence Agency (CIA) and the right-hand man of Matsutaro Shoriki, was sent to Director Allen Welsh Dulles:

> Not only is Japan the first, but the only nation so affected. In each instance, America was responsible and, as result [sic], the fear of A-bomb harbored by Japanese people is second to none in the world. The bitterness people feel toward United States for its use of the bomb is deep-seated, and taking advantage of this existing sentiment, the communists clearly are succeeding in their anti-US and peace propaganda offensives.[22]

The incident, in addition to the history of the two atomic bombings, posed a great hindrance and ironic contradiction to what the US had been propagating to the world. USIS Tokyo had to wrestle with these adverse circumstances and "move" Japanese public opinion dramatically toward a pronuclear and pro-American stance.

Miraculously, by the end of 1955, Japan did wholeheartedly embrace nuclear power. The Japan Atomic Energy Commission was established on January 1, 1956, and, in May, the Science and Technology Agency was created. Both were headed by Shoriki, the founder of Nippon Television Network, the owner of *Yomiuri Shimbun*, and the CIA agent code-named "PODAM."[23] Japan's turnaround was primarily due to the tremendous success of the Atoms for Peace campaign, supported by this strong-willed Japanese media tycoon, whose economic pursuits and political ambition happened to coincide with the interests of the US.[24] His newspaper *Yomiuri* embarked on a mission to enlighten the Japanese public about this new technology of advanced science in aligning itself with USIS (and the CIA): it sponsored in Tokyo, from August 12 to August 22, 1954, the exhibition *Dare nimo wakaru genshiryoku-ten* (*Anyone Can Understand Atomic Energy Exhibit*); on May 13, 1955, the lecture "Genshiryoku heiwa riyo daikoenkai" (Grand Lecture on Peaceful Uses of Atomic Energy); and from November 1, 1955, the exhibit *Genshiryoku heiwa riyo hakurankai* (*Atoms for Peace Exhibit*).[25] Because of its tremendous success in Tokyo, *Atoms for*

Peace traveled around Japan, each stop sponsored by a local newspaper. The most symbolic event that signaled Japan's complete turnaround was the exhibition held from May 27 to June 17, 1956, at Hiroshima Peace Memorial Museum, drawing 119,500 visitors. The museum's displays of artifacts related to the atomic bombing were temporarily removed to make room for the exhibit.[26] USIS publicized the exhibits "with a filming of the exhibit and a campaign of publications, radio and television shows."[27] The film, entitled *Power for Peace* (1956), ends with the narrator's forward-looking words, "a promise of a richer, fuller tomorrow."[28] USIA reported to the US Congress, quoting *Japan News*, that its activities "had the effect of 'replacing the vague and menacing picture of the atomic mushroom with a shining vision of a happier, healthier, more prosperous mankind.'"[29] As the replacement at Hiroshima Peace Memorial Museum epitomizes, Shoriki's *Yomiuri* and USIS strove to outmode a vision of atomic apocalypse. Together they led Japan to turn its eyes away from the trauma of the past—the war and nuclear devastation—and to gaze on the coming future, the future of peace, progress, and prosperity, healed completely by the magical power of atoms.

Ten years after the surrender and three years from the end of occupation, what Japan needed was willpower to look forward. USIS Tokyo invited the Japanese to embrace such power conflated with atoms and America. "The change in opinion on atomic energy from 1954 to 1955 was spectacular," boasted USIA officials: "Through an intensive USIS campaign, atom hysteria was almost eliminated and by the beginning of 1956, Japanese opinion was brought to popular acceptance of the peaceful uses of atomic energy. . . . Substantial progress has been made in improving Japanese opinion towards the US."[30] USIS succeeded in winning the hearts and minds of Japanese people, and Japan willingly succumbed to the US-led vision, aspiring to become an equal member of the nuclear world family. Indeed, since its first application in 1952, Japan had been attempting to gain accession to the United Nations until finally being admitted on December 18, 1956.

Yet the success of the Atoms for Peace campaign was not the only factor that changed Japanese public opinion. It was against this backdrop that Faulkner and Steichen came to Japan, inevitably involved in the US foreign policy toward Japan. The timing was not accidental. Faulkner's participation in the Nagano Seminar on American Literature from August 6 to 15, 1955, overlapped with a major antinuclear—thus potentially anti-American—event. The first World Conference against Atomic and Hydrogen Bombs convened in Hiroshima from August 6 to August 9, in Osaka on August 13, and in Tokyo on August 15.[31] On the other hand, Steichen's Japanese version of *The Family of Man* was scheduled to coincide with the *Atoms for Peace* tour in Japan. From March 1956 to the summer of 1957, *The Family of Man* traveled around dozens of Japanese cities, while *Atoms for Peace* toured eleven cities between November 1955 and August 1957.³² Coming at the height of anti- and pronuclear movements, Faulkner's visit and Steichen's exhibit played their parts in US atomic diplomacy. Both cultural programs supported the Atoms for Peace campaign in, to quote Eisenhower's campaign speech from 1952, "more subtle, more pervasive, more complete" ways.

Impressions of Japan and *The Family of Man*, 1955-1956

"Our tragedy today is a general and universal physical fear . . . : When will I be blown up?"³³ Between man's mere endurance and prevalence, the speaker says, he will take the latter and help man prevail "by lifting his heart."³⁴ The rhetoric of fear and choice found in Faulkner's Nobel Prize banquet speech on December 10, 1950, anticipated that of the "Atoms for Peace" speech, which set the keynote of USIA's global psychological warfare of the mid-1950s.

The American master-narrative penned by the Eisenhower administration was, by emphasizing "the theme that all humanity was united in the common plight," aimed at consolidating and extending the nuclear world family of the Western free bloc. The "Atoms for Peace" speech was revised several times and was a collaborative effort between the president and his advisors: John Dulles, Strauss, and Jackson, who was by this time special assistant to the president. Although all the previous drafts had assured that, if attacked, the US military would "feel free to use atomic weapons," this assurance was deleted in the final editing.³⁵ By removing the statement that could be misconstrued as belligerence, Eisenhower made it easier for audiences to identify the US as the facilitator of the peaceful uses and the Soviet Union as that of the destructive uses of nuclear energy: "It must be put into the hands of those who will know how to strip its military casing and adapt it to the arts of peace. The United States knows that if the fearful trend of atomic military buildup can be reversed, this greatest of destructive forces can be developed into a great boon, for the benefit of all mankind."³⁶ The overall rhetoric is as simple as this: by instilling the fear of nuclear annihilation in the audience's minds, the speaker urges the audience to choose between peace and war, a prosperous future and the end of humanity, and American democracy and Soviet communism. Unless one is suicidal, the choice seems obvious. Thus, the speech presents the world as two families, led by two opposing patriarchs. One of the many aims of the "Atoms for Peace" campaign was to promote the US as an apostle of peace and to seek transnational alliances, all the while continuing the competition with the Soviets in the nuclear arms race.

In Japan, however, just as Eisenhower had deleted the phrase that made too strong an impression, USIS Tokyo needed to understate the modern universal fear to accommodate the situation of Japan, where the memories of nuclear destruction by the hands of the US were all too vivid. Rather than to incite nuclear anxiety, it had to eradicate nuclear fear. A close examination of the editing and the censorship of USIS Tokyo reveals the overall US psychological strategy.

Based on Faulkner's essay "Impressions of Japan," the USIS motion picture unit produced a fourteen-minute, black-and-white documentary film on Faulkner's visit to Japan.[37] Directed by Harry Keith and scripted and narrated by Jack H. Shellenberger, this "documentary" was, like any other such film, heavily constructed.[38] The opening scene of Faulkner's arrival was reenacted on the last day of his departure at Haneda Airport, borrowing an unused aircraft from Northwest Airlines. The wives and children of foreign-affairs officers played the roles of travelers, and several USIS local staff members performed the roles of journalists. To simulate the scene where Faulkner in the car is driven along a winding mountain road, Faulkner had to sit on "the rear seat of a car which was being bounced up and down by hand," and for realistic effects, "a branch of a tree was waved rhythmically to cast its shadow upon the car and the novelist."[39] Most importantly, although almost all the narration of the film is composed of extensive quotes from Faulkner's three addresses delivered and distributed at Nagano, Faulkner's words are taken freely out of the original contexts and interjected into the scenes of the film, functioning as imposed captions. The film was composed to follow the authorial intent of US foreign policy.

One example of such editing can be seen in the following sequence. The camera captures Faulkner having an impromptu session at the Nagano Japan-America Cultural Center, with its library visitors mainly comprising high school students. In this informal session, which Faulkner himself had proposed to hold, the students posed candid questions: "What is your opinion about the atomic bomb?" Other questions ranged from the discrepancy between American democracy and the US military bases in Asia, to the ineffectual politics of the American occupation forces.[40] In the film, however, the whole scene is shown in pantomime, and the voiceover interprets the scene for the audience: "The young students prying and prodding with their questions, wanting some message which they could call truth." The truth that Faulkner offers is, the narrator suggests, "that each must seek not for a mere crutch to lean on, but to stand erect on his own feet believing in his own toughness and endurance, realizing that man's hope is in man's freedom not given as a gift but as a right and a responsibility to be earned." By combining three different passages from "To the Youth of Japan" into one, USIS makes Faulkner's words, which in their original context referred to man's prevalence in continuing efforts and to the writer's responsibility to speak the universal truth, come to sound more like a direct message to post-occupation Japan, urging the nation to stand on its own feet and of its own free will.

Consecutively, the scene moves to one of the sessions in the Nagano Seminar. While the camera slowly pans from left to right showing Japanese academics all clad in *yukatas* and fanning themselves busily, the voiceover reads almost verbatim from the last passage of Faulkner's "Message Given at Nagano":

> The Japanese did not even want another intellectual. What they wanted was just a human being who spoke not their same intellectual language, but who could write books which met their standards of what writing must be, yet who in trying to communicate, human being to human being, spoke in a mutual language much older than any intellectual tongue because it is the simple language of humanity.

This passage, which advocates a people-to-people communication, perfectly ventriloquizes the objective of the State Department's Exchange of Persons Program. The phrase that concludes the second sentence in Faulkner's address, however, was omitted: "of mankind, of man's hope and aspiration which has enabled him to prevail above his condition and fate and *his own self-created disasters*."[41] This line, which could be received as a vague allusion to, or even a justification of, the droppings of the atomic bombs, was superseded by the voiceover: "What phases of Japan do you seek to explore?" "Humanity. Faces." This exchange between a Japanese professor and Faulkner was apparently dubbed because the lines do not match the movement of their mouths. The answer applied to Faulkner's mouth speaks for the theme of the film: portraits of the family of man. The scene that follows, a series of close-up faces of Japanese farmers in Nagano, bears the message that, despite their superficial differences, even those Far-Eastern country people have something in common with the great American Nobel Prize–winning author, who in Japan repeatedly called himself a farmer.[42]

In *Impressions of Japan*, USIS Tokyo emphasized the theme of the multicultural world family. In its editing process, while the cacophonous voices that disrupted the American master-narrative were silenced or omitted, Faulkner's words that resonated with US policy were highlighted, taken freely out of their original contexts. In so doing, the agency spread the peaceful message of building mutual understanding and friendship between diverse cultures by "the simple language of humanity." In its semiannual report to the Congress, USIA singled out *Impressions of Japan* as the film that "helped strengthen US cultural ties with the rest of the free world."[43]

Similar editing was performed at the exhibit *Za famiri obu man: warera mina ningen kazoku* (*The Family of Man: We All Are a Family of Man*). Cosponsored by Nihon Keizai Shimbun (Nikkei), MoMA, and USIS, the Japanese version was made possible by the initiative of Nikkei, which had been seeking a suitable event to commemorate the eightieth anniversary of its founding. Yoshitake Terauchi, head of the Planning Department, first contacted the US Embassy and underwent a complicated negotiation process involving organizations such as the State Department, USIS, MoMA, and Japan Ministry of Foreign Affairs. The Japanese organizing committee was formed; Steichen, then director of the Department of Photography at MoMA, came to inspect the arrangements, all expenses covered by Nikkei.[44] Though over thirty photographs taken by Japanese photographers were added, the compiled version closely followed Steichen's direction at MoMA.[45]

The conceptual design of *The Family of Man* was perfectly in tune with Eisenhower's "Atoms for Peace" speech. Believing that photography is "the only universal language we have, the only one requiring no translation," Steichen organized pictures and captions to "let them speak together."[46] The captions consisted of quotations, and the customary information such as name, title, date, place, materials, and dimensions was absent. In the MoMA version, in the center of the exhibit hall were the central theme pictures, six various-sized panels of family photographs, shot in the US, Italy, Japan, and Bechuanaland. The caption to this arrangement read: "Sioux Indian: 'With all beings and all things we shall be as relatives.'" These family albums emphasize the theme of the multicultural world family, overcoming differences and animosities. Near the exit was a dark room, where the visitor would see inside the illuminated transparency of the nuclear explosion's fireball at Enewetak Atoll, Marshall Islands, the only color photograph in the whole exhibit (see figure 12.1). The next section consisted of nine panels of close-up faces, including one taken a day after the atomic bombing of Nagasaki. The caption to this section was a quotation from Bertrand Russell: "The best authorities are unanimous in saying that a war with hydrogen bombs is quite likely to put an end to the human race. . . . [T]here will be universal death—sudden only for a fortunate minority, but for the majority a slow torture of disease and disintegration."[47] Confronting these nine faces, one

Figure 12.1. Wayne F. Miller, Miller's wife and children in front of the panel of a hydrogen bomb at the exhibition *The Family of Man* at MoMA, New York, February 1955. Image copyright © Wayne Miller/Magnum Photos. Image source: Wayne Miller/Magnum Photos/Aflo.

Figure 12.2. Installation view of *The Family of Man* at Nihombashi Takashimaya Department Store, Tokyo, March 1956. Image source: Takashimaya Archives.

would notice, out of the corner of one's eye, another panel in the rear: a dead soldier, facedown, taken at Enewetak. The exhibit ends with a wall-length panel of the UN General Assembly and various-sized portraits of children.[48] Thus, with the accent placed on the nuclear holocaust, both explicit and implicit narratives of the exhibit pose a question: between the doomed end of humanity and a prosperous future for children, which path would you take? The best-known photograph of the exhibit, *Peruvian Flute Player* by Eugene Harris, featured in six different-sized panels in the exhibit, framed the obvious answer.[49] Using the same rhetoric of Eisenhower's speech, Steichen's photographic narrative played accompaniment to the Atoms for Peace campaign.

Though it faithfully followed this MoMA version in almost all respects, the Japanese exhibit differed in one significant way. The picture of the hydrogen bomb was removed and replaced by photographs representing atomic disasters. The committee made a large photographic panel documenting Nagasaki near ground zero a day after the explosion, taken by Yosuke Yamahata, with four small panels attached to it (see figures 12.2, 12.3, 12.4, 12.5, and 12.6). Among them was Yamahata's picture of a mother and son, holding rice balls in hand. Since the boy's close-up face appeared among nine facial portraits in the MoMA version, they put the picture back into its original context and background.

This panel became a center of controversy. When Emperor Hirohito was to visit the exhibit on May 23, 1956, at the invitation of the US Embassy and escorted by Ambassador Allison, Nikkei screened six

Figure 12.3. Yosuke Yamahata, *Mother and Child Near Takaramachi, Nagasaki, August 10, 1945*. Image copyright © Shogo Yamahata. Image courtesy of Shogo Yamahata.

Figure 12.4. Yosuke Yamahata, *Wounded People Waiting for Help Near Iwakawamachi, Nagasaki, August 10, 1945*. Image copyright © Shogo Yamahata. Image courtesy of Shogo Yamahata.

photographs related to atomic bombs with a white cloth to block the emperor's view. The veiling made headline news, and three days later, at the request of Steichen, the panel was dismantled.⁵⁰ As for this last-minute change, the story rests on a misunderstanding between Steichen and the Japanese committee. Steichen publicly commented that he regretted he was misunderstood to have given consent to add new photographs and that he requested the removal because one particular incident could not express the general meaning without falsifying it.⁵¹ On the other hand, *Nihon Keizai Shimbun hachijunenshi* (*The Eighty Years' History of Nihon Keizai Shimbun*) (1956) officially records that it was Steichen himself who had proposed to replace the transparent panel of the hydrogen bomb with photographs taken in Japan, saying that Japan was the only victim country of atomic bombs and that the MoMA version of the panel was too beautiful to express the fear of nuclear bombs. The book somewhat laboriously explicates that the decision to curtain off the Japanese version of the panel was nevertheless made because it was mounted without Steichen's final consent, though the Japanese organizing committee understood that it had been given full authority to do so. Nikkei stresses that it adopted a cautious approach at the official visit of the emperor because the panel was, after all, not definitely authorized by Steichen.⁵² However, Ihei Kimura, a famous photographer and an organizing committee member, claimed that Steichen had entrusted them with the selection of substitutes.⁵³ These competing accounts, to a certain degree, corroborate the story of misunderstanding.

 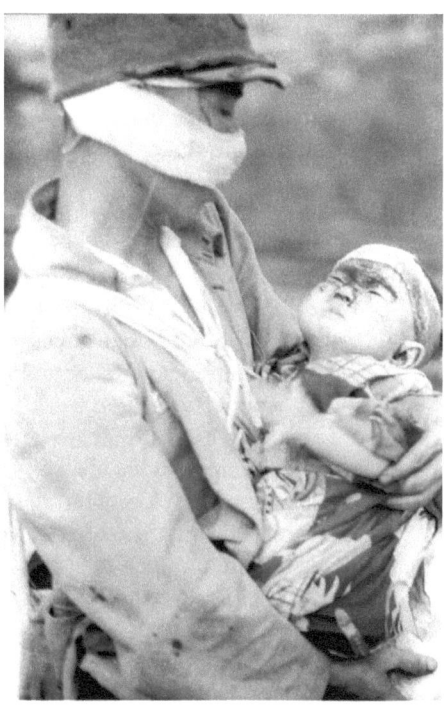

Figure 12.5. Yosuke Yamahata, *Boy Carrying His Wounded Brother on His Back Near Nagasaki Station, Nagasaki, August 10, 1945*. Image copyright © Shogo Yamahata. Image courtesy of Shogo Yamahata.

Figure 12.6. Yosuke Yamahata, *Father Looking for a Doctor to Treat His Wounded Baby Near Takaramachi, Nagasaki, August 10, 1945*. Image copyright © Shogo Yamahata. Image courtesy of Shogo Yamahata.

However, the true story behind the curtain was US censorship. Shellenberger would later recall Allison's initial reaction to the Nagasaki panel: "Well, that won't do, that's got to go. I can't imagine that we could use that photo in this exhibit. It would be enormously insulting."[54] Arthur W. Hummel, Jr., Deputy Public Affairs Officer, revealed nearly forty years later that Steichen indeed had given the committee "permission to add some local photographs," contrary to his contract with USIA that stated the Japanese version be "exactly the same" as the one touring worldwide. The curtaining-off was the result of a compromise, "finally and painfully negotiated at the very highest level," since the Government could not tolerate "six or eight horror photos of Hiroshima and Nagasaki."[55] The photographic testimonies of atomic disasters, along with the dissenting Japanese voices, were safely silenced; the pacified version of *The Family of Man* toured around Japan, spreading the beatific vision of mankind as one.

In the Japanese version of *The Family of Man*, USIS Tokyo emphasized the theme of the peaceful and prosperous world family. Under its supervision, while Steichen's curatorial decisions that were consistent with the American master-narrative were highly appreciated, his direction that went against it was forced to be retracted. By removing the scenes of atomic disasters, the agency propagated the peaceful message that nations can build mutual understanding and friendship as an extended family: "We shall be as relatives." For USIA, this kinship was synonymous with the ever-growing transnational alliances of the Free World. USIA reported to the US Congress: "It was shown in Amsterdam, in Tokyo (audiences averaged 10,000 a day) and in Paris, where even the Communist intellectual weekly, *Les Lettres Françaises*, called the exhibit 'wonderful.'"[56]

Therefore, not only in the Atoms for Peace campaign but also in both the film *Impressions of Japan* and the exhibit *The Family of Man*, USIS Tokyo made efforts to obliterate the traumatic memories of the past and replace them with a therapeutic picture of a bright new future, "a shining vision of a happier, healthier, more prosperous mankind." The film and the exhibit served as effective "visual aids" of US education in postoccupation Japan.

Indeed, all three USIA overseas information programs were in "concerted action" under US foreign policy toward Japan. The statement of "US Policy toward Japan," adopted by the NSC and approved by Eisenhower on April 9, 1955, defines the US basic interest in Japan as "a strong Japan, firmly allied with the United States."[57] OCB's *Outline Plan of Operations with Respect to Japan* paraphrases this objective: "The US wants a friendly, cooperative and strong Japan." To achieve this objective, "We should play on this theme of free world cooperation." It was a policy of placation and persuasion:

> In our operations we must persuade the Japanese that it is to Japan's benefit to do the things we want done.... Since the Japanese are nationalistic and independence-minded, we must play up the advantages to them of developing their political, economic and military strength.... At the same time we should stress the theme of continued cooperation with the US and the free nations as Japan recovers its strength.

The instruction also adds, "Japanese sensitivity on all nuclear matters requires the most careful handling."[58] Under this overall strategy, in all its information activities, USIS Tokyo played on the theme of transnational kinship and dealt with nuclear problems. In so doing, the agency succeeded in winning the "minds and wills" of Japan, as the formerly occupied country aspired for more freedom and autonomy. For post-occupation Japan, the call to join the nuclear family of the Western free bloc was simply irresistible.

Faulkner and His (Trans)National Families

In hindsight, USIS activities in the mid-1950s were what paved Japan's road to becoming a pronuclear and pro-American nation. It would certainly be overstating the case to say that Faulkner's visit and Steichen's exhibit were what changed Japan's public opinion about atoms and America. Nevertheless, they indeed were catalysts that "moved" the Japanese audience in favor of the US as a promoter of peace, freedom, and prosperity. Faulkner and Steichen, in their humanist beliefs, told America's story and became spokespeople and icons for "the family of man." The agency efficiently exploited their cooperation and touched a chord with Japanese people by playing on the all-encompassing humanist theme as the truth onto which they should hold. The immense popularity and success of this American master-narrative attest to the fact that the song was what the Japanese at that time wanted to hear and to sing themselves.

How much Faulkner himself believed in this multicultural world family we can only speculate. He correctly understood the mission of USIA, according to the letter he sent to Harold E. Howland, an officer of the State Department: he would "help give people of other countries a truer idea than they sometimes have, of what the US actually is."[59] During his stay in Japan, Faulkner had promised Leon Picon, Book Translation Officer, that he would not "let USIS down." In the last few days of his visit, Faulkner asked Picon, "Have we met all the requirements, done all the things we're supposed to do?" He was sincerely trying to fulfill what was expected of him and, according to Picon, made a "rip-roaring success."[60] USIS "distributed Mr. Faulkner's writings, produced 15 hours of radio programs and made a motion picture for countrywide showing through theaters, on television and by private organizations."[61] Faulkner and USIS fought like good Cold Warriors. After Faulkner's visit to Japan, USIA Director Theodore Cuyler Streibert, in November 1955, commended USIS Tokyo in a message headed "Exploitation of Faulkner Visit": "The Agency believes this is an example of a well-coordinate [sic] effort to make the most of a given opportunity. The extensive plans for follow-up through the centers, films, books, press and publications, radio and exhibits are well calculated to keep the Faulkner momentum rolling as long as possible."[62]

The Japanese print media ensured that the "Faulkner momentum" would last. The Japanese publisher Kenkyusha published *Faulkner at*

Nagano in 1956, compiling all of Faulkner's interviews, sessions, and addresses in Japan—except the one at the Nagano Cultural Center—and his Nobel Prize acceptance speech into one book. The accounts of Faulkner's visit appeared in newspapers and magazines, and those articles were full of the word *ningen*, meaning "human being," "mankind," and "personality" in Japanese. The idea of common humanity appealed so much to Japanese intellectuals that they eagerly erased Faulkner's racial and cultural differences in their reminiscences: "Every Japanese—without any exception—was so attracted to him because of his Oriental, likable, and sincere personality." One even went further to say that Faulkner looked like "a familiar Japanese old man."[63] For many Japanese who had heard him talk, Faulkner became a member of their "family of man."

On April 25, 1957, however, Faulkner, long done with his Far East mission, was speaking to the youth of America. At Mary Washington College, asked if he thought Japanese and American writers share the same problems, Faulkner answered, "I'm sure their problems were the same problems, but their culture is—is so different. It's a culture . . . completely alien to—to me, to any Occidental, but I—I never did touch the Japanese." Although the perplexed questioner insisted that "the published book about it [*Faulkner at Nagano*] sounded as though you had touched them very much," Faulkner concluded his answer: "we simply could not communicate."[64] He may have been whistle-blowing that there was something deceitful behind the American master-narrative, which he had so faithfully followed less than two years before, advocating the "simple language of humanity." In any case, the growing laughter of the audience attests that Faulkner, a great writer of human minds and wills, was also a great orator who could move and unite an audience instantaneously, by giving it what it wanted to hear.

NOTES

1. For related discussion of Faulkner's role as a cultural ambassador in Japan, see Joseph Blotner, "William Faulkner, Roving Ambassador," *International Educational and Cultural Affairs* (Summer 1966): 1-22; Takako Tanaka, "The Global/Local Nexus of Patriarchy: Japanese Writers Encounter Faulkner," in *Global Faulkner: Faulkner and Yoknapatawpha, 2006*, ed. Annette Trefzer and Ann J. Abadie (Jackson: University Press of Mississippi, 2009), 116-34; Wai Chee Dimock, "Faulkner Networked: Indigenous, Regional, Trans-Pacific," in *Faulkner and History: Faulkner and Yoknapatawpha, 2014*, ed. Jay Watson and James G. Thomas, Jr. (Jackson: University Press of Mississippi, 2017), 3-20; Greg Barnhisel, "Packaging Faulkner as a Cold War Modernist," in *Faulkner and Print Culture: Faulkner and Yoknapatawpha, 2015*, ed. Jay Watson, Jaime Harker, and James G. Thomas, Jr. (Jackson: University Press of Mississippi, 2017), 158-74.

2. Dwight D. Eisenhower, "The Need for Psychological Warfare: Speech of the Republican Presidential Candidate (Eisenhower) at San Francisco, October 8, 1952 (Extracts)," in Clarence W. Baier and Richard P. Stebbins, eds., *Documents on American Foreign Relations 1952*, vol. 14 (New York: Harper & Bros., 1953), 99-100.

3. For detailed discussion of Eisenhower's psychological warfare, see Kenneth Osgood, *Total Cold War: Propaganda Battle at Home and Abroad* (Lawrence: University Press of Kansas, 2006); and Frances Stonor Saunders, *The Cultural Cold War: The CIA and the World of Arts and Letters* (New York: New Press, 1999).

4. *USIA Second Report to Congress, January–June 1954* (Washington, DC: US Government Printing Office [GPO], 1954).

5. NSC 165/1, October 24, 1953, in Lisle A. Rose and Neal H. Petersen, eds., *Foreign Relations of the United States (FRUS) 1952–1954*, vol. 2, part 1 (Washington, DC: GPO, 1984), 1753.

6. "Propaganda, n.3," *Oxford English Dictionary Online*, June 2007, Oxford University Press, www.oed.com/view/Entry/152605, accessed April 26, 2019.

7. Dwight D. Eisenhower, "Atoms for Peace Speech," December 8, 1953, International Atomic Energy Agency, www.iaea.org/about/history/atoms-for-peace-speech, accessed April 26, 2019.

8. Jack Masey and Conway Lloyd Morgan, *Cold War Confrontations: US Exhibitions and Their Role in the Cultural Cold War* (Baden, Switzerland: Lars Müller, 2008), 46.

9. Lewis L. Strauss, Memorandum for the President, September 17, 1953, in Rose and Petersen, *FRUS 1952–1954*, vol. 2, part 2, 1219.

10. NSC 5507/2, March 12, 1955, in David S. Patterson, ed., *FRUS 1955–1957*, vol. 20 (Washington, DC: GPO, 1990), 46–55.

11. See Nicholas J. Cull, *The Cold War and the United States Information Agency: American Propaganda and Public Diplomacy, 1945–1989* (Cambridge, UK: Cambridge University Press, 2008), 106.

12. "Fukushima and Hiroshima, Part 3 (Special)," July 25, 2011, Hiroshima Peace Media Center, The Chugoku Shimbun, accessed November 30, 2019, www.hiroshimapeacemedia.jp/?p=28535.

13. *The Film Program of the United States Information Agency* (Washington, DC: United States Information Agency, 1956), 3.

14. *Yomiuri Shimbun*, March 16, 1954, morning edition, 7 (in Japanese).

15. *Yomiuri Shimbun*, October 6, 1954, morning edition, 7 (in Japanese).

16. *Mainichi Shimbun*, September 24, 1954, extra edition, 1 (in Japanese).

17. For example, Richard A. Ericson, Jr., then Foreign Service Economic Officer for the US Embassy in Japan, recalls that, after the incident, there was "this enormous explosion of feeling against the United States." "It was a serious economic disruption in addition to being a psychological body blow to Japan." See his interview by Charles Stuart Kennedy, March 27, 1995, in Foreign Affairs Oral History Collection (FAOHC), Association for Diplomatic Studies and Training (ADST) (1998), 41, www.adst.org/OH%20TOCs/ERICSON,%20Richard%20A.toc.pdf?_ga=2.177519717.1718971626.1575024157-971965901.1574443125, accessed July 6, 2019.

18. Rose and Petersen, *FRUS 1952–1954*, vol. 2, part 2, 1379–80.

19. David W. Mabon and Harriet D. Schwar, eds., *FRUS 1952–1954*, vol.14, part 2 (Washington, DC: GPO, 1985), 1636.

20. Mabon and Schwar, eds., *FRUS 1952–1954*, 1643–44.

21. Mabon and Schwar, eds., *FRUS 1952–1954*, 1649.

22. Hidetoshi Shibata, abridged memorandum quoted in Message to the Director of the US Central Intelligence Agency, December 31, 1954, "Shoriki, Matsutaro" files, vol. 1, no. 29, CIA FOIA Electronic Reading Room, www.cia.gov/library/readingroom/document/519cd81c993294098d51649b, accessed November 26, 2019.

23. See declassified CIA files under "Shoriki, Matsutaro," CIA FOIA Electronic Reading Room, www.cia.gov/library/readingroom.

24. Walter Nichols, Field Supervisor, who first approached Shoriki about sponsoring the *Atoms for Peace* exhibit, assumed that his support was primarily economically motivated,

mingled with an ambition for fame: "if he could catch the other two major papers [*Asahi* and *Mainichi*] out in left field still promoting this bugaboo view of atomic energy, while he could bring the public around to a dramatic comprehension of both the commercial and peaceful potential for this powerful new genie, he would have scored a real coup and carved out a place in history for himself." G. Lewis Schmidt, Acting Public Affairs Officer, considered Shoriki's motive to be political: he "wanted more than anything else to be the first head of Japan's Atomic Energy Commission." CIA officials considered that his motive had changed from economic to political. In December 1954, an unnamed officer reported to the director: "Shoriki ambitious, desires to be power in Democratic Party, dreams of cabinet post." A year later, in December 1955, an unnamed officer commented on Shoriki's enormously grown "appetites": "When we first began dealing with [Shoriki], his main apparent interest was in the completion of the all-Japan microwave system as a vehicle for the extension of his television operation. Since then, he has branched out into atomic energy. He is now talking about becoming Prime Minister." See Nichols, interview by G. Lewis Schmidt, October 10, 1989, in FAOHC, ADST (1998), 49–50, www.adst.org/OH%20TOCs/Nichols,%20Walter.toc.pdf?_ga=2.244814149.1718971626.1575024157-971965901.1574443125, accessed July 6, 2019; Schmidt, interview by Allen Hansen, February 8, 1988, in FAOHC, ADST (1998), 22, www.adst.org/OH%20TOCs/Schmidt,%20Lewis.toc.pdf?_ga=2.52924648.1718971626.1575024157-971965901.1574443125, accessed May 2, 2018; [Author's name left blank], Message to Director of the US Central Intelligence Agency, December 31, 1954, "Matsutaro, Shoriki" files, vol. 1, no. 28, CIA FOIA Electronic Reading Room, www.cia.gov/library/readingroom/document/519cd81c993294098d5164a2, accessed November 26, 2019; and [Author's name left blank], Dispatch to "Chief, F[ar] E[ast]," December 9, 1955, "Matsutaro, Shoriki" files, vol. 2, no. 43, CIA FOIA Electronic Reading Room, www.cia.gov/library/readingroom/document/519cd81c9932 94098d516569, accessed November 26, 2019.

25. *Yomiuri Shimbun hachijyunenshi* (*The Eighty Years' History of Yomiuri Shimbun*), ed. Yomiuri Shimbunsha Shashi Henshushitsu (Tokyo: Yomiuri Shimbunsha, 1955), 32, 95, 724 (in Japanese). The lecture held at Hibiya Public Hall—chaired by Shoriki and given by John Jay Hopkins, president of General Dynamics, Dr. Ernest Orlando Lawrence, 1939 Nobel Laureate in physics, and Dr. Lawrence R. Hafstad, director of Reactor Development Division, US Atomic Energy Commission—was broadcast live on Shoriki's Nippon TV.

26. "Evolution of the Hiroshima Peace Memorial Museum, Part 2: Exhibition on Atomic Energy," Hiroshima Peace Media Center, The Chunichi Shimbun, www.hiroshimapeacemedia.jp/?p=92003&query=Atoms+for+Peace, accessed July 6, 2019. For historical accounts of the *Atoms for Peace* exhibit in Hiroshima, see Ran Zwigenberg, "'The Coming of a Second Sun': The 1956 Atoms for Peace Exhibit in Hiroshima and Japan's Embrace of Nuclear Power," *Asia-Pacific Journal* 10.6.1 (February 2012): 1–16.

27. See *USIA 6th Report to Congress, January 1–June 30, 1956* (Washington, DC: GPO, 1956), 5.

28. US Information Agency film reel (1956), Record Group 306, Moving Images Relating to US Domestic and International Activities, 1982–1999, Motion Pictures (RDSM), National Archives at College Park, US National Archives, www.youtube.com/watch?v=h3UBVlUNY9 o&list=ULOvoHwefzHww&index=17&app=desktop, accessed March 20, 2019.

29. See *USIA 6th Report to Congress*, 5.

30. Quoted in Osgood, *Total Cold War*, 179.

31. See *Yomiuri Shimbun*, July 12, 1955, morning edition, 7 (in Japanese); *Yomiuri Shimbun*, August 4, 1955, morning edition, 7 (in Japanese); and *Yomiuri Shimbun*, August 16, 1955, morning edition, 7 (in Japanese).

32. See Yoko Tsuchiyama, "Visions utopiques de l'énergie nucléaire dans l'exposition *The Family of Man* et sa présentation au Japon dans les années 1950," in *Japon Pluriel 11*, ed. Jullien Martine and David-Antoine Malinas (Arles, France: Editions Philippe Picquier, 2017), 260n18.

Faulkner, Atomic Diplomacy, US Visual Education in Post-Occupation Japan   233

33. William Faulkner, Nobel Prize Banquet speech (December 10, 1950), in *Faulkner at Nagano*, ed. Robert A. Jelliffe (Tokyo: Kenkyusha, 1956), 204.

34. Faulkner, *Faulkner at Nagano*, 206.

35. Ira Chernus, *Eisenhower's Atoms for Peace* (College Station: Texas A&M University Press, 2002), 94. Also see Atoms for Peace Draft #5, November 28, 1953, C. D. Jackson Papers, Box 30, "Atoms for Peace-Evolution (5)," www.eisenhowerlibrary.gov/sites/default /files/research/online-documents/atoms-for-peace/atoms-for-peace-draft.pdf, accessed July 6, 2019; and Chronology of Atoms for Peace Project, September 30, 1954, C. D. Jackson Papers, Box 29, Atoms for Peace-Evolution (1), www.eisenhowerlibrary.gov/sites/default /files/file/atoms_Binder9.pdf, accessed November 27, 2019.

36. Dwight D. Eisenhower, address to the 470th Plenary Meeting of the United Nations General Assembly, December 8, 1953, www.iaea.org/about/history/atoms-for-peace-speech, last accessed November 30, 2019. For historical accounts of the Atoms for Peace speech and campaign, see Richard G. Hewlett and Jack M. Holl, *Atoms for Peace and War, 1953–1961: Eisenhower and the Atomic Energy Commission* (Berkeley: University of California Press, 1989); Chernus, *Eisenhower's Atoms for Peace*; Martin J. Medhurst, "Atoms for Peace and Nuclear Hegemony: The Rhetorical Structure of a Cold War Campaign," *Armed Forces and Society* 23 (1997): 571–93; and Mara Drogan, "The Nuclear Imperative: Atoms for Peace and the Development of US Policy on Exporting Nuclear Power, 1953–1955," *Diplomatic History* 40.5 (November 2016): 948–74.

37. USIA, *Impressions of Japan* (1955), film reel, Record Group 306, Moving Images Relating to US Domestic and International Activities, 1982–1999, Motion Pictures (RDSM), National Archives at College Park.

38. See Schmidt, interview by Allen Hansen, 14, 26; Leon Picon, interview by G. Lewis Schmidt, October 30, 1989, FAOHC, ADST (1998), 17, www.adst.org/OH%20TOCs/Picon,%20 Leon.toc.pdf, accessed May 22, 2017; Jack Shellenberger, interview by G. Lewis Schmidt, April 21, 1990, in FAOHC, ADST (1998), 5, www.adst.org/OH%20TOCs/Shellenberger,%20 Jack.toc.pdf, accessed October 30, 2019.

39. Jack H. Shellenberger, "William Faulkner: STAG (Short Term American Grantee)," *Foreign Service Journal* 54.1 (January 1977): 10, 30.

40. See Jun'ichi Nakamura, "Kokosei to kataru W. Faulkner" (W. Faulkner Talking with High School Students), *The Youth's Companion* 10, no. 7 (1955): 10–13 (in Japanese).

41. Jelliffe, *Faulkner at Nagano*, 177; emphasis added.

42. For example, Faulkner said on August 4, 1956, "I am a farmer, a country man and I like to write" (Jelliffe, *Faulkner at Nagano*, 194).

43. *USIA 6th Report to Congress*, 10.

44. "'Za famiri obu man' wo omou" (Thinking of "The Family of Man"), *Rekurieishon* 8, National Recreation Association of Japan (1956): 54–55 (in Japanese).

45. See Ihei Kimura's comment in "Omunibasu zadankai: saikin no wadai wo kataru" (An Omnibus Round-Table: Talking about Recent Topics), *Asahi Camera* 41, no. 6 (June 1956): 125 (in Japanese).

46. Edward Steichen, "Photography: Witness and Recorder of Humanity," *Wisconsin Magazine of History* 41, no. 3 (Spring, 1958): 160.

47. The quotation is from Bertrand Russell's famous speech "Man's Peril from the Hydrogen Bomb," first aired on a BBC radio broadcast, December 23, 1954, later published as "Man's Peril from the Hydrogen Bomb" in the *Listener* 52 (December 30, 1954): 135–36. The same sentences can be found in the Russell-Einstein Manifesto, issued on July 9, 1955.

48. See figure 12.6, "Floorplan and synopsis of The Family of Man," first published in *Popular Photography* (May 1955), reprinted in Allan Sekula, *Photography Against the Grain: Essays and Photo Works, 1973–1983* (Halifax, Nova Scotia: Press of the Nova Scotia College of Art and

Design, 1984), 92; installation views, "The Family of Man," MoMA, www.moma.org /calendar/exhibitions/2429, last accessed November 30, 2019; and the master checklist, "The Family of Man," MoMA, www.moma.org/documents/moma_master-checklist_325962.pdf, accessed September 9, 2018.

49. See the master checklist, "The Family of Man."

50. *Asahi Shimbun*, March 23, 1956, evening edition, 7 (in Japanese); *Asahi Shimbun*, March 27, 1956, morning edition, 11 (in Japanese).

51. *Asahi Shimbun*, March 27, 1956, evening edition, 3 (in Japanese).

52. See *Nihon Keizai Shimbun hachijunenshi* (*The Eighty Years' History of Nihon Keizai Shimbun*), ed. Nihon Keizai Shimbun Shashi Hensanshitsu (Tokyo: Nihon Keizai Shimbun, 1956), 655 (in Japanese).

53. See Ihei Kimura's comment in "Omunibasu zadankai," 127 (in Japanese).

54. Shellenberger, interview by G. Lewis Schmidt, 10.

55. Arthur W. Hummel, Jr., interview by Charles Stuart Kennedy, April 13, 1994, FAOHC, ADST (1998), 38, www.adst.org/OH%20TOCs/Hummel,%20Arthur%201994.toc.pdf?_ga=2 .137232560.1686619593.1575244233-1971965901.1574443125, accessed October 30, 2019.

56. *USIA 6th Report to Congress*, 14.

57. NSC 5516/1, April 9, 1955, *FRUS 1955–1957*, vol. 23, part 1, ed. David W. Mabon (Washington, DC: GPO, 1991), 55.

58. *OCB Outline Plan of Operations with Respect to Japan*, February 8, 1956, NSC Staff Papers, OCB Central Files, Box 48, OCB 091 Japan (File #4) (6), 4–5, www.eisenhowerlibrary .gov/sites/default/files/research/online-documents/declassified/fy-2011/1956-02-08.pdf, accessed June 6, 2019.

59. Blotner, "William Faulkner, Roving Ambassador," 6.

60. Leon Picon, interview by G. Lewis Schmidt, October 30, 1989, FAOHC, ADST (1998), 17–18, www.adst.org/OH%20TOCs/Picon,%20Leon.toc.pdf?_ ga=2.126611917.1195873210.1578653435-1971965901.1574443125, accessed May 22, 2017.

61. *USIA 5th Report to Congress, July 1–December 31, 1955* (Washington, DC: GPO, 1956), 8.

62. See the reproduced document in Barnhisel, "'Put Someone in Charge of His Liquor' and Other Foreign-Service Rules for Handling William Faulkner," *The Vault* (February 26, 2015), slate.com/human-interest/2015/02/william-faulkner-biography-the-writer-s-overseas -tour-during-the-cold-war.html, last accessed November 30, 2019.

63. Blotner, "William Faulkner, Roving Ambassador," 7, 8.

64. See the audio recording and transcript, April 25, 1957, Mary Washington College, Fredericksburg, tape 2, in Stephen Railton, *Faulkner at Virginia*, © 2010 Rector and Visitors of the University of Virginia, faulkner.lib.virginia.edu/display/wfaudio08_2.html, last accessed December 12, 2019.

About the Contributors

Josephine Adams is a doctoral candidate at the University of Virginia. She is completing her dissertation on forms of time in the twentieth-century American novel.

Jeff Allred is associate professor of English at Hunter College/CUNY and associate professor of digital humanities at the CUNY Graduate Center. He has published work in modernist studies, American studies, and digital humanities in *American Literature, American Literary History, Criticism*, and *Transformations*, among others. He is author of *American Modernism and Depression Documentary* (2010).

Garry Bertholf is assistant professor in the African American Studies Department at Wesleyan University. His work, which was recently supported by an Andrew W. Mellon Visiting Faculty Fellowship in the Humanities Unbounded Initiative at Duke University, has appeared or is forthcoming in *Anthurium: A Caribbean Studies Journal*, the *Journal of Popular Music Studies, south: a scholarly journal* (formerly the *Southern Literary Journal*), *Viewpoint Magazine, Diacritik, The Martyr's Shuffle*, the *Philosophical Quarterly*, and the Nation Divided series at the University of Virginia Press. His first book manuscript is titled "The Black Charismatic: Demagoguery and the Politics of Affect."

Maxwell Cassity is a PhD candidate in the English Department at Syracuse University. His dissertation, "Novel Epidemics: Contagion and Metaphor in Ethnic American Literature," examines how the language and cultural imagination of epidemic shaped notions of race and resistance in experimental twentieth-century fiction of the United States.

John N. Duvall is Margaret Church Distinguished Professor and editor of *MFS: Modern Fiction Studies* at Purdue University. His books include *Faulkner's Marginal Couple: Invisible, Outlaw, and Unspeakable Communities* (1990) and *Race and White Identity in Southern Fiction* (2008). He is also author of a new edition of Faulkner's collection of detective fiction, *Knight's Gambit*, based on previously unknown typescripts.

Katherine Henninger is Russell B. Long Associate Professor of English at Louisiana State University. She is the author of *Ordering the Façade: Photography and Contemporary Southern Women's Writing*. Work on her current monograph, *Made Strangely Beautiful: Southern Childhood in US Literature and Film*, has been supported by a fellowship from the National Endowment for the Humanities.

Maude Hines is professor of English and chair of Black studies at Portland State University. Her teaching and research focus on African American literature, critical childhood studies, and the Southern Gothic. Her work appears in *Children's Literature, The Lion and the Unicorn, American Quarterly, College Literature*, and various anthologies. She is president of the Children's Literature Association.

Robert Jackson is James G. Watson Professor of English at the University of Tulsa. His most recent book is *Fade In, Crossroads: A History of the Southern Cinema* (2017). He is currently at work on a book about the relationship between James Baldwin and Robert F. Kennedy and its influence on the history of race relations in the United States.

Julie Beth Napolin is assistant professor of digital humanities at the New School. Her book manuscript, titled "The Fact of Resonance," proposes a theory of aural phenomena in the works of Conrad, Du Bois, and Faulkner. In 2018–19 she was a Mellon Postdoctoral Fellow in the Price Lab for Digital Humanities at the University of Pennsylvania, working on a project titled "The Sound of Yoknapatawpha: An Acoustic Ecology."

Rebecca Starr Nisetich is associate professor and director of the honors program at the University of Southern Maine. Her scholarship is based in race and ethnic studies, and her published work concerns representations of identity in American literature and culture. Her articles have appeared in *African American Review, Studies in American Naturalism*, and in a collection of essays on Kate Chopin. Her book project explores representations of racial indeterminacy in early twentieth-century American literature.

George Porter Thomas is a Marion L. Brittain Postdoctoral Fellow at the Georgia Institute of Technology. He is currently writing a book about the depiction of time and race in William Faulkner, Toni Morrison, Juan

Rulfo, and Cormac McCarthy. His work has appeared in *Mississippi Quarterly*, *Mediations*, and *American Studies*.

Jay Watson is Howry Professor of Faulkner Studies and Professor of English at the University of Mississippi, where he has directed the Faulkner and Yoknapatawpha Conference since 2012. He is author of three books, most recently *William Faulkner and the Faces of Modernity* (2019), and is editor or coeditor of ten published or forthcoming volumes on Faulkner's work.

Yuko Yamamoto is associate professor of American literature at Chiba University, Japan. Her articles have appeared in Japanese and in English in a number of journals and books, including *Studies in English Literature*, *Studies in American Literature*, the *Faulkner Journal of Japan*, the *Journal of Modern Periodical Studies*, and *Faulkner and Hemingway* (2018).

Index

Page numbers in **bold** refer to figures.

Absalom, Absalom! (Faulkner), 6, 34, 61, 139; appendix, 63; childhood and innocence in, 51; comparisons to Antigone, 92-93, 95-96, 98; death and burial in, 95-96, 103; encounter in, 51; ending, 69, 102; endpapers, 127; exile in, 93; family and role of genealogy in, 6, 11, 15, 62-63, 88, 96-98, 101-3, 139; future Americans in, 58, 62-64; gender in, 15, 86-103; grief and mourning in, 88-89, 92-93; identity in, 98; incest in, 130; inspiration for, 86; marginal figures in, 13, 62; master-slave relationship in, 100; miscegenation in, 63-64, 69, 100, 130, 139, 141; monumentality in, 15, 88-90; motherhood in, 94-95; patrimony in, 139-40; politics of family, 92-93, 97-98, 100, 103; queerness and desire in, 99-102, 105n33; race in, 58, 62, 88-89, 100, 102; Southern Gothic in, 11, 29, 35, 45n19; southern guilt in, 64; suicide in, 96, 102
Adamic myth, 144n3
Adams, Josephine, 14
Adventures of Huckleberry Finn, The (Twain), 33
African American Falkners, 10
Allison, John M., 218-19, 225, 227
Allred, Jeff, 15
America: A Family Matter (Gould), 60
American Dilemma, A (Myrdal), 61
American Negro, The (Thomas), 60
American Negro: His Past and Future, The (Barringer), 60
Anderson, Sherwood, 3
"anti-genealogies," 142
Antigone (Sophocles), 90-96, 98-100; death and burial themes in, 91, 95, 99; family in, 91-92, 100; feminine lament in, 91; queerness in, 92, 95

Appiah, Kwame Anthony, 17, 132-33
As I Lay Dying (Faulkner), 37, 73-83; childhood in, 49; death and burial in, 73-74, 76-78; ending, 74; epidemiological epistemology reading of, 19, 178; extinction in, 130; family and role of genealogy in, 77, 78, 84-85n17; grief and longing in, 77-78, 80-82; identity in, 80, 82-83, 84-85n17; monologues and narration in, 14, 74-81, 83-84n9; spatial heatmap of, **177**; "spotted horses" in, 177-78; temporal shifts in, 49, 75-76, 78, 83-84n9; use of italics in, 80-81, 85n19
Atomic Energy Commission, 21, 217, 219; Science and Technology Agency, 21
Atoms for Peace campaign, 20-21, 215-21, 225; primary goal of, 218
Atoms for Peace exhibit, 21, 217, 221

Baker, Houston A., Jr., 59, 69
Baldwin, James, 19, 50-51, 194; on Faulkner, 194; on white supremacy, 55
"Barn Burning" (Faulkner), 151, 169; children and childhood in, 12; class issues and, 56n10; family and role of genealogy in, 49; Southern Gothic in, 12; temporal markers in, 48-49; white supremacy in, 12
Barnett, Ned "Uncle Ned," 196-97
Barr, Caroline, 9, 122-23
Barringer, Paul, 60
"Bear, The," 122-24, 129, 136, 142, 147-63; alternative genealogy in, 149; animal-man relationships in, 147-63, 166n19, 166n25; blood/blood mediation in, 148-51; death in, 156-61; family and role of genealogy in, 147-49, 151-52, 158-60,

239

166n21; fetishization of race in, 148–49, 156–57, 160–61, 166n23; incest in, 160; intersexuality in, 153, 155–56, 160–61; miscegenation, 147, 149, 155, 161; narration, 153–54; patrimony in, 147, 149, 151–52, 154, 158; power dynamics in, 155; queerness in, 147–63, 166n26; race in, 147–48, 151, 156–57, 160; sexual exploitation in, 152
Bernstein, Robin, 40
Bertholf, Garry, 19–20
Bethlehem Christian Methodist Episcopal Church, 199, **200**, **207**
Bianchi, Emanuela, 100
Bikini Atoll, Marshall Islands, 218, 224
biological determinism, 4
Birth of a Jungle: Animality in Progressive-Era US Literature and Culture (Lundblad), 149
Biss, Eula, 192n37
Black Twitter, 119
Blaine, Diane, 74
Bleikasten, Andre, 11, 75
Blood Work (Salvant), 127
Blotner, Joseph, 207–8
Body Farm (Knoxville, Tennessee), 34
Boston Evening Transcript, 58
Brooks, Cleanth, 10
Brooks, Peter, 73
Boy Carrying His Wounded Brother on His Back Near Nagasaki Station, Nagasaki, August 10, 1945 (Yamahata), **227**
Buchanan, Pat, 44n17
Buddenbrooks (Mann), 5
Buddy, Jim, 205, **206**
Bush, George H. W., 44n17
Butler, Judith, 126, 132
Butler, Samuel, 4, 92, 94, 96–97, 99

Caldwell, Erskine, 28
Capote, Truman, 28
Carby, Hazel, 104n18
Carter, Virginia "Gee Gee," 12, 26, 35, 41
Cassity, Maxwell, 18–19
Castronovo, Russ, 127
CBS, 195, **196**, **201**, **205**, **206**
Centers for Disease Control and Prevention (CDC), 170
Central Intelligence Agency (CIA), 219
Chandler, Edwin, 4
Charbrier, Gwendolyn, 10
Chauncey, George, 155

Chauvin, Derek, 104n8
Chesnutt, Charles W., 13, 28, 58, 59–62, 69, 70
Child, Benjamin, 181–82
Civil War, 28, 34, 87, 143, 174; class structures post-, 175–76
Clarke, Deborah, 11, 116
Cold War, 20–21, 132, 216
Commins, Saxe, 198
Confederate monuments, 87, 104n18
contagion. *See* epidemiology/contagion
Cook, Kennard, 211
COVID-19, 19, 168
Cowley, Malcolm, 17
Crenshaw, Kimberlé, 70
critical consciousness, 89
critical race theory, 70
Cross, William, 50
Culture Wars: The Struggle to Define America (Hunter), 44n17

Dare nimo wakaru genshiryoku-ten (*Anyone Can Understand Atomic Energy Exhibit*), 219
"Dark House" novels, 142
Darwinism, 7, 149–50, 164n9
Davis, Angela, 95
Davis, Thadious M., 11, 196
Dedalus, Stephen, 7
Deleuze, Gilles, 142
Derrida, Jacques, 121n11, 166n19, 186
Descent of Man (Darwin), 150
Daigo Fukuryu Maru (*Lucky Dragon No. 5*), 218
Digital Yoknapatawpha (DY) project, 19, 169–90; data tools, 170–71; MapIt function, 171; mapping Snopes epidemic, 169–90
Dirt and Desire (Yaeger), 27, 31
discourse networks, 109, 127
"Ditch, The" (Mann), 32
Du Bois, W. E. B., 132
Dulles, John Foster, 217–19, 221
Duvall, John N., 3, 6, 18

Echo, 120n3
Eisenhower, Dwight D., 20, 216–17, 221–22, 224–25
Electra-complex, 94
Ellison, Ralph, 28, 119
Epidemiology: A Very Short Introduction (Sarraci), 170

epidemiology/contagion, 170; eugenic metaphor of contagion, 174; language of, 174-75; reading, 170-76; social control through, 172
Ethridge, Robbie, 139
Evans, Walker, 30

Falkner, Billy, 4
Falkner, "Chooky," 198
Falkner, Dean, 4, 86
Falkner, Jimmy, 198
Falkner, John, 9, 198
Falkner, Maud, 8, 197
Falkner, Murray Charles "Jack," 197
Falkner, W. C., 196
Family of Man, The (Steichen), 20-21, 215, 220-29; censored version of, 227-28
Father Looking for a Doctor to Treat His Wounded Baby Near Takaramachi, Nagasaki, August 10, 1945 (Yamahata), **227**
fatherhood. *See* paternalism/fatherhood/patriarchy
Fathering the Nation (Castronovo), 127
Faulkner, Estelle, 196, **197**
Faulkner, Jill, 196, **197**, 198
Faulkner, Mississippi (Glissant), 141-42
Faulkner, William, **196**, **197**, **206**; 1934 will, 194; 1940 will, 196, 197; 1951 will, 19, 20, 198; 1954 will, 20, 198, 199; Antigone and, 90-96; birth, 3; "Black families," 10; on blood, 127-28; childhood, 9; contagion metaphors in work, 168-90; as cultural ambassador in Japan, 20-21, 215-30; death, 20; on extinction/environmental degradation, 125-26, 132; father's death, 8; financial issues, 8-9, 122; "future Americans," 62-69, 70; interview with Marshall J. Smith, 3; language choices, 47-48; lineage, 3, 8; Native American representation in work, 139-41, 145n8, 145nn11-12; Nobel Prize, 215, 221, 230; "outbreak narrative," 172-73; "southern" identity, 132-33, 144; subversive genealogies, 136-44; use of childhood in writing, 48, 50-51, 55; use of female characters in writing, 94, 99-100
Faulkner and the Ecology of the South (McHaney), 125
Faulkner and Whiteness (Watson), 175

Faulkner and Yoknapatawpha Conference, 20, 92; "Faulkner's Black Families in Oxford and Lafayette County," 201-7; "Faulkner's Families," 200; "Faulkner and Slavery," 199
Faulkner and Yoknapatawpha series, language choices in, 47
Faulkner at Nagano, 229-30
Faulkner's Families: A Southern Saga (Charbrier), 10
Federal Land Bank of New Orleans, 210-11
Ferguson, Ally Ann, 69-70
Fiedler, Leslie, 25, 27
Flags in the Dust (Faulkner), 5, 37, 127
Floyd, George, 103n8
Ford Foundation, 195, **196**, **201**, **205**, **206**
Foucault, Michel, 7, 91, 144nn5-6
Franklin, Benjamin, 93
Frederickson, George M., 60, 71n13
Freedom Riders, 119
Freudianism, 7, 94, 148-50, 164n9
Fruge, Don L., 208, 212
Fugitives, 121n22
"Future American, The" (Chesnutt), 58-61, 69-70

Galloway, Patricia, 6, 139
Galsworthy, John, 4
Games of Property: Law, Race, Gender, and Faulkner's Go Down, Moses (Davis), 196
Gardner, Alexander, 28
Garner, Eric, 103n8
Gates, Henry Louis, Jr., 63
Genealogical Fictions (Welge), 125
genealogical novels, 5
"Genshiryoku heiwa riyo daikoenkai" (Grand Lecture on Peaceful Uses of Atomic Energy), 219
Genshiryoku heiwa riyo hakurankai (*Atoms for Peace Exhibit*), 219-20
Gensuibaku Kinshi Shomei Undo Zenkoku Kyogikai (National Council of Signature-Collecting Campaign to Ban Atomic and Hydrogen Bombs), 218
Glissant, Éduoard, 10-11, 141-42
Go Down, Moses (Faulkner), 6, 61, 122, 133; alternative genealogy in, 149; animal-man relationships in, 147-63; "Barn Burning," 12, 48-49, 56n10, 151; "The Bear," 122-24, 129, 136, 142, 147-63;

blood/blood mediation in, 128–29, 141, 148–51; class issues in, 140; classification of, 123–24; "A Courtship," 17, 139–40; death in, 157–59; dedication, 122–23; "Delta Autumn," 13, 18, 67, 131, 148, 154, 161–62; family and role of genealogy in, 10–11, 13, 16–18, 66–69, 123–26, 128, 131–33, 136, 138–43, 147–49, 151–52; family estrangement in, 16, 18, 130–31; fetishization of race in, 148–49, 162–63; "The Fire and the Hearth," 123, 128; future Americans in, 58, 66–69; "Go Down, Moses," 123; incest in, 18, 130, 138; inspiration for, 9; marginal figures in, 13, 58, 62; miscegenation, 18, 67, 130, 138–39, 141, 147, 149, 158, 161–62; "The Old People," 123, 125, 128, 139–41, 151; "Pantaloon in Black," 123, 158; patrimony in, 8, 9, 139–42, 147, 149, 151–52, 162; postracialism rhetoric in, 68; queerness in, 67, 147–63; race in, 58, 62, 66–69, 147–48, 151, 162–63; "Was," 123, 130–31
Go Down, Moses and Other Stories (Faulkner), 123
Go Set a Watchman (Lee), 25, 32; white consciousness in, 26, 31
Godden, Richard, 152–53
Goddu, Teresa, 27–28, 30, 36
Gold, Joseph, 176
Goldberg, Sylvan, 126
Gone with the Wind (novel/film), 107
Gothic America (Goddu), 27–28
Gould, Charles, 60
Grant, Madison, 60
Greenfield Farm, 9, 19–20, 194–212; African American tenant farmers on, 9, 194, 199–209, 211–12; Faulkner's purchase of, 210; Oil and Gas Mining lease, 210–11; "Sectional Index to Lands," **211**, 212
Greenfield Farm Project, 208–10; advisory board, 210; blueprint for, **209**, 210
Guattari, Félix, 142

Haas, Robert K., 8–9, 123
Hamblin, Robert, 197
Hamlet, The (Faulkner): epidemiological epistemology reading of, 19, 169, 171–72, 177, 180; opening scene, 143; sexuality in, 174; spatial heatmap of, **180**, 181, **187**, 192n32; "spotted horses" in, 177–78, 180–81

Handley, George B., 11
Haneda Airport, 222
Haraway, Donna, 154
Harker, Jaime, 99, 100
Harris, Eugene, 225
Harris, Trudier, 29
Hartman, Saidiya, 208
Harvard University, 33–34
Hays, J. N., 170
Helms, Jesse, 44n17
Henninger, Katherine, 11, 12, 48
Hergesheimer, Joseph, 4–5
Hines, Maude, 12–13, 37–39
Hirohito (emperor), 225
Hiroshima Peace Memorial Museum, 21, 220
Hitler, Adolf, 131
Hold Still (Mann), 25, 32; childhood in, 26; Massey Lectures, 33–34; white consciousness in, 26, 35
Hollins College, 34
Holly Springs National Forest, 199
House Behind the Cedars, The (Chesnutt), 60–62
Howe, Irving, 74, 175
Howland, Harold E., 229
Hudson, Bill, 30
human exceptionalism, 150
Hummel, Arthur W., Jr., 227
Hunter, James Davison, 44n17
Hurricane Dorian, 96–97
Hurston, Zora Neale, 119, 121n22, 199

I'll Take My Stand (Twelve Southerners), 121n22
Immediate Family (Mann), 33, 34
Immunity: An Inoculation (Biss), 192n37
Impressions of Japan, 20, 21, 215, 221–29; editing/censoring, 223–24
"Impressions of Japan" (Faulkner), 222
In My Father's House (Appiah), 132
incest and genealogy, 129–30
institutional memory, 86
Intruder in the Dust (Faulkner): family in, 6; paternalism in, 9; Southern Gothic in, 35–36; white consciousness in, 35–36
Invisible Man (Ellison), 119
Irwin, John T., 11
Isenberg, Nancy, 174

INDEX 243

Jackson, Al, 3
Jackson, C. D., 216, 221
Jackson, Robert, 16, 17
Jakobson, Roman, 113
Japan Ministry of Foreign Affairs, 224
Japan-America Cultural Center, 222
Japan News, 220
Jones, Tommy, 206
J. R. Cofield Collection, 196
"Justice, A" (Faulkner), 47, 49–50, 139–42

Kaepernick, Colin, 104n12
Kavaloski, Joshua, 84n9
Keith, Harry, 222
Kendi, Ibram X., 61
Kenkyusha, 229
Kimura, Ihei, 226
King Lear (Shakespeare), 93
Kinney, Arthur F., 10
Kittler, Friedrich, 15, 109, 127
Ku Klux Klan, 117
Kuboyama, Aikichi, 218

Laughlin, Clarence John, 30
Lee, Harper, 25–26, 31–33, 48
Les Lettres Françaises, 228
Les Rougon-Macquart cycle (Zola), 4
Leslie, John O., 210
Levander, Caroline, 29
Light in August (Faulkner), 34, 61, 137; automaton imagery in, 52–53; children and childhood in, 12, 51–52; encounter in, 53; family and role of genealogy in, 11, 13, 52–53, 62, 64–66; fate in, 52–53; future Americans in, 58, 64–66; marginal figures in, 13, 58, 65; material presence of blood in, 66; miscegenation in, 64–66; race in, 47, 51, 53, 58, 62, 64–66, 72n19; racialized hysteria in, 64; Southern Gothic in, 12; white supremacy in, 12
Lloyd, Christopher, 34, 40
Loichot, Valerie, 11
London, Jack, 164n9
López, Ian Haney, 61
Loreaux, Nicole, 86
Louis Daniel Brodsky Collection, 197
Lundblad, Michael, 149–50, 164n9

Macauley, Rose, 4
Mainichi Shimbun, 218

"Mama's Baby, Papa's Maybe: An American Grammar Book" (Spillers), 94–95, 98
Mammy Callie, 10
Mann, Sally Munger, 11–12, 25–27, 30, 32–33, **42**, 46n29; on Faulkner, 36, 40; formal techniques, 34–35
Mann, Thomas, 5
Mann, Virginia, 41
Mansion, The (Faulkner): class issues in, 185; epidemiological epistemology reading of, 19, 169, 185–90; final passage, 189–90; opening note, 190; race in, 185; sexuality in, 185; spatial heatmap, **187**
Mary Washington College, 230
Masters, Edgar Lee, 4
Matthews, John T., 119, 157
McHaney, Thomas L., 125–26
McJunkins, Alvis, 20, 198–99, 203, **204**, **205**, **211**, 212
McJunkins, Alvis, Jr., 204, **205**
McJunkins, Ardelia, 203, **204**, **205**
McJunkins, Barbara, **203**
McJunkins, Bertha, 205
McJunkins, Buford W., 212
McJunkins, Charles (Alvis's son), 20, 200, **203**, **204**, **205**, 212; childhood home, **207**; interview with, 201–7
McJunkins, Charles "Big Charlie," **202**, **203**
McJunkins, Charles "Little Charlie," 20, 198, 202–3, **206**
McJunkins, Dana, 204, **205**
McJunkins, Dewayne, 204
McJunkins, Elmetria, 204
McJunkins, George, 205, 212
McJunkins, Julie, **203**
McJunkins, LaTasha, 199
McJunkins, Lawrence Arenza "Renzi," 20, 195, **196**, 197, 198, **201**, **202**, 205, **206**, 207, **211**, 212; former home of, **200**, **201**; headstone, 199, **200**, 208
McJunkins, Ray, 204, **205**
McJunkins, Sally, 201, **202**, **203**
McJunkins, Sheldry, 204, **205**
McJunkins, Starling O., 212
McJunkins, Theron, 20, 200, 204
McNeeley, Linder G., 210, 212
McWilliams, Dean, 60
Meatyard, Ralph Eugene, 30
Melville, Herman, 137
Mendelian genetics, 4

"Message Given at Nagano" (Faulkner), 223, 230
Miami Herald, 96
Michaels, Walter Benn, 72n23
Miller, Wayne F., **225**
miscegenation, 130
Mitchell, Koritha, 47
Modern Language Association, 4
monumentality, 14–15, 86–87
Morrison, Toni, 27
Mosquitoes (Faulkner), 3, 6
Mother and Child Near Takaramachi (Yamahata), **226**
Mothers in Mourning (Loraux), 86
Moynihan Report, 10
Murphy, Robert, 219
Museum of Modern Art (MoMA), 215, 224, **225**, 226; Department of Photography, 224
Myrdal, Gunnar, 61

Nagano Cultural Center, 230
Nagano Seminar on American Literature, 220, 223
Napolin, Julie Beth, 14
Narcissus, 120n3
Nashville Agrarians, 132
National Endowment for the Arts, 44n17
National Geographic, "The Changing Face of America," 59
National Security Council (NSC), 216–17; US Policy toward Japan, 228
Native Americans: genocide of, 25; guilt regarding, 25, 28; representation in Faulkner's work, 139–41, 145n8, 145nn11–12
New Critics, 132
New Historicism, 145n6
New Yorker, 114
Nietzsche, Friedrich, 144n5
Nigrescence, 50
Nihombashi Takashimaya Department Store, **225**
Nihon Keizai Shimbun (Nikkei), 224–26; Planning Department, 224
Nihon Keizai Shimbun hachijunenshi (*The Eighty Years' History of Nihon Keizai Shimbun*), 226
Nippon Television Network, 219
Nisetich, Rebecca, 13

Nixon, Angelique V., 96
Norris, Frank, 164n9
Norris, Kathleen, 5
Northwest Airlines, 222
Not Quite White (Wray), 174–75
nuclear bombs, 21; arms race, 222; movement to ban, 218–19

Ober, Harold, 122
O'Connor, Flannery, 28
Oedipus Rex (Sophocles), 91–96; death and burial themes in, 91, 95; family in, 91–92; feminine lament in, 91; queerness in, 92, 95
oikos, 15, 89, 92, 101–2
Omnibus, 195, **196**, **201**, **205**, **206**
"one-drop rule," 127
Operations Coordinating Board (OCB), 217; *Outline Plan of Operations with Respect to Japan*, 228
Oxford English Dictionary, 216

Pantaleo, Daniel, 103n8
Parrish, Susan Scott, 125–26
Passing of the Great Race, The (Grant), 60
paternalism/fatherhood/patriarchy, 11, 107; legacies of, 7; southern, 8, 195–96, 212
patriarchy. *See* paternalism/fatherhood/patriarchy
Pearl Harbor, bombing of, 123
Pearson, Norman Holland, 45n21
Peeker, Aili Pettersson, 52
Pendergrass, David, 210
Perrine, Laurence, 37
Peruvian Flute Player (Harris), 225
phatic dimension of language, 113–14
Picon, Leon, 229
plot versus plotting, 73–74
PMLA, 4
PODAM, 219
polis, 15, 86, 92, 101, 105n23, 172
Polk, Noel, 11, 152
Portable Faulkner (Cowley), Compson Appendix, 17, 139
Porter, Carolyn, 11
Porter, Katherine Anne, 28
post-Blackness, 69
postracialism, 13, 58–70; identity and, 69; problems with, 69–70; racial assimilation and, 59; whiteness and, 59, 72n23

Power for Peace (1956), 220
Precarious Life (Butler), 126
propaganda: Soviet, 21, 217; United States, 216-21
Puskus Creek, 199
Pylon (Faulkner), 6

racial assimilation, 59, 60
racial definition, 60
racial essentialism, 61, 72n23
racial subjectivism, 60
Ramsey, William, 69
Random House, 8-9, 123
Ratliff, V. K., 19
Reading for the Plot (Brooks), 73
"Red Leaves" (Faulkner), 17, 139-40
Reivers, The (Faulkner), 21; "ditch" metaphor in, 49-50, 53-54; encounter in, 50-51; family and role of genealogy in, 21, 167n30; racism in, 50; sex in, 8; white identity development in, 50
Republican National Convention, 44n17
Requiem for a Nun (Faulkner), 139; family and role of genealogy in, 21; Southern Gothic elements in, 25
Rising Tide of Color, The (Stoddard), 60
Rogin, Michael, 17, 137
Romantic Era, 32
Ross, Jim Buck, 208, 212
Ross, Stephen, 75-76, 80
Rowan Oak, 10, 194, 196, **197**, 199; Caroline Barr's funeral at, 10; designated National Historic Landmark, 194
Russell, Bertrand, 224

Saldivar, Ramon, 126
Salvant, Shawn, 127
Sanctuary (Faulkner), 37, 157; epidemiological epistemology reading of, 19, 177-79; race in, 178-79; sexual language in, 157; spatial heatmap of, **179**; "spotted horses" in, 177
Sarraci, Rodolfi, 170
Saudek, Robert, 195, **196**, **201**, **205**, **206**, 212
Sedgwick, Eve Kosofsky, 149, 164n9, 165n16
Seeing Race Again (Crenshaw), 70
Shellenberger, Jack H., 222
Shibata, Hidetoshi, 219
Shklar, Judith, 17, 137-38, 144n3
Shoriki, Matsutaro, 219, 220

Simmons, K. Merinda, 59, 69
Sinclair, Upton, 164n9
slavery, 28; African American families and, 10, 97, 137; chattel, 47; guilt of, 25, 28, 30, 48; records, 137; white supremacy and, 47; women and, 95, 97
Smith, Marshall J., 3
Snopes family: anxieties regarding, 174-76; autoimmunological dynamics of, 186-89; as contagion, 168-90; Flem Snopes, 182-85; sexuality, 174; symptomatic, 176-82; as white trash, 174-75, 189
Snopes-watchers, 19, 173, 176, 182
Soldiers' Pay (Faulkner), 6
Sontag, Susan, 172, 184
Sophocles, 90-96
Sound and the Fury, The (Faulkner), 34, 36-37, 86; childhood in, 5; class issues in, 5, 33; "Compson Appendix," 139; ending, 87; eugenics in, 5; family and role of genealogy in, 10; inspiration for, 4, 5; language in, 47-48; monumentality in, 86-87; narration of, 37; paternalism in, 8; suicide in, 103
Southeast Missouri State University, 197
Southern Gothic, 11-12, 25-43; appeal of, 27-28, 30; children/childhood and, 12, 40, 42-43, 48; function of, 41; hauntology of, 31-32, 41-43; iconography, 28-29; national innocence and, 36, 40-41; not-knowing in, 48-49; "operatic" rhetorical structures of, 52; racial oppression and, 30-31, 41-42; revelatory strategies of, 36; scary-sexy aspect of, 36, 40, 42; spectatorship of, 29-30; white supremacy in, 48
Spillers, Hortense J., 10, 29, 51, 86, 94, 97-98
St. Peter's cemetery, 10
state power, 89
"Statement of Policy on Peaceful Uses of Atomic Energy," 217
Steichen, Edward, 20-21, 215, 220-29
Stern, G. B., 5
Stevens, Gavin, 19, 176
Stewart, W. L., 210-11
Stoddard, Lothrop, 60
Stone, Phil, 197
Stowe, Harriet Beecher, 33
Strauss, Lewis L., 217-18, 221
Streibert, Theodore Cuyler, 229

"subversive genealogy," 17, 136–44; in "Dark House" novels, 142
systematic management, 113, 114

Tatum, Beverly, 50
Terauchi, Yoshitake, 224
Terrible Picture, The (Mann), 40, 46n29
"That Evening Sun" (Faulkner), 11, 36–38; absurdness/instabilities of Blackness in, 39; childhood in, 36–37; class issues in, 38; "ditch" metaphor in, 53–55, 57nn27–28; language in, 48, 57n26; learned obliviousness in, 41; narration, 48; racism in, 39, 48; Southern Gothic in, 37–40; temporality in, 54; "what happened" element of, 39–40; whiteness in, 38–40, 54
"That Evening Sun Go Down" (Faulkner), 38–39; class issues in, 53–54; degrees of not-knowing in, 38–39; race in, 47, 53; whiteness in, 53–54
Their Eyes Were Watching God (Hurston), 121n22
Thérèse Raquin (Zola), 122
These Thirteen (Faulkner), 36
Thomas, George Porter, 17
Thomas, William Hannibal, 60
Thompson-Chandler house, 4
Till, Emmett, 34
Time magazine, "The Future Face of America," 59
Tinnie, Wallis, 48
To Kill a Mockingbird (Lee), 31, 33, 36; racial innocence in, 48
"To the Youth in Japan" (Faulkner), 223
Totem and Taboo (Freud), 150
Town, The (Faulkner): character-location markers, 183; disease spread in, 183–85; epidemiological epistemology reading of, 19, 176, 179–85, 188; role of secrecy in, 184–85; spatial heatmaps of, 181, **182**, **187**
Towner, Theresa M., 173
Trigg-Doyle-Falkner house, 3
Trouble with Post-Blackness, The (Baker, Simmons), 59
Trump, Donald, 104n11
Turner, R. Gerald, 210
Twain, Mark, 28, 33
Twitter, 104n11
"Two Virginias, The" (Mann), 12, 41, **42**, 43

Uncle Tom's Cabin (Stowe), 33
United Nations General Assembly, 217, 225
United States Census, 20
United States Congress, 220, 228
United States Customs and Border Protection, 96–97
United States Embassy, Japan, 218, 224–25
United States Federal Census Collection and Public Records Index, 198
United States Information Agency (USIA), 215–18, 221, 224, 227, 229
United States Information Service (USIS), 20, 218, 220, 223, 229; Tokyo, 218–20, 222–23, 228–29
United States State Department, 216, 218, 224, 229; Exchange of Persons Program, 216, 223
University of Maryland, 4
University of Mississippi, 4, 199, 208, 210; Bondurant Hall, 208; Delta Psi house, 4
University of Virginia, 169, 196
Unvanquished, The (Faulkner), 107–19, 122; "Ambuscade," 47–48, 110–11; Black knowledge in, 111; Civil War backdrop, 109–10, 112, 114–15; family and role of genealogy in, 15–16, 108, 109–10; film rights, 9; gender dynamics, 116–17, 119; marginal characters in, 108; patriarchy in, 108, 118; race in, 110, 116, 119; "Raid," 111; relevance of character names, 116; "Riposte in Tertio," 111; role of media in, 16, 108–10, 112–17, 119; "Skirmish at Sartoris," 116; systematic management in, 113–14; voting procedures in, 117–19; weaponization of noise in, 118–19; white supremacy in, 108, 111, 116

Wald, Priscilla, 172–73
Walker, Alice, 199
Wasson, Ben, 8
Watson, Jay, 175
Way of All Flesh (Butler), 4
WCKT, 194
Weinstein, Philip M., 5
Welge, Jobst, 125
Wells, Dean Faulkner, 198
When Species Meet (Haraway), 154
white trash, 174–75, 189
Wilkins, Sally Murry, 4
"William Faulkner," *Omnibus*, 195

William Faulkner Memorial Highway, 199
William Faulkner: The Yoknapatawpha Country (Brooks), 10
Williams, Tennessee, 28
Wilson, Payne, 197–98
woods, lauren, 104n10
World Conferences against Atomic and Hydrogen Bombs, 220
World War II, 131, 220, 222; bombing of Hiroshima and Nagasaki, 21, 218, 224–25, 227
Wounded People Waiting for Help Near Iwakawamachi, Nagasaki (Yamahata), **226**
Wray, Matt, 174–75
Wright, Richard, 28

Yaeger, Patricia, 26–27, 29–31, 36, 41–43, 50, 116
Yamahata, Yosuke, 225, **226**, **227**
Yamamoto, Yoko, 20–21
Yomiuri Shimbun, 218–20
Young, Trudy McJunkins, 20, 199–200, **203**, **204**, **205**; childhood home, **207**; interview with, 201–7
Young, William, 199–200

Za famiri obu man: warera mina ningen kazoku (*The Family of Man: We All Are a Family of Man*), 224
Žižek, Slavoj, 148
Zola, Emile, 4, 122
Zucker, A. E., 4, 7

www.ingramcontent.com/pod-product-compliance
Lightning Source LLC
Chambersburg PA
CBHW030618230426
43661CB00053B/2048